Imprinting the South

Imprinting the South

SOUTHERN PRINTMAKERS AND THEIR IMAGES OF THE REGION

1920s–1940s

Lynn Barstis Williams

The University of Alabama Press • Tuscaloosa

Manufactured in Korea

Designer: Michele Myatt Quinn
Typeface: Garamond

The paper on which this book is printed meets the minimum requirements of American National Standard for Information Sciences-Permanence of Paper for Printed Library Materials, ANSI Z39.48–1984.

Library of Congress Cataloging-in-Publication Data

Williams, Lynn Barstis, 1946–
Imprinting the South : southern printmakers and their images of the region, 1920s–1940s / Lynn Barstis Williams.
p. cm.
Includes bibliographical references and index.
ISBN-13: 978-0-8173-1560-3 (cloth : alk. paper)
ISBN-10: 0-8173-1560-8
1. Southern States—In art. 2. Prints, American—Southern States—20th century. 3. Regionalism in art—Southern States. I. Title.

NE962.S65W55 2007
769.975—dc22 2006024308

Contents

Preface vii

1 Printmaking in and from the South 1

2 Imagery of the South 19

3 The Printmakers 39

Appendix: Southern Connections 161

Glossary 183

Selected Bibliography 185

Endnotes 195

Index 205

Color images follow page 38

Preface

MY INITIAL INTEREST IN IMAGES of the South in prints began with the shock I experienced upon first viewing George Biddle's lithograph titled *Alabama Code—Our Girls Don't Sleep with Niggers* at a print fair in Atlanta shortly after I moved to Alabama in 1989. That interest flamed again when I was compiling a subject index for my *American Printmakers, 1880–1945: An Index to Reproductions and Biocritical Information* (1993). About the time that book project wound down, I bought some lithographs of southern scenes by James Routh, who was born and raised in the South. Since I knew from information supplied by the gallery that he was still living, I contacted him. He seemed pleased that some of his works from fifty years ago had found an appreciative home and readily supplied information about their creation and identity. He also mentioned other southern artists, including Lamar Baker and Carroll Cloar, whom he knew in the late 1930s when he studied in New York at the Art Students League. Thus began the hunt for more southern printmakers and their southern scenes along with information about them. Feeling at loose ends when my index was finally out of my hands and encouraged to publish as a faculty member of a university, I began thinking of articles, and ultimately, another book centered on the southern printmakers and their images of the South.

Having developed a persistent interest in southern culture during the past quarter century that I have lived in the South, my first wish for this book is that it be a contribution to the emerging field of southern studies. The regionalism and social realism that dominated American Scene realism for approximately a quarter century, from the 1920s to the late 1940s, frequently focused on the South as the most distinctive region of this country and the most problematic as well. In addition to catalogs on individual artists, curators and scholars have explored this focus in a few general exhibition catalogs. A small catalog, *Southern Works on Paper, 1900–1950* (1981), covered some outstanding examples in prints and drawings, while the more extensive *The American Scene and the South* (1996) surveyed the broader spectrum in paintings, prints, drawings, and photographs from seven of the southern states. The major printmakers who worked in Charleston have been brought to wider attention by Martha Severens's *The Charleston Renaissance* (1998) and more recently, Stephanie Yuhl's more broadly based *A Golden Haze of Memory* (2005), as well as a dissertation on southern art of the interwar period by Mariea Dennison. At the time this book manuscript went to the publisher, a collection of essays based on papers at a 1987 North American Print Conference, *Printmaking in New Orleans,* was awaiting publication. This book attempts to tie such various localities in the South together to identify broader trends.

Two contrasting regionalist or geographical approaches to cultural studies can be identified. One examines works of artists from a particular region, while the other focuses on region or place as a subject of the work. This book attempts to meld the two approaches in the first chapter, but the second chapter places emphasis on the South as subject. Of what real importance is the fact that artists were born or lived in the South if the region and its culture had no influence on their work?

Individual printmakers, highlighted by an entry with a reproduction of one of their prints, have been selected because they had sufficient documented biographical contact with the South and pictured it in their print oeuvre, generally in at least three prints. Quality and interest of the print oeuvre also played a role. Occasionally the presumption that an image is southern is my hypothesis, because not all works have titles that denote geography, and other information pointing to a southern locale may not be available. Selecting a print to represent the artist's southern experience or view of the region has been challenging, to the extent that I have changed by mind, in some cases as many as a half a dozen times. I have, however, tried to choose prints not only for their inherent interest and quality but also for their representational or exceptional position in the body of prints depicting the South and its culture. Over half have come from my own personal collection and that of my friend Stephen Goldfarb. Others have been found in institutional collections or those of private individuals willing to have their works reproduced in this publication.

A word or two should be said about titles, which can be problematic, as artists not infrequently gave different titles to the same print. Titles given in italics below the print are those that appear on the particular impression used. Other titles are noted in the reference notes. If no title is given, the title established in a catalogue raisonné or other major catalog is given in brackets. Otherwise, my simple descriptive title is given in brackets.

Since the central experience impacting southern history was secession from the union and subsequent defeat in the Civil War, the South, for purposes here, includes the former Confederate states with the exclusion of Texas. The Lone Star state hosted so many printmakers of the period that it deserves a book of its own. Only in the few instances where there is some overlap with the Southeast are they listed in the Southern Connections section in the back. Black printmakers of the period who migrated to the North but created southern images have also been included as southerners as they undoubtedly would have wished to be.

As a librarian I have intended that this book serve as a reference tool for those seeking information about individual printmakers as well as an interpretive study. For reference purposes the reader must access the Appendix titled Southern Connections, an Index and Dictionary to Printmakers, where I have supplied an alphabetical list of printmakers of the era who had contact with the South and noted the extent to which they made images of the South. There a page reference leads to information about the printmaker in the central section or information in the case of those who have not been singled out for an individual entry accompanied by a reproduction. As much as possible, I have tried not to duplicate standard biographical information available in the major art dictionary for the period: the three-volume, second edition of Peter Falk's *Who Was Who in American Art* (1999), as that reference set is readily available in most academic and large public libraries. However, as information in exhibition catalogs and articles is not readily available to collectors, I have summarized those works here with emphasis on images.

The exact dates for the chronological scope of this study are somewhat arbitrary. That scope generally begins sometime around the end of World War I when many American artists returned from Europe and more came south to vacation or reside and produced prints influenced by what they saw and experienced in this region. It ends with the waning of realistic, figurative prints in small format, which occurred gradually among southern artists during the late 1940s, although the extent to which such a general tendency prevailed varied from artist to artist. My original intention was to end in 1945 with the end of World War II, since that point marked the end of an era in American as well as southern history; however, a few artists in Alabama produced excellent lithographs in the years 1945–49, so I could not resist extending the scope slightly to include them. The true chronological finale of this study is the advent of abstract expressionism, generally seen to occur with the onset of the 1950s.

Compared to the post–World War II era when American fine prints achieved world-renowned status, those produced during the first half of the twentieth century may appear to their detractors as a populist enterprise attempting to lure the American masses from their apathy toward art by novel ventures to produce inexpensive impressions. One occasionally hears the American Scene period scorned for the prevailing realistic, easily comprehensible style that is said to lapse into mere illustration. However, this realistic, figurative style in both painting and printmaking underwent a vast expansion during a period between two world wars—from the narrow range of themes and iconography that had prevailed during the nineteenth century as American art began to develop its own national character apart from its European origins. The result was a body of work that is possibly the most reflective of American mass culture, with all its charm, banality, degradation, and naiveté, in the history of American art. Due to the movement known as regionalism, which prevailed in the 1930s and into the 1940s as well, much of the art created reflected a culture that is truly regional in character and should be examined with such regional emphasis. Such is my intent in this study of the South through the fine art prints, which focuses on aspects of its culture in their imagery.

Many people are to be thanked for their help and encouragement with this project. First I should thank those associated with my employer Auburn University Libraries. The library deans and department heads under whom I have worked have been most supportive in my research on southern printmakers over the course of ten years. This includes three library deans or directors—William Highfill, Stella Bentley, and Sheri Downer, as well as department heads Glenn Anderson, Marcia Boosinger, and Dwayne Cox. My colleagues who have served on the Library Research Advisory Committee through the years have also supported my research financially through the grants that this committee has allocated to this project. I am also grateful to the Office of Research at Auburn University for making a grant-in-aid available to me.

Librarians and staff at other institutions must also be thanked, above all those at Historic New Orleans Collection, especially Sally Stassi, who have answered my numerous inquiries tirelessly through the years. Diana Brown at the St. Charles Public Library in St. Charles, Illinois, shared with me the results of her research on Victoria Hutson Huntley for an exhibition of that artist's lithographs. Staff at the North Carolina State Archives sent me numerous newspaper articles on Mabel Pugh as did staff at the Polk Museum of Art for Kent Hagerman. Ellen E. Knight of the Town Clerk's Office, in Winchester, Massachusetts, searched local street directories, vital records, and newspaper indexes for information on Walter Ronald Locke and sent the results in multiple e-mails to me.

Among museum professionals I thank Bill Eiland, Director of the Georgia Museum of Art, University of Georgia, for the early encouragement he gave to my efforts to collect prints of the South and to write a book on the subject. Paul Richelson, Chief Curator and Assistant Director at the Mobile Museum of Art, also furthered this project. He went out of his way to arrange an interview with Doris Alexander shortly before she died and gave me an opportunity to study and write on Roderick MacKenzie for an exhibition catalog. Other curators, registrars, and other assistants in museums, including the Montgomery, the Gibbes, and Historic New Orleans, have graciously arranged visits so I could view prints and obtain information.

Art dealers whom I have come to know through years of collecting have also helped supply information in various ways. First is David Allen (David Allen Fine Arts), who helped me build up a southern print collection by calling me when he found prints I was looking for. He also shared information he obtained and supplied photocopies. Others I should name are Lee Stone (M. Lee Stone Fine Prints) for sharing letters and answering inquiries, Wayne Kielsmeyer (Covington Fine Arts Gallery) for supplying an article, Herbert Halpern (Herbert Halpern Fine Arts) for information and general encouragement with this project, and Don Smith (Donald C. Smith Fine Arts) for sending me information from his recently published bibliography, while it was still being compiled. Finally I have to thank the artists or their descendants who have shared the stories of their lives and printmaking activity so generously and encouraged me to continue working on a book about them. I have made every attempt to contact relevant copyright holders and others who might have contact information about them to obtain permission to reproduce images. I regret that in a number of instances I have not been able to reach the appropriate people.

Above all, my words of thanks must be directed to my friend Stephen Goldfarb without whose help and encouragement this book would probably have not reached its final stage. In addition to preparation of the endnotes and bibliography for which he is largely responsible, he assisted with the historical research and tirelessly edited the text at every stage. He joined me in collecting prints to use for research purposes and accompanied me on many research trips to museums and some interviews with individual printmakers or their descendants. In addition he served as my initial photographer and helped me label and organize professionally photographed images. As my companion, research assistant, editor, critic, and shrink, his encouragement and support never flagged.

Imprinting the South

1

Printmaking in and from the South

WITH ITS REGIONALIST ACCENTS, the American Scene movement, which arose in the 1920s, peaked in the 1930s, then waned in the 1940s, wove varied regions of the United States, including the South, into a broader and denser American artistic fabric. Due to a strong impetus toward external, visual exploration, increasing numbers of American artists viewed the South—the most rural, impoverished, and isolated region of the country—with both aesthetic and sociological interest. During this same period, an artistic revival of print media meant that more artists who explored the South pictured the region in prints: first in etchings followed by woodcuts, wood engravings, linoleum cuts, lithographs, serigraphs, and even a few monotypes.

Numerous views of the South appear on an expanding print market during the Great Depression, which envisioned prints as affordable art for a growing population of American art consumers. This book investigates the southeastern segment of that graphic activity, which knit the South more tightly to a national artistic culture. Indeed the period from the 1920s through the 1940s constituted the first great age of the American figurative, realistic print to which the South contributed both artists as well as subjects. Few other periods in the history of printmaking produced such an extensive range of local imagery that historically documented a period and culture in all its regional variations.

BEGINNINGS: THE ETCHING REVIVAL

Prints of southern place, often reproductive in nature, can be traced back to some of the earliest explorations of the region; however, the late nineteenth-century movement identified as the "Etching Revival" serves as a good starting point to discuss their evolution toward the twentieth century.[1] Countering the sweep of the industrial revolution, whereby prints had become almost exclusively commercial media, artists in the late nineteenth century revived the fine art print, choosing seventeenth-century etchings by Rembrandt as their beacon. This development, known as the Etching Revival, drifted from France and England to American shores, settling in the Northeast during the 1880s.[2]

Spurred by dealers, collectors, and artists in Europe, especially the American expatriate, James McNeill Whistler, a number of American painters took up the etching needle to express their personal response to a subject. Societies to promote etching were organized as articles about the medium appeared in periodicals.[3] Some painter-etchers became itinerants, seeking new vistas to explore, and since a warm, southern climate has always enticed Yankees mired in long, cold, northern winters, a few turned to the southeastern coast, most easily accessible by boat or train, to whet their artistic eye. A leading art historian's comment that "the phenomenon of the artist as winter resident was—and still is—an important part of the history of painting in the South" applies equally well to prints.[4]

Northeast Florida appears to have been the prime southern attraction for etchers of the 1880s. Northeastern landscape artists, such as Thomas Moran and his wife Mary Nimmo Moran, Stephen Parrish, and George Smillie, became early Florida tourists who etched delicate, panoramic vistas they viewed from steamboats as they plied the St. John's River and visited old St. Augustine.[5] Later in the decade, the oil magnate and financier Henry Flagler built the Hotel Ponce de León in St. Augustine, where he welcomed artists to promote tourism on the eastern coast of Florida. Otto Bacher, known for his Venetian etchings, accepted Flagler's invitation and delineated the hotel's elaborate facade in etchings, which were hung in the hotel lobby.[6] Bacher's etchings of the Ponce de León continued a European architectural etching tradition that touched New Orleans in the 1880s and reached other southeastern seaports after World War I.

As the major commercial center of the South, New Orleans had, by the 1880s, a relatively active, organized art community centered on painting.[7] With the revival of etching underway, more artists versed in the intaglio printmaking process arrived. Joseph Pennell, the most prominent exponent of etching in the United States, visited in 1882 on an assignment from *Harper's* to illustrate an article on the city by George Washington Cable, a local author. In his article Cable claimed that New Orleans was "without pretension or intention, picturesque and antique" with a "quaint Southern-European aspect."[8] Etchers like Pennell could not resist such pictorial appeal. Pennell made a series of etchings of the homes in which Cable's characters lived and some of the Mississippi River, which he explored on a cruise.[9]

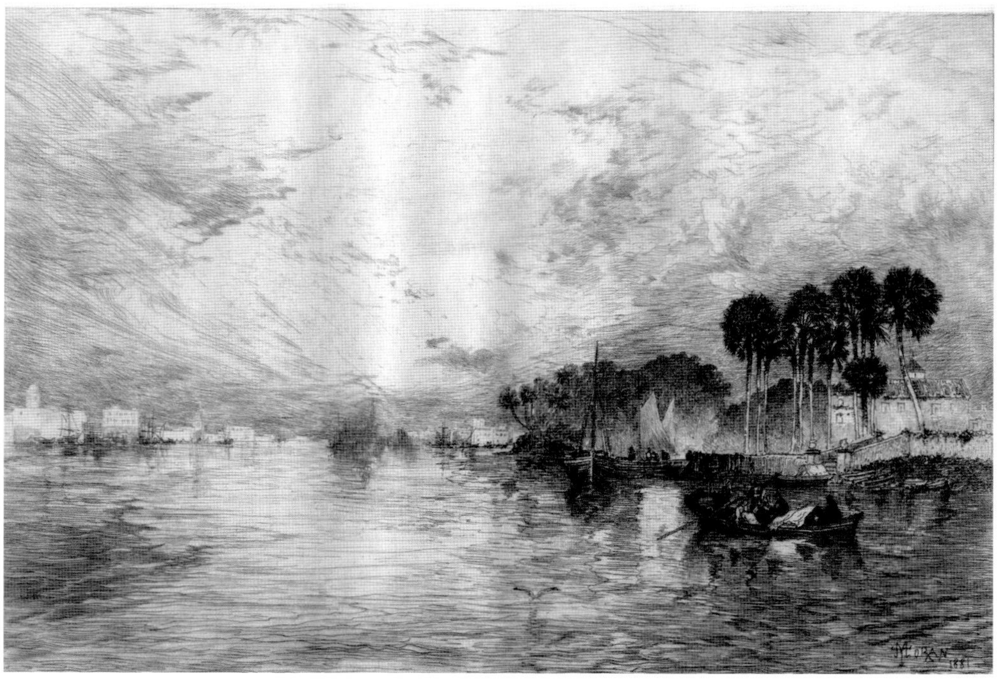

A. Thomas Moran, *Morning on the St. John's, Florida,* etching, 1886, 5 ⅝ x 8 ½ in., collection of Lynn Barstis Williams.

In 1884 William Woodward came to New Orleans from Massachusetts to teach art at Tulane University, and his brother Ellsworth followed a year later. In 1887 both brothers helped establish Sophie Newcomb College for women where Ellsworth headed the art department and William taught etching.[10] Ellsworth began etching scenes of the French Quarter, particularly the French market, and years later, during his retirement in the 1930s, reprinted from those early plates.[11] Robert Bledsoe Mayfield, who arrived in 1891 to work as an editor at the *Times-Democrat,* began to etch views of the French Quarter as well as activity on the docks.

While the southern coast began to attract more northern etchers, young southerners with an artistic bent headed north or abroad for training, which increasingly included printmaking as the twentieth century began. As art was considered an acceptable endeavor for well-born, southern women, some artists were female, including a few from Alabama, such as Anne Goldthwaite, who became etchers. However, women who sought art training shortly after the turn of the century had to surmount gender prejudice. When Goldthwaite first attempted to enroll in an etching class at the National Academy of Design in New York City, she met with rejection. The director excluded women, he explained, not because he considered them less capable, but because matrimony too often diverted them from their art careers.[12] Although the competing Art Students League accepted women, it did not offer an etching class until 1921 when Joseph Pennell joined the faculty.[13] The League became the preferred school for southern artists to learn printmaking from the 1920s until the 1940s.

Etching was not the only print medium that artists from the South were interested in learning; an artistic revival of relief prints was also underway. Renewed exploration of the woodcut began in the late nineteenth century due to interest in the Japanese tradition of color woodcuts. Decorative embellishment of fine press books by William Morris and his acolytes in the Arts and Crafts movement also spurred interest in the medium. Wood

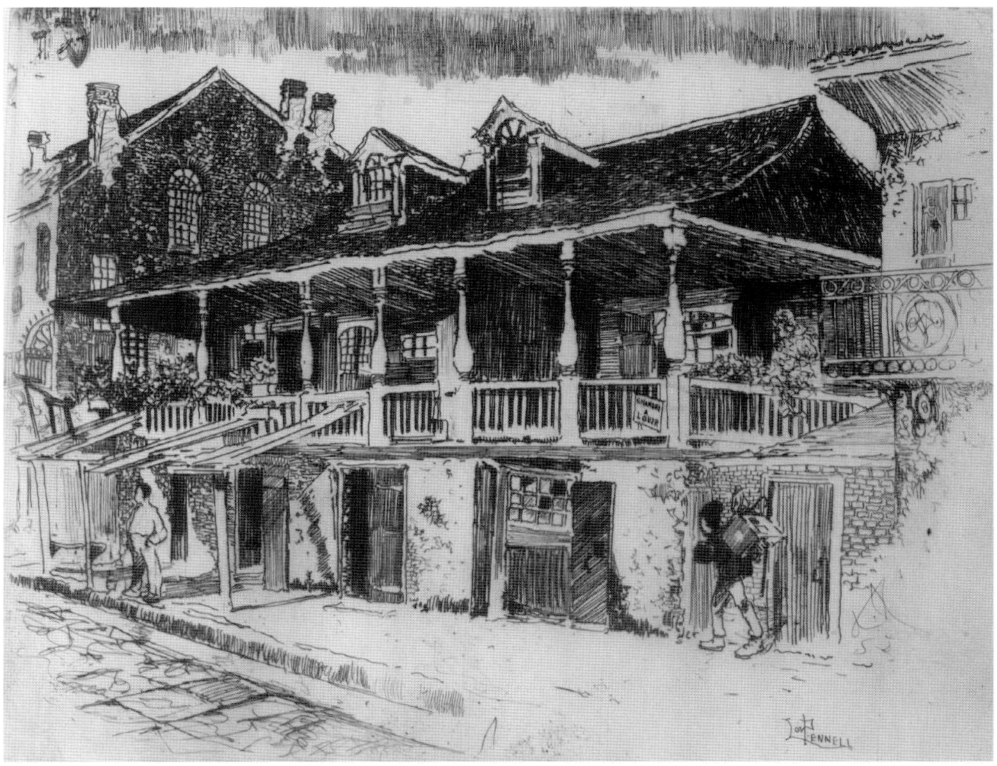

B. Joseph Pennell, *Madame John's Legacy,* etching, c. 1882, 5 ⅞ x 7 ⅞ in., collection of Stephen Goldfarb.

engravings, made on the end grain instead of the plank side of a piece of wood, had become the major media for illustrations, both in periodicals and books. By the end of the nineteenth century, photo-mechanical print processes had superseded the commercial value of hand-executed prints. When the American etching revival began, a small group of American illustrators were attempting to raise wood engraving to a fine art through finesse in technique.[14] Printmakers would succeed with such efforts from the 1920s through the 1940s in both book illustrations and individual fine prints.

Wood carving and wood engraving had been considered acceptable art media for women from the mid-nineteenth century, and some, like Helen Hyde, traveled to Japan to learn Japanese techniques.[15] Anna Heyward Taylor, a young woman from Columbia, South Carolina, became interested in woodcuts in 1904 when she heard a lecture about Japanese prints while studying in London; some ten years later she also traveled to Japan to study the technique.[16] The Woodwards began teaching wood carving in evening decorative art classes for women soon after they arrived in New Orleans.[17] The art curriculum they established at Newcomb College included such woodwork instruction. Unlike etching, which requires pressure from a rotary press to print a metal plate, prints made by carving in relief can be "spooned," or printed by hand with pressure from the back of a spoon or another suitable tool, which appealed to exponents of handcraft methods. Women students at Newcomb, along with their female instructors, produced book plates, calendars, greeting cards, and free-standing prints.[18]

Two prominent Newcomb instructors, Henrietta Bailey and Sadie Irvine, faced their wood plates with a new synthetic medium, linoleum. More easily carved than wood, linoleum democratized printmaking further in the first half of the twentieth century. By the 1920s articles began to appear in magazines, such as *School Arts,* explaining linoleum's ease in making prints, while books serving as instruction manuals followed. Charles William Smith, a Virginia artist, published *Linoleum Block Printing* in 1925. Although impressions from linoleum plates cannot always be distinguished from those made from the plank side of wood, southern artists appear to have taken advantage of the medium's advantages. Among the few using this medium to earn their living by illustrating books was Mabel Pugh, originally from North Carolina.

A Broader Coastal Area

By the second decade of the twentieth century, organizing efforts resurged with new societies or clubs to exhibit prints, sell prints, and offer training as well, since the few museums, art schools, and art organizations offered only scant opportunities. After the founding of the Chicago Society of Etchers in 1910, others followed in major northern and West Coast cities: the California Society of Etchers (San Francisco, 1912); the Print Makers Society of California (Los Angeles, 1914); the Brooklyn Society of Etchers and Print Club of Philadelphia (both in 1916); and the Cleveland Print Club (1919).[19] Although this print society movement meandered southward at a slow, attenuated pace, the historic southeastern coast increasingly enticed members of such clubs from other parts of the country seeking picturesque views on which to hone technical skills and venues in which to sell their creations.

With its French Quarter architecture associated with Old World, European vistas, New Orleans continued as the most popular southern haunt for artists. By 1910, New Orleans had an art museum, named after its benefactor Isaac Delgado (now the New Orleans Museum of Art). In 1916 a midwestern artist, Louis Oscar Griffith, spent a winter in the city and exhibited his etchings at the Delgado Museum.[20] However a print society did not appear in New Orleans until the end of the 1930s, and, according to one local art authority, the city lagged in its appreciation of print media. In 1921 Gideon Stanton, an artist as well as a trustee of the Delgado Museum, responded to a letter from Ralph Pearson, a member of the Chicago Society of Etchers, who asked about opportunities to sell prints in the city. Stanton wrote, "I regret exceedingly that there is no dealer in New Orleans to whom I could recommend you to send any of your work to sell. Although this is a comparatively large city, it is woefully behind in any real appreciation of graphic art."[21]

Leaders of New Orleans art community, such as the Woodwards, promoted a broad spectrum of arts and crafts, rather than focusing on prints. However, Stanton wrote to Pearson that the New Orleans Art Association, formed in 1905, had been organizing one exhibit devoted to prints for which sales were "fairly good," so he encouraged Pearson to send some impressions for one of their exhibitions.[22] The year Stanton wrote to Pearson, Ellsworth Woodward organized the Southern States Art League, which, until 1950, provided artists residing in the South opportunities to exhibit and sell prints, along with paintings, sculptures, and crafts, in various southern cities. A year later, in 1922, the New Orleans Arts and Crafts Club was founded; members established the New Orleans School of Art, which provided an etching press as well as classes, demonstrations, and exhibitions in the following years.

Urban development in New Orleans spurred print production too. As skyscrapers shot up near the French Quarter in the 1920s and "progress" threatened historic landmarks, efforts began to rescue and restore the Vieux Carré, which had sunk into a swamp of squalor and decay, threatening the antique charm that George Washington Cable noted in his 1883 article. With writers such as Lyle Saxon and Sherwood Anderson extolling the Quarter's assets, encouraging artists as well as writers to encamp in its dilapidated buildings, the district metamorphosed into a bohemian art colony during the 1920s.[23]

Visiting artists increasingly streamed into New Orleans. Among them were Mabel Dwight, who visited her childhood home in 1928, and from records of their etchings, Anne Goldthwaite and Loren Barton also visited. The pattern of an artist first visiting for a short period, then returning for an extended stay became common. More painters arrived versed in etching, including George Castleden and Knute Heldner, both of whom set up studios after initial visits to taste the Quarter's fare. By the late 1920s two new residents, Alice Standish Buell and Gerry Peirce, were teaching etching at the New Orleans School of Art.[24] Etchings and relief prints worked hand-in-hand with photographs to supply affordable mementos of visits to the Quarter for a burgeoning tourist trade.

The onslaught of the Great Depression in the early 1930s lured even more artists making prints to the Vieux Carré, largely due to its inexpensive housing.[25] As one writer concluded, New Orleans was "the poor man's Paris, the Paris of the South."[26] The Quarter became home for more artists from other parts of the South who took up etching: Eugene Loving from Texas and Alvin Sharpe from Kentucky. Carl Hancock sojourned every summer from Arkansas.[27] Morris Henry Hobbs abandoned his Chicago home for the Quarter at the end of the 1930s, and others from the Chicago area—Charles Wilimovsky, Leon Pescheret, and Hubert Morley—made visits.[28] Artists continued to visit through the 1940s. Philip Kappel came to produce a book from his etched Louisiana views, while Charles Surendorf made repeated visits from California at the end of that decade to take advantage of the city's visual appeal.

Printmakers native to the city, including Newcomb instructors Henrietta Bailey and Sadie Irvine, tended to be women, who were less mobile than men. By the late 1930s they were showing their color relief prints in the exhibitions of the New Orleans Art Association as well as the Southern States Art League. Caroline Durieux also studied and taught at Newcomb. As male artists from other regions increasingly came and went during the 1920s and early 1930s, Durieux, following her husband's business career abroad, made contacts in Mexico and New York, which launched her into lithography. Although in other parts of the country lithography increasingly became the favored print medium during the 1930s, printmakers working in the South adopted this planographic medium much more slowly.

In 1939, soon after Morris Henry Hobbs settled in the Quarter, he along with Clarence Millet, Charles Reinike, and David Bowman organized the Louisiana Society of Etchers, a final spark of the etching society movement, which had continued to develop through 1930s, extending even to smaller cities.[29] By the end of the 1930s, many of these etching societies were considered staid and conservative, shunning the modernist, experimental styles gradually influencing American prints, though such artistic conservatism appealed to the conservative South. Hobbs became the first president of the Louisiana Society of Etchers, which suggests he led efforts to organize on its behalf.[30] Actively involved in the Chicago Society of Etchers and the American Society of Etchers, he evidently thought New Orleans could benefit from a local organization devoted exclusively to prints.

Active membership in the organization was limited to residents of Louisiana or artists from other areas who worked in New Orleans for at least part of the year. The association's bylaws called for patron members who would receive an annual presentation or gift print in exchange for their support, a common print society practice. The organizers also planned lectures and demonstrations for the benefit of both artist and patron members. With headquarters located in several rooms in a building that also housed the New Orleans Art League, the society offered an etching press and other printing equipment for the use of members. During its first year, twenty printmakers joined the association, which held an annual exhibition every year of its three-year existence. The short-lived organization died in 1941, as many members joined the war effort, though Hobbs continued to mentor the novice in intaglio media.[31]

A good overview of how far the French Quarter had traveled as an art colony since the early 1920s can be found in an unpublished autobiography by Charles Surendorf, a frequent visitor after World War II. After an initial visit in 1947, Surendorf returned in 1948 with a good selection of matted linoleum engravings made from sketches during his first trip the preceding year. He contacted dealers to whom he marketed his views of local New Orleans subjects and managed to sell some to galleries; however, he frequently encountered opposition to the prices he was asking. New Orleans, he concluded, is "crowded with artists, all trying to eek out a meager food-and-rent living, and the competition makes for cutthroat reduction in art prices" as they strive to sell their art to tourists. Surendorf concluded New Orleans was a poor market for his prints, and those depicting New Orleans subjects sold more easily in California, where he had a home and permanent studio.[32]

On the Atlantic coast, a few female etchers discovered Charleston, which bloomed as a printmaking hub in the early 1920s, a development noted in an early survey of southern graphic arts.[33] Although the etching revival of the 1880s had by-passed Charleston, the movement's resurgence in the second decade of the twentieth century struck the charming old seaport with a more definitive stroke than New Orleans.[34] As a number of art historians have recounted, two prominent women etchers, Ellen Day Hale of Philadelphia and Gabrielle de Veaux Clements of Baltimore, began to winter in Charleston during World War I, when naval combat in the Atlantic Ocean discouraged travel to Europe. In addition, Helen Hyde, known for her Japanese-inspired woodblocks, visited in 1916 to explore local southern views for some etchings, and in 1917 Bertha Jacques, an etching enthusiast and president of the Chicago Society of Etchers, arrived to arrange an exhibition at the Gibbes Memorial Art Gallery. This convergence of artists versed in etching and woodcuts encouraged and tutored local Charleston artists, notably Alice Ravenel Huger Smith.[35] Smith in turn taught and encouraged other local artists such as her friend Elizabeth O'Neill Verner.[36]

As the 1920s began, etching took root as a major facet of what has been termed the "Charleston Renaissance," a flowering of literary and visual arts in the city.[37] In 1920 the Carolina Art Association hired Alfred Hutty as its director and shortly thereafter, he caught the etching fever, teaching others once he mastered its technique.[38] With encouragement and support from Ellen Hale and Gabriele Clements, who were undoubtedly familiar with the etching society movement across the country, Charleston artists organized the first print society in the South. Clements, Hale, Smith, Hutty, and Verner, along with four others participants, founded the Charleston Etchers' Club in 1923 with a few others joining in the following years.[39] Like other etching societies, the association had annual exhibitions and made a press available for members' use; however, it did not adopt other practices that became common, such as establishing patron members, offering an annual presentation print to stimulate sales, or arranging "circuits," exhibitions of members' work that traveled to other cities. The organization remained exclusively local, both in membership and exhibitions, which were held annually from 1923 to 1928 and again in 1933.[40]

Many of the members of the Charleston Etchers' Club made only a few prints, but Hutty, Verner, and Antoinette Rhett produced a significant number of etchings. While Rhett abandoned etching soon after the organization's demise in the early 1930s, Hutty and Verner continued their production through the following decades, rivaling each other in their views of Charleston and its environs. At the end of the 1920s Anna Heyward Taylor set up a studio in the city as well, which continued to attract winter residents and other tourists.[41] Artists opened studios on Atlantic Street, a narrow lane paved with oyster shells in the historic district that became a genteel art colony, where Elizabeth Verner's studio served as a frequent tourist stop.[42]

Like New Orleans, Charleston's historic charm attracted a stream of visiting artists who sketched its sights and also fanned out to nearby lowland terrain for rural views. Sojourns of Prentiss Taylor, Childe Hassam, Charles William Smith, George Biddle, and Palmer Schoppe have been documented.[43] From images of Charleston in their print oeuvre, a number of others—Leon Pescheret, Victoria Hutson Huntley, Georges Schreiber, Katherine Merrill, and Alice Rumpf—can be counted among those who made prints from visits.

In historic St. Augustine, local artists formed a small arts association called the Galleon Club in 1924. It soon died but a new arts club organized in its wake in 1931. The organization, which changed names a number of times, collaborated with the local business community to restore St. Augustine to its former status as a winter artist's colony and thereby enhance its tourist appeal. Through the 1930s and 1940s members attempted to attract artists to the city, particularly those who worked in Provincetown during summers, such as Blanche Lazzell as well as Tod Lindenmuth and his wife Elizabeth Warren.[44] As in Charleston and New Orleans, prints became important media to provide inexpensive tourist mementos and publicize the town's attractions. Elizabeth Warren along with Walter Yeomans, Dano Jackley, and Edith Oliver depicted the town through intaglio while Celia Reid, Edith Oliver, and Blanche Lazzell did so in woodcuts.[45] Meanwhile, other areas of Florida attracted printmakers as well. On the west coast Walter Ronald Locke settled in Tarpon Springs and Polly Knipp Hill in St. Petersburg, while Kent Hagerman moved his etching production to Lakeland in the central part of the state.

From the mid-1920s through the next two decades, other areas of the coastal Southeast attracted artists who produced views of the region in prints. J. J. Lankes moved to the Chesapeake Bay area of Virginia from Buffalo, New York, in 1925, while Charles William Smith relocated to Richmond from his home in western Virginia. Both created a series of relief prints that depicted Virginia life in the historic coastal area, while Smith depicted his native Blue Ridge Mountain region as well. The tidewater area also lured northern etchers such as Earl Horter and Samuel Chamberlain.

Farther south Christopher A. D. Murphy began a wide-ranging project to etch scenes of his native Savannah in 1925, and visiting artists occasionally depicted that city. If Mobile, Alabama, did not lure visiting artists, it did nurture a native etcher, Marian Francis Acker, who launched her project to render Mobile's architectural heritage in etchings in the early 1930s. In the 1940s Walter Anderson made block prints on wallpaper strips farther west in Ocean Springs, Mississippi. As in Charleston and New Orleans, artists appear to have launched sketching forays from coastal ports to explore the surrounding lowland area for interesting images for their prints.

A few printmakers working on the coastal South, such as Elizabeth Verner and J. J. Lankes, had occasional opportunities to illustrate books about the South by other authors.[46] Verner, Lankes, and other southern printmakers publicized their prints and the region further by publishing their own books that compiled reproductions of their prints. Visual tours of the South through prints were nothing new. However, whereas northern artists illustrated earlier books, such as *Picturesque America,* which were published in the North, southern printmakers increasingly contracted with local publishers or printers to produce books exclusively of their work during the 1920s through the 1940s to publicize the traditional South.[47]

These southern, geographic artist books included varying amounts of text commenting on the imagery of the prints. Published locally, none appeared in fine print editions featuring high quality paper and fine type design with original impressions, as the aesthetic private press movement, which William Morris initiated, hardly touched the South during this era. Evidently, the expense such productions entailed, together with a limited market and lack of trained, interested, fine printers, discouraged such books for the South, unlike elsewhere in the country.[48]

Charles William Smith and J. J. Lankes led the trend at the end of the 1920s by using their relief prints of Virginia, mostly of the tidewater area, and Smith continued with a book on Charleston in 1933. Etchers in historic cities followed suit during the 1930s and 1940s.

In 1938 New Orleans etchers William Woodward and Carl Hancock published books of their etchings, while Hancock brought out three other pamphlets celebrating the historic city.[49] In Mobile, Marian Francis Acker published *Prints of the Past* in 1932 and *Etchings of Old Mobile* in 1938. During the 1940s similar books of Charleston and Savannah by Elizabeth O'Neill Verner and Christopher Murphy respectively appeared, while a northeastern etcher, Philip Kappel published another of Louisiana in 1950. Samuel Chamberlain included some drypoints of Williamsburg with his photographs of the town for his book published in 1947.[50] By 1950 it becomes evident that books of prints, as well as photographs, publicized the traditional South, particularly its historic urban architecture.[51]

Expansion Inland

By the 1920s, the inland New South cities of Nashville, Atlanta, and Birmingham had surpassed all the older coastal ports except New Orleans in population.[52] If these cities lacked the picturesque, tourist appeal of older seaports to attract visiting artists, they still provided a relatively warm climate and some employment opportunities that lured a small number of artists who were making prints by the 1930s. Sophonisba Hergesheimer came to Nashville from Pennsylvania and Frank Hartley Anderson to Birmingham from Massachusetts, while Richard Coe, an Alabama native, settled in Birmingham after his studies in the North and abroad.

By the 1930s cities such as Birmingham and Nashville had enough art patronage to foster genuine artistic communities, and local art organizations were formed.[53] These organizations encouraged teaching, creating, and exhibiting art in a sufficiently broad scope to encompass prints. In Nashville, Sophonisba Hergesheimer, Mayna Avent, and Ernest Pickup became friends as artists and members of the Studio Club of Nashville. Hergesheimer agreed that she would introduce Pickup to lithography if he taught her to make wood engravings, and she encouraged him to exhibit his prints in national shows.[54]

Birmingham saw the most significant organizing effort for prints in the South in 1935, when Frank Hartley Anderson founded the Southern Printmakers Society to bring print exhibitions to the region and also to raise standards for art. Birmingham could boast of an active art club, founded in 1907; by the mid-1930s, a sizeable number of artists were active, including a small number of printmakers.[55] However, Anderson did not gather a local group together, as did artists in Charleston and New Orleans. Instead he used a national art periodical, *Art Digest,* which featured a regular section devoted to prints, to recruit artists across the country and to publicize the organization's exhibitions. He relied on local newspapers for publicity in cities hosting the society's circuit exhibitions.

In a 1936 *Art Digest* article, Anderson announced his goal of showing the best among print work to the South, where few galleries, museums, and art schools existed. Part of his objective involved raising standards, standards set in the Northeast or abroad, for southern artists, who, often, did not master etching or relief media beyond a rudimentary level. Ellsworth Woodward articulated the same concern for quality in art produced in the South in an annual address to the Southern States Art League a few months earlier.[56] Furthermore, like other promoters of fine prints in the 1930s, Anderson believed strongly that the public should have more opportunity to buy good, affordable art, and prints offered a means to do so.[57]

As an early subscriber to *Art Digest,* Anderson had undoubtedly learned of other print societies continuing to sprout throughout the country, because components of his program, such as patron or associate members, presentation prints for monetary support, and prizes, had become standard practice for such organizations.[58] The society held its first exhibition in 1936 at the Birmingham Public Library, prior to a tour of other southern cities. For the Birmingham venue Anderson was able to arrange for a group of prints by major national figures, such as Rockwell Kent and John Steuart Curry to be included. However, because of prior arrangements, this group could not be included in the circuit to other southern cities.[59] On the roster of artists in later exhibitions, the only name that stands out for strong national recognition is John Taylor Arms, a leading exponent of technical mastery in the conservative etching tradition.

The exhibitions Anderson organized traveled not only to cities throughout the South but also to other parts of the country. By 1937 the society had fifteen exhibitions circulating, mostly in the South and the Midwest.[60] When he accepted a position in Atlanta with the Army Corps of Engineers in 1938, Anderson transferred the Southern Printmakers to Mountain Hall, a large house in Mount Airy, Georgia, that had been his wife's family home in the mountain foothills of north Georgia. The couple kept the organization going from that location until Anderson entered the military in 1942.[61] By 1940 the number of artists exhibiting had more than doubled, with membership among southern artists remaining a minority. Those southern printmakers included a few such as Alfred Hutty, Elizabeth O'Neil Verner, and J. J. Lankes who were recognized nationally due to participation in national shows. Among those from beyond the South, Anderson attracted a fair number of lesser-known, conservative artists, such as Grace Albee or Leo Meissner. Very obscure names appeared on lists of exhibitors as well.

Anderson's organization obviously could not compete with the many other print societies across the country in attracting artists with a national reputation, particularly as modernism was making considerable headway in New York by 1940; yet it gave those continuing to work in a traditional, realistic style, among them many southern printmakers, new exhibition venues. Southern imagery does not appear to be particularly common among the prints exhibited; however, some exhibiting members who were not southerners, such as Leon Pescheret, Ella Fillmore Lillie, and Leo Meissner, produced prints with southern imagery at some point in their printmaking career, so the organization may have encouraged or reflected their contact with the South.

The name of Wilmer Jennings, a black printmaker from Atlanta, appeared in a list of exhibiting artists in the 1940 brochure of the Southern Printmakers, but this tidbit of racial integration was an anomaly. Had they been aware of the name's racial identity, southern viewers, with their conservative racial mores, might have shunned the organization's exhibitions. Black artists like Jennings and his teacher Hale Woodruff could not exhibit their prints with art organizations in the South, and only the Harmon Foundation provided significant exhibition venues from 1926 to 1933 for black artists.[62] Even in a relatively liberal, southern city like Atlanta, black people had difficulty gaining entrance to the High Museum.[63] Artists coming to the South from other regions of the country confronted legal segregation, even in the freewheeling, cosmopolitan French Quarter of New Orleans. In his autobiography Charles Surendorf noted that he inadvertently sat at a table with colored diners in a French Quarter restaurant and "was nearly thrown out on his ear." Surendorf concluded that "the liberal minded northerner soon realizes he must keep his mouth shut and observe the customs of 'Rome.'"[64]

Black artists making prints in the South were few in number, and most worked in relief media of wood and linoleum, which did not require a press for printing. Foremost among them was Hale Woodruff, who came to Atlanta to establish the art department at Atlanta University in 1931. Woodruff taught his students to make relief prints, as he did, since they did not have a press available, and he nurtured a distinguished practitioner in this medium: Wilmer Jennings.[65] To counter the racial barriers he and his students faced in exhibiting their work or visiting museums and galleries, Woodruff organized annual exhibitions for black artists at Atlanta University beginning in 1942. In 1944 money was donated for an award in sculpture and graphics and a few, such as Jenelsie Holloway, exhibited prints.[66]

Artists active in small southern towns and rural outposts here and there in the South also engaged in printmaking, usually etching, during the 1930s and 1940s. Kent Hagerman continued his etching career in Lakeland, Florida, where he came on a circuitous route that jumped from Ohio to Denver to central Florida. James Fowler Cooper set up an etching studio on the family farm he inherited in rural Williamson County, South Carolina. A number of female printmakers worked in the unlikely region of northern Alabama. Mary Wallace Kirk made etchings at her home near Tuscumbia, Mildred Nungester managed to produce lithographs from her home in nearby Decatur, and Ida Ten Eyck O'Keeffe, the sister of Georgia O'Keeffe, produced monotypes during her brief appointment in the art department at Athens College. Later in the 1940s and early 1950s, a black printmaker, Claude Clark, also made linoleum cuts during the years he taught at Talladega College near Talladega, Alabama. Such activity in an area that would be considered a cultural backwater is surprising in an era when the only art museum in the state of Alabama was a fledgling institution begun in 1930 in an old high school building in Montgomery!

The Great Depression offered some southern artists time to make prints due to unemployment. Both Frank Hartley Anderson and Ernest Pickup took up carving wood plates to make prints in order to occupy spare time that resulted from lack of employment. In sales, prints gained some advantage over paintings since as multiples they were less expensive. One scholar observed, "Prints became an attractive medium to express cultural sophistication when more expensive objects had to be resisted."[67]

New commercial enterprises such as Associated American Artists (AAA) sprang up in New York City to print and market impressions at inexpensive prices to a broader segment of the American public. Founded in 1934, AAA contracted with individual artists to produce editions of 250 impressions in lithography or etching, which were sold for as little as five dollars per impression in mass commercial outlets like department stores.[68] AAA contracted with only a few southern artists: Walter Ronald Locke, a Florida winter resident, was among the first, and John McCrady, who had a New York reputation, followed when he began making lithographs in the 1940s.[69]

Southern artists in parts of the South harboring a weak or barely existent market for art, such as northern Alabama, rural South Carolina, or even Atlanta, created editions of merely five or ten impressions due to minimal chances of selling their work. Mildred Nungester commented to the author that she only sold her prints in Decatur, Alabama, when Tennessee Valley Authority (TVA) personnel came to the region.[70] Moreover, copper plates or those of wood were limited to small editions unless they were steel faced by galvanic action.

Printmakers working in small localities may not have had access to such procedures as Celia Cregor Reid did. Even for artists working in New York, good quality printing paper such as Rives was expensive, a factor that limited edition size.[71]

Associated American Artists publicized imagery of the South through their large editions by such artists as Thomas Hart Benton and Georges Schreiber, who traveled through the South and pictured the region in their paintings and lithographs. The increasing availability of automobile transportation and improved roads undoubtedly accounts for much of the American Scene movement as artists had access to remote areas not served by railroads. Although the South held a reputation for poor, even dangerous, roads at the end of World War I, by the mid-1920s southern roadways had improved to such an extent that twelve well-known, national highways traversed the South.[72] Thomas Hart Benton documented his artistic exploration of southern back roads, even into the mountains, which he began in 1928, with many more artists following in the 1930s and 1940s.[73] The South's reputation for cultural distinctiveness that constituted an antidote to modern, industrial, and even liberal, civilization in the North incited such exploration.[74] Artists from the South, like James Routh and Lamar Baker, explored the region as well, setting out from a home base like Atlanta to view more remote rural areas, which they interpreted in prints. Frequently, such visual exploration occurred through grants. Howard Cook received a Guggenheim travel grant, while James Routh and Robert Gwathmey benefited from the Julius Rosenwald Foundation. New Deal projects financed the travels of Georges Schreiber and Philip Reisman.[75]

North Versus South

New Deal art programs gave many more artists the opportunity to make prints and exposed more of the public to print media. Both the Public Works of Art Project (PWAP), 1933–34, and the later Federal Art Project of the Works Progress (later Projects) Administration (WPA/FAP), 1935–43, specifically allocated funds for prints.[76] The WPA/FAP established a Graphic Arts Division through which studios were set up across the country. In such major art centers as New York and Philadelphia the FAP established well-equipped graphic arts workshops, where artists could experiment with new techniques with technical assistance from experienced printers. On the largest workshop in New York, artists experimented with both screen printing (to make what Carl Zigrosser termed "serigraphs") and color lithography, media with which American artists, unlike those in Europe, had previously done little work. The FAP sponsored community art centers throughout the South in both white and black communities, such as that in New Orleans, in order to extend cultural resources beyond the Northeast and other major art centers to the artistically disadvantaged. In addition, the agency circulated exhibitions of prints executed through the project's largesse to various community centers in small towns and cities throughout the South and elsewhere.[77]

From a scan of state correspondence files, it does not appear that much printmaking of significance occurred on various FAP projects in southeastern states.[78] A few comments in those files suggest studios established here and there acquired an etching press, usually donated. For example, when a press was given to the Florida FAP in Jacksonville, etchings were made and demonstrations of the process were given to the public. However, the director of the program in Washington, Holger Cahill, did not believe there were enough good etchers on the Florida project to warrant purchase of good, foreign made, etching paper.[79] Richard Merrick, who made etchings on the Florida project, stated that most artists on its rolls were commercial artists or hacks, not true, professional artists.[80] On the Virginia FAP, headquartered at Richmond, the state director inquired about an assistant for a graphic arts workshop for which people in Richmond were eager. She added that silkscreen equipment and a lithograph press were available in her studio, which had adequate space; nevertheless, no further documentation appears that mentions artists actually producing prints in such a facility.[81]

As one would expect, the largest number of prints appear to have been produced on the Louisiana FAP in New Orleans, where a lithographer, Caroline Durieux, had been appointed director in 1939. Although the FAP there set up an art school with a gallery at its headquarters in a restored building of the French Quarter, no evidence indicates that either an etching or a lithographic press was available for artists to use.[82] In an interview about the New Orleans program, Durieux explained that although the Louisiana project had a gallery where works produced through the project could be exhibited, artists worked in their own studios. Later, a room in the Quarter provided space for those artists making silkscreen posters for the war effort. Durieux also noted that the New Orleans project was one of the few in the South that included blacks.[83] A relatively small number of artists working on the project produced prints, primarily etchings; of these, Lawrence Arthur Jones is the only one who can be identified as African American. His early etchings from that New Orleans period suggest that little technical help was available to him there. Knute Heldner and Alvin Sharp also produced etchings on the FAP, but names attached to other prints on the lists, such as Hal Story and Catherine Howell, are very obscure. Howell and Story produced lithographs, possibly using commercial printers.

A number of black artists from the South who joined the FAP graphic arts division in Philadelphia reaped the benefits of working with other accomplished printmakers at a well-equipped workshop that provided technical assistance. Four of the five black artists on this project—Dox Thrash, Claude Clark, Samuel Brown, and Raymond Steth—were born in the South and had migrated to the North. Thrash, along with Hugh Mesibov and Michael Gallagher, experimented with the carborundum stone, a tool that had been used for grinding lithographic stones, and applied it to the intaglio processes of etching and mezzotint, producing a large body of impressive prints as a result. Claude Clark and Raymond Steth also used this process. Only Thrash has been the subject of a catalogue raisonné, which suggests that he was the most prolific in applying the then new carborundum process and documenting southern black experience in print media.[84]

Although a few FAP community centers in the South appear to have had an etching press, none had a well-equipped graphic arts workshop with a press for lithography and printers trained to aid artists, such as those set up in New York and Philadelphia.[85] In the 1930s lithography gradually replaced etching as the most popular medium for fine prints, in part because the larger edition size lithography facilitated meant impressions could be sold more cheaply—essential during the Great Depression. For artists, lithography posed technical difficulties since the chemistry involved in printing with acid required more expertise than printing relief plates or intaglio with an etching press. With no graphic arts workshop comparable to that which the FAP established in New York and Philadelphia or printers trained for artists, artists in the South interested in lithography were at a distinct disadvantage. As

Clinton Adams points out in *American Lithographer, 1900–1960: The Artists and Their Printers,* finding and training commercial printers to print lithographs for artists took time, even in New York, during the early decades of the twentieth century.[86] By the 1930s printers like George Miller were available in New York and other major cities, but not in the South.

By the late 1930s more southern artists were learning lithography at the Art Students League in New York and other art schools such as the Colorado Springs Fine Arts Center. When they returned to the South, they adopted various solutions to the challenge of obtaining plates, traditional Bavarian limestones, and having their lithographs printed. Although purchasing stones by mail and shipping them to a printer when the drawing was completed was both cumbersome and expensive, the process seems to have been fairly widespread.[87] From New Orleans, Caroline Durieux shipped her stones to George Miller in New York, and she likely encouraged John McCrady to ship his eastward as well. When they began printmaking programs at Alabama universities in the 1940s, Maltby Sykes and Richard Zoellner shipped their stones, as well as those of their students, to printers in cities outside the South. In his article "Recollections of a Lithographile," Sykes comments that, "The importance of work done on stones shipped, processed, and printed by professional printers—mail-order lithography, as it might be called—has not been fully appreciated."[88] Mildred Nungester adopted a variation of this process. When she returned to Decatur, Alabama, after studying lithography at the Art Students League, she ordered zinc plates from a commercial printing company in Birmingham and after drawing her scenes on them, sent them back to be printed.[89]

By 1940 some artists in the South, like those elsewhere, managed to purchase their own lithography press as commercial firms were discarding equipment and replacing it with newer offset technology. James Routh, who served as Will Barnet's assistant in lithography at the Art Students League, was able to purchase his own Fuchs & Lang press for twenty dollars after he returned to Atlanta around 1940. Routh took it to his parents' home, cleaned and oiled the parts, and with the advice of Barnet, reassembled the press and got it working. He explained that printing lithography requires two people because one person has to keep the stone wet, so he enlisted the help of family and friends for that task.[90] Doris Alexander purchased her own press in 1945 in Philadelphia, where she studied lithography, and had it shipped to Columbia, South Carolina. She installed the press in her home where there was barely enough space for it to be operated.[91] She printed her own work after 1945, one of few women to do so, as a significant degree of upper body strength is required to crank the traditional lithographic press.[92]

With the FAP experimentation in color lithography and applying the commercial screen-printing process to fine art prints, or serigraphs, color began to appear in American prints to an extent that had not occurred before. Southerners making prints in New York, like Robert Gwathmey and William Henry Johnson, took advantage of these developments to produce some of the finest serigraphs of the period. Johnson was particularly prolific, producing his serigraphs at the Harlem Community Art Center supported by the FAP. Although FAP community art centers in the South expressed interest in the screen-printing methods, often asking the national headquarters in Washington for manuals and instructions, and small workshops, like that in New Orleans, produced some for the war effort, little of artistic note was accomplished in the region. Artists did express interest in learning. In the early 1940s

Joe Clancy taught the screen-print process to students at the Dixie art colony in rural Alabama, who produced impressions as a group, which all signed.[93]

If printmakers working in the South created little of significance in color lithography and serigraphy before 1950, artists working here and there in the South did produce color prints through more traditional methods, particularly in the relief media of wood and linoleum. Women artists at Newcomb College printed wood and linoleum carved plates inked with color. Charleston was a small center for the color woodblock due to the outstanding work of a few women, especially Alice Smith, who learned the Japanese technique of applying color through registration of multiple colored wood plates. Anna Heyward Taylor practiced both the Japanese method and the white line technique pioneered by B. J. O. Nordfeldt in Provincetown. A significant number of southern women artists summered in Provincetown, noted for color block printmaking due to Nordfeldt's influence. Mabel Pugh, Mary Tannahill, Sophonisba Hergesheimer, and Mayna Avent all sojourned in Provincetown through this period, and all experimented with color prints in the Nordfeldt method at one time or another.

Hand coloring some impressions of etchings and relief prints also appears fairly common. Among those in New Orleans, Alvin Sharpe produced hand-tinted aquatints, while Clarence Millet's block prints appear hand colored. Roderick MacKenzie hand colored areas of his large lithographs of steel mills in a thin wash of watercolor. Polly Knipp Hill hand colored some of her etchings, although this may have been in her later years, while Edith Walker Oliver is known for her hand-colored etchings of historic architecture, many of St. Augustine.

Culturally conservative, the South neither cultivated innovative artists nor attracted them to any discernable extent before 1950. Artists making prints in the South as well as those who visited tended to be traditional etchers. Even in the French Quarter of New Orleans, with its freer, bohemian mores, a number of the printmakers who congregated to picture its sights never achieved much beyond a competent, if mediocre, level, mostly in etching. Although one prominent abstract artist associated with the German Bauhaus, Josef Albers, found refuge at Black Mountain College in Black Mountain, North Carolina, in the 1930s and 1940s, he did not develop a printmaking program or exert any modernizing influence in southern printmaking.[94] A touch of modernist creativity can be detected in some of the relief prints Hale Woodruff made in Atlanta, like *Relics* and *Georgia Woodlands,* a result of his previous exposure to modern art in Paris. The creative spirit that modernism reflected is most emphatically represented in the linocut designs of Walter Anderson, although they reach beyond modernist style to more eclectic influences and his own isolated spirit.

More research needs to be done to determine to what extent the Maitland Art Center, located near Orlando, Florida, fostered experimentation in printmaking. Jules Andre Smith, a New England etcher, established the center around 1935 with his friend Duke Banca through the largesse of the Bok Foundation. The center's mission was to serve as a laboratory studio to promote experimentation in modern art. Fellowships lasting from four to nine months were extended to three to five resident artists per year from 1938 until 1958. Smith, whose eyesight was failing by 1935, shipped one of his etching presses to the facility for residents' use since he had abandoned etching.

Carson Davenport, a Virginia printmaker, received one of the first fellowships in 1938, but what influence it had on his prints is not known. Other artists known for innovative approaches in modern art—Ralston Crawford, Milton Avery, and Boris Margo—were also residents by 1950. Milton Avery and Boris Margo made abstract monotypes, and while in residence, Margo probably made the experimental cellocuts for which he is well known.[95] Frank Besedick made his etchings of Florida during his residency or after, but they are firmly traditional. No clear evidence indicates that he or any other artist used the etching press at Maitland.[96]

A small number of artists from the South who left for New York, the center of experimental art activity, soaked up a degree of modernism that influenced their print style. In the 1920s stylized African art influenced the bold, simple, black-and-white forms of James Lesesne Wells' linoleum prints, which can be considered part of the Harlem Renaissance. In the early 1930s Charles William Smith abandoned traditional, scenic prints of his native Virginia to experiment with a new method of combining abstract forms in relief when he taught at Bennington College. Smith's experimentation was probably the result of living and exhibiting in New York from 1933 to 1936. If purely abstract works like those of Smith and Albers have scant relationship to the South, compositions produced by such artists as Robert Gwathmey and Walter Anderson incorporated a semi-modernist, experimental idiom in simplified forms, undoubtedly due to the influence of a New York avant-garde as well as foreign sources. Lamar Baker and Carroll Cloar used new conceptions of pictorial space in their montage compositions.

Equally significant, artists from the South traveling beyond the South to study and work confronted increasingly critical perspectives on the South pervading art circles, particularly in New York during the 1930s. H. L. Mencken's scorn for the South and its cultural achievements, which became more vituperative with the Scopes Trial in 1925, is well known.[97] The artistic left, increasingly strong in New York and other art centers in the 1930s, promulgated egalitarian social, and democratic political values that were at odds with those that pervaded the conservative and hierarchical South. Artists associated with the left often incorporated their social, political perspectives in their prints.[98] The publicity the Communist Party gave to the Scottsboro case drew national attention to the worst of southern racial mores, which fed the national campaign to make lynching a federal crime. Artists of the left centered in New York increasingly attacked the South through their prints, as George Biddle did in his lithograph *Alabama Code* and Harry Sternberg in his lithograph *Southern Holiday,* both of which the Scottsboro Case inspired.[99]

A popular instructor in etching, lithography, and composition at the Art Students League from 1933 until 1961, Sternberg taught a number of southern artists including James Routh, Lamar Baker, Carroll Cloar, Mary Wallace Kirk, and Elizabeth Catlett just after she had lived and worked in the South.[100] His influence might be reflected in critical perspectives toward the region in the prints of some of these students. Routh remarked that Sternberg often engaged him in arguments about the South, and Sternberg himself confessed that a "cloying sweetness" in the work of some of his southern students provoked a degree of annoyance on his part, which he did not repress.[101]

From his perspective Sternberg was encouraging his southern students to think critically and reflect such thinking in their art. About two of them, Lamar Baker and James Routh, Sternberg wrote:

> Lamar Baker gradually did come around to dealing with the real world and did some strong and handsome prints that touched on some of the problems of the South. He and James Routh were curious and open minded, hungry to learn, so that when I pushed them to deal with the real world in their art they opened their eyes and hearts. It was, I know, very difficult because of their deep loyalty to the South. I was not trying to convert them any more than I was trying to bend the point of view of many of my other students who came from places like Japan and Israel. I only wanted my students to learn to *see* and not to avoid.[102]

Sternberg's words suggest that in his view, artists from the South tended to idealize the South in their art, avoiding critical perspectives. New York artists were not the only ones to display critical attitudes toward the South. Mildred Nungester drew on her sketches of southern scenes when she made lithographs as a student at the Colorado Springs Fine Arts Center in 1943–44. She claimed that a degree of prejudice against the South existed among the instructors there, such as Arnold Blanch, who considered her "hopelessly sunk in Southern culture" because of her subject matter.[103]

Cultural pressure from the South to avoid addressing its problems through art came from various directions, not least of which was a defensive cultural heritage since the abolitionist attacks of the 1830s. The Southern States Art League, which offered membership to artists residing in the South for at least five years, continued that inclination by encouraging members to produce positive images of the region. The organization tried to stem the artistic drain from the South, and also to encourage southern artists to depict southern subjects and to portray what the South had suffered as well as the progress it had made.[104] Articles and reviews of native, southern artists, such as Elizabeth O'Neill Verner, which appeared in local southern newspapers and magazines, often cite their theme as the beauty and charm of the South.[105] Recent scholarly investigations claim that southern art of the period aimed to reinforce the racial status quo and class structure in the region.[106] Depicting flaws of former Confederate states would hardly earn a favorable response from fellow white Southerners.

The commentary Elizabeth Verner and Marian Acker supplied for their books featuring etchings of their native cities of Charleston and Mobile respectively suggests that native southern women may have been more committed to this goal than their male counterparts. Gender expectations imposed a decorative, beautifying agenda on the female artist. Those living in the South would most likely accept such an agenda given the region's conservative mores and psychological need to enhance its image after a demoralizing defeat in the Civil War. The imagery and styles that evolve in print oeuvres as well as artistic biographies described in the entries that follow lend some credence to this idea.

Stylistic or political extremes were, however, at the far fringe of artistic activity for the vast majority of artists who came from the South or to the South in depicting aspects of its culture from the 1920s through the 1940s. For many artists, prints remained a sideline of their artistic expression, noted in an early discussion of graphic arts in the South.[107] Sketches were often made on site in some southern location and then, back in the studio, wherever that might be, a painting was often made with one or more prints produced as well. The paintings and prints were frequently compositions produced from a number of sketches as well as artistic imagination. Hovering somewhere between high and popular art depending on the artist, prints of this era continued to have a reproductive function, to some extent, extending two-dimensional creations to larger numbers of the public. Sold more widely and cheaply as multiples than paintings, they provided additional income for artists. If they only contributed significantly to a tourist economy on the urban, coastal South, articles in local newspapers about individual artists testify that prints promoted civic pride in other cities and enhanced a sense of cultural progress through diversity in artistic media for the region.

At the end of his essay "The Southern Heritage," Charles W. Ramsell notes that at the end of the nineteenth century and beginning decades of the twentieth, the South was swept into national currents as increasing ease of travel allowed southern youth of sufficient means to study at northern schools and colleges, while northern scholars and other professionals found employment in the South.[108] Artists can be considered part of such interlocking mobility among the professional classes, which bound the South more tightly to a national visual culture, even if sectional strains remained. The increasing number of artists with southern connections who made prints, multiples of their images at less expensive prices, tightened this nexus as their southern imagery and biographical connections created more threads that knit the South to the larger American cultural arena.

Scanning Peter Falk's *Who Was Who in American Art* for southern biographical connections would probably disclose many printmakers who were born in the South, and left the region for training and employment elsewhere with nary a trace of their southern origins detected in their imagery. Ella Gregory's early study of printmaking in the South mentions Lewis Allen from Alabama among the region's noteworthy graphic artists.[109] Yet examination of examples of Allen's prints in publications yields little suggestion of southern places in titles or imagery. Lucille Douglass, also born in Alabama, spent the early part of her career there, but her etching oeuvre depicts scenes reflecting her later years spent traveling through the Orient.

The printmakers highlighted here with reproductions of their work have a documented biographical connection to the South and views of the region in their prints based on observation as well as imagination. Their imagery can be significant in understanding how the South was viewed in a painful era of its history that was marked by post–Civil War poverty as well as Jim Crow laws legitimizing racial segregation. Photographs of the region taken during the Depression era by Walker Evans and other documentary photographers, as well as those with more romantic, poetic proclivities such as Clarence Laughlin, have been highly celebrated; yet the multiple images created by the artistic hand in revived print media also deserve recognition.

2

Imagery of the South

In an essay published in 1964, George Tindall, one of the foremost historians of the early twentieth-century South, proclaimed there were "few areas of the modern world that have bred a regional mythology so potent, so profuse and diverse, even paradoxical, as the American South."[1] With such a mythological complex well developed by the 1920s, artists turning to the South for subjects confronted a wet, fecund natural environment with an underdeveloped and weakly industrialized economy, and a strict racial caste hierarchy as well. Nevertheless, printmakers were almost invariably well-trained educated artists exposed to various broad national and international artistic currents; hence, southern culture rarely appears through its isolating emblems, the Confederate flag or segregation signage, but, more often, as part of a larger cultural arena with ties forged to the rest of the nation.

By the end of the nineteenth century, imagery of lowland swamps and plantations had suffused enough paintings and popular prints of the South to create a romantic, idealizing iconographic tradition that coincided with a sentimental, nostalgic strain in southern literature. In subsequent decades, as more artists made prints and looked to the South for subjects, traces of that romantic vein continued to appear. A European graphic tradition centered on historic, architectural vistas along with a burgeoning preservation movement encouraged increasing numbers of printmakers to apply that tradition to historic buildings of the urban southeastern coast. In addition, by the first decades of the twentieth century, rising socialist influence that championed a social underclass—the "common man"—turned increasing numbers of artists to its plight as well as to its mores. Scholars have also identified a backlash against "modernity," accelerated change wrought by technological advancement, that idealized a tradition-bound "folk" and their folkways that artists, writers, and collectors were intent on documenting.[2] In their book *I'll Take My Stand* (1930), the Vanderbilt Agrarians represent the most vocal expression of this viewpoint.

The Natural World

As art historians have frequently remarked, the South's warm climate fostered growth of flora and fauna that supplied a fecund source of imagery to artists who created scenes of a natural paradise.[3] The South was the only region of the country that included an extensive area of low wetlands in the form of marshes or swamps that harbored a rich panoply of wildlife. Before the Civil War naturalist artists such as Mark Catesby, William Bartram, and John James Audubon embarked on scientific explorations, traveling through the Southeast in quest of new species. After the Civil War painters such as Joseph Meeker and Martin Johnson Heade made their way southward to render the swamps of Louisiana and the wetlands of Florida, with moss-hung oaks and pines breaking the horizontal sweep of their landscapes or "swampscapes."

Still a primarily rural region during the first half of the twentieth century, artists tended to turn to the same low, wet terrain when they investigated the natural world. Most who did so appeared to have visited or resided in the two urban art centers of New Orleans and Charleston, and from there traveled to the surrounding lowlands for their subjects. But as more artists moved to Florida to take advantage of the warm climate, they pictured its flora and fauna as well. The most notable among them for original style, Walter Anderson, resided on the Mississippi coast at Ocean Springs.

In the first half of the twentieth century, relatively few artists turned to birds of the coastal lowlands for emphasis in print imagery, as did Victoria Hutson Huntley, who donned the role of artist-explorer like her earlier male predecessors who explored the southern lowlands. Huntley explored the Florida Everglades when she lived in the Orlando area during the 1940s. Around the same time that Huntley investigated avian species of the Everglades, Morris Henry Hobbs was making large, polished aquatints of birds hovering over the Louisiana swamps. Occasionally one finds such coastal wildlife in prints by other artists, such as Kent Hagerman or Adolf Dehn. Visually impressive shapes of species such as egrets, herons, and pelicans with long, curvaceous necks and pointed beaks appear to have attracted most artistic attention; however, the low, close-up viewpoint we see in Huntley's lithograph was highly unusual (Fig. 1).

While Huntley made trips from central Florida to the exotic terrain of the Everglades during the 1940s, Walter Anderson sailed to Horn Island, a barrier island off the Mississippi coast to observe its bird life. Realistic representation of southern species did not engage Anderson's artistic sensibility as much as the opportunity for rhythmic, decorative patterns (Fig. 2). Anderson has achieved renown for his outstanding sense of design as well as for the unusual material he selected or found for prints: the back of wallpaper strips that often resulted in an unusually elongated format and large size for the period.

Most prints of the period were relatively small in size, so when nature appeared, it usually did so in small slices of botanical life, either flowers or trees. Although Walter Anderson worked images of trees and plants as well as birds into his creative compositions, botanical prints with particular species in close-up view on a flat, undifferentiated ground tended to be the province of women. Women artists had appropriated still life as well as flowers to their artistic oeuvre since the seventeenth century in Holland.[4] When those in the South turned to prints, they often chose flowers for their imagery, probably because images would likely be close at hand in their domestic sphere. A number of women carved wood or linoleum blocks for prints of their floral compositions. Wood carving and wood engraving, still life, and other decorative arts became associated with women artists over the course of the nineteenth century in America, and this gender tradition extended into the early twentieth century South as well.[5]

Botanical forms can supply simple images to delineate, but the best prints of this genre or artistic category distinguished themselves by their striking compositions, whether the asymmetrical compositions influenced by the Japanese bird and flower woodcuts or more frontal, symmetrical views. South Carolina women artists associated with the Charleston Renaissance—Anna Heyward Taylor and Alice Ravenel Huger Smith in woodcut as well as Antoinette Rhett in etching—have been celebrated for their outstanding compositions in Japanese asymmetrical designs; however, women artists in other areas of the South deserve attention for their flower prints from wood or linoleum blocks: Sadie Irvine in New Orleans; Sophonisba Hergesheimer and Mayna Avent in Nashville; Mabel Pugh of Raleigh, North Carolina; as well as Edna Reed Whaley in Columbia, South Carolina. The symmetrical approach to composition is evident in Mayna Avent's color woodcut of irises in contrast with the asymmetrical design in Antoinette Rhett's colored etching of hollyhocks (Figs. 3 and 4, color plate).

Fewer southern printmakers chose the more complex, formal still life of plants within a specified three dimensional setting by which both Sophonisba Hergesheimer and Charles William Smith distinguished themselves in their chosen media. Hergesheimer was undoubtedly influenced by her Peale family tradition in Pennsylvania, which included some of the best early American still life painters. Her formal still life compositions, which she transferred from painting to lithography, proclaimed her skill in creating traditional, three-dimensional space for the objects she combined and placed on a draped, tabletop setting. The large southern magnolia, which she so often placed in foreground, was a favorite flower subject for southern women artists, probably because it was so commonly associated with women, beauty, and the South (Fig. 5).[6]

By the early 1930s Charles William Smith began to distinguish himself with simple still life objects in an interior window setting through which an exterior background, whether in the form of a landscape or cityscape, is discernable (Fig. 6). North Carolina artist Hobson Pittman also used this composition pattern for linocuts that juxtaposed contrasting inside/outside, foreground/background views. Another North Carolina printmaker, Mary Harvey Tannahill, made simpler still-life compositions of flowers in a vase through color block prints that echoed early folk art styles.

Trees were probably the most common natural subject matter in prints of the South. Instead of depicting the broad vistas typical of the late nineteenth-century coastal scenes, printmakers tended to narrow their scope to focus on a small range of individual specimens of pines, cypress, or oak, such as we see in *Cypress* by Henrietta Bailey (Fig. 7). Moss dripping from branches of oak or cypress had become almost an archetypal visual icon that denoted the natural world of the Deep South since the swampscape paintings of the late nineteenth century. Even if documentary evidence did not exist that Mabel Dwight's lithograph of a graveyard is a New Orleans scene, we would know a southern coastal location due to the moss-hung live oaks that dominate its imagery.

The distant nocturnal scene with simple images of trees and a moon became somewhat of a formula, which Bailey and her colleague Sadie Irvine carved into linoleum plates as well as on clay for pottery decoration. Alice Ravenel Huger Smith also created a few similar landscapes in color woodcuts.[7] Although such landscape views in color relief prints are relatively scarce, they are significant as extensions in print media of the tendency to romanticize the coastal wetlands and to rely on simple imagery of tree, moss, and moon to do so.

Both Sadie Irvine and Hale Woodruff reveal a somewhat similar compositional strategy in displaying a dense range of cropped tree trunks across a lowland swamp scene. Irvine's *Marsh Maple,* with diagonally splaying branches, individualized leaf forms, and a few crooked trunks reveals a naturalistic bent on the artist's part (Fig. 8). Irvine conveys distance or depth in space by placing shadowy tree forms, perhaps with hanging moss, in a muted background. By contrast, Hale Woodruff's linoleum cut *Georgia Woodland,* exhibits a more modernist, flattened composition whereby depth in space is represented by higher elevation on the two-dimensional picture plane (Fig. 9). Woodruff also simplifies his pine trees by aligning trunks, branches, and needles along a rigid horizontal and vertical axis. Walter Anderson created equally distinctive compositions with trees in linoleum cuts. In such works he fashions his typical rhythmic pattern established through repetition and parallel alignment of forms.

Trees are also found in other print media, particularly etchings, the most commonly practiced print medium in the South. In addition to his prints of Charleston focusing on people and architecture, Alfred Hutty is also known for his countless images of trees: from thin, southern pines to expansive, sturdy oaks punctuated by graceful peaks of moss that enhanced the romantic image of the South.[8] Many of Hutty's etchings were landscapes in which little else besides trees in the foreground receive emphasis. Elizabeth O'Neill Verner and James Fowler Cooper also created etchings in which peaks of moss hanging from live oaks beautified a southern scene. When placed within such a romantic context, Mabel Dwight's lithograph of a New Orleans graveyard gains some satirical import as its straight pointed moss hangs like a sinister screen across the top of the picture space (Fig. 11).

Hutty inspired some of his students, such as Walter Ronald Locke and Elizabeth White, to render trees in etchings. Living on the west coast of Florida, Locke was one of the few artists to highlight the Florida palm in a large number of prints. Like his mentor Hutty, Locke often combined architectural structures with tree imagery, placing the tree in the foreground so it can compete for attention with distinctive architecture, such as a lighthouse (Fig. 10). As the sharp etching needle on metal allows minute detail in a way that other print media do not, individual leaf forms can easily be discerned in Locke's tree imagery.

The landscapes we see in the lithographs of Buell Whitehead and James Routh are rural inland scenes that have lost much of the romantic aura associated with coastal views highlighting the natural world. Both relate to agrarian themes that were common in landscape prints of the 1930s, particularly those of the Midwest. Routh's expanse of cotton rows in the hilly foreground shows productive control over nature that can be seen in many other views in prints highlighting human labor involved in cultivation of cotton and tobacco. Routh was one of the few printmakers of this era who also pictured destruction of the natural environment by industry and erosion, such as we see in Whitehead's lithograph of an eroded hillside in south Alabama (Figs. 32 and 33). Erosion of soil became a dire problem in the South by the 1930s. A 1934 survey of soil conditions in the region showed that over half of the rural land, something over 150 million acres, suffered from erosion, and we occasionally see evidence of erosion in prints and paintings.[9]

Mountain vistas begin to enter print iconography during the 1920s and become more frequent in the 1930s and 1940s. By the mid-1920s a national highway system linked the mountain South to other areas of the country, making its vistas more accessible to the gaze of artists and other viewers.[10] Chauncey Ryder appears to have been among the first to depict the mountains of Tennessee and North Carolina beginning around 1920.[11] Richard

Zoellner along with William Woodward, Harrison Cady, and Leon Pescheret all deployed the high mountain viewpoint for panoramic scenes of the mountains of eastern Tennessee and western North Carolina in their chosen print media. Often a small cabin denotes isolated human habitation. In most such mountain as well as piedmont views during this era, nature usually appears tame, controlled, or even molested by human hand, rarely in the more natural, untouched state typical of coastal scenes. In Doris Alexander's view of a quarry, the opposite pole of mountain heights, human work on the land has fashioned dark, beautiful, yet slightly disturbing depths of space (Fig. 39).

Architectural Vistas

In prints of the South from the 1920s through the 1940s, the land and its vegetation more often provides a setting, sometimes an embellishment, for architectural forms and human activities, which take center stage. Architecture usually provides the most specific indication of place in prints through this era. Among the most numerous are those that reflect interest in a historic architectural legacy along the southeastern coast, particularly in Charleston and New Orleans but including tidewater Virginia, Savannah, St. Augustine, Mobile, and other small outposts of early settlement. Numerous etchings, along with woodcuts, linoleum cuts, wood engravings, and a few lithographs from this period, reveal interest in historic buildings and support for an expanding historic preservation movement among those who were visually aware.

The books that southern printmakers published of their prints emphasized historic architecture and contributed to an expanding body of architectural literature, particularly architectural histories, during the 1930s.[12] Commentary written by printmakers, from Charles William Smith's preface in *Old Virginia in Block Prints* to the more extensive text supplied by Elizabeth Verner and Marian Acker in their books, testifies that nostalgia for the traditional South motivated architectural prints for memory, celebration, and preservation. Martha Severens has shown how visual art nurtured the preservation movement in Charleston, but drawings, paintings, photographs, and prints picturing the southeastern coast, from Virginia to New Orleans, clamored to capture structures in danger of vanishing.[13]

The South led the country in preserving entire historic districts in cities during the 1920s and 1930s. In both Charleston and New Orleans concerned citizens organized historic preservation societies in the 1920s, which led to enactment of the earliest historic preservation ordinances in the country.[14] Etchers, such as William Woodward and Morris Henry Hobbs in New Orleans and Elizabeth Verner in Charleston, regarded their prints as deliberate contributions to preservation movements in those cities.[15] William Woodward produced a series of drypoints from earlier crayon sketches, which were sold in an edition for the benefit of the Vieux Carré Commission that had organized to preserve the quarter's historic character.[16] Elizabeth Verner, a charter member of Charleston's Society for the Preservation of Old Dwellings, offered etchings to the organization for sale at fundraisers.[17] Although Savannah and Mobile did not lead in preservation efforts, the etchings of Christopher Murphy and Marian Acker respectively encouraged historic preservation in those cities. The commentary on individual buildings that Acker supplied in her books makes her concern with preservation clearly evident.

In Virginia the massive project that began in the late 1920s to restore Williamsburg through the funds provided by the Rockefeller Foundation changed the character of historic preservation efforts nationally.[18] Both Charles William Smith and J. J. Lankes selected Williamsburg buildings for some their prints in the late 1920s, when most of the restoration was still in the planning stage. Alice Rumph, an etcher with roots in Georgia and Alabama, began etchings of Williamsburg landmarks before 1934 and placed them in the Colonial Williamsburg Foundation gift shop where they sold well.[19] In 1938, as the second phase of the restoration project began, William Perry, the lead architect for the Williamsburg restoration project, commissioned a New England printmaker, Samuel Chamberlain, to sketch restored buildings, from which Chamberlain made a number of drypoints (Fig. 22).[20] Perry was obviously aware that multiple images drawn by an artist could provide an important publicity tool for the project. Other etchers such as Leon Pescheret and Earl Horter were also drawn to historic Williamsburg for images.

Although most such artistic support for architectural preservation occurred at historic coastal cities, occasionally prints were used at more isolated points farther inland. For example, Mabel Pugh's *Rock House Ruins* was reproduced on a program to unveil a historic marker for the central North Carolina remnant, thus fostering historic architectural memory (Fig. 23).[21]

Such architectural prints of the South are part of a conservative printmaking tradition, particularly associated with etching. Europe's old-world architecture lured American painter-etchers of the late nineteenth century as well as those referred to as the second generation or second etching revival in the early decades of the twentieth.[22] Etchers such as Samuel Chamberlain, Earl Horter, and Morris Henry Hobbs, traveled to Europe and rendered picturesque views with emphasis on old-world structures whose elaborately carved detail challenged their technical expertise. Some, like Chamberlain, Hobbs, and Horter, veered toward American architecture of the southeastern coast after such European forays. The linocut oeuvre of Mabel Pugh indicates that this geographic transfer of architectural iconography from Europe to the Southeast occurred in relief media as well, although to a lesser extent. Architectural print historians discussing national trends have emphasized modern architectural wonders like skyscrapers and bridges in New York that captured the imagination of printmakers working there, but they have tended to disregard interest in historic American architecture.[23]

To many young New York artists of the 1930s, like Jacob Kainen, the conservative printmaking tradition was "deadening . . . a timid, ineffectual echo of the past," and to a major American print historian, artists who worked within it were "victims of a dominating heritage handed down by the European artist-etchers."[24] To artists exploring the historic southeast, however, the tradition served as a felicitous vehicle to heighten consciousness of an architectural legacy increasingly threatened by progress and decay. Architectural prints of old southeastern seaports often bear a subtitle with the word "Old" followed by the name of the city: "Old New Orleans" or "Old Mobile," indicating artists were cultivating historic, picturesque associations to heighten historic appeal. Often minor visual evidence of decrepitude, such as flaking plaster, was apparent in an overall scene of genteel or elegant shabbiness. Prints usually idealized and romanticized deteriorating buildings by focusing on stylized features with delicate or soft lines, tonal contrast, embellishing vegetation, or color. In a few rare instances printmakers depicted advanced decay for a more dramatic form of romantic interest, as in Mabel Pugh in *Rock House Ruins* (Fig. 23).

Urban architectural views, termed *vedute* in the Italian tradition, can be differentiated according to breadth of view. Those of the coastal south, like the views of natural scenery, tended to narrow in focus, eschewing the panoramic view to capture stylistic details that distinguished a particular building. As we see from the prints shown here, many printmakers focused on monuments or landmarks, identified by name in a title, with historic significance for a city or locale. Often such landmarks were early churches, reflecting the importance of the church in southern culture. St. Michaels and St. Philips provided subjects for many etchings of Charleston by Hutty and Verner, and they appeared in woodcuts by Anna Heyward Taylor as well (Figs. 17 and 18). J. J. Lankes and Charles William Smith often chose churches of tidewater Virginia for subjects of their relief prints, as their books testify. Christopher Murphy's book on Savannah shows that he pictured its residential landmarks such as the Green House in addition to historic public buildings like Chatham Academy that we see here (Fig. 20). In New Orleans secular landmarks such as Madame John's Legacy, the Napoleon House, and the French Market seem to outnumber those of the St. Louis Cathedral, suggesting a more secular culture there. Historic cemeteries, such as the St. Louis Cemetery in New Orleans seen in Surendorf's wood engraving or that attached to St. Philips church in Charleston, supplied rarer iconography in prints (Fig. 16).

Some views encompassed smaller segments of architectural space. In New Orleans this was often the interior courtyard as well as the dark passageway or antechamber through which it was accessed, often guarded by a wrought or cast iron gate, such as we see in H. Alvin Sharpe's view of Demarchy's Court (Fig. 14). The courtyard served to link the main house with a carriage house and slave, or later, servants', quarters. For artists and their patrons, the courtyard not only represented the city's French and Spanish heritage with a strong, private domain in its historic residential core, it also celebrated the restoration of the Quarter, as courtyards had been filled with junk and trash during the period of its decline. Restoring a building meant beautifying the courtyard, often planting native species for which garden clubs gave advice, and we see such floral displays in Clarence Millet's color block print.[25] Some courtyards, such as that at 628 Toulouse Street, seen in Millet's *Claiborne Court,* where a number of artists had studios, appear repeatedly (Fig. 15). Artists usually centered their courtyard views around an elegant entrance, whether a heavy, rounded archway, a curving staircase, or a patterned, iron gate.

The wrought or cast iron gate with its elaborate grillwork became even narrower focal points for prints of New Orleans, Charleston, and Mobile, principally in etchings whose thin, delicate lines easily captured such fine detail. Some with strong elegant patterns, such as Sword Gate in Charleston and Wishing Gate in New Orleans, became tourist attractions in their own right and appear frequently in etchings by various artists. Patterned iron gates received as much attention from Charleston printmakers, although due to Charleston's English architectural heritage, iron gates tended to be exterior. Anna Heyward Taylor's woodcut of St. Philips seen through the wrought iron gate protecting its cemetery shows that relief media could project ironwork patterns as well (Fig. 18).

Interest in the entrance as a subject for prints did not limit itself to the patterned iron gate. Particularly in Charleston, artists pictured the wood door, and not just the elegant high style variety that we see as a focal point in Elizabeth Verner's view of the Ravenel house. Elizabeth Curtis's book of photographs, *Gateways and Doorways of Charleston* (1926), might account for some of the attention Charleston artists gave to the exterior entrance.

Windows became focal points for prints only occasionally. We see a rare example of the barely distinguishable, plain, sashed window in the background of Charles Smith's still-life composition, through which he frames a generalized mountain landscape (Fig. 6). Smith uses a similar sash window setting for his woodcut *Charleston Window* published in the 1933 issue of the periodical *Colophon,* and he gives more emphasis to an elegant arched window in the woodcut *Washington House Window* published in his book *Old Charleston.* A few other examples can be cited in which artists celebrated the arched fan window, a distinguishing feature of Federal architecture. Both Hobbs and Eugene Loving rendered the large fan window in the house at 628 Toulouse Street, New Orleans, the same address featured in Millet's color print. In a few other cases the arched window appeared above or within a door. In Verner's *Ravenel Doorway* a small fanlight, which is heightened by value contrast in the lower center of the composition, supplies much of her etching's aesthetic appeal (Fig. 19).

In the opposite visual direction, artists elongated perspectives to encompass urban street scenes, which projected a feel for a city by blending a range of adjoining buildings, walls, and gates that lined the street and its sidewalks. Hobbs's view of the Labranche Building represents one of the most distant of such views in this period. As in this composition, such scenes were usually structured on a diagonal, and they frequently captured a clip of a building or balcony corner on the opposite side of the street in the immediate foreground. In Hobbs's *Iron Lace, Old New Orleans* this corner is only the underside of an eave, but sometimes it included a fragment of elegant iron pattern (Fig. 12). Less frequently artists chose a tunnel structure from the center of the street, as Hutty did for his popular etching of Church Street in Charleston, *Charleston Spires.*[26] In St. Augustine, Avila Street, around which the historic core of the city centered, became the landmark that most printmakers depicted, undoubtedly for its tourist appeal.[27]

Frequently human figures are added to enliven the scene, but if the artist wished to emphasize the architecture, they remained small in proportion so as not to detract from the building facades and to provide scale as well. Such figures tended to be stock or stereotypical, and their dress and race suggests two contrasting emphases: either the contemporary or the traditional. As in Christopher Murphy's scene and that of Eugene Loving, artists sometimes included figures in contemporary attire to imply that the old world city was host to contemporary life. More often figuration leaned toward the traditional with stereotypical female figures appearing in tandem with the old world character of the architecture. These women frequently sport a long dress with apron as they stroll on a sidewalk or appear in courtyard views, as in Millet's color linocut. Servants' quarters adjacent to interior courtyards justified their placement in such private locales.

Printmakers enlivening street scenes with figures usually chose black females strolling along a sidewalk before building facades. Such figures are particularly prominent in Charleston prints. The flower woman balancing a basket on her head, such as we see in Verner's *Ravenel Doorway,* became a stock figure in Charleston views. Some scholars have regarded these black flower women primarily as decorative accessories that create an old South ambiance.[28] Similar stereotypical figures appear before traditional architecture in other southern coastal locations, such as Mobile and Virginia towns, as obvious icons denoting the old urban South. In etchings of Mobile by Marian Acker, the strolling black woman, delineated with simple contour drawing, balances a bundle of wash instead of flowers; a similar female figure also appears in relief prints by Charles William Smith that picture Virginia towns and Charleston streets. Whites often commented on the skill black women demonstrated in balancing heavy, cumbersome loads on their heads, an African custom, and such imagery testifies to their admiration, at least to some degree.[29] The image appears in a different context in Dox Thrash's color mezzotint *Monday Morning Wash* (Fig. 41). Thrash, an African American printmaker, we recall, makes the laundress balancing her bundle along with her co-worker the central focus of the print, placing them against a humble, rural cabin, which suggests their own home territory.

A few artists in New Orleans and Charleston offered fresh views of the human figure in an architectural setting, resisting stereotypical configurations. Architecture in prints often provides the setting for the subject, rather than being the subject itself.[30] Caroline Durieux's *Desirée* provides an example, as the older, white woman rarely appears in prints of artists associated with the South (Fig. 44). A few artists who depicted the black figure did so in a way that emphasized their racial plight in the South by placing them against an architectural background. For example, two artists who visited Charleston, Georges Schreiber and Victoria Hutson Huntley, place a black figure outside an entrance to suggest racial exclusion in lithographs. Schreiber places a black man in formal attire outside a store that has moved in *The White House,* and Huntley, an old woman seated under a portico before an elegant, monumental stairway on Meeting Street. A multifigured lithograph by Aaron Bohrod, known as *New Orleans Street,* features a jaunty, young black girl facing the viewer in the foreground with a black woman and elderly white woman walking in the background before houses that suggest a rare view of the lower garden district. The female figures of various ages suggest a coming-of-age scenario.[31]

For an inland southern city, Nashville, whose beginnings date to the late eighteenth century, could boast of some early nineteenth-century landmarks, which Ernest Pickup pictured in wood engravings (Fig. 24). Yet views of inland southern cities are scattered and scarce in prints. Some of the rare architectural impressions of such New South cities as Birmingham and Atlanta define them through images of plain, utilitarian architecture, such as the gas towers that appear in Richard Coe's etching (Fig. 25). Artists in Birmingham, like Coe, saw the pictorial potential of panoramic *vedute* from its surrounding mountains. Coe uses a compositional format similar to that of Pickup in placing modest structures in the lower foreground at the foot of more imposing ones in the background. Skyscrapers shot up in New South cities as well as in the older, coastal ports, but they rarely appear in prints of the South as they do in the background of Coe's etching. Hale Woodruff's linoleum cut of an Atlanta street scene, usually entitled *Returning Home,* is a rare architectural view of the black neighborhood in that city.[32] Woodruff's view is distinctive for its emphasis on rickety, plain, wood housing in Atlanta.

Equally rare are views of the small town. According to one historian, small market towns and cities dominated the urban pre–World War II South, yet we see only an occasional print highlighting this small-scale urban scene.[33] Relief prints by J. J. Lankes and Charles William Smith, many focusing on homes and churches in the historic settlements of Virginia, can be considered small town views, according to their titles. The tidewater area of Virginia from which they drew their subjects was still primarily rural at the end of the 1920s, with numerous small towns dotting the landscape. Farther south Kent Hagerman etched architectural views of Lakeland, a small city in Florida. Titles of prints by other Florida etchers indicate a small town setting, although the emphasis is on the human action in the foreground, instead of architecture defining place. The title of Polly Knipp Hill's etching of a flooded yard locates the scene in Arcadia, Florida, while Frank Besedick's churchyard scene specifies Eatonville, Florida. James Fowler Cooper's etching *Saturday Night* does not point to a specific place, but the importance of Saturday events in southern life is usually a small town phenomenon.

When printmakers shifted from historic urban architecture of the coast, they usually turned to the humble, plain, vernacular architecture in the countryside. The two-story farmhouses we see in an etching by Mary Wallace Kirk and a woodcut of J. J. Lankes's represent this transition from city to countryside (Fig. 27). More common in the upper South than the lower, the two-story dwelling sometimes evolved from the simple one- or two-room cabin.[34] However, as represented in prints, the two-story house often provides some rare indication of rural, middle-class status due to its size and additions, which indicated a degree of prosperity (Fig. 26).[35] The urban architectural imagery in old coastal cities usually represents structures associated with an upper-class elite, who often owned the large land holdings that formed plantations cultivated by tenants or sharecroppers. We do occasionally see representation of the porticoed plantation house in prints of this era, but not as often as one would expect, given the mythology associated with the structure, reinforced by the popularity of Margaret Mitchell's saga of the Civil War, *Gone With the Wind,* in the novel and the subsequent film, during the 1930s.

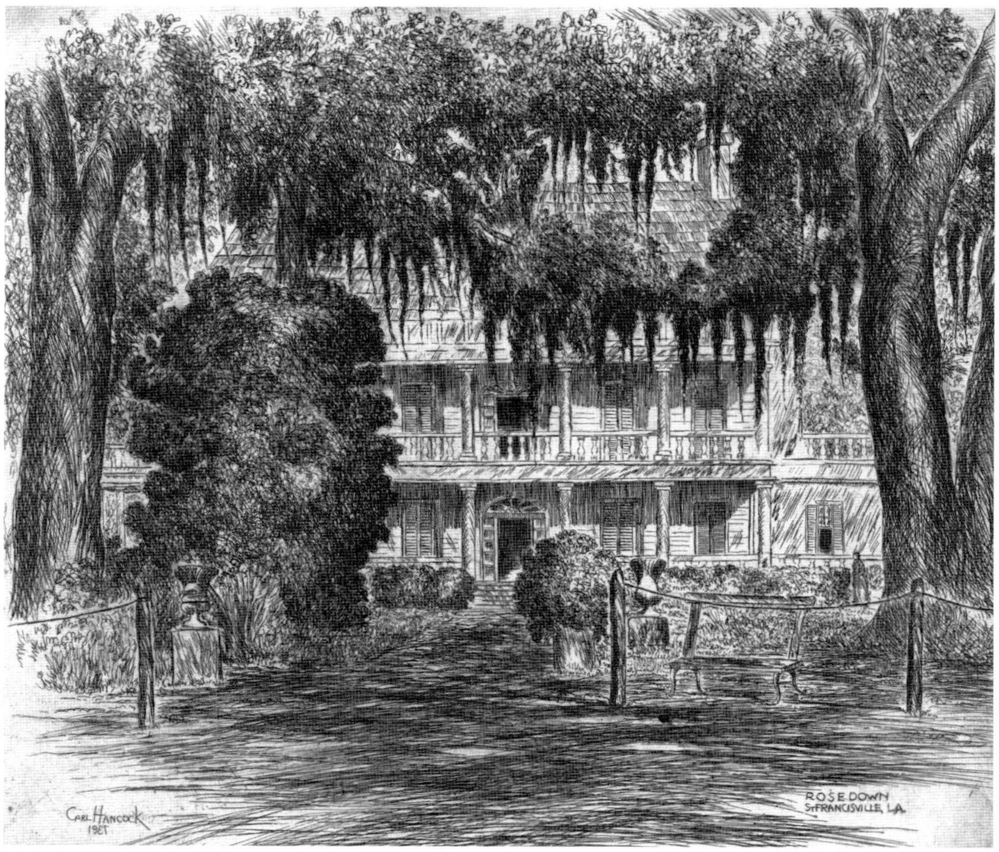

C. Carl Hancock, *Old Plantation House, Rosedown, St. Francisville, LA,* etching, 1937, 9 ⅛ x 10 ⅞ in., courtesy of Myrtie Engelkes and from the collection of Stephen Goldfarb.

Artists representing the South architecturally saw most interest in extremes or contrasts, and when they turned from the elegant, stylized building on the urban coast where they often lodged, they looked not to a two-story rural farmhouse, the plantation mansion, or utilitarian structures of inland cities, but to small one-story dwellings or the tiny shacks where an underclass of poor farm laborers lived. In his autobiography, Thomas Hart Benton remarked, "The beauty of southern homes has filled both song and story for years, yet the greater part of the houses of the South are dilapidated shacks with no grass in the yard and no flowers within miles."[36] Undoubtedly the dire poverty of the South during the Great Depression years, publicized by Roosevelt's pronouncement that the South was the nations "number one economic problem," accounts for some of this interest.[37] Such ordinary dwellings of the southern underclass have as long a legacy in prints of the South as that of urban coastal landmarks. They surface in the prints of the commercial press of the mid-nineteenth century, and in the 1880s Joseph Pennell pictured such in an etching of Pilot Town, Louisiana.[38] Only in the 1920s, 1930s, and 1940s, however, do such structures appear with considerable frequency.

The cabin sitting in the swamps in the drypoint by Knute Heldner (Fig. 28) as well as that on rocky terrain in the wood engraving of Clare Leighton (Fig. 29) show that this small dwelling appears in prints of all regions of the South, from the Appalachian Mountains through the piedmont to the coastal plains, from all angles and in numerous media. Derived from the housing of the white yeoman farmer on the frontier, as well as that for slaves in the antebellum period, such dwellings were usually occupied by sharecroppers or tenant farmers after the Civil War until economic forces and technological change made such housing obsolete after World War II.[39]

Sometimes landowners boarded over nineteenth-century log cabins with planks, but after 1900 many built less substantial structures of planks nailed to corner posts, which they scattered over their property.[40] As the views by Dox Thrash, Raymond Steth, Wilmer Jennings, and William Henry Johnson demonstrate, black printmakers from the South tended to represent their southern roots pictorially through this structure, yet white figures appear in conjunction with the cabin as well. Surrounding trees, as in the view by Heldner, suggest an isolated rural location, though some cabins pictured in prints could have been situated in urban areas. African Americans in southern cities occupied housing that resembled the cabins of sharecroppers more than the tenements of northern ghettos.[41]

Looking at all the cabin views that appear on the following pages, we see various styles, often in the background, like the square, blue structure in William Henry Johnson's serigraph, which has no architectural appendages or embellishment whatsoever (Fig. 42). However, the cabin appears most often in a simple, cottage style with sloping roof over a front porch and a gable on the side, a style to which architectural historians have given various names, such as "cat slide," "spraddle roof," or even "witch's hat," as terminology for vernacular architecture has not been standardized.[42] The house in the drypoint by Knute Heldner is typical. With a chimney often on the gable side, the cabin sometimes sat on rock or brick pilings, which are evident in the wood engraving by Leighton.

Differences in illumination also give cabin views different emphases. Touches of red and green brighten Thrash's carborundum mezzotint, but his cabins in black and white carborundum media usually sit in darkness, suggesting the dreary side of their occupants' existence. Thrash's best prints of the structure tend to show the dilapidation or run-down condition in loose boards or sections out of plumb. Other printmakers, such as Elizabeth O'Neill Verner, brighten cabins with suggestions of full sunlight along with trees that gracefully frame the architecture. Such differences in light, embellishments, and structural delineation point to gradations in rural poverty as well as the artist's view of the entire cultural matrix, which the cabin represented. With surrounding trees, particularly moss-hung oaks, or even mountains, the small cabin could appear as picturesque as the elegant, high-style dwelling.

Because the dwelling was so small, printmakers frequently show that much of the life of the people who lived within occurred outdoors.[43] Tools or even pieces of furniture may surround the structure, emphasizing the meager interior space for storage. Human figures often appear on the porch, as in the views by Heldner and Leighton, or standing in the yard nearby. Because the house was considered the female domain, the figures are frequently women with children nearby, as in the wood engraving by Leighton. Women also appear involved or associated with domestic tasks. Frequently this work involves clothing, especially laundry. In Thrash's *Monday Morning Wash* we see two women tending to weekly laundry, a scene that has some historical resonance if one considers that the laundress was one of the few occupations open to African American women (Fig. 41). In a color etching of a Tennessee mountain scene by Leon Pescheret, a white woman sits at a spinning wheel on the porch.

When a man appears nearby, he often sits unoccupied, showing that males considered their home a place where they were free of domestic labor. We see such scenarios in close-ups that focus on figures against an architectural background suggesting the cabin or shack, such as in Claude Clark's *Sharecroppers* or Wilmer Jennings's *Lazy Bones* (Figs. 30 and 43). Both views imply that the humble shack was a place of domestic work for the woman, whereas it supplies rest, relaxation, or idleness for men, although Jennings may be satirizing such a viewpoint. Other prints that are cabin close-ups feature women in the foreground working on a porch. Barbara Latham's wood engraving of a mountain woman is probably the best example.[44] We see a similar scene without an explicit cabin setting in Georges Schreiber's *Evening in North Carolina* but with more human drama as another figure, an idle male, is juxtaposed against the working woman (Fig. 40). Polly Knipp Hill's *June Flood in Arcadia* indirectly refers to the domestic work of women but appears to move up the social ladder to a more middle-class setting with a small cottage in the background of the lively neighborhood scene (Fig. 54).

If the tenant cabin frequently came into view during tours of the southern countryside before 1950, surely barns, sheds, and country churches did so as well. Yet such rural architectural structures appear rather infrequently in prints, much less frequently than the simple cabin. Barns have been a subject for innumerable, hackneyed, country scenes in paintings, but their appearance in prints of the South, such as we see in Richard Zoellner's scenic lithograph from a high mountain viewpoint, is rare. Another type of rural architecture, the small, unpretentious rural church, does appear fairly often but usually in the background of a genre scene, such as in Frank Besedick's view of Eatonville (Fig. 58). Many printmakers—Thomas Hart Benton, Elizabeth Verner, Caroline Rohland, and Anna Heyward Taylor—depicted the humble church structure with a broader perspective that indicated an isolated country setting.

Genre or Human Activity Scenes

In art history, the term "genre" has traditionally denoted scenes depicting aspects of everyday life, usually with figures representing the middle class or lower class. Genre scenes are rarely seen in fine art prints of the South before the World War I. However, an agrarian tradition had developed in nineteenth-century genre paintings and commercial prints that portrayed an African-southern underclass working in the cotton fields or adjacent to their cabins. This iconographic tradition merged with another that demeaned blacks as jolly entertainers, a subject of numerous recent studies.[45] Both created the sociologically "picturesque" in what has been described as "the picturesque cotton South."[46] The prints of the South that began to appear at the end of World War I and the decades that followed continued such iconography of southern genre focusing on a poor black population, but increasingly bestowed their subjects with a more serious, respectful treatment.

In the 1930s and 1940s blacks became, according to one authority, "irresistible regional symbols for artists and writers" depicting the South.[47] In 1900, 90 percent of the African American population lived in the South and by 1940, even after substantial migrations northward, three-fourths continued to reside in the region. For increasing numbers of white artists viewing the South as fertile, artistic territory, a highly visible black population offered the opportunity to continue what has been described as a "voyeuristic fascination with black culture" as exotic and other that began in the nineteenth century.[48] By the 1930s, however, the iconographic spectrum of prints broadened somewhat to embrace white southerners in a broader range of everyday activities. Genre imagery tended to fall into three broad categories of activity: working, playing, and praying, with the majority of participants still brandishing dark skin and falling into the lower social orders.[49]

Work became the major theme of genre prints of the 1930s throughout the country. Although a large category of southern genre prints in the 1930s and 1940s continued the earlier pictorial tradition showing figures engaged in agricultural work, we see a greater range of treatment with less emphasis on the picturesque. In the 1930s the Southeast was still an agrarian region with a majority of its income derived from agriculture and the largest percentage of the population in agriculture of any region of the country.[50] Moreover, southern farms were the smallest, poorest, and least mechanized in the nation. Much of the soil had been depleted by over cultivation, and the boll weevil had exacted its toll on the cotton crop.[51] With depressed prices for cotton from the 1920s through the 1930s, farmers labored long and hard for minimal returns, much of the labor supplied by women and children.[52] Such circumstances did not easily lend themselves to picturesque views of the "happy darky," such as we see in the late nineteenth-century paintings of William Aiken Walker, but conditions for blacks in the post-Reconstruction era South hardly did so either.

Agricultural prints of the 1930s and the following decade emphasized the rudimentary nature of work on southern farms through images of traditional hand labor, such as the simple plow, hoe, and wheel forms in William Henry Johnson's serigraph *Deep South.*[53] With cotton continuing as the region's major cash crop through the 1940s, the farm laborer appears frequently in various phases of cotton cultivation with workers hoeing, picking, hauling, or weighing this commodity, as in the lithographs by Routh, Benton, and Baker shown here. Tobacco, the most labor-intensive, southern crop, cultivated mainly in the upper South and often by blacks, occasionally appears, as in Robert Gwathmey's serigraphs based on views of coastal North Carolina (Fig. 35). A few southern printmakers extended southern agricultural iconography beyond cotton and tobacco, as did Anna Heyward Taylor who included rice cultivation in a historic view. James Fowler Cooper, who had an etching studio on his farm near Kingstree, South Carolina, extended views of agricultural labor on the part of both black and white workers to such activities as threshing peas and slaughtering hogs, while Alfred Hutty drew large, black, female figures pounding rice, pressing sugar cane, and digging potatoes in the low country near Charleston.

Such farming figures tend to display bending postures from varied perspectives, which can easily suggest bending or bowing in response to higher powers, both in the vicissitudes of weather as well as social hierarchy. Hauling the crop on one's back, like the two staggering figures in Benton's lithograph seen from the rear, easily denotes the burdened worker (Fig. 34). Mabel Dwight shows men hauling bananas in a frontal view and James Fowler Cooper depicts shrimpers hauling their catch in nets. However, not all artists emphasized the harsh side of such labor in agricultural prints, and Charleston printmakers were among those who projected a measure of ease.[54] Anna Heyward Taylor, for example, orchestrates bending backs with sheaves of rice in a rhythmic flow in *Harvesting Rice,* while Elizabeth O'Neill Verner removes the harshness of field labor by placing black workers at a distance under gracefully draped, moss-hung oaks in *Low Country* and *Under the Oaks.*[55] James Fowler Cooper suggests strength and endurance by the strong bodies of his male workers, both black and white, as do lateral views of large foreground figures of cotton pickers in lithographs by Georges Schreiber and Mildred Nungester.

Industrial scenes, so common in prints of other regions during the American Scene period of the 1930s, appear less frequently in prints of the South, which is not surprising given the primacy of agriculture in the region. Nevertheless, industry did exist in the South and not only in known industrial centers like Birmingham, Alabama. Artists scattered here and there throughout the region produced prints for commerce that depicted local industries. During the early years of his career from 1927 to 1931, for example, Charles William Smith made color linocuts of Richmond businesses, including factories and their operations, for the covers of *Richmond Magazine.*[56] Among Kent Hagerman's many etching commissions in Florida were those for the Florida-Louisiana Red Cypress Company, which pictured logging and milling of lumber, while John McCrady executed lithographs picturing oil refineries in Baton Rouge, Louisiana, commissioned by Standard Oil.[57]

Prints shown here represent rare views of various segments of the South's industrial economy: the steel industry in Birmingham, the textile industry throughout the South, the shipping and boating business at many seaports, and quarries scattered here and there. Circumstances regarding the production of Roderick MacKenzie's lithographs of the Birmingham steel mills, one of which we see here (Fig. 37), are not as well documented. MacKenzie's interior views of Birmingham steel mill operations, similar to his pastels from the 1920s, are traditional, realistic constructions compared with Lamar Baker's more modernist, montage compositions, incorporating imagery relating to the textile industry as well as cotton agriculture (Fig. 36). Celia Cregor Reid's views of the shrimping industry in St. Augustine, usually in a traditional realistic style, occasionally found an echo in river views, such as those of John McCrady featuring boats on the Mississippi (Fig. 38).

Images of figures resting from work, usually male, such as we see in William Henry Johnson's serigraph *Deep South* or *Farmers Day of Rest,* were almost as frequent as those picturing active workers (Figs. 42 and 43). Those images varied from figures lying on a porch of a shack in a southern siesta to dreamers, such as the young man in Schreiber's tension-laden scene. Such views reach beyond gender division of domestic labor in cabin views to touch upon southern stereotypes. In the eighteenth and nineteenth centuries, it was widely believed that the warm southern climate induced a certain laziness among Southerners, a view that has not been entirely discredited.[58] Later historians of medicine documented that the "lazy South" may well have been based on a group of diseases—malaria, hook worm, pellagra—that were endemic in the South but very rare in the North.[59] White figures taking a nap among the fields as a break from work appeared in the work of some Midwestern regionalists, such as John de Martelly, so extending the theme to the South was natural, though black figures were usually chosen in such southern scenes.[60] Moreover, crops such as cotton only required work during six or seven months of the year, with many workers finding little to do during other months.[61] The Great Depression of the 1930s also generated significant unemployment and hardship in the South as elsewhere in the country. However, we rarely see direct references to the dire straights of the unemployed in scenes such as breadlines that were common in prints of northern cities.

The linoleum print by Elizabeth Catlett and the lithograph by Mildred Nungester constitute rare images that show the figure at rest while traveling or waiting to travel on public transportation. Urban mass transportation, whether on buses, subways, or trains, interior or exterior, comprised an important subject of the New York urban realists, but although buses, streetcars, and trains also transversed southern cities and towns, that modern transportation experience left few trails in southern art. More commonly, artists cultivated an image of a traditional, rural South by depicting the mule-drawn cart, such as we see in views by Anne Goldthwaite (Fig. 45). The mule, a mainstay of traditional southern agriculture, was the primary means of locomotion for the typical sharecropper.[62] The northern urban realists emphasized the isolation and anonymity of urban life, a theme which Nungester treats in her view of people in close proximity, but isolated in their own psychological space as they await their train. Her scene in a train station also allows a rare view of southern middle-class life, as only the middle and upper classes would probably have had the money for such travel in the South, and the region had a shortage of professional, clerical, and skilled classes compared to other regions of the country (Fig. 46).[63] Yet Nungester's view could represent any station in the country at that time. Elizabeth Catlett's depiction of riding a bus could refer only to the South; the sign "Colored Only" was a distinctive aspect of public transportation in the South: legally mandated segregation in separate public facilities known in the vernacular as Jim Crow (Fig. 47).

In spite of the widespread practice of segregating public facilities throughout the South, specific visual references, such as we see in Catlett's linocut, rarely occur in prints. Most often when artists focused on southern racism in prints, they did so through images of racism's most virulent form, lynching, which was most common in the South, where African Americans comprised the most frequent victims.[64] Two New York exhibitions organized in 1935 to publicize and elicit support for efforts to make the practice a federal crime accounted for the number of prints with imagery associated with lynching in the mid-1930s. The NAACP organized one exhibition while the John Reed Club and other leftist organizations arranged the other.[65] Among the black artists contributing prints to *An Art*

Commentary on Lynching, the exhibition organized by the NAACP, were two from Atlanta, Hale Woodruff and his student Wilmer Jennings, both of whom offered relief prints on the theme.

Southern associations are not explicit in the lynching prints of Woodruff and Jennings, but a few white printmakers in New York pointed explicitly to the South through titles they chose for prints on the theme of lynching. Harry Sternberg, who participated in both exhibitions, entered *Southern Holiday* for his lithograph of a castrated black male roped to a column. Boris Gorelick labeled a montage composition *Strange Fruit,* the title of a song referring to lynching in the South that became popular in the 1930s, while Prentiss Taylor titled

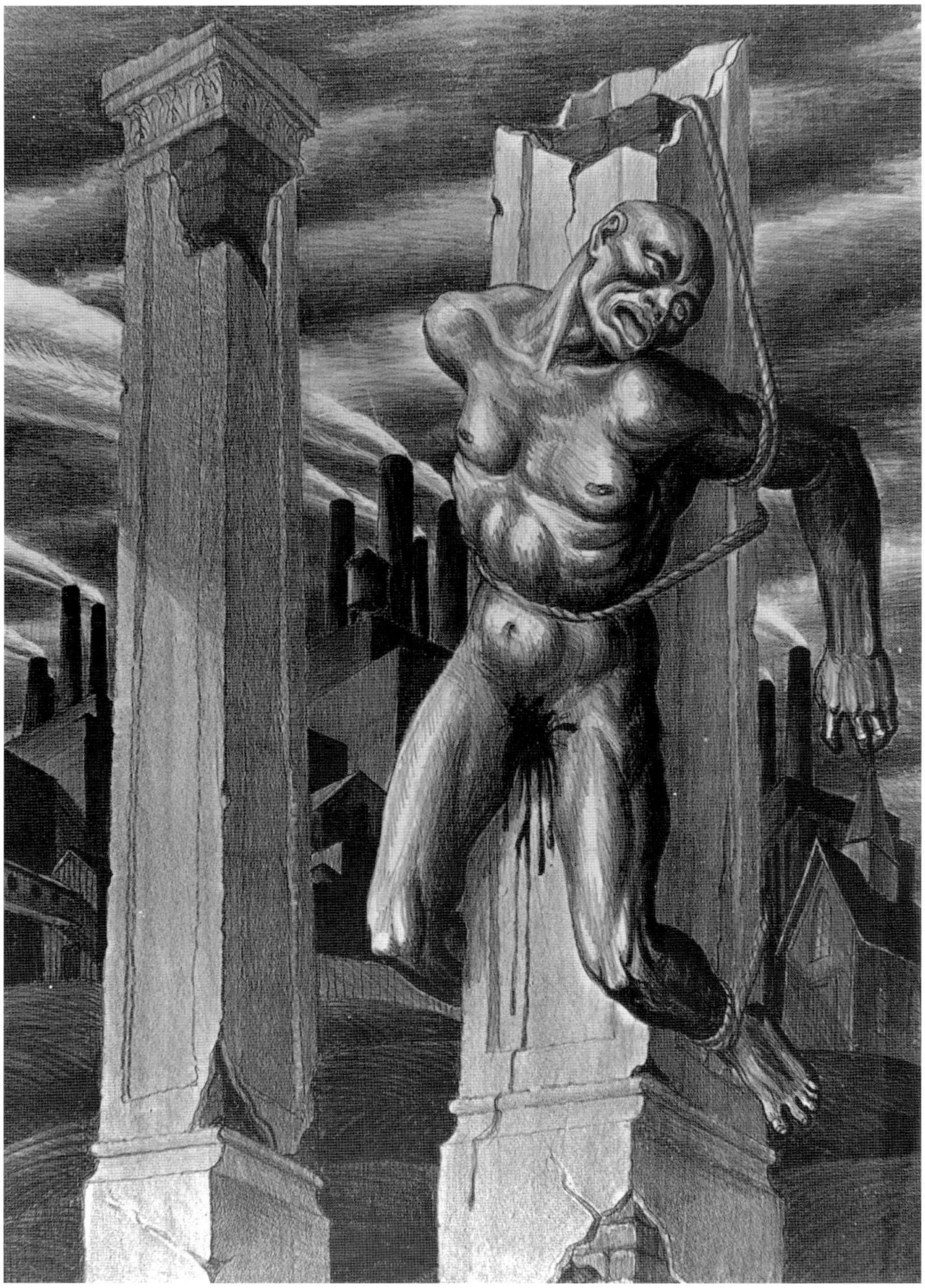

D. Harry Sternberg, *Southern Holiday,* lithograph, 1935, 21 ¾ x 15 ¾ in., courtesy of the Estate of the Artist and the Susan Teller Gallery, New York, and from the collection of the Edwin A. Ulrich Museum of Art, Wichita State University Foundation Art collection.

his image of a crucified black figure *Christ in Alabama,* one of the four lithographs he made to protest the conviction of the nine black youths accused of rape in the Scottsboro case.[66] Philip Reisman titled his lynching scene simply *South.* George Biddle blatantly condemned the South through the title he chose for a caricature of a southern, white couple: *Alabama Code—Our Girls Don't Sleep with Niggers* (Fig. 49). Both *Christ in Alabama* and *Alabama Code* were offered to the NAACP exhibit on lynching. Walter White, executive secretary of the NAACP, accepted *Christ in Alabama* but thought the title and imagery of Biddle's lithograph too subtle and ambiguous for inclusion.[67]

Rarely do native white southern artists treat such themes of terror.[68] Furthermore, by the late 1940s, interest in these themes appears exhausted on the national scene for the time being. However, Homer Casteel, who was only beginning his printmaking career in the late 1940s, uses the abstraction coming into stylistic hegemony to simplify his juxtaposed images of the white hooded figure with a black figure hanging from a rope to emphasize covert operations. He does not, however, point explicitly to his home region of the South through a title, yet the subject has the utmost relevance to the South (Fig. 48).

We also see the life of leisure extended to social interaction and specific activities in southern genre scenes of the 1930s and 1940s. John McCrady, Caroline Durieux, Polly Knipp Hill, and Kent Hagerman were among the few southern printmakers, all of them white, who depicted such social interaction through leisure activity among middle-class whites. Durieux stands as one of the few southern printmakers who depicted a socially elite, white culture in such varied settings as the parlor, dining room, plantation garden, or concert hall. She did so through caricatures and satirical genre scenes in which she exaggerated features, above all facial features, to reflect smug, snobbish attitudes, although compassion emanates from *Desirée,* a woman down on her luck. In her satirical bent Durieux allies herself with other women printmakers on the national scene, such as Mabel Dwight or Peggy Bacon, who lampooned middle-class social typology somewhat more gently.

Street life, often with public revelry, constituted one large iconographic category in prints of the South, and Mardi Gras scenes were among the most prominent. John McCrady's Mardi Gras scene, *Carnival in New Orleans,* with a chain of figures dragging each other across the foreground, displays the strongest satire among the prints on view here (Fig. 51). McCrady, Caroline Durieux, and Ralph Wickiser were commissioned to create a book of drawings and lithographs commemorating Mardi Gras day, or Fat Tuesday, depicting Mardi Gras revelry.[69] Morris Henry Hobbs and Charles Surendorf also rendered Mardi Gras revelry with a slightly satirical touch, while Celia Reid commemorated the "Day in Spain" fiesta on Aviles Street in St. Augustine with a woodcut.[70] Satirical views of a white middle-class social culture in Florida public spaces can be seen in a number of etchings by Polly Knipp Hill. Here we see her subtle satire in a domestic scene of children taking advantage of a minor disaster to have some fun.

Prints reveal more artistic interest in depicting street life among a lower-class black community, which artists subjected less often to satire. James Fowler Cooper's small etching *Saturday Night,* like Prentiss Taylor's *Horlbeck Alley,* shows numerous small conversation groups lined up across storefronts seen from a distance (Fig. 50). Saturday was a day when country folk came to town to sell their produce, buy needed items, and socialize, and it became a minor theme in southern art of the period. An aquatint by Clarence Millet bears the title *Saturday Night,* as do lithographs by Dallas artist Elizabeth Walmsley and by Mildred

Nungester, which move closer to storefronts and focus on fewer interacting figures. A number of other prints, such as Adolf Dehn's street scene in Key West or Charles Surendorf's *Conversation,* do not picture a specific day's events, yet echo Cooper's in their depiction of the vitality of African southern street or neighborhood life.

The communal meal provides a specific activity by which to compare contrasting treatments of black and white social experience in prints. We see the dinner as a dignified rite among the black community of two social levels in the lithograph by Raymond Steth and the wood engraving by Frank Hartley Anderson shown here. *Southern Barbeque* by Steth shows a typically southern country feast about to occur among poor country blacks, who appear to constitute a family (Fig. 56). They circle around a pig on a spit with their home, a cabin, in the background. Frank Hartley Anderson's *Church Supper* provides not only a contrasting indoor location but also suggestions of a middle-class milieu in the black community, which is pictured much less frequently in prints (Fig. 57).

Depictions of the meal partaken by white figures shift toward the satirical in treatment. Polly Knipp Hill's *Picnic on the Beach* is particularly southern and symbolic in its associations of racial differentiation. Black figures providing amusement for whites, a typical scenario in nineteenth-century pictorial views, are relegated to the periphery outside a shed that shelters the whites who frolic in its inner sanctum.[71] In a 1939 lithograph titled *Dinner,* Caroline Durieux deflates a high-style meal with a ridiculously elaborate centerpiece in the middle of a dining room table around which white figures are gathered.

Other specific pastimes add to a picture of leisure between work and sleep, even though the common laborer worked long hours, often from sunup to sundown. Music produced by the common folk comprised perhaps the most frequently depicted pastime depicted in prints during an era where "Free delivery of mail brought mail order catalogues from Chicago offering cheap guitars, mandolins, and banjos" as appreciation for folk, country, and blues music of the South escalated.[72] African Americans assigned to roles as musical entertainers appeared in nineteenth-century American genre paintings,[73] and they continued to surface, more often strumming guitars than plucking banjos in prints of the twentieth century by white and black artists. Some African American artists from the South—Hale Woodruff, William Henry Johnson, and Dox Thrash—included such images in their print oeuvre, as did white artists James Fowler Cooper, Frank Hartley Anderson, and Barbara Latham. Richard Zoellner, who created images of southern guitar players in an angular, modernist style at the end of the 1940s, remarked that he first experienced genuine folk music when he came to Alabama and heard black musicians in country bars.[74] White musicians were not utterly neglected, however. Howard Cook's ensemble of three white instrumentalists we see here is one of the strongest images that diverges from the typical racial iconography (Fig. 52). African Americans dancing became another stereotype in American prints of the 1930s and 1940s, but few had a rural, southern setting, as does Palmer Schoppe's *Grapevine Twist* with musicians accompanying figures by beating drums and clapping hands (Fig. 53).

The importance of religion and the church in southern life has often been seen as a mark of southern cultural distinctiveness. As Howard Odum wrote, "the way of the South has been . . . the way of religion" as the South has continued a religious culture "more literally and aggressively than any other region of the nation."[75] As religious subjects for their prints, artists looked primarily to the southern black church and its culture that we see pictured in the background of Frank Besedick's view of Eatonville, Florida, and in *Church Supper* by Frank Anderson. Besedick emphasizes the common theme of African American sociability in his view of church life in a small southern town (Fig. 58). Other external views of the humble church and its parishioners by Elizabeth Verner and Thomas Hart Benton use a higher viewpoint to encompass a broader, rural setting. Artists may have chosen the black country church for subjects of their prints due to the decline of the white rural church, which occurred with the advent of the automobile and better roads. White country parishioners moved to towns or drove to churches there, whereas black churches remained relatively small in the open country through the 1930s.[76] Such geographic factors may have made the black country church seem untainted by modern civilization and, thus, an expression of folk tradition.

Other prints focused on religious rituals, above all the outdoor baptism of adults by immersion in a natural pond, a custom common in the South at least into the 1970s. The primacy of baptism over communion as a Christian ritual distinguishes southern Christianity from its practice elsewhere. Southern evangelical Protestants also emphasized that only conscious, decision-making adults are suitable for this rite, which often involves total immersion.[77] Although midwestern and southwestern artists such as John Stuart Curry and Peter Hurd depicted the outdoor baptism among whites in their lithographs, when artists centered this subject in the South, they selected black participants. Prentiss Taylor's lithograph *"—In Whom I Am Well Pleased"* serves as an example (Fig. 59), as do prints by Howard Cook, Clare Leighton, or Frank Hartley Anderson that were often based on first-hand observation in the South. Taylor depicts the baptismal rite and church service among southern blacks as a highly spiritual, emotional experience.[78]

In a number of lithographs by Carroll Cloar, such as *The Preacher,* a variety of white religious practices are visible in small scenic segments dominated by the central figure, often the preacher (Fig. 60). Cloar includes adult baptism among the practices he depicts. But he also shows adults prostrating themselves in prayer on benches, as well as foot washing, a less common Christian ceremony that evangelical sects of the South sometimes practiced.[79] Cloar's emphasis on the figure of a preacher was not unusual in prints. Relief prints by Wilmer Jennings, Frank Hartley Anderson, Isaac Friedlander, and Margaret Law highlight a black preacher leading a congregation, usually with hand lifted in a dramatic gesture, emphasizing the importance of the preacher in the black community. What is clear in a number of Cloar's views of white religiosity is a critical, derogatory perspective on the preacher that is lacking in interpretations of black religious experience.

In *An Artist in America,* Thomas Hart Benton observed, "If anywhere in the world the Christian faith is still touched with the hand of God it is among the southern Negroes of the back country who cling to traditional ways. *They alone* set it in unstereotyped beauty [italics mine]."[80] One scholar confirms that artists projected contrasting views of white and black religious experience in prints: "The ecstatic nature of black worship was endlessly fascinating to white elites; unlike the behavior of white revivalists, which was generally despised; the former was deemed authentic and natural, the latter had the quality of rancid snake oil."[81] Benton's lithograph *The Meeting,* George Bellows's *Benediction in Georgia,* or Mabel Dwight's *Brothers* lend some credence to such hyperbolic commentary, which does apply to a few of the religious lithographs of Carroll Cloar, such as *The Preacher* or *Hellfire.* Both feature upper torsos of the white preacher in the center of the image area. Whereas the ranting preacher in *Hellfire* points to a fanatic evangelist, the smug, direct expression along with hand gestures in *The Preacher* suggest tight control over the masses seen in pews in the background.

Some of the favor white artists gave to black spiritual life has been attributed to increasing interest in "Negro" spirituals during the interwar period.[82] In Charleston, a Society for the Preservation of Negro Spirituals was organized in 1922. The organization staged performances throughout the country, and in 1931 published a collection of spirituals titled *The Carolina Low Country,* although theirs was not the first collection of African American song.[83] On the one hand, artists such as John McCrady, Mildred Nungester, and, above all, Ruth Starr Rose reflected this interest through their lithographs that illustrated specific spiritual titles, such as "Swing Low, Sweet Chariot," through scenarios with black figures. On the other hand, liberal ridicule of aspects of conservative white Christianity, such as H. L. Mencken's diatribes against the Scopes "monkey trial" in 1925, novels such as Sinclair Lewis's *Elmer Gantry,* along with press reports of such white religious leaders such as Billy Sunday, undoubtedly provoked cynicism toward conventional Christianity and evangelical, fundamentalist sects on the part of a liberal, northeastern, artistic establishment that caused relative neglect and disparagement of white spiritual experience, at least in the South.

Graphic interpretations of religious texts, such as spirituals or biblical passages, extended representation of southern black culture beyond the boundaries of realism to more imaginative realms. However, the vast majority of prints depicting southern culture in the interwar period and immediately after did so through realistic, contemporary views and most, whether from the hands of both southern and northern artists, had a positive or neutral tenor with a few critical notes. Commentators on the South of this period, from Thomas Hart Benton to W. J. Cash, note the contradictions in the southern mind and culture, contradictions that endow the South with much of its cultural interest.[84] Such contradictions are seen in prints between a romantic, ideal South of lush vegetation, elegant historic architecture, and close communal life and a South of poverty, racial injustice, and environmental degradation.

Both white and black printmakers showed the greatest interest in African southern or black life, which they reflected in a sympathetic light. Black life appears arduous in its simple, physical labor; it is beset as well by racial exclusion and oppression yet compensated by spiritual and communal attributes in religious practice as well as leisure. Such communal solidarity with mutual solace and support has been noted by historians of African American cultural heritage.[85] Images of a communal black culture might also be considered part of what Richard Powell describes as the "construction of a pictorialized folk past" that became evident during the 1930s and 1940s.[86] When one turns to the dominant white, southern culture, generalizations are more problematic. A more critical, satirical slant tends to be cast on southern whites, particularly those of the upper or middle class, which dovetailed with a large category of satirical prints of the 1930s.[87] Views of a lower-class white culture are too sparse and diverse to coalesce in any such simple, composite view. When one considers the imbalance in the number of black and white subjects, one is forced to conclude with historian Wayne Flynt that southern whites tend to be "Dixie's forgotten people" in prints.[88]

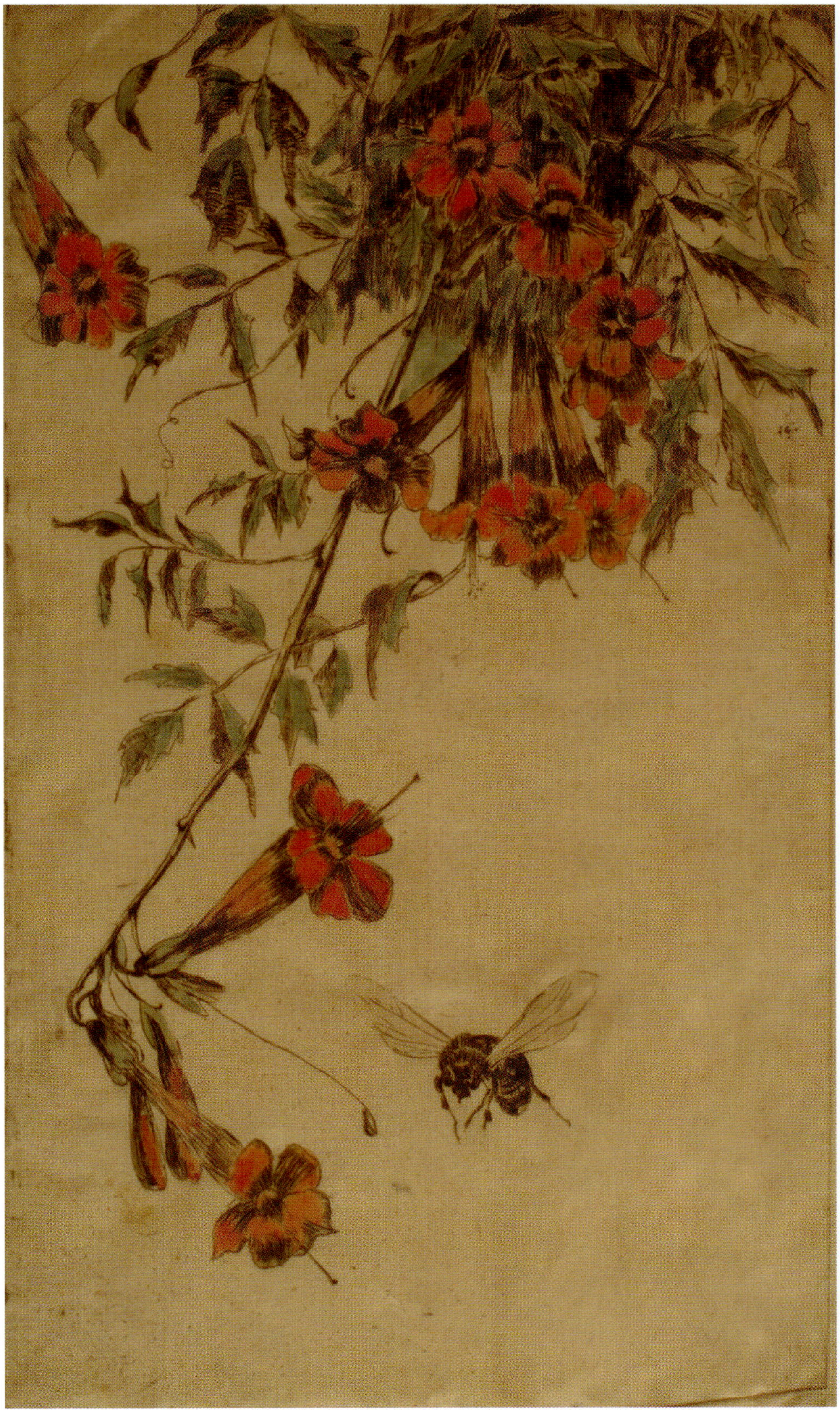

Antoinette Rhett, [Trumpet Vine and Bee], etching with hand color, 10 ½ x 6 ½ in., courtesy of David Allen and from the collection of Lynn Barstis Williams.

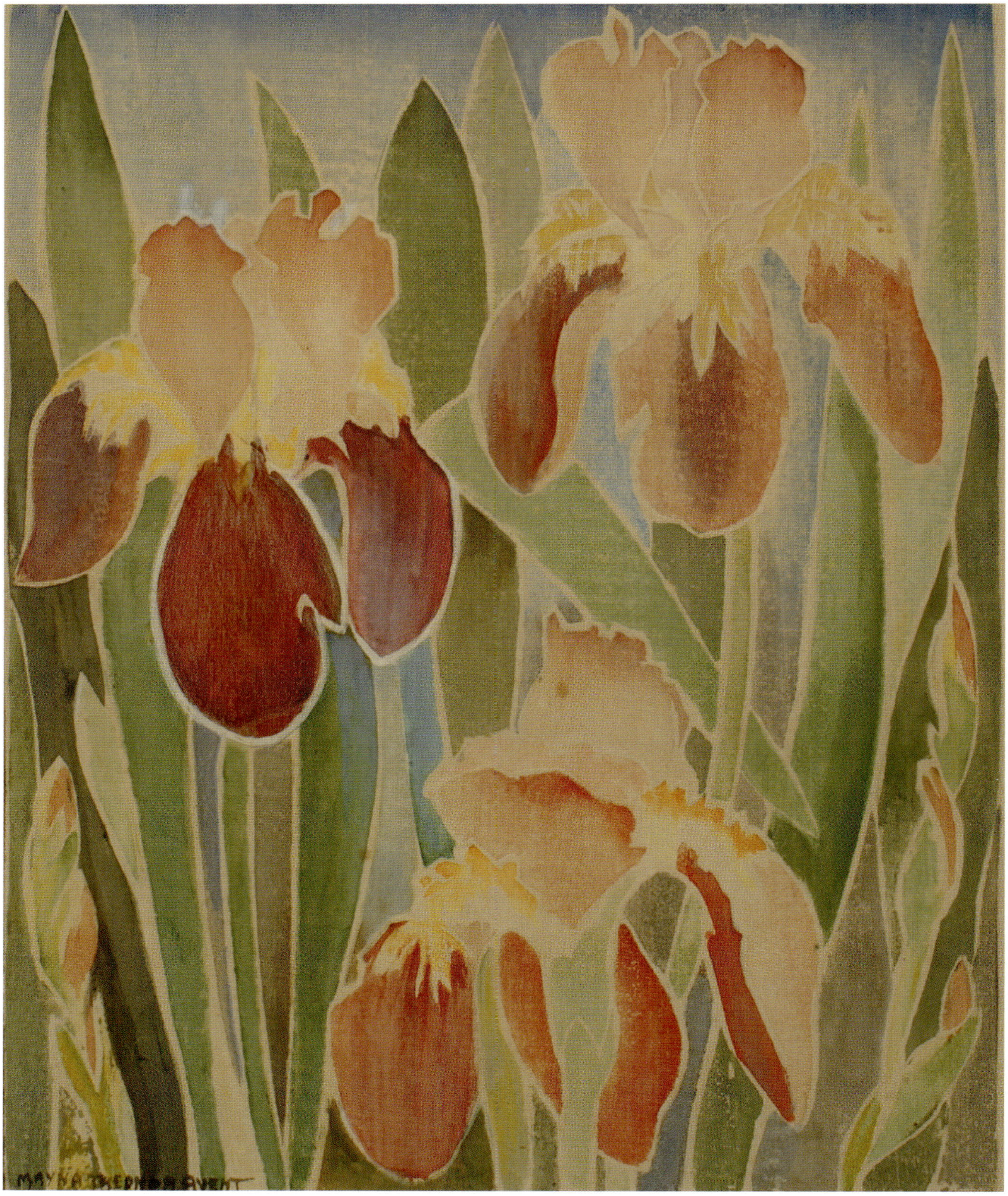

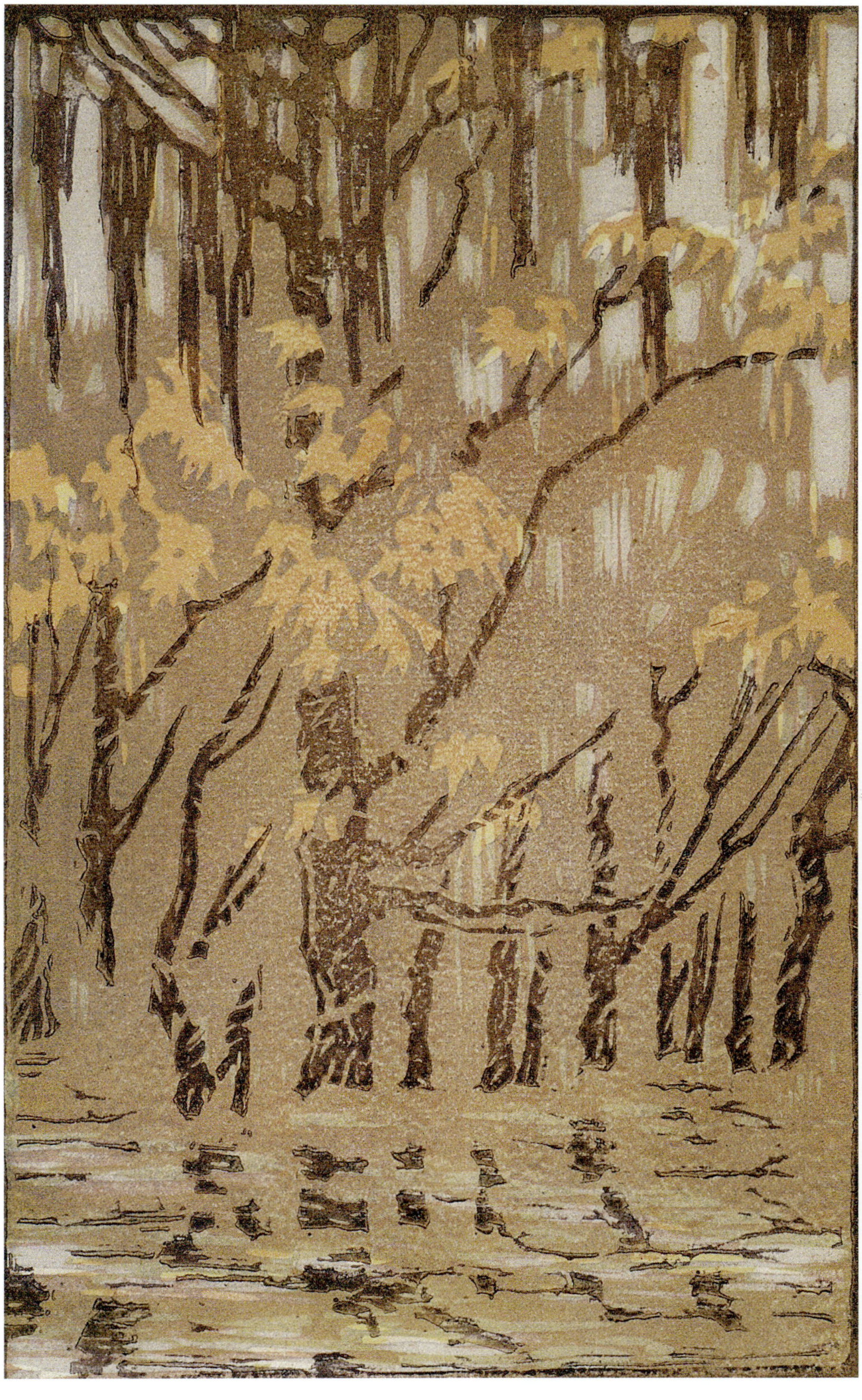

Opposite page:
Mayna Avent, [Irises], woodcut, 12 x 10 in., courtesy of the Avent Family and from the collection of Ann Avent.

Left:
Sadie Irvine, *Marsh Maple,* color linoleum cut, c. 1920, 11 ⅛ x 7 ⅛ in., collection of the Louisiana State University Museum of Art; gift of Dr. A. Brooks Cronon Jr. and Diana Cronan.

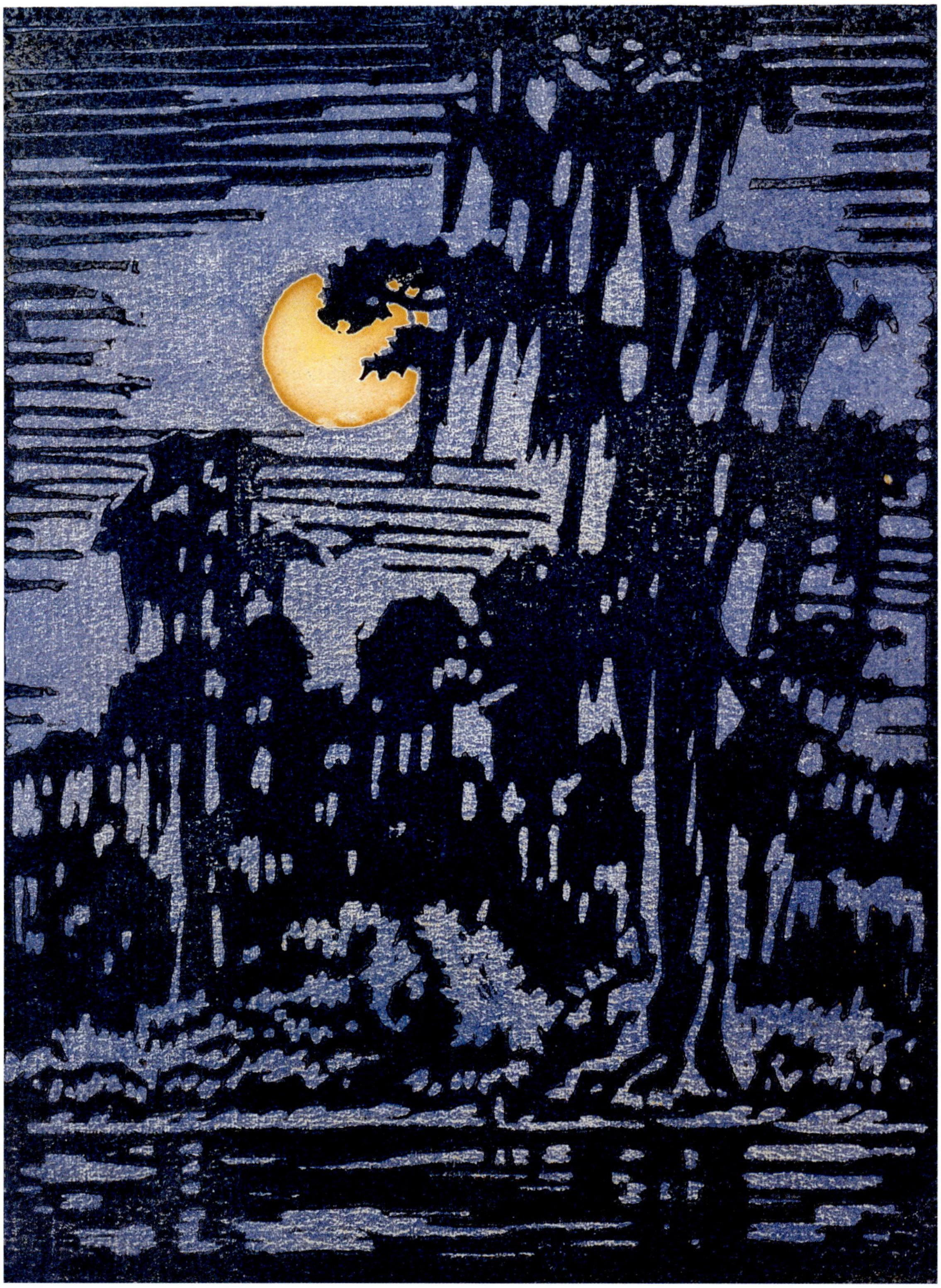

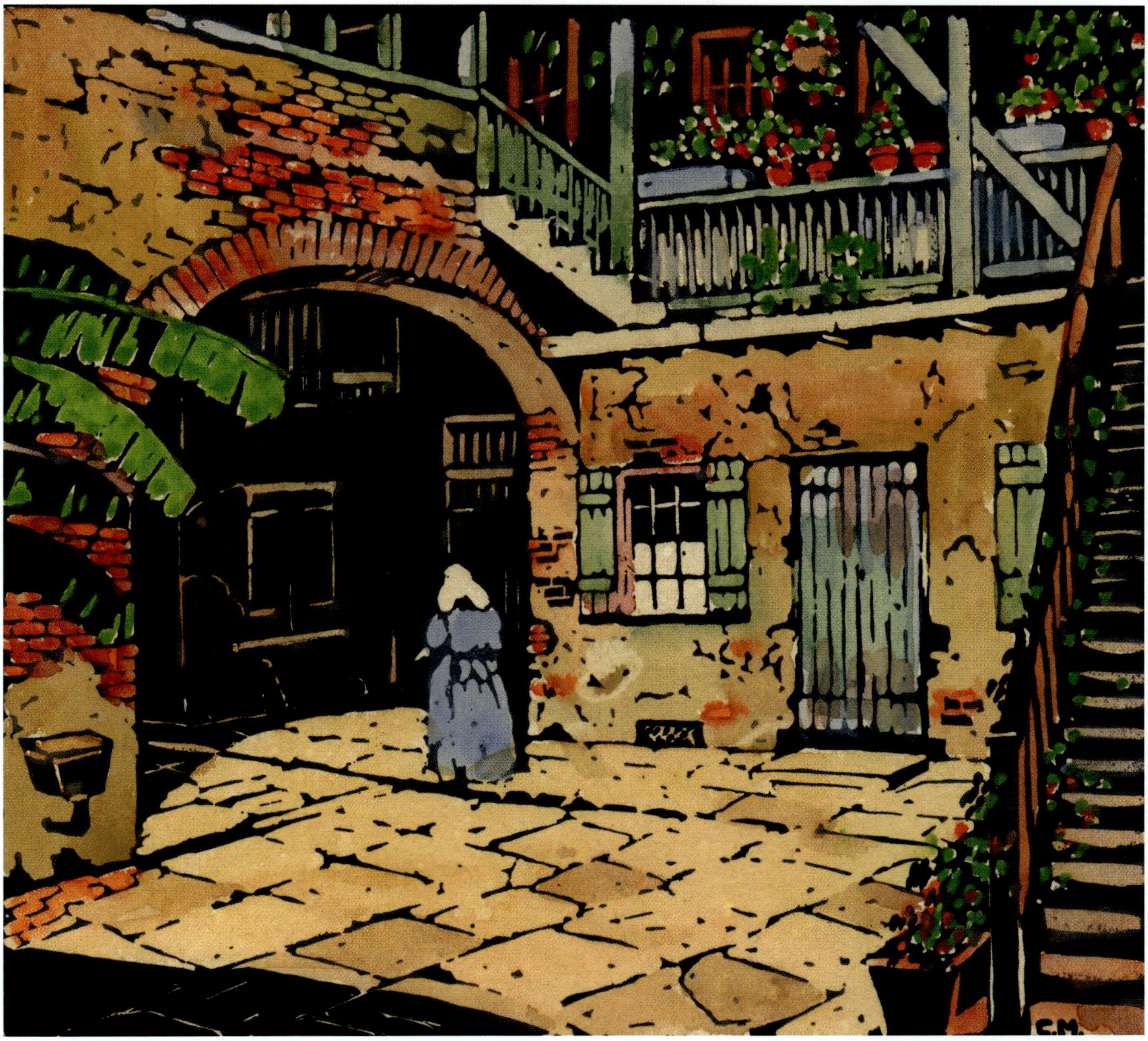

Opposite page:
Henrietta Bailey, *Cypress,* woodcut, c. 1911, 8 x 5 ⅞ in., collection of the New Orleans Museum of Art; gift of J. Norcom Jackson Jr., 91.165.

Above:
Clarence Millet, *Claiborne Court,* hand-colored linoleum cut, c. 1933, 5 ⅞ x 6 ½ in., collection of Lynn Barstis Williams.

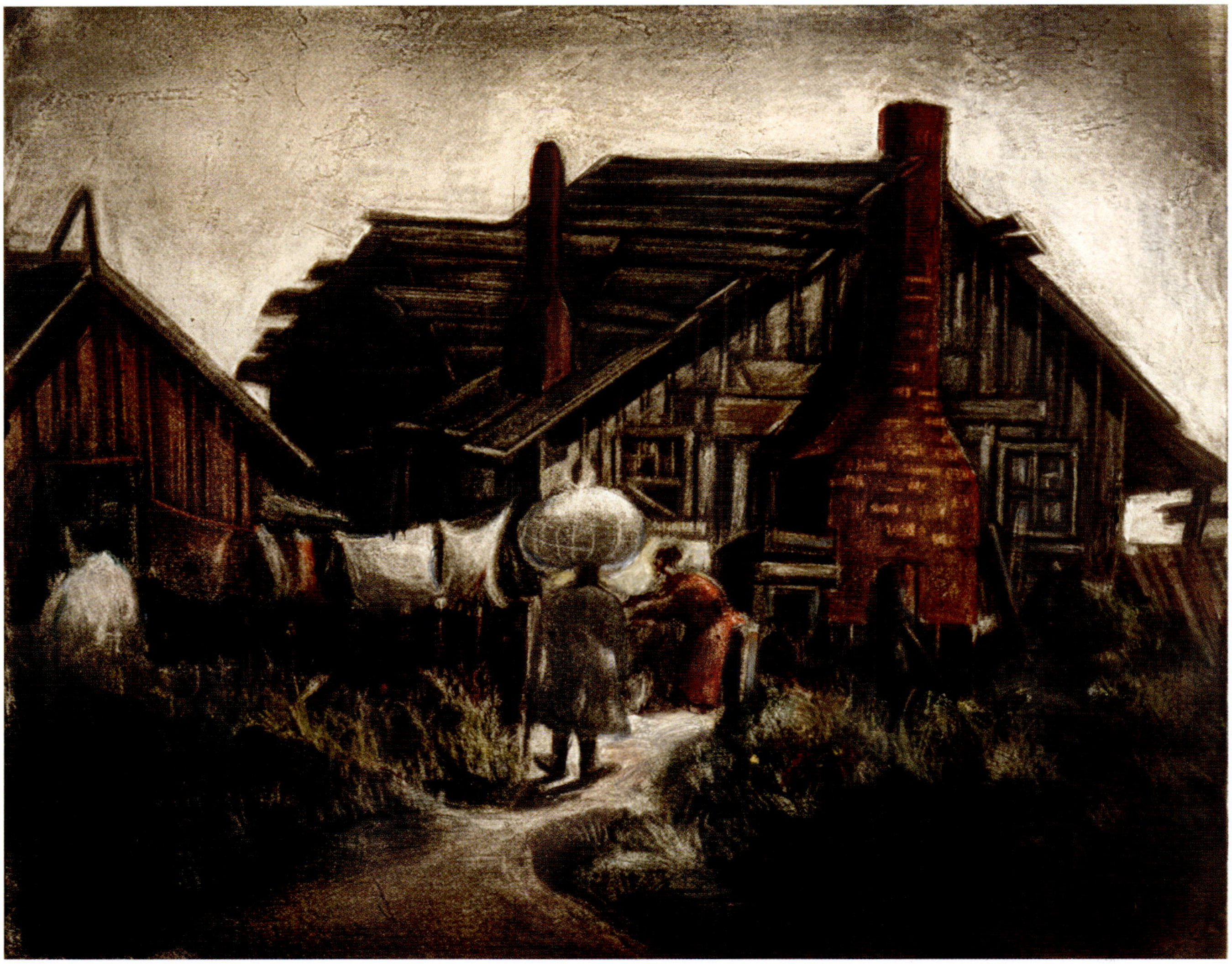

Above:
Dox Thrash, *Monday Morning Wash,* color carborundum mezzotint, c. 1939, 11 x 14 in., collection of the Philadelphia Museum of Art purchased with the Thomas Skelton Harrison Fund.

Opposite page:
Robert Gwathmey, [Tobacco Farmers], serigraph, 1947, 13 ½ x 10 ½ in., art © Estate of Robert Gwathmey/Licensed by VAGA, New York, NY and from the collection of Lynn Barstis Williams.

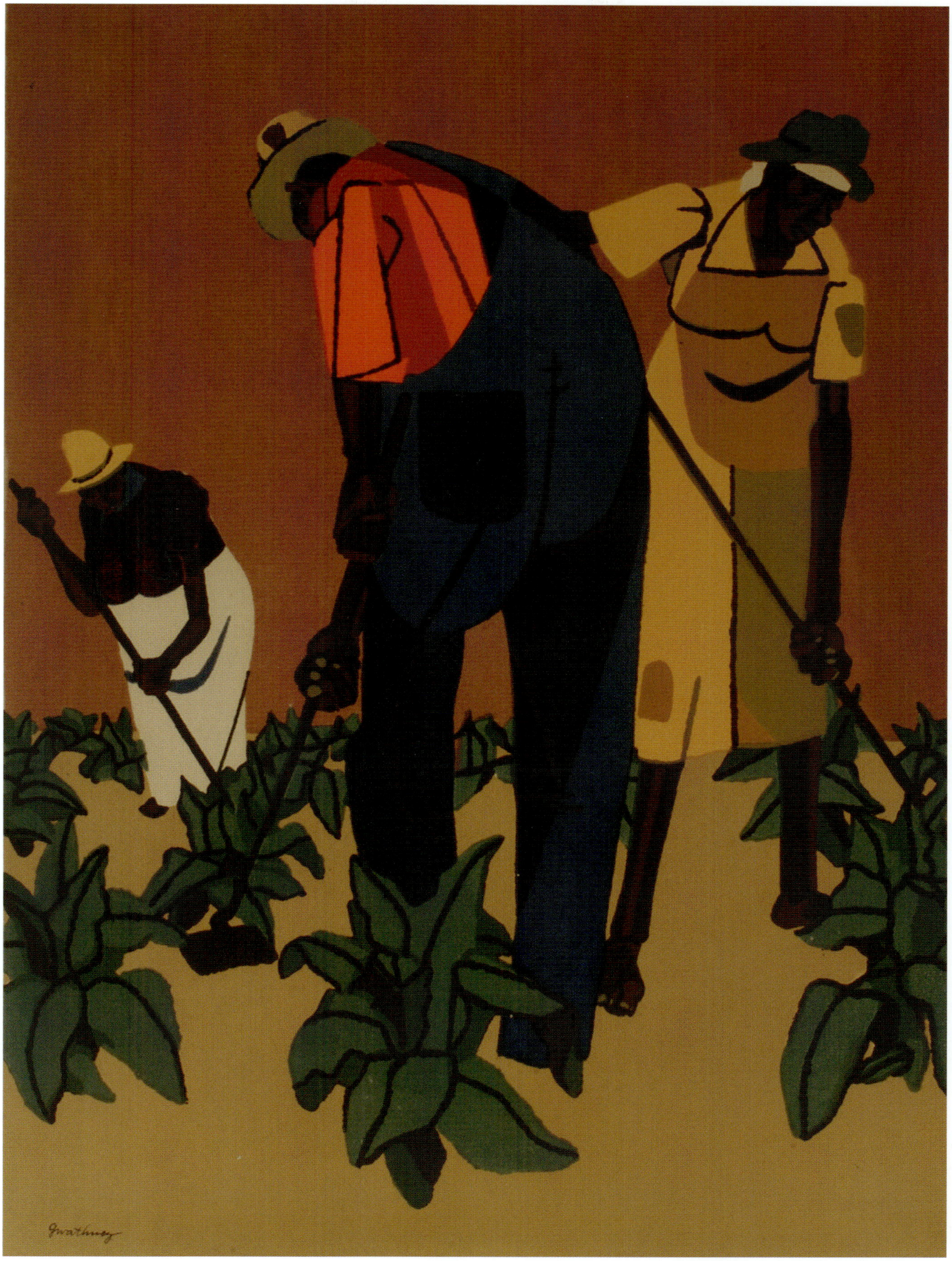
Gwathmey

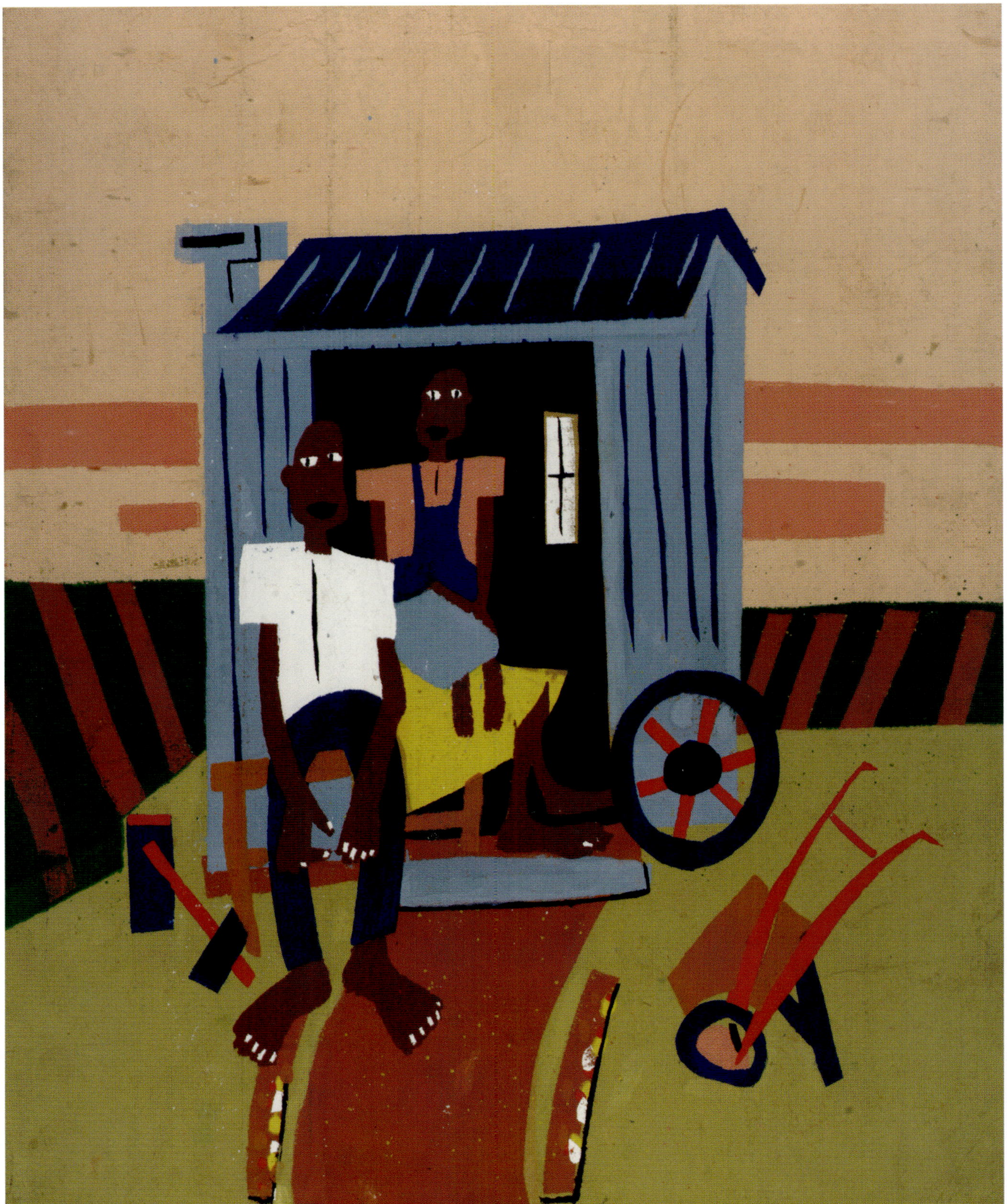

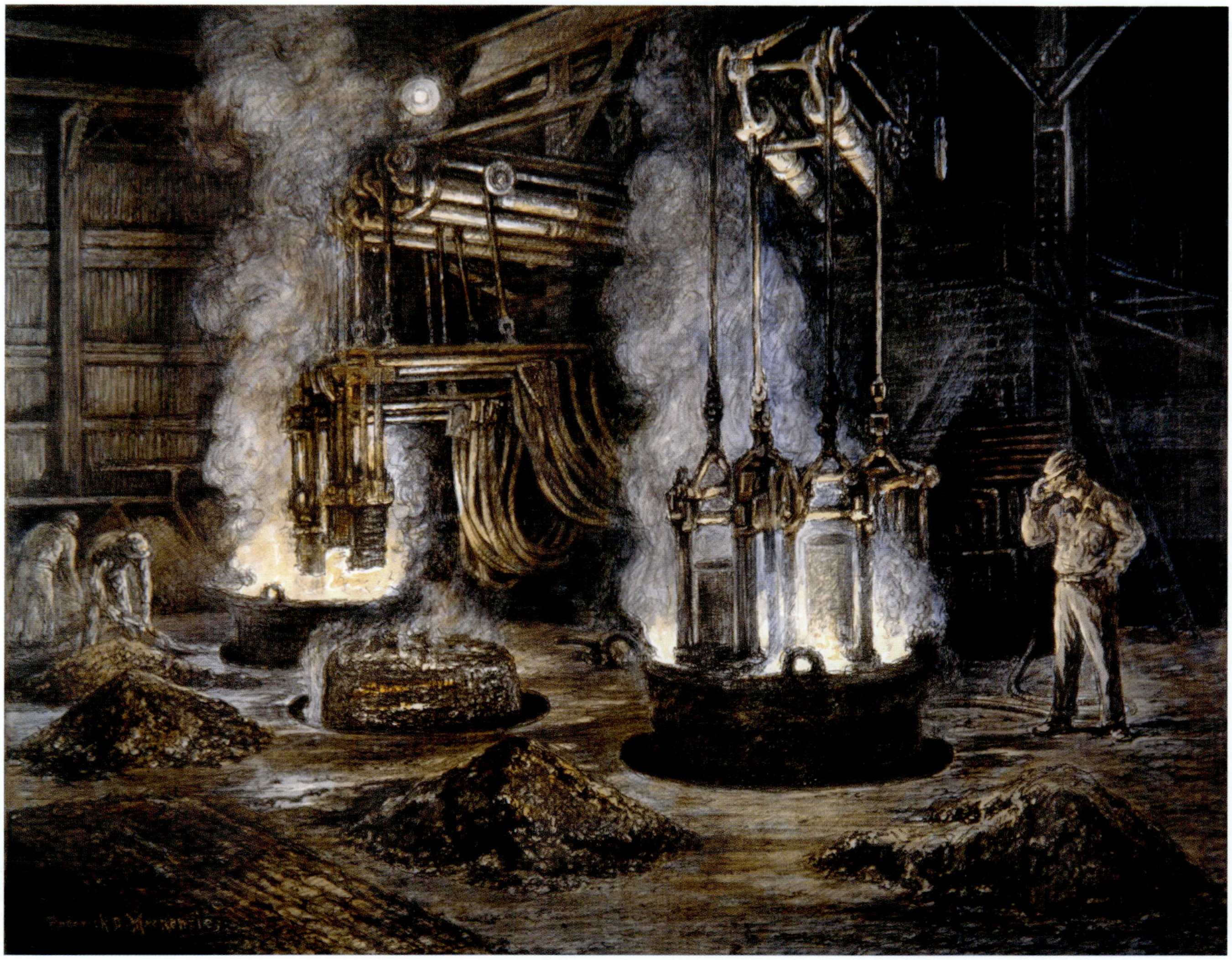

Opposite page:
William Henry Johnson, *Deep South,* serigraph, c. 1940, 17 ⅛ x 14 ⅛ in., collection of the Smithsonian American Art Museum; gift of the Harmon Foundation.

Above:
Roderick MacKenzie, *Soaking Pit,* hand-colored lithograph, c. 1932, 28 ¼ x 36 in., collection of the Birmingham Museum of Art, Alabama; gift of Mr. Herbert Ryding.

3

The Printmakers

Victoria Ebbels Hutson Huntley (1900–1971)

Born in northern New Jersey, Victoria Ebbels grew up in New York City and entered the Art Students League at the early age of twelve. She continued her studies there, as well as at the New York School of Fine Arts; however, with the death of her father she entered Teachers College of Columbia University to prepare for a teaching career. She secured a position at the College of Industrial Arts in Denton, Texas (now Texas Woman's University), which she held for two years in the early 1920s. In 1925 she returned to New York and became Mrs. Hutson. After that marriage ended in 1933, she married Ralph Huntley with whom she spent the rest of her life.

With the encouragement of Carl Zigrosser, Huntley took up lithography in 1930 and learned the technical process from George Miller. From 1934 to 1946 she taught art in various private schools in the New York City area and produced a considerable number of lithographs, some on industrial themes.[1] In 1946 she and her family moved to Fern Park, in the Orlando area of Florida, where they remained until 1953. During the year 1946–47 Huntley taught at nearby Rollins College. With a grant from the National Institute of Arts and Letters, in 1947 she traveled to the Everglades to study its bird life. A Guggenheim grant awarded in 1948 enabled her to travel through other parts of the South; two lithographs of Charleston in 1949 are associated with these travels. After her years in Florida, Victoria Huntley accompanied her husband to Illinois and then back to New Jersey.[2]

After her studies in the Everglades, Huntley made a considerable number of lithographs depicting the birds of the region. While some present distant, panoramic views of birds in their wetlands setting, others move closer to a small number of species that occupy most of the image area. *In the Everglades; Detail, Cuthbert Rookery,* done in 1948, is notable for its low, close-up examination of several species. Cuthbert Rookery was a major nesting area for wading birds within the Everglades. Perched on an odd-shaped tree in the foreground are three white herons almost at ground level. Those in the nest in the background toward the upper left are probably intended to be the white ibis, which are smaller than egrets and have curved bills.[3] Through value contrast in the foreground, Huntley highlights the sinuous shapes of the white herons as well the black sweeping form of the tree against an indefinite background in a gray tonal range.

Notes

1. F. A. Whiting Jr., "Victoria Hutson Huntley," *Magazine of Art* 31 (November 1938): 639–40; "Victoria Hutson Huntley (1900–1971)" Stone and Press Gallery, New Orleans, LA, Catalog #10, October 1990.
2. "'The Lithograph Speaks Many Languages': A Retrospective of the Prints of Victoria Huntley," June 1, Gallery of Fine Art, Washington, DC, November 16–December 6, 1974; "Victoria Hutson Huntley (1900–1971)"; [Diana Brown], "A Place in Time," A Retrospective Exhibition, St. Charles Public Library, St. Charles, IL, available at http://www.st-charles.lib.il.us/low/artju199.html, accessed July 1, 2002.
3. Tom Webber letter to author, June 5, 2000; Roy Woods e-mail to author, September 9, 2001.

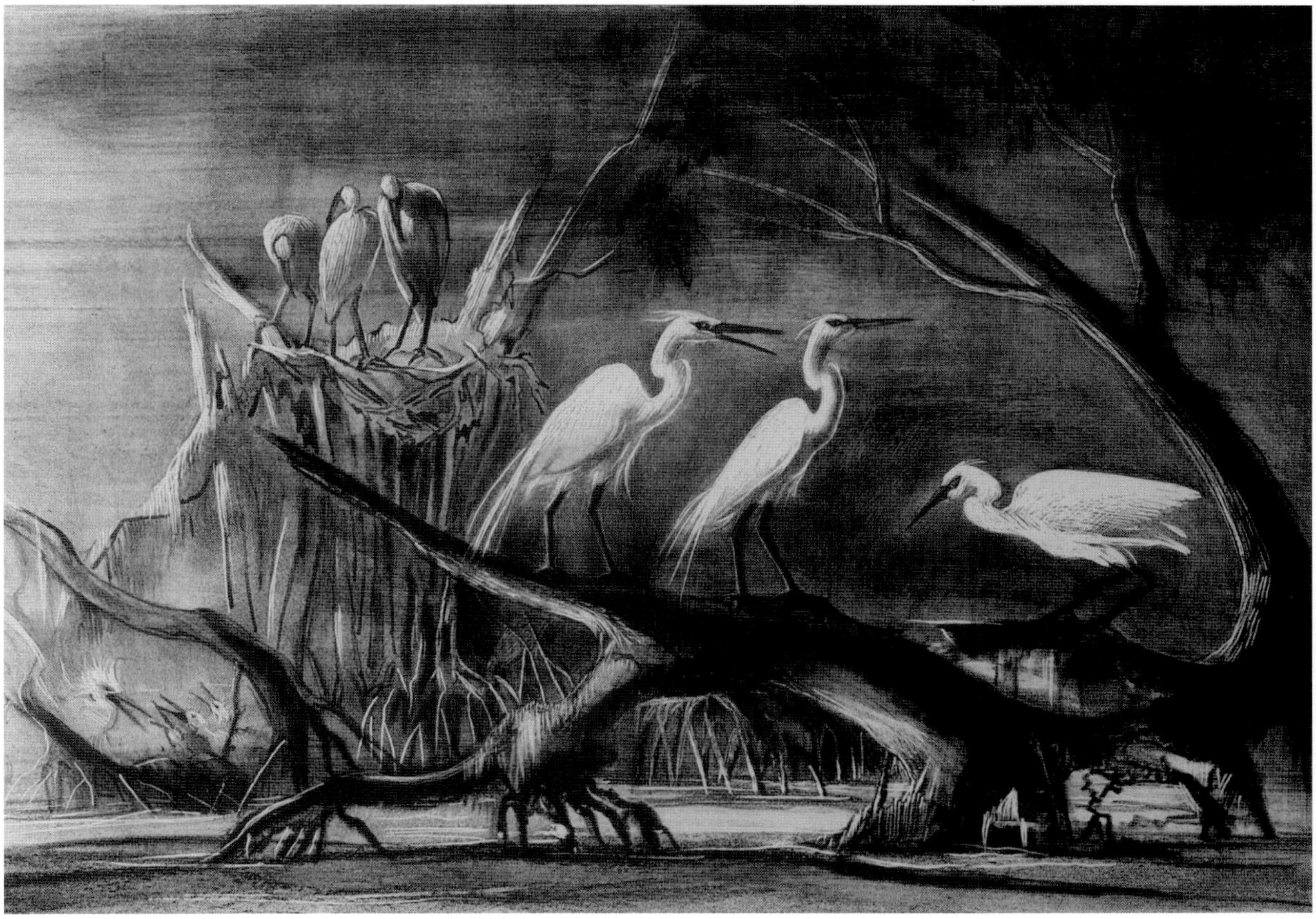

1. Victoria Hutson Huntley, *In the Everglades; Detail, Cuthbert Rookery,* lithograph, 1948, 9 ⅝ x 13 ¾ in., courtesy of Matteo Ledinic and from the collection of Lynn Barstis Williams.

Walter Inglis Anderson (1903–1965)

One of the South's most distinctive printmakers, Walter Anderson has been celebrated for his watercolors of birds, but his talent for design extended to many other media, including block prints from linoleum strips. Anderson had a sound artistic education, attending the Pennsylvania Academy of the Fine Arts from 1923 to 1928, followed by travel through Europe financed by a Packard award and a Cresson travel grant. Returning to his parents' summer home in Ocean Springs, Mississippi, where he worked as a decorator in his brother's Shearwater Pottery, he began to make block prints. After three years confined to a mental institution, Anderson settled on the Oldfields' Plantation in Gautier, Mississippi, with his wife and children in 1940. From 1940 to 1949 he made approximately three hundred block prints from pieces of linoleum, which he reputedly garnered from shipyards in nearby Biloxi. He printed many of them on the back of wallpaper samples (unfortunately a highly perishable medium), which accounts for their unusually large size and elongated format. A number that he made from 1945 to 1949 are "monumental": from 60 to 100 inches in length in a long strip format. He printed the pieces by hand using a pipe filled with sand for pressure.[1]

As linoleum accommodates less fluidity than paint, Anderson's designs for prints exhibit a more schematic style with flat, contour drawing in heavy, controlled lines that emphasize decorative pattern. According to his daughter, the style of his block prints reflects the influence of Mexican design and the book *A Method for Creative Design* (1926) by Adolfo Best-Maugard, which claims that all art can be reduced to seven organic motifs.[2] The pelican in view here, like Anderson's other print imagery, is less a naturalistic presence than an opportunity for bold design. Dense scale patterns in interweaving sections create a fluid, graceful, visual rhythm filling almost the entire picture space. For his southern print imagery Anderson drew not only on Gulf coastal flora and fauna that he saw around him but also on the human figure. Men and women are seen in rhythmic compositions of Biloxi, Mississippi, hikers and bicyclists on the beach.[3]

Notes

1. Carole E. Thompson, "Walter Anderson: Prints from Mississippi," *Print Collector's Newsletter* 20 (May–June 1989): 54; Patricia Pinson and Mary Anderson Pickard, "The Art of Walter Anderson," in *The Art of Walter Anderson,* ed. Patricia Pinson (Jackson: University Press of Mississippi and the Walter Anderson Museum, 2003), 145.
2. Mary Anderson Pickard letter to author, September 1995; Pickard, introduction to *Birds by Walter Anderson* (Jackson: University Press of Mississippi, 1990), xiv.
3. *A Catalogue of Block Print Designs by Walter Inglis Anderson* (Family of Walter Anderson, 1988) reproduces the linoleum cut designs and establishes titles of the prints.

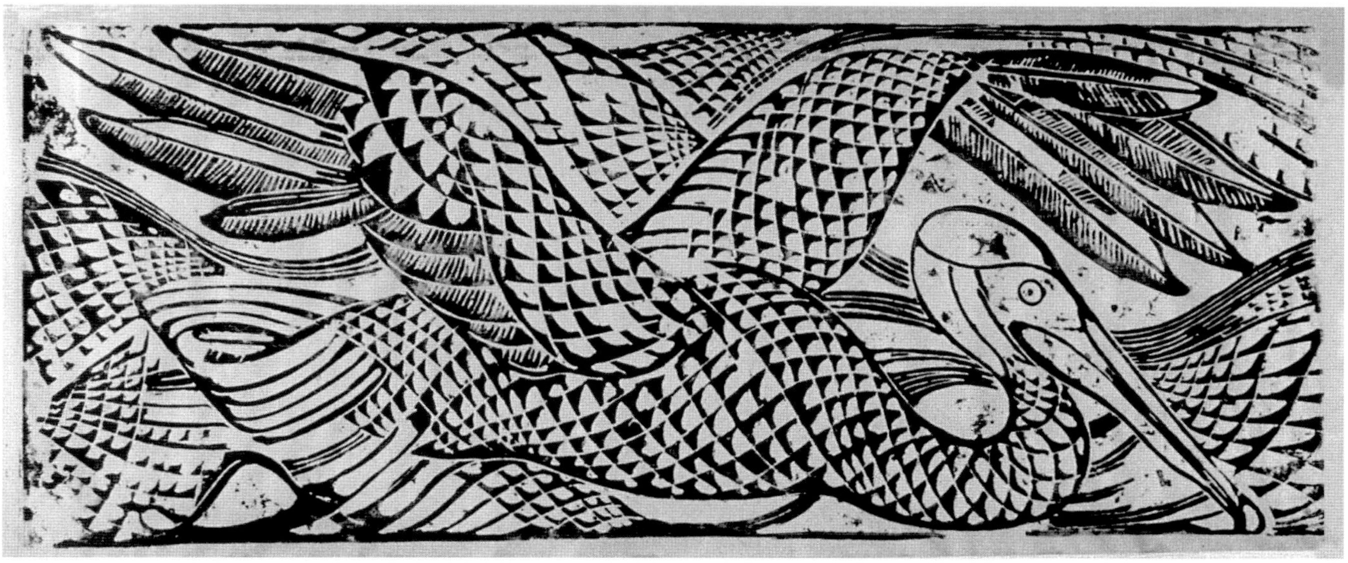

2. Walter Anderson, [Horizontal Pelican], linoleum cut, 1945, 21 x 61 in., © Family of Walter Anderson and from the collection of the Walter Anderson Museum of Art.

Antoinette Rhett (1884–1964)

Antoinette Rhett was born in Baltimore and was educated at Converse College in Spartanburg, South Carolina. She moved to Charleston when she married Arthur Rhett. When Alfred Hutty came to Charleston, she took a life-drawing class from him at the Gibbes Museum and learned etching from Hutty as well. Rhett became a founding member of the Charleston Etchers Club, and she first exhibited her etchings with that organization. In the late 1920s she broadened her exhibition venues to other organizations in the South and beyond, including the Southern States Art League and the Chicago Society of Etchers. According to her friend and fellow member of the Charleston Etchers Club, Selma Tharin Dotterer, Rhett abandoned printmaking in the mid-1930s to raise cocker spaniels.[1]

Rhett often combined etching with drypoint and chose many of the same subject categories as Hutty: the architecture of Charleston and the flora of the surrounding lowland area. Often she combined the two in compositions similar to those of Hutty. However, her most distinguished etchings were asymmetrical compositions in the Japanese bird and flower tradition that combined floral blooms on stems or thin branches with small fauna, such as bees or butterflies, on the wing. Compositions by Rhett ally themselves somewhat with those of Alice Smith in design, so the Japanese tradition influencing Smith likely influenced Rhett as well. Here we see this in the heavy cluster of blooms and leaves of hollyhock in the upper right from which a thin branch descends diagonally into the image area. The bee in mid-air, which appears headed toward two blooms, endows the composition with a hint of imminence. Rhett often hand colored her etchings with watercolors and some, like the example here, exhibit strong saturated hues. These have a light, delicate touch, which is reinforced by the thin paper on which they are printed.[2]

Notes

1. Selma Tharin Dotterer telephone interview with author, March 1994.
2. Severens, *Charleston Renaissance,* 44.

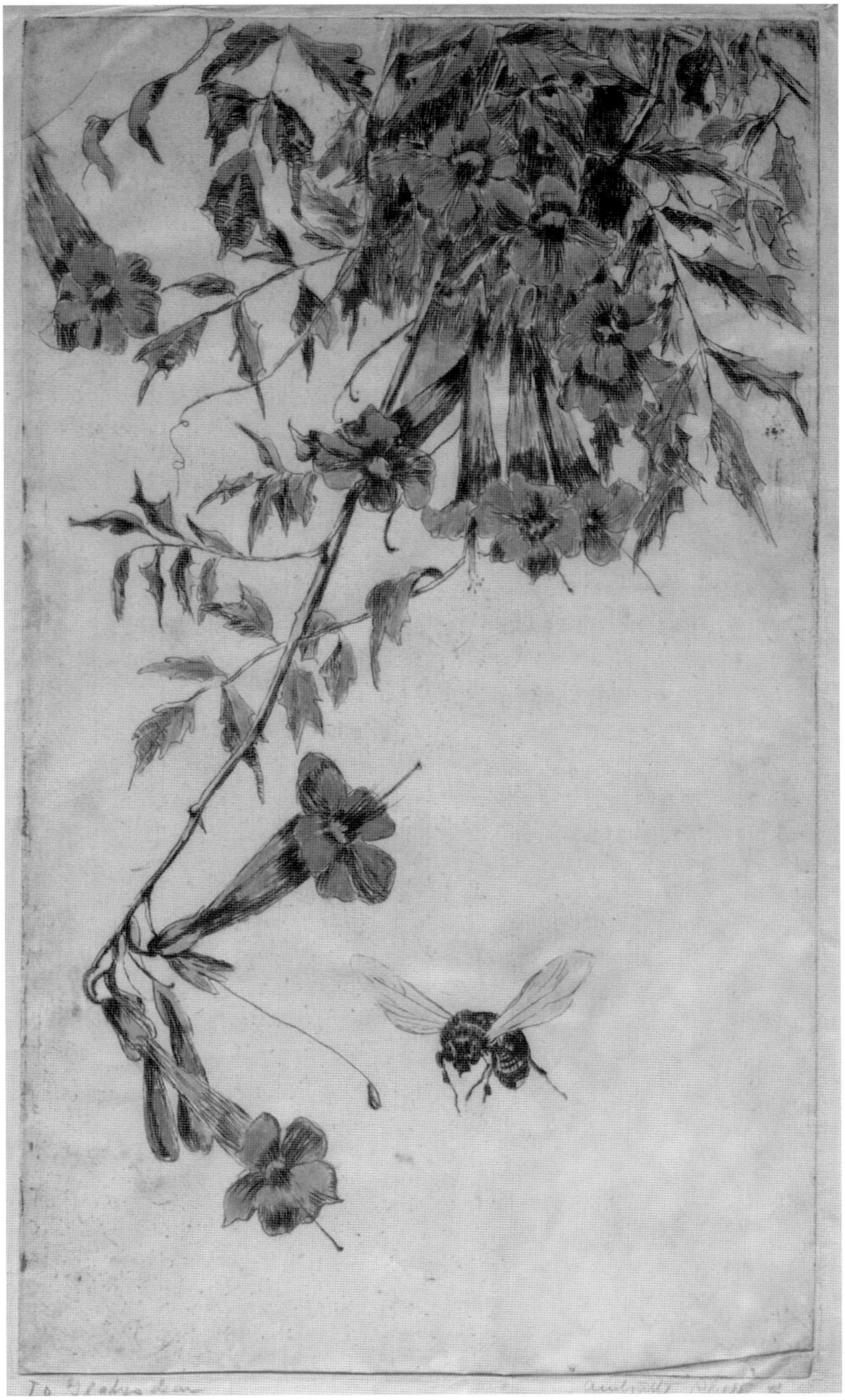

3. Antoinette Rhett, [Trumpet Vine and Bee], etching with hand color, 10 ½ x 6 ½ in., courtesy of David Allen and from the collection of Lynn Barstis Williams.

Mayna Treanor Avent (1868–1959)

Mayna Treanor Avent combined rearing a family with a career as an artist in central and east Tennessee. Born in Nashville not long after the Civil War, she grew up on Tulip Grove Plantation in the Nashville vicinity. After studying at the Cincinnati School of Design, she went to Paris around 1888, where she spent two years studying at the Académie Julien. Returning to Nashville, she married in 1891 and two children followed. Avent continued to work as a painter, retiring from family responsibilities to a studio, which she set up in the attic of her home. In 1918 her husband bought a log cabin retreat in the Smoky Mountains, which she used as her summer studio.

Sometime in the mid- to late 1920s, Avent accompanied her artist friend Sophonisba Hergesheimer on a trip to Provincetown, Massachusetts, where they studied color printmaking from wood blocks. She was interested in learning the Japanese technique of printing from multiple blocks, but judging from the prints she produced, she also learned the single block, white line method pioneered by B. J. O. Nordfeldt in Provincetown. A small body of woodcuts resulted on which she worked until sometime in the 1940s. She rarely sold or exhibited her prints but usually gave them as gifts to family and friends.[1]

Mayna Avent chose similar subjects for her prints as she did for her paintings: floral compositions, portraits, and landscapes. During summers she often depicted the one-room, nineteenth-century cabin where she worked in the mountains, deploying varied perspectives as well as techniques in the application of color to achieve the same impressionist objective as her painted landscapes. From the few examples available by which to judge her floral prints, she uses a frontal, basically symmetrical composition. Made on a pine block, some of whose horizontal grain lines are evident in the impression, *Irises* exemplifies the white line technique associated with Provincetown. The woodcut is particularly lovely for the range of subtle variation in contrasting, complementary hues in watercolor ink. Avent outlines the composition with a narrow black border punctuated by orange square corners.

Notes

1. Mayna Nance letter to author, July 10, 1996; James C. Kelly, *Portrait Painting in Tennessee,* Special Issue of *Tennessee Historical Quarterly* 46 (Winter 1987): 260.

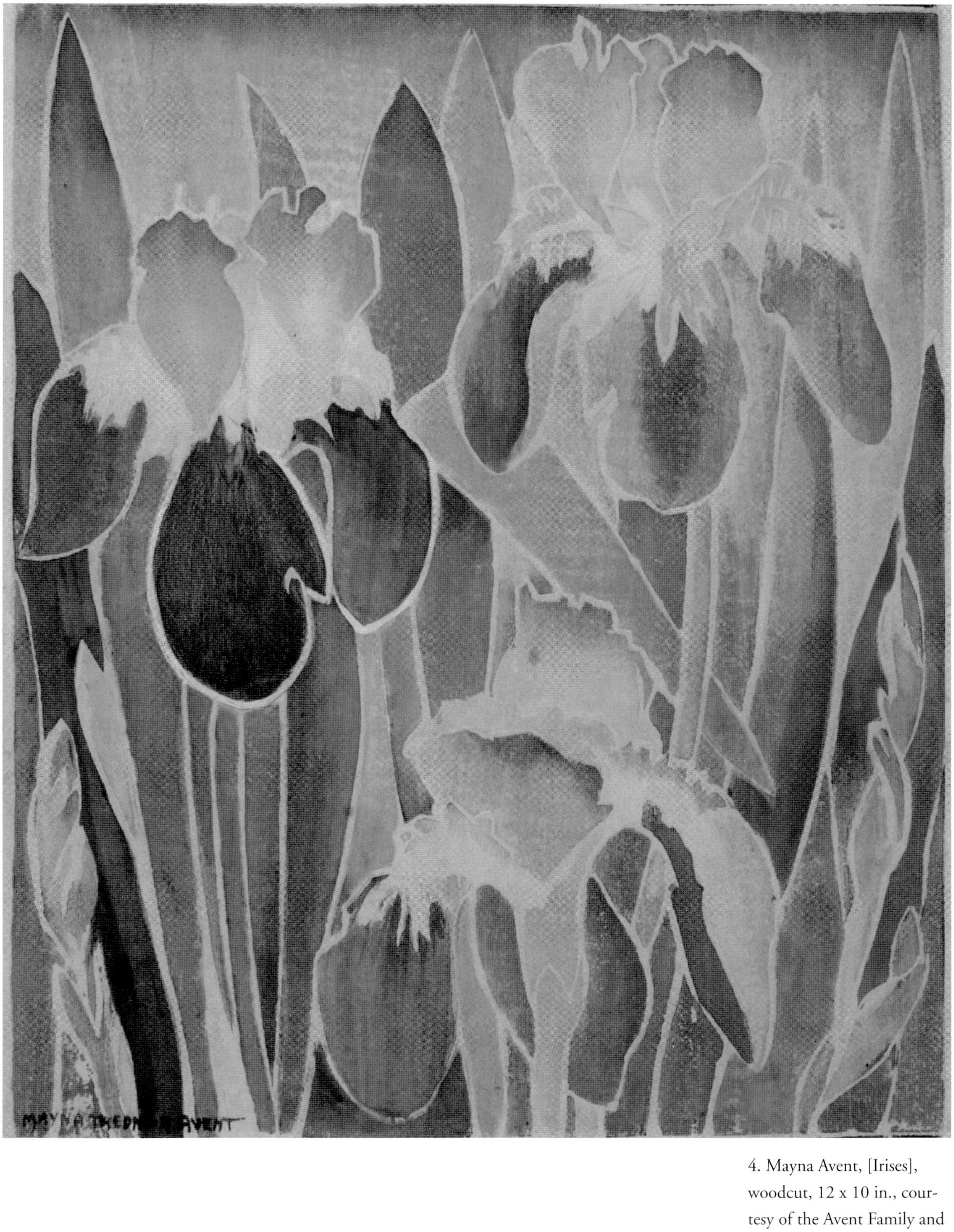

4. Mayna Avent, [Irises], woodcut, 12 x 10 in., courtesy of the Avent Family and from the collection of Ann Avent.

Ella Sophonisba Hergesheimer (1873–1943)

Ella Sophonisba Hergesheimer was the great-great-granddaughter of Charles Wilson Peale. She inherited the name Sophonisba from one of his daughters, whom he named after the Italian Renaissance artist Sophonisba Anguissola. Born in Allentown, Pennsylvania, and reared in nearby Reading, she received solid art training at the Pennsylvania Academy of the Fine Arts and won scholarships to study for three years in Europe. Hergesheimer came to Nashville in 1907 on a commission from Vanderbilt University to paint the portrait of Bishop Holland McTyeire, one of that institution's founders. She liked the city so much that she decided to remain.

Working in a studio in her apartment above a store, she earned her living by painting portraits, but she also specialized in still lifes. Between portraits, Hergesheimer made aquatints and relief prints through which she experimented with design. Her relief prints were "gorgeously colored," one by one, in a meticulous manner.[1] Most were of botanical subjects, which she learned to sketch early in her life as her parents had a conservatory adjacent to their home in Reading.[2] In the early 1930s Hergesheimer turned to lithography.

Hergesheimer made a number of lithographs featuring traditional still-life arrangements on the Victorian marble tabletop that we see here, which was probably in her studio. These compositions are highly polished in an immaculate, three-dimensional style, with a number of them featuring the southern magnolia, a flower she loved. She magnifies the magnolia bloom, which is always placed in the foreground. *A Southern Magnolia* juxtaposes the white bloom with undulating dark leaves against a darker, straight-sided, utilitarian jug to suggest certain basic oppositions in life: beauty versus plainness, pleasure versus work, or transience versus durability. Although she was a portrait painter, Hergesheimer made only one known portrait print: that of her live-in cook, housekeeper, and companion, Jenny Mae, whom she rendered seated at the same marble-topped table.[3]

Notes

1. Christine Sadler, "Nashville Woman Artist Paints Wholeheartedly and Systematically," *Nashville Banner,* July 5, 1932.
2. Kate Talbot, "Artist Who Takes," *Nashville Banner Magazine,* February 26, 1938.
3. Beverly St. John, "Ella Sophonisba Hergesheimer, 1873–1943," unpublished typescript supplied to author by Beverly St. John; Beverly St. John telephone interview with author, July 7, 2000. *Jennie May* can be seen in Pohl, *In the Eye of the Storm,* 26.

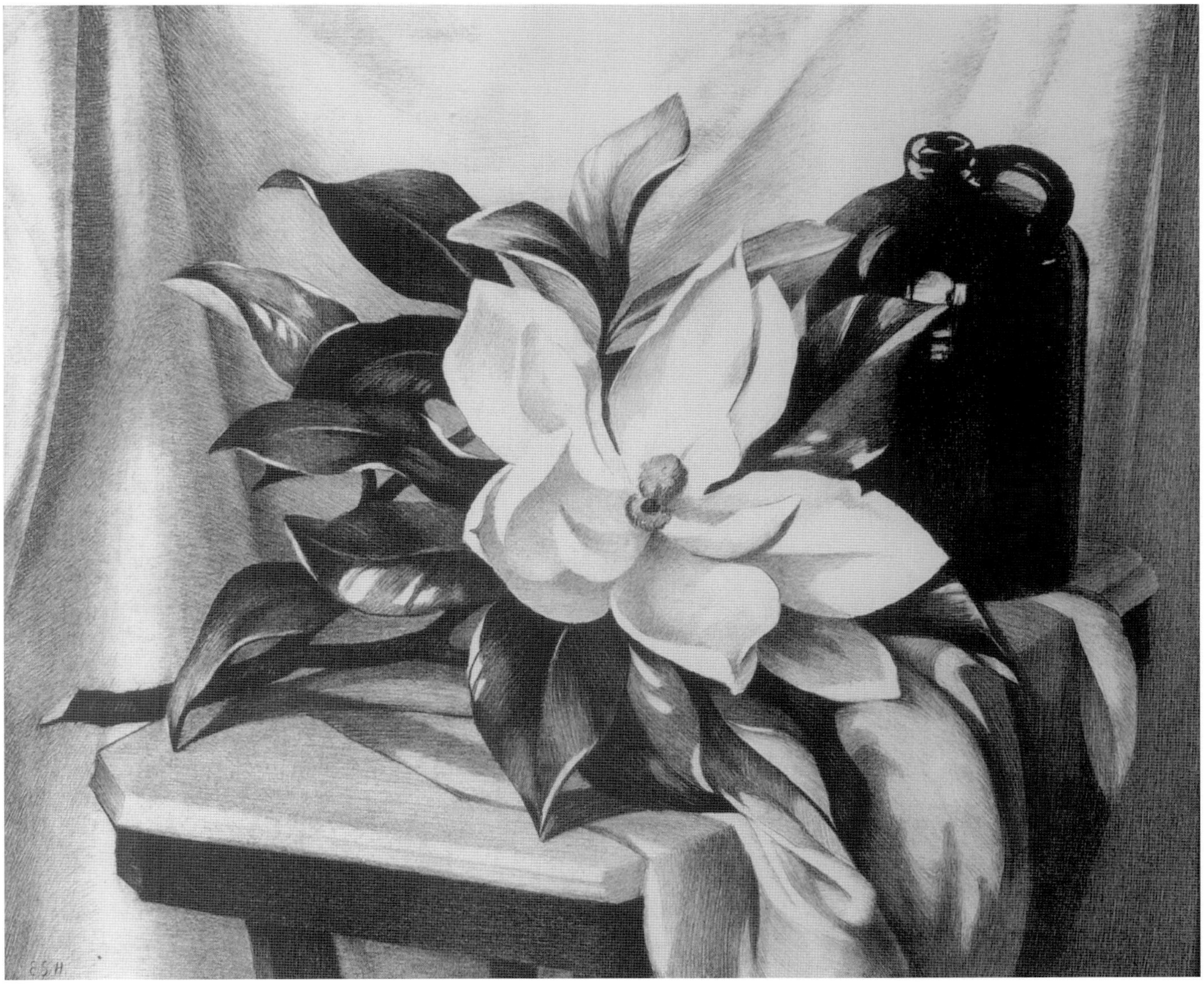

5. E. Sophonisba Hergesheimer, *A Southern Magnolia,* lithograph, c. 1939, 14 x 17 in., collection of Lynn Barstis Williams.

Charles William Smith (1893–1987)

Charles William Smith distinguished himself in relief printmaking, which he carried from realistic representations of southern places to innovative, abstract techniques. Smith grew up in Waynesboro, Virginia, and entered the University of Virginia in 1911. After two years he transferred to the Corcoran School of Art (now Corcoran College of Art and Design) and then finished his studies in 1917 with a certificate from the Yale University School of Fine Arts. From his father, a patternmaker, he learned to carve wood and linoleum plates. After serving in World War I, Smith returned to Waynesboro in 1919 to work as a commercial artist and teacher.[1]

In 1925 Smith moved to Richmond, where he worked for a local printing firm and as an independent commercial artist, continuing to teach as well. He published *Linoleum Block Printing* in 1925 followed by other books composed of images of his relief prints of the historic South. *Old Virginia in Block Prints* appeared in 1929. Smith passed the winter of 1931–32 in Charleston, which he pictured in woodcuts that appeared in *Old Charleston* (1933). *The University of Virginia: Thirty-Two Woodcuts* followed in 1937. After his Charleston visit, Smith moved his commercial art business to New York, where he exhibited his Virginia and Charleston prints. While teaching at Bennington College from 1936 to 1946, he began to experiment with abstract design using moveable wood block sections. He cut up blocks from which earlier prints had been made to create abstract shapes, which could be rearranged in varied compositions. From 1946 to 1963 he taught at the University of Virginia, where he served as the first chairman of the art department.[2]

During his early artistic career, the traditional Virginia life Smith knew, from the mountains of the Shenandoah Valley to the tidewater lowlands, appeared in his traditional scenic prints, many of them with an architectural focus. In addition he created compositions in which such scenes are viewed from an interior perspective through a window before which he renders a still life. In *Country Window* Smith brings a tabletop still life with potted plants before a sash window, behind which a generalized mountain landscape is barely discernable. The play of sharp leaf forms against diamonds in textiles, rectangles in windowpanes, and gentle mountain curves reflects his growing interest in abstract design that culminated in 1939 with his landmark book, *Abstractions.*

Notes

1. Wm. Sergeant Kendall letter to J. Howard Smith, May 7, 1917; Thomas C. Colt Jr., "Charles William Smith," unpublished typescript, September 10, 1947; Charles William Smith files, Alderman Library, University of Virginia; Marsha Blakemore, "Waiting Still Bores Artist of 70 Years," *Richmond Times-Dispatch,* March 26, 1978; *Block. Ink. Paper.: The Prints of J. J. Lankes and Charles W. Smith,* The Library of Virginia, Richmond, VA, June 4–December 1, 2001.
2. William Bainter O'Neal, *Charles Smith: Prints and Paintings* (Charlottesville: University of Virginia Press, 1958), 1–3; "Brings 'the Virginia Scene' to New York," *Art Digest,* December 15, 1931, 21; "Virginian Pictures His Home and Hills," *Art Digest,* November 15, 1935, 21; Robin Davenport telephone interview with author, August 14, 2004.

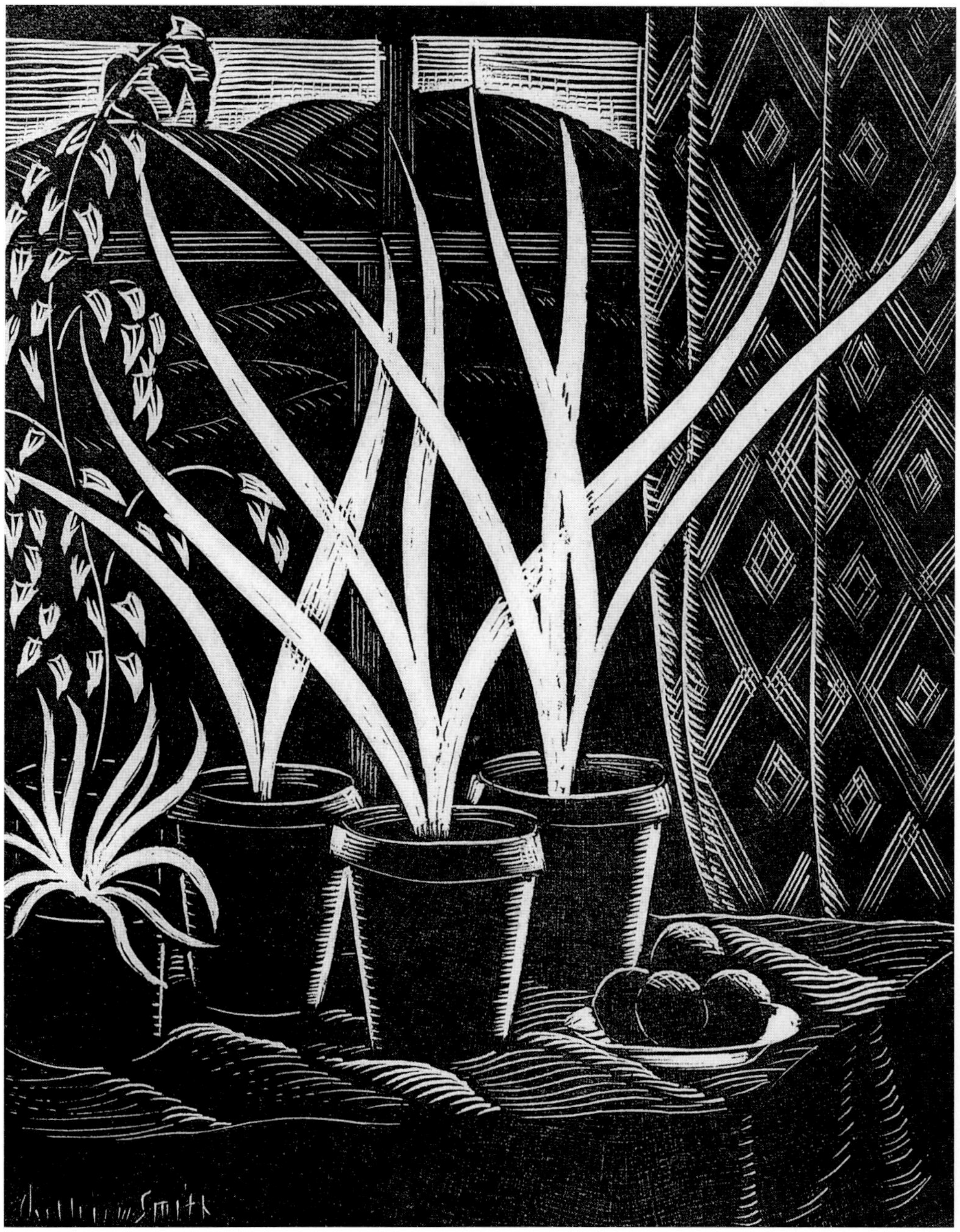

6. Charles W. Smith, *Country Window,* wood engraving, c. 1930, 7 ½ x 6 in., courtesy of Robin J. Davenport and from the collection of the Miriam and Ira D. Wallach Division of Art, Prints and Photographs; The New York Public Library; Astor, Lenox, and Tilden Foundations.

Henrietta Davidson Bailey (1874–1950)

Along with Sadie Irvine, Henrietta Bailey was one of the long-time Newcomb pottery decorators, and like Irvine she also made and exhibited relief prints. Bailey began working at the pottery in 1902 when she was a student in the art school of Newcomb College, from which she graduated in 1903. In 1904, while working as a pottery decorator, she won a scholarship to study at Ipswich, Massachusetts, with Arthur Wesley Dow, a major figure in color relief printmaking. Bailey acquired or perfected her skill in color relief prints through Dow. She returned to New Orleans and taught block printing, bookbinding, and other crafts, first as a part-time teacher on the art faculty at Newcomb from 1908 to 1926 and then full-time from 1926 to 1938.[1] She began exhibiting her relief prints in 1930 and continued through the decade in annuals held by the Art Association of New Orleans and the Southern States Art League. She also lectured and demonstrated both etching and relief printmaking methods for New Orleans arts organizations, such as the Arts and Crafts Club.

Cypress is a romantic swamp scene with strong contrast between highly saturated colors that, according to secondary sources, seems to be common in her prints. A review of an exhibition of her block prints in April 1931 noted "misty overcast in Louisiana swamps and bayous" with "beautiful effects with moonlight, sunlight, and early morning overtones." This review singled out a moonlight scene in which a moon shines through the top branches of a "midnight blue" live oak as one of the most "stunning," which seems to be the print on view here.[2] Archival evidence shows many of her prints bore titles of trees of the southeastern lowlands as well as other Louisiana subjects, such as *Madisonville Street* and *Mississippi River.* Unfortunately, very few impressions of her prints are available in public institutions to further the study of Bailey's printmaking methods, subjects, and style.

Notes

1. Bragg and Saward, *Newcomb Style,* 22, 57; Ormond and Irvine, *Louisiana's Art Nouveau,* 150–51.
2. Bragg and Saward, *Newcomb Style,* 58, 61; Ormond and Irvine, *Louisiana's Art Nouveau,* 151.

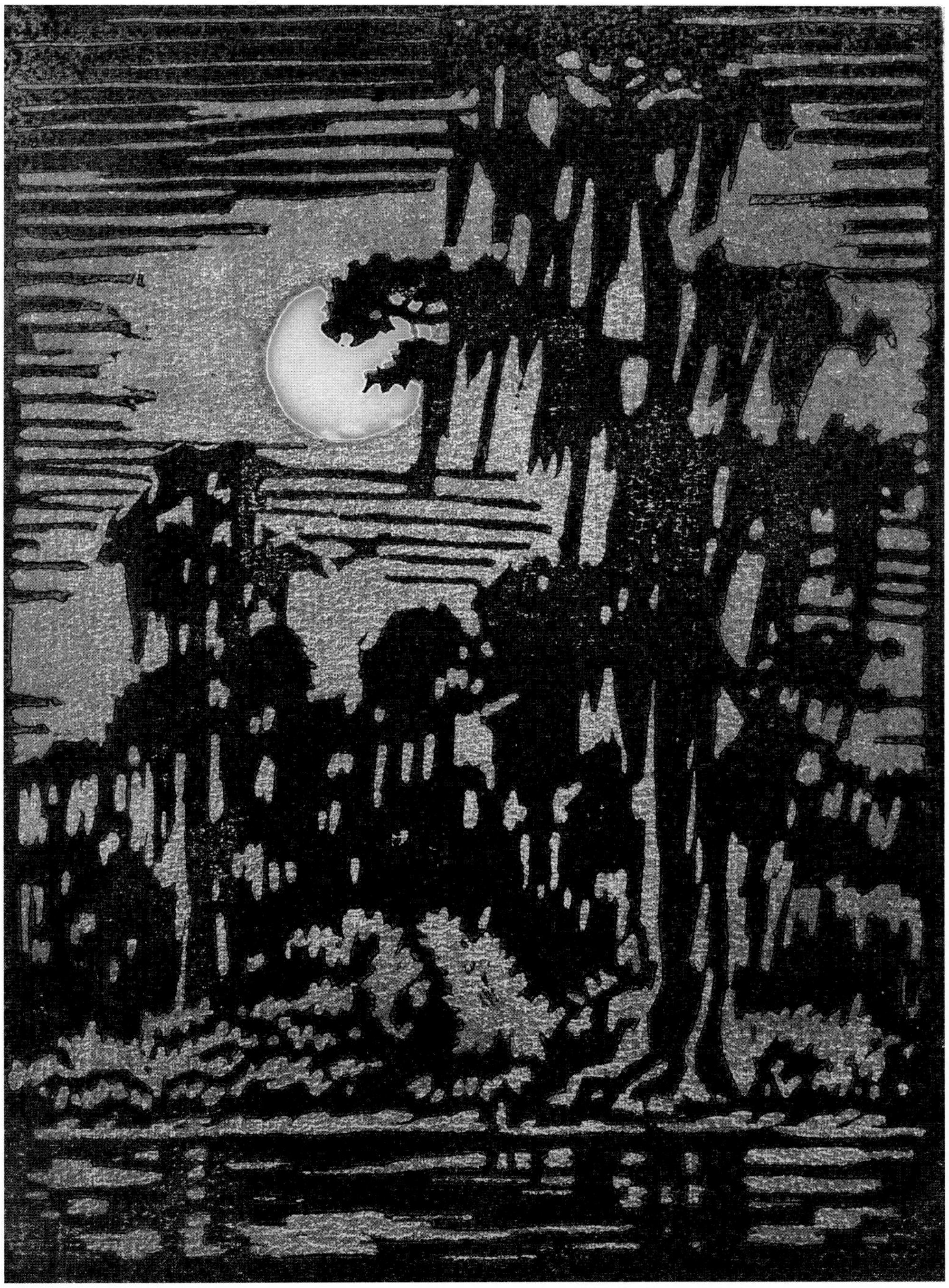

7. Henrietta Bailey, *Cypress,* woodcut, c. 1911, 8 x 5 ⅞ in., collection of the New Orleans Museum of Art; gift of J. Norcom Jackson Jr., 91.165.

Sadie (Sarah Agnes Estelle) Irvine (1887–1970)

An accomplished decorator of Newcomb pottery, Sadie Irvine also excelled in the color relief print, like her fellow decorator Henrietta Bailey. Her stepmother recognized her art talent and after Sadie graduated from high school, enrolled her in Newcomb College, from which she graduated in 1906. After studying at the Art Students League in New York, she returned to New Orleans in 1908 to work at Newcomb Pottery. She also taught in the Newcomb art department, progressing to head the ceramics department until she retired in 1952. She then taught at the Academy of the Sacred Heart in New Orleans until 1967.[1] Exactly when Irvine began to make relief prints is not known, but she exhibited impressions during the 1930s in the annual exhibitions of the Art Association of New Orleans and the Southern States Art League, along with her pottery. She used linoleum slabs backed by wood for her plates and printed them using delicate color.[2]

Irvine's print iconography tends to fall into two groups: the natural imagery that she used for her pottery and portraits. In the first category she usually made simple compositions with close-ups of flowers or landscapes highlighting trees, often against a moonlit sky. With tree imagery of dark parallel verticals scattered with orange maple leaves in the foreground against a muted, diffused background, *Marsh Maple* appears to be one of Irvine's more complex landscape compositions. She exhibited this print in the 1932 Southern States Art League annual.[3] Her portraits were usually head views of her friends and family, rendered economically through strong dark lines. She was one of the few artists to depict the white child in portrait prints. Irvine also produced numerous small bookplates in relief prints.

Notes

1. *Sadie Agnes Estelle Irvine Memorial Show, 1906–1960* (New Orleans: Louisiana Craft Council, April 1–10, 1971); Poesch, *Newcomb Pottery,* 100; Bragg and Saward, *Newcomb Style,* 26; *Newcomb College Arts and Crafts Sales Exhibition,* 58.
2. Ormond and Irvine, *Louisiana's Art Nouveau,* 134.
3. The print appears in the exhibition catalog with the title *Marsh Maples.*

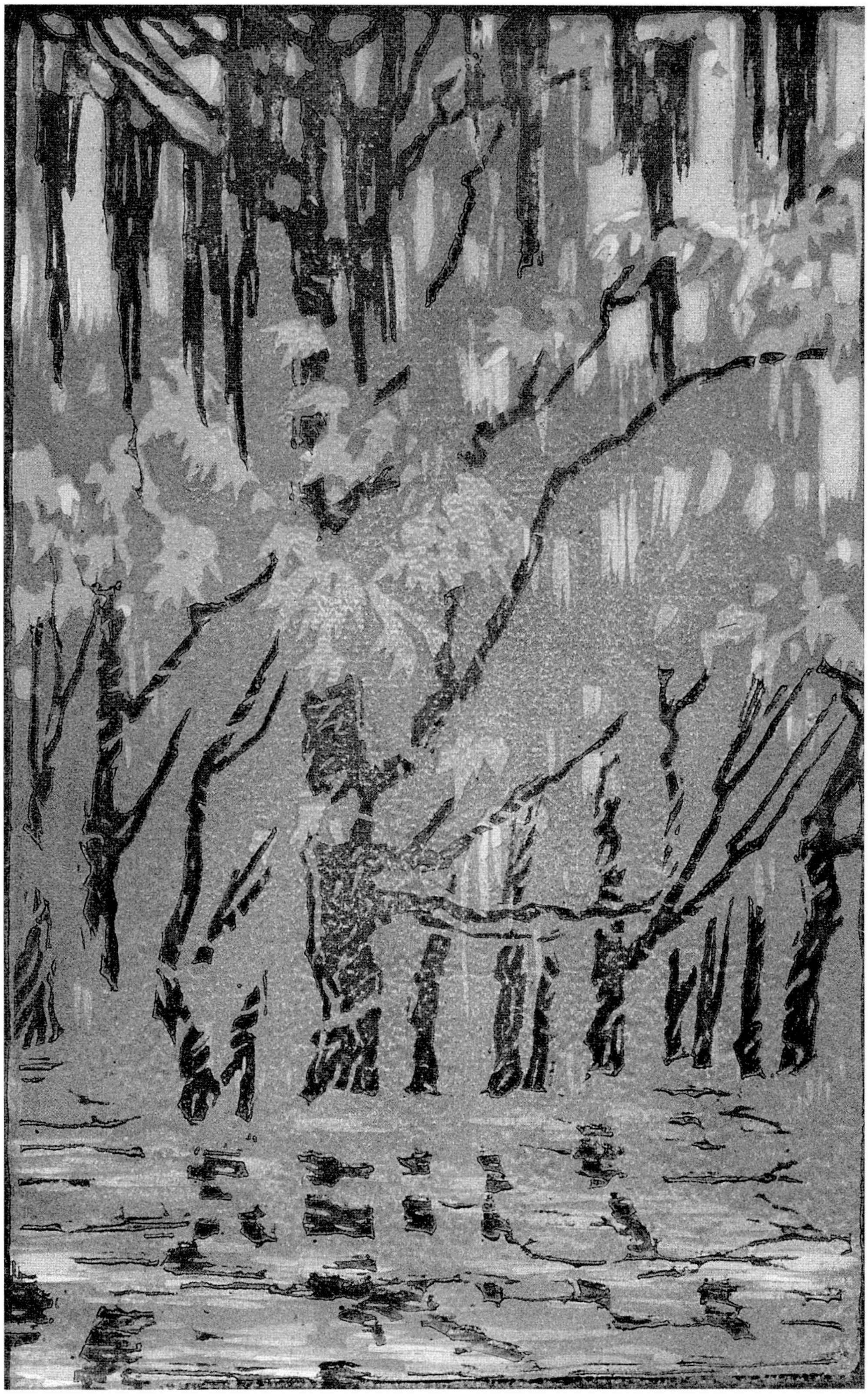

8. Sadie Irvine, *Marsh Maple,* color linoleum cut, c. 1920, 11 ⅛ x 7 ⅛ in., collection of the Louisiana State University Museum of Art; gift of Dr. A. Brooks Cronon Jr. and Diana Cronan.

Hale Aspacio Woodruff (1900–1980)

Born in Cairo, Illinois, Hale Woodruff grew up in Nashville, where his widowed mother brought him as a young child. He began his art career drawing cartoons for his high school newspaper, an experience that helped him do the same for an African American newspaper in Indianapolis, where he began working in 1919. Employed at various odd jobs to be able to afford tuition, Woodruff began studying at the John Herron Art Institute in Indianapolis in 1920 and exhibited his paintings there as well. In 1926 he won the first bronze medal from the Harmon Foundation, a monetary reward that he used with other funds to travel to Paris. He remained in France until 1931, studying at the Académie Scandinave and the Académie Moderne.[1]

Woodruff returned to the South from France when he was offered the opportunity to establish the art program at Atlanta University. In addition to teaching his students to make prints from wood and linoleum blocks, he used both media for his own creative work from 1933 to 1939.[2] At least some of these were apparently done through a WPA grant. In 1943 Woodruff left Atlanta when he won a grant from the Julius Rosenwald Foundation to study in New York. In 1946 he took a teaching position at New York University, where he remained until his retirement in 1967.[3]

Woodruff saw his art program at Atlanta University closely connected with the South, particularly its segregated African American population. In an interview, he stated that he and his students were interested "in expressing the South as a field, as a territory, its peculiar run-down landscape, its social and economic problems, the Negro people."[4] Of ten relief prints from the 1930s, *Returning Home* (also titled *View of Atlanta* or *Atlanta Street Scene*) has been reproduced most often to exemplify Woodruff's concern with the social environment. It shows the dilapidated housing of an African American neighborhood.[5] Run-down buildings along with mules and musicians were common motifs in Woodruff's southern iconography. *Georgia Woodlands,* possibly a swamp scene, appears to be the only work of his Atlanta print oeuvre focusing solely on the South's natural environment. Aligning his dense pine forest rigidly along a vertical axis, perpendicular to the horizon plane, Woodruff suggests a natural barrier resisting human penetration. The emphasis on formal structure reflects his interest in modernist experimentation, which appears with a light touch here and there in his southern prints. Woodruff also made a number of views of buildings on the Atlanta University campus in a more conventional, realistic style.[6]

Notes

1. *Hale Woodruff:* 9–12. Due to an incongruity between chapter headings and the table of contents, it is difficult to cite specific authors in this catalog.
2. Woodruff used linoleum blocks for all his prints except for *Blind Musician.* E. T. Williams telephone interview with author, September 12, 2004; E. T. Williams written communication with author, September 25, 2004.
3. *Hale Woodruff:* 32–33, 73.
4. "Black Beaux-Arts," *Time,* September 21, 1942, 74.
5. See *Alone in a Crowd,* 31, and King-Hammond, "WPA Black Printmakers," 218.
6. The exhibition catalog *Homage to Hale Woodruff,* Waddell Gallery, Atlanta University, 1981, includes reproductions of two prints and lists seven of Atlanta University.

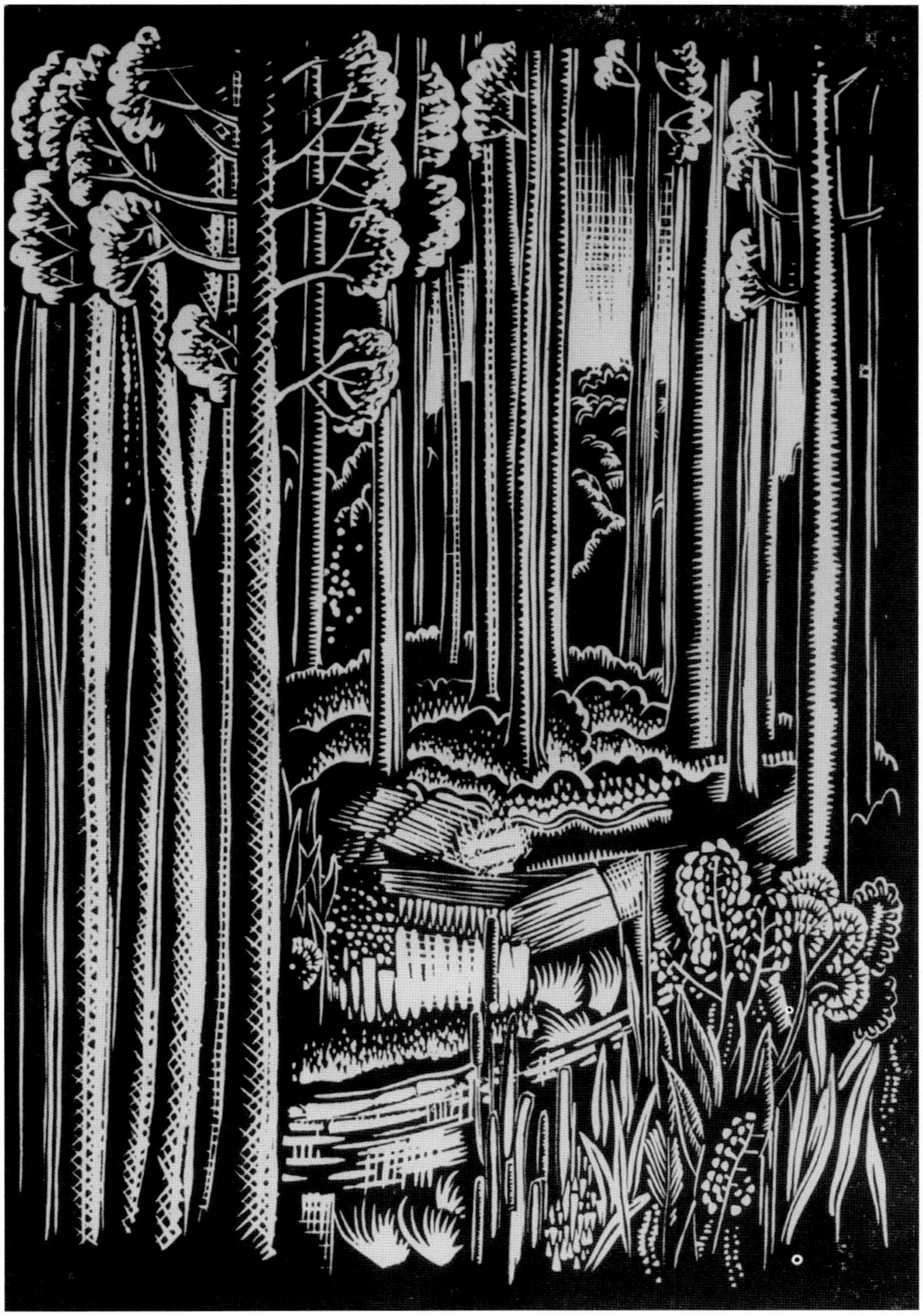

9. Hale Woodruff, *Georgia Woodlands,* linoleum cut, c. 1935, 11⅞ x 8 ⅝ in., courtesy of Elnora, Inc. and from the collection of Stephen Goldfarb.

(Walter Ronald) W. R. Locke (1883–1949)

Walter Ronald Locke, known as W. R., grew up in Winchester, Massachusetts, where he lived until about 1910.[1] He studied under a Boston painter, Louis Kronberg, but abruptly ended his art training and ceased artistic activity for twenty-two years. Coming South for his health, he met Alfred Hutty, who taught him to etch. Locke established a studio and home on the Florida west coast at the mouth of the Anclote River near Tarpon Springs, while his summers were spent in "the New England hill country."[2] He became so proficient in realistic, detailed etchings that Associated American Artists selected three of his southern scenes—*Along the Gulf of Mexico, Eucalyptus Tree,* and *In Old Savannah*—for their first editions issued in 1934.[3]

Locke appears to have traveled to various parts of north Florida and nearby states, judging by the imagery and titles of his etchings. He often described himself as a naturalist who could not tolerate urban life and spent twelve of his early years away from civilization, working as a lumberjack in the Pacific Northwest. His love of the natural world surfaced in images of trees and, according to his own testimony, he spent months studying a specific variety before undertaking an etching in which he pictured its features with exacting detail. Locke struggled with a form of palsy, which caused him to become somewhat of a recluse and made finesse with the etching needle particularly challenging.[4]

Trees, often varieties of the Florida palm, are almost always placed in the foreground of Locke's compositions, but he often includes architecture as well. In *Anclote Light,* the lighthouse, which towers in the center background above the trees, competes for our attention. The wrought iron lighthouse on Anclote Key, a three-mile-long island covered with tropical vegetation, which Locke visited almost daily in a small skiff, went into service in 1887 and was discontinued in 1952.[5] The two buildings in the background, which served as residences for the lighthouse keeper and his assistant and their families, are no longer extant.[6]

Notes

1. Ellen E. Knight e-mail to author, October 8, 2002.
2. Paul Hidey, "Tree Artistry," *American Forests* 47 (September 1941): 410–12; Locke's mother's 1934 obituary in the *Winchester Star* indicates that she was living with her son Walter Ronald who was proprietor of the Woodstock Inn in Woodstock, NY, where Hutty also wintered. Locke, however, was not a member of the Woodstock Artists Association.
3. "Associated American Artists: Prints for 20th Century Americans," *Journal of the Print World* 25 (Summer 2002): 46.
4. Dale and Nancy Smerkar letter to Burton Moore, October 24, 2004, in possession of David Allen Fine Prints.
5. Love Dean, *Lighthouses of the Florida Keys* (Key West, FL: Historic Florida Keys Foundation, 1992), 18. Locke offered some information about himself and his prints on the descriptive slips attached to the back of etchings issued by AAA.
6. Ray Jones and Bruce Roberts, *Gulf Coast Lighthouses: Florida Keys to the Rio Grande* (Old Saybrook, CT: Globe Pequot Press, 1998), 40.

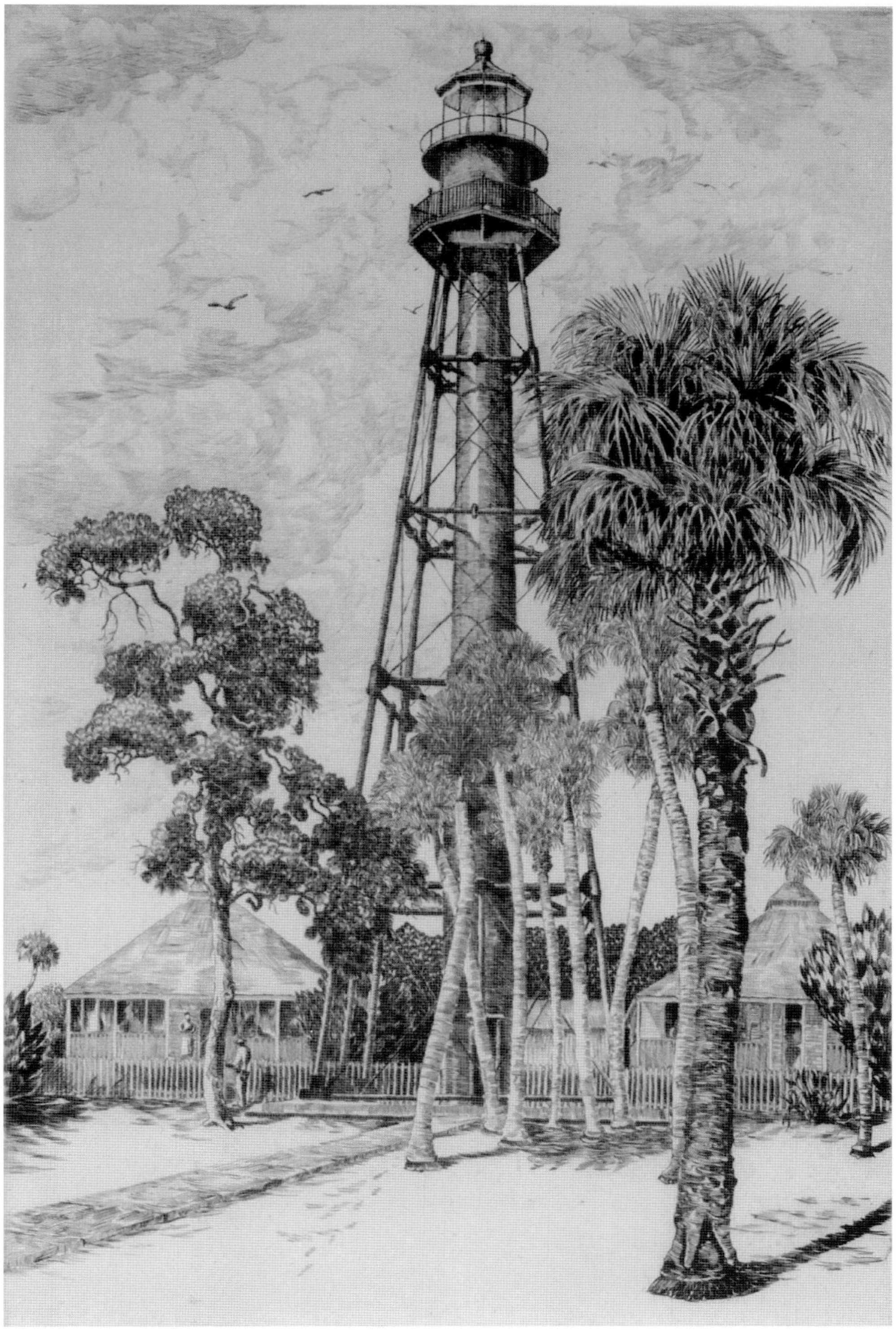

10. W. R. Locke, *Anclote Light,* etching, 12 ¼ x 8 ⅜ in., collection of Stephen Goldfarb.

Mabel Dwight (1875–1955)

Mabel Dwight, one of the most acclaimed American women printmakers of the late 1920s and 1930s, was best known for her satirical lithographs of the American Scene. Born in Cincinnati, Ohio, Dwight spent some of her early years in the South, as her family moved to the New Orleans suburb of Carrollton in the 1880s, where Dwight attended a convent school. Around 1893 the family moved to San Francisco, and Dwight enrolled in the Hopkins Institute of Art for one year. After a year of travel, she settled in New York, where she spent most of her artistic career. That career was undistinguished until she began her lithography oeuvre at the age of fifty-two with the encouragement of her friend Carl Zigrosser, who promoted her work through the Weyhe Gallery that he managed.[1]

In 1927 Dwight traveled to Paris to learn the art of lithography at the Atelier Duchâtel and made her first lithographs in that city. At the end of 1928, shortly after her return to New York, she embarked on a trip to New Orleans with a friend. She wrote to Zigrosser that New Orleans was a "wonderful place for an artist" and that she "saw some things there that I simply must do."[2] When she returned to New York she made two lithographs from her sketches. One was *Derelict Banana Men, New Orleans,* a view of the working poor set in the Old French Market of the city.[3] The other was the view of the graveyard we see here. Dwight was evidently impressed by huge, moss-hung live oaks, whose crowns she crops in a close-up view of their presence in the graveyard. With a curtain of moss threatening to overtake small, unstable gravestones, the view becomes a satiric comment on human aspirations toward remembrance and immortality in the face of an aggressive nature.

Notes

1. See Susan Barnes Robinson and John Pirog, *Mabel Dwight: A Catalogue Raisonné of the Graphic Work* (Washington, DC: Smithsonian Institution Press, 1997), 1–51 and 153–56, for biographical information and critical appraisal of her lithographs.
2. Robinson and Pirog, *Mabel Dwight,* 21, 87.
3. The catalogue raisonné of Robinson and Pirog clarifies that Dwight did two lithographs of banana men: one of New Orleans in 1928 and the other made from a sketch in Brooklyn in 1936, both with basically the same setting.

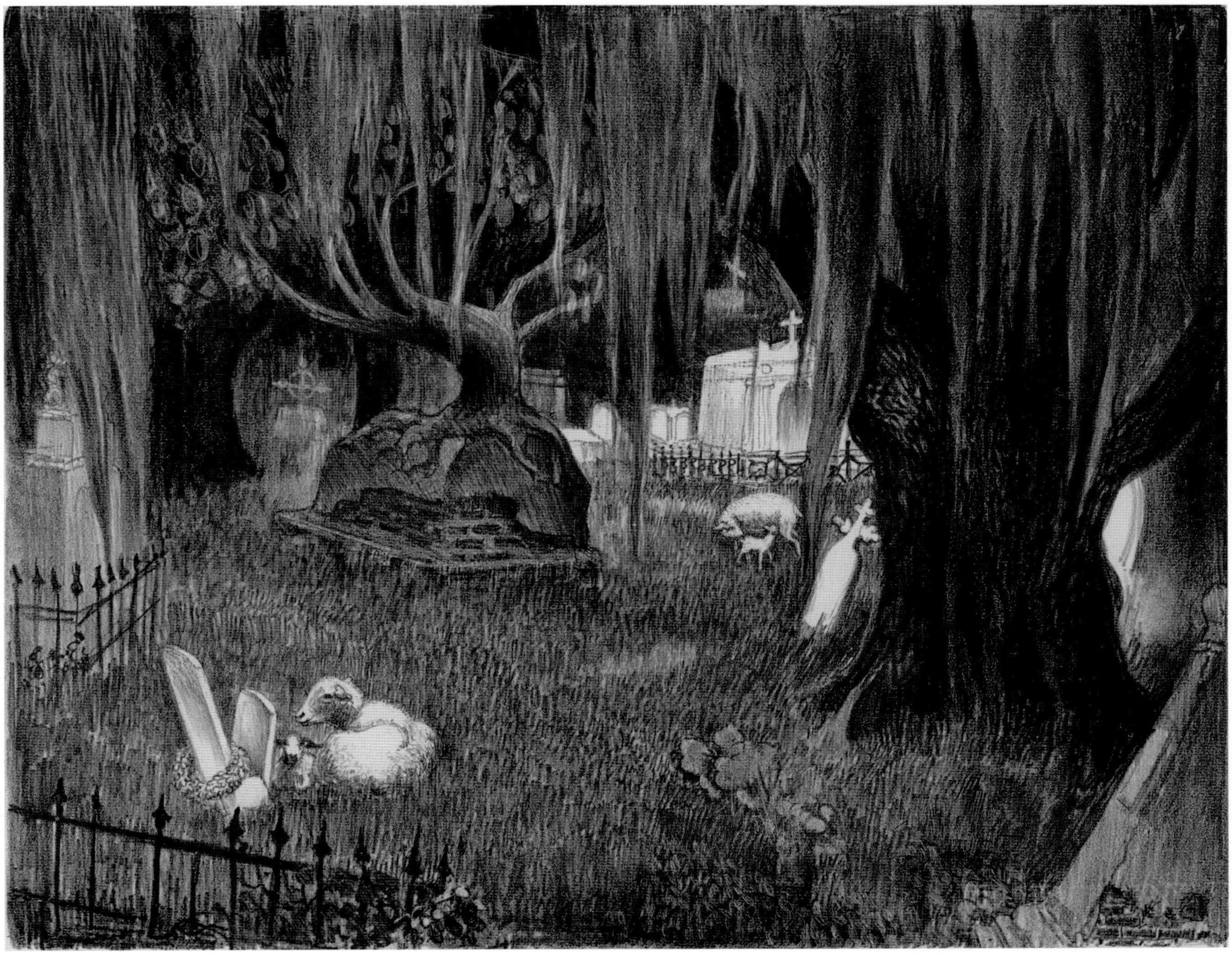

11. Mabel Dwight, *Old Southern Graveyard,* lithograph, 1929, 9 ⅞ x 12 ⅝ in., collection of Lynn Barstis Williams.

Morris Henry Hobbs (1892–1967)

The most important architectural etcher of New Orleans, Morris Henry Hobbs, trained as an architect in Chicago. He took only three months of evening classes in art and drawing at the Art Institute of Chicago, but drew and painted in his spare time during his early years as a practicing architect in Chicago. After serving in France during World War I and losing most of his hearing to influenza, Hobbs resumed his architectural career, moving to Toledo, Ohio, in 1921, where he first studied etching with J. Ernest Dean. After he returned to Chicago in 1925, he selected Ralph Fletcher Seymour as his etching tutor. Hobbs perfected his technical knowledge of the medium during a study tour in France and England in 1930. When he returned to this country, he developed special etching tools for his own use and a miniature press to easily demonstrate the etching process to students. During the 1930s he exhibited extensively on a national level and managed to support himself and his family through his art.[1]

Hobbs worked in the full range of intaglio printmaking of the time: drypoint, aquatint, and mezzotint, often with masterful effects. In 1938 he traveled to New Orleans to do a series of etchings of the French Quarter, and the following year he decided to make the city his permanent home. Concerned with what he saw as inaccurate restoration efforts, he aimed for historical accuracy in rendering buildings to leave a visual record for future generations.[2] In 1939 he exhibited thirty-six etchings, aquatints, and drypoints of "tranquil Old New Orleans" at the Smithsonian Institution.[3] *Iron Lace,* which depicts the well-known Labranche building at the corner of St. Peter and Royal streets, exemplifies views in which he delineates a range of buildings at a distance from the street. The cast iron balconies of the Labranche building are considered some of the finest examples in the French Quarter, and few etchers have captured its cast iron pattern from the distance that Hobbs did. In the late 1940s Hobbs turned to depicting the wildlife of the Louisiana swamps as a subject for aquatints with etching in a larger format.

Notes

1. *Morris Henry Hobbs: Prints and Drawings,* December 2, 1975–January 13, 1976, Morris Henry Hobbs file, Williams Research Center, Historic New Orleans Collection; Kheel, "Morris Henry Hobbs," passim.
2. Kheel, "Morris Henry Hobbs," 61.
3. "Old New Orleans as Seen by Etcher Hobbs," *Art Digest,* October 15, 1939, 24.

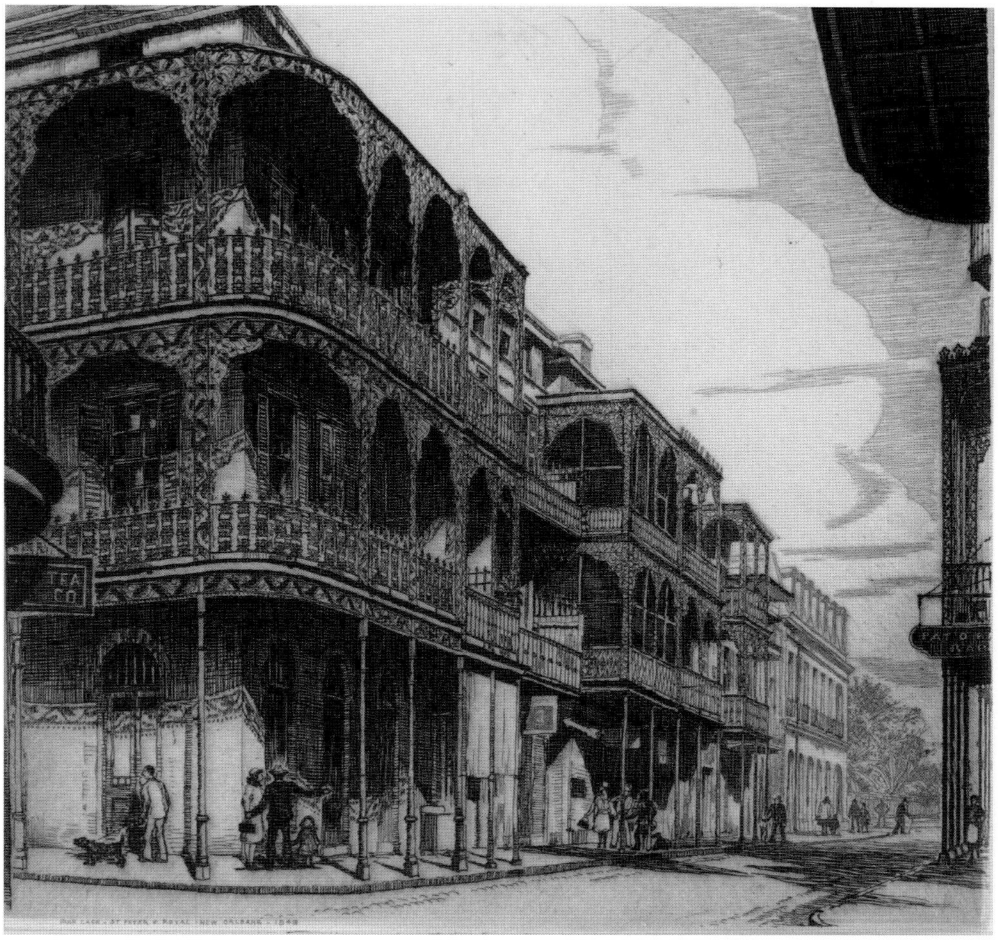

12. Morris Henry Hobbs, *Iron Lace, St. Peter and Royal, Old New Orleans,* etching, c. 1939, 5 ⅞ x 5 ¾ in., collection of Stephen Goldfarb.

Eugene E. Loving (1908–1971)

Little information is available about either the life or artistic career of Eugene Loving. He was born in Round Rock, Texas, and moved to New Orleans in 1931. Judging from his absence in dictionaries of Texas artists, he had no reputation as an artist before that date. His name surfaces in New Orleans newspapers not for his art, but because of a few scrapes with the law. In 1933, in the depths of the Great Depression, a twenty-five-year-old Loving was part in a trio that held up beer parlors in the early morning hours, for which he and his partners were arrested.[1] Six years later in 1939, Loving made the front page again when he pleaded guilty to a robbery, which he had committed in 1933. A judge placed him on probation because he had never been in trouble before the robbery and had behaved himself since.[2] In 1939 Loving became a member of the Louisiana Etchers Society, and he also exhibited with the all-male New Orleans Art League, serving as secretary in 1949.[3] In that year he published *Old New Orleans Calendar,* consisting of ten plates, and a reproduction of his etching *Pirates Alley* appeared in *Print Collector's Quarterly;* otherwise, there is little evidence that Loving exhibited nationally.[4]

Loving became one of the most prolific etchers of the French Quarter, as his etchings typically indicate an edition size of one hundred. Most are views of courtyards that highlight wrought iron gates in small formats. *Iron Lace Balconies, Old New Orleans,* another view of the Labranche building, is one of Loving's larger, more complex etchings. The style bears a striking resemblance to many of the French Quarter etchings of Morris Henry Hobbs, suggesting that Loving may have come under Hobbs's influence after Hobbs moved to New Orleans. Considerable skill is evident here in the intricate patterns of cast iron and shadow as well as the human figures passing on the street, which are absent in his smaller etchings. Loving usually included the subtitle "Old New Orleans" after more specific indications of place in his titles.

Notes

1. "Hold-Up of Beer Parlors Laid to Trio of Suspects," *New Orleans Times-Picayune,* May 29, 1933.
2. "Admits Robbery of 6 Years Ago, Wins Probation," *New Orleans Times-Picayune,* April 20, 1939.
3. "Re Elect H. E. Turner," *New Orleans Item,* April 8, 1949.
4. *Print Collector's Quarterly,* February 1949, 62; *Old New Orleans Calendar* (New Orleans: Harmanson's, 1949).

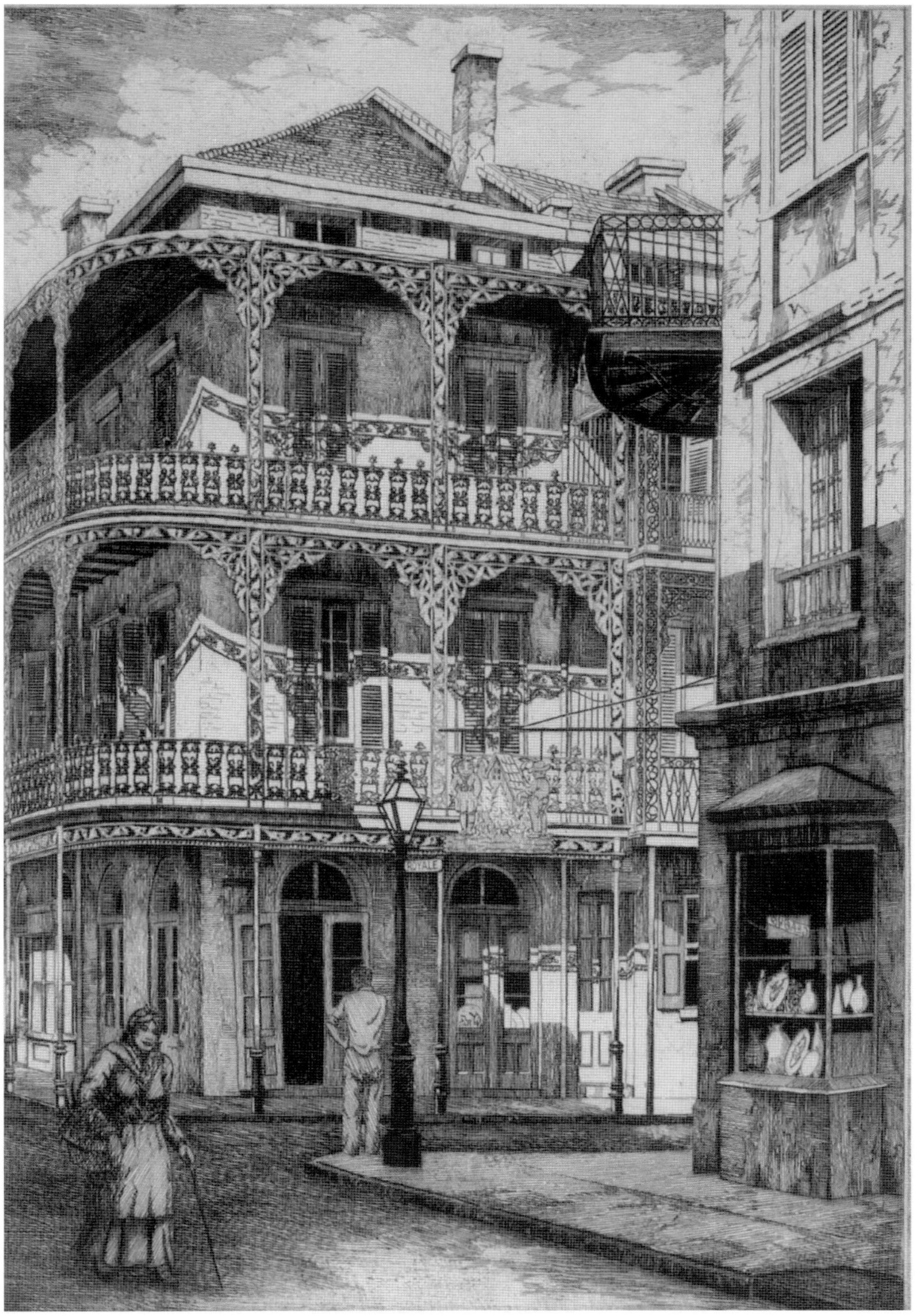

13. Eugene E. Loving, *Iron Lace Balconies, Old New Orleans,* etching, 9 ⅞ x 7 ⅛ in., collection of Stephen Goldfarb.

H(erbert) Alvin Sharpe (1910–1982)

H. Alvin Sharpe is better known in New Orleans popular history for the aluminum doubloons, which he designed for Mardi Gras carnivals beginning in 1959, than for his finely crafted, intaglio prints of the 1930s and 1940s. Sharpe was born in southern Kentucky and lived in various parts of that state until the age of fourteen, when he joined the merchant marine. He spent the next seven years traveling the high seas and probably harbored in New Orleans at times, as he settled there to work as an artist in 1931. During his early years in Kentucky, Sharpe had begun sketching, a practice he continued as a sailor along with painting. Without any formal art training whatsoever, Sharpe taught himself the intaglio processes of etching and aquatint. He made impressions from more than one hundred plates in his studio in the French Quarter, which he sold as mementos to tourists. When the WPA art project was established in New Orleans, Sharpe signed up, making etchings, which were placed in government buildings. In 1939 he joined the Navy and served during World War II, returning to New Orleans in the early 1950s.[1]

Among the architectural etchers working in New Orleans, Sharpe stands out for his mastery of the aquatint process, which he combined with etching. His aquatints are fairly large in format, like *Toulouse Street Court* shown here. The subject was more commonly known as Demarchy's Court and Stairway, part of a building dating to 1807. The elegant, sweeping "S" curve of the interior stairwell was a feature admired by both artists and tourists.[2] Sharpe's view of the stairway and courtyard in the distance is exceptional for the value contrasts in the patterns projected by light and shadow, which emphasize the majestic curving line of the stairway in contrast to the delicate pattern of wrought iron grillwork in the distance. Like a number of other artists who were residents of the French Quarter, Sharpe's imagery in his aquatints also extended to the Louisiana swamps.

Notes

1. "Doubloon-Pioneer H. Alvin Sharpe Dead at 72," *New Orleans Times-Picayune,* October 21, 1982.
2. Lynn, *New Orleans,* 88.

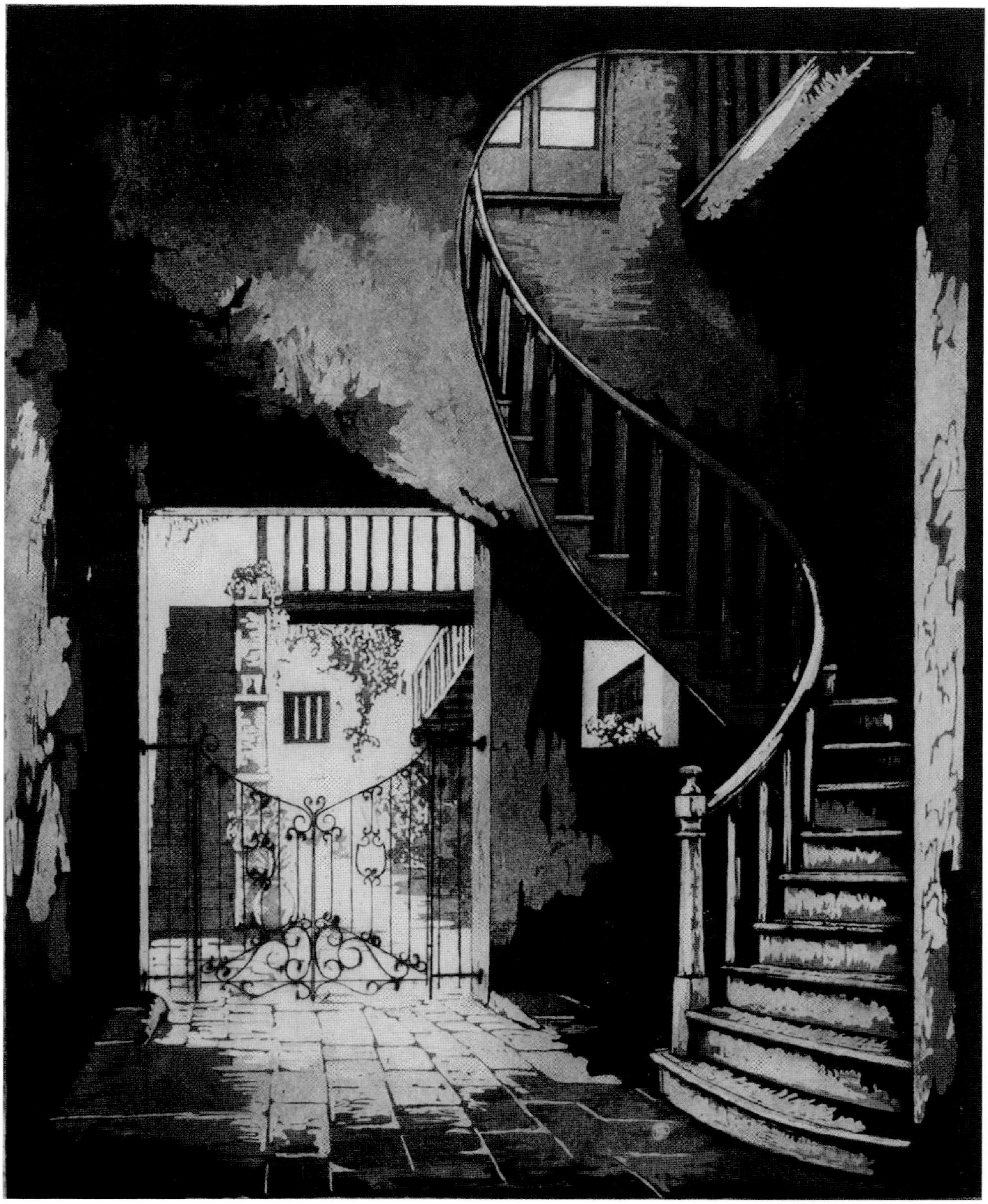

14. H. Alvin Sharpe, *Toulouse Street Court, Old New Orleans,* aquatint with etching, 11 ⅝ x 9 ⅞ in., collection of Stephen Goldfarb.

Clarence Millet (1897–1959)

From the small town of Hahnsville, Louisiana, Clarence Millet migrated to New Orleans in 1914 to find work and paint as a hobby. One account states he was working as an apprentice at an engraving company and another, as a wrapper and shipping clerk in a store, when midwestern etcher Louis Oscar Griffith and his friend Robert Grafton encouraged him to work at art full-time. After spending two years in New York studying at the Art Students League, Millet returned to New Orleans in 1924 and opened a studio. He was a founding member of the Arts and Crafts Club, where he taught night classes, and became active in other New Orleans arts organizations. In his later years he opened an art shop at 628 Toulouse Street, which he operated until his death.[1]

Millet undoubtedly picked up printmaking easily, having had work as an engraver. He worked in both intaglio and relief printmaking media and a number of his prints were of the same views as his paintings.[2] Millet was one of a small number of printmakers working in the French Quarter who pictured traditional architectural scenes in relief prints, some of which were used to illustrate Stanley Clisby Arthur's *Old New Orleans.* Such is the case with *Claiborne Court,* identified in the guidebook as Courtyard of Maison Jacob at 628 Toulouse Street, where Millet opened his art shop. The book acknowledges, however, that tradition mysteriously associates the building with Governor Claiborne, as we see from the title of this impression.[3] Millet adds the typical old-world touch of New Orleans printmakers by including a female figure in a long dress. This impression has been hand painted with watercolor to suggest the bright light of midday, whereas another impression of the same print shows a more subdued different color schema. One cannot assume, however, that Millet painted the prints. Millet also made some etchings and aquatints, which he exhibited with the Louisiana Society of Etchers.

Notes

1. Henry W. Krotzer Jr., *250 Years of Life in New Orleans* (New Orleans: Friends of the Cabildo, Louisiana State Museum, 1968), 67; "Clarence Millet," Clarence Millet file, Morris Museum of Art, Augusta, GA.
2. Pennington, *Downriver,* 171.
3. Arthur, *Old New Orleans,* 72–73.

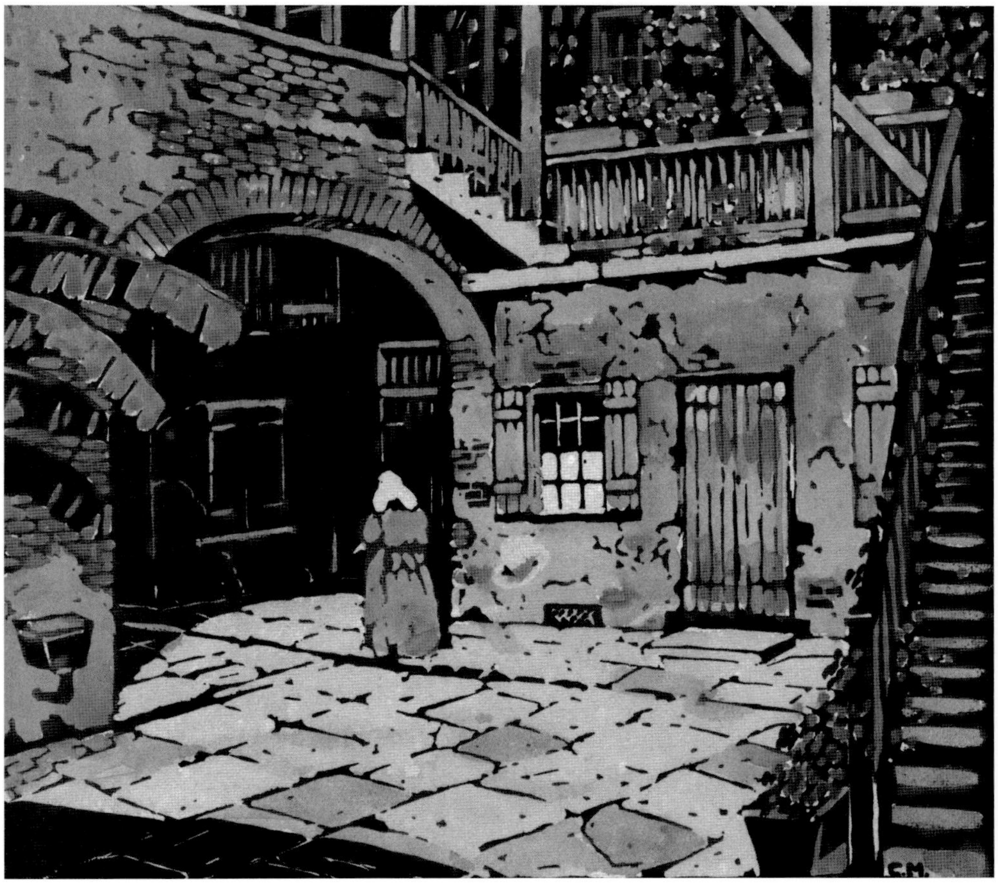

15. Clarence Millet, *Claiborne Court,* hand-colored linoleum cut, c. 1933, 5 ⅞ x 6 ½ in., collection of Lynn Barstis Williams.

Charles Frederick Surendorf (1906–1979)

An Indiana native, Charles Surendorf led a peripatetic existence across the country during his early years, like many artists. He studied at the Art Institute of Chicago, the Art Students League, Ohio State University, and also with various individual instructors. In 1937 he made his first sketching trip from his studio in San Francisco to Columbia, California, an early settlement in the Sierra gold mining territory. In 1946 he established a residence and studio in this community, which remained as his home base during subsequent years and as one subject of his prints.[1] Surendorf began making what he termed linoleum engravings "as a hobby to keep himself occupied on rainy days."

He became interested in visiting New Orleans when his secretary at a San Francisco Art Festival, a frequent visitor to the French Quarter, vividly lauded the district's appeal for artists. His first visit took place in 1947. He rented a studio for several months so he could paint local subjects and sketch sights as subjects for prints. When he returned to California, he made around twenty linoleum prints, which he considered "some of the best series of prints to ever come from my graver." He sent impressions of three prints to various print exhibitions around the country held by museums, and a number won awards. In the following year he returned to New Orleans to experience Mardi Gras and to sell his prints. In 1949 he returned to New Orleans to live for a year with a new bride, an experience that was not financially rewarding, as he found it increasingly difficult to sell his work at a price to make a profit. Moreover, his bride complained about the many roaches in the Quarter![2]

Surendorf crafted both architectural and genre views of New Orleans in his linoleum engravings. *St Louis #1,* a view of one tomb in the St. Louis Cemetery near Basin Street, was the first relief print he produced from his New Orleans sketches. He wrote in his unpublished autobiography that, "the large concrete vault was leaning with age and neglect," emptied, with the "tomb entrance . . . open to the rain and sun and the bones of occupants long removed." The fence surrounding the vault and rusty urns was in a similar state of disrepair.[3] To convey such dilapidation in his linoleum engraving, Surendorf places sections of fence, urns, and other objects at angles in the plot before the vault positioned in a somewhat modernist, flattened picture space. A black cat wandered across the foreground during his sketching, and he included it as a small element of life in a scene that emphasizes the finality of death on earth.

Notes

1. Cindy Surendorf e-mail to author, October 24, 2002.
2. Surendorf, "Artist Autobiography," 3–7, unpublished typescript, courtesy of Surendorf Gallery.
3. Surendorf, "Artist Autobiography," 7–8.

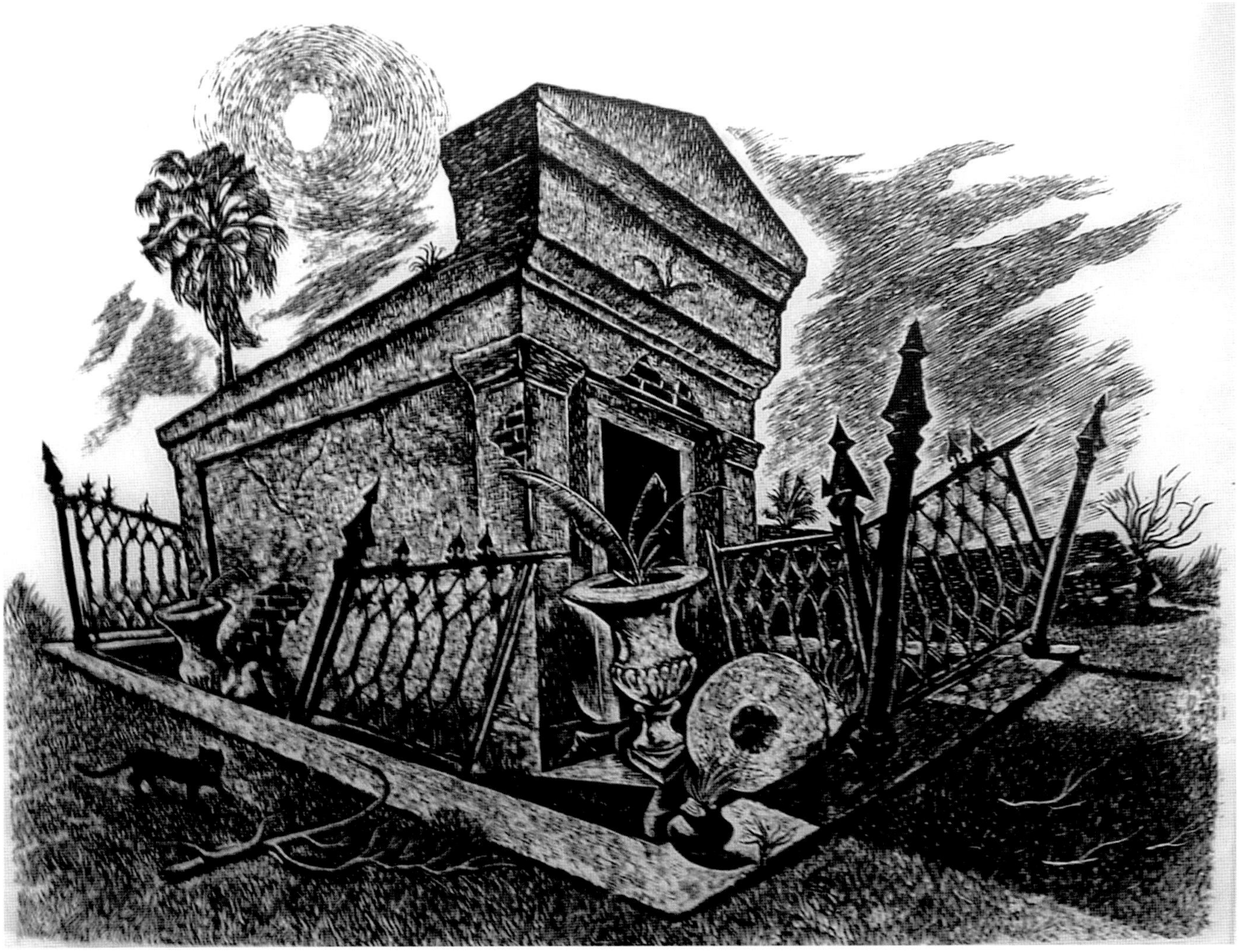

16. Charles Surendorf, *St. Louis #1, New Orleans,* linoleum engraving, c. 1947, 13 ¼ x 16 ½ in., courtesy of the Surendorf Gallery and from the collection of C. L. Surendorf.

Alfred Heber Hutty (1877–1954)

Alfred Hutty's comment to his wife upon first viewing Charleston—"Come quickly, have found heaven"—has become legendary. Hutty wandered eastward toward the artist colony of Woodstock, New York, from his native midwestern roots in Grand Haven, Michigan, Kansas City, and St. Louis, where he had established a career as a stained glass designer. Searching for a warmer locale in which to paint during winters, he discovered Charleston in 1919 and became one of its foremost etchers. Hired the following year as director and instructor of its art school by the Carolina Art Association, Hutty and his wife made Charleston their winter home, which alternated with summers in Woodstock until 1951. He became a founding member of the Charleston Etchers' Club and a very prolific printmaker of the South, making lithographs as well as etchings that advertised the charm of Charleston and its surrounding lowlands.[1] Competition with Elizabeth O'Neill Verner to be considered the city's premier printmaker may have spurred some of this productivity.

The beauty of Charleston enhanced by elegant architecture and abundant vegetation seems to have inspired Hutty's interest in etching.[2] In views such as *Old St. Michaels,* he created the ambiance of a mellow, old, urban South. A loose yet lively line often softened by drypoint accomplished much of this effect.[3] Highly polished plates that leave white paper background free of ink suggest intense southern sunlight and provide the maximum tonal contrast for strongly inked images that include areas of cast shadow. Although trees frequently stand alone as central subjects of Hutty's prints, architectural etchings such as *Old St. Michaels* frequently include branches laden with foliage that meander across the foreground to embellish and soften angles of buildings. Small black figures in the foreground often appear as well. Another category of genre prints emphasizes their activities through large figures in the foreground.

Notes

1. The most complete biographical information on Hutty can be found in Saunders and McAden, *Alfred Hutty and the Charleston Renaissance,* 13–16. See comments by Severens in *Charleston Renaissance* for the most complete critical appraisal of Hutty's prints to date. A catalogue raisonné by Johnson Hagood of Carolina Galleries is underway.
2. Birge Harrison, "Old Charleston as Pictured by Alfred Hutty," *The American Magazine of Art* 13 (1922): 483.
3. Severens characterizes Hutty's line as "animated"; *Charleston Renaissance,* 61.

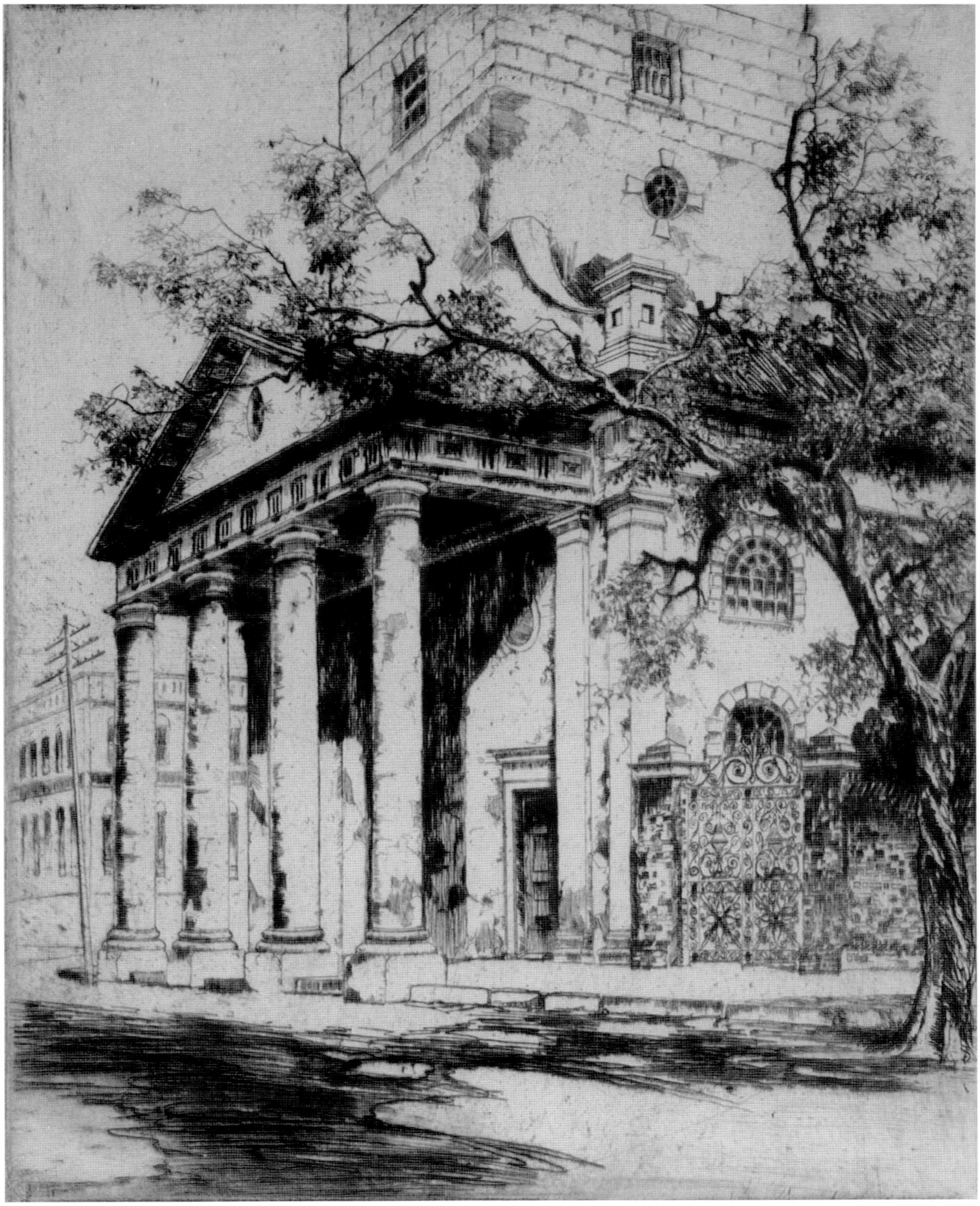

17. Alfred Hutty, *Old St. Michaels,* etching, 1928, 10 ⅜ x 8 ⅝ in., courtesy of Carolina Galleries and from the collection of Stephen Goldfarb.

Anna Heyward Taylor (1879–1956)

Anna Heyward Taylor of Columbia, South Carolina, found subjects for her relief prints in world travel as well as in her native South Carolina. After obtaining her bachelor's degree from South Carolina College for Women in 1897, she traveled in Europe, studying with William Merritt Chase in both London and Holland. In 1914 Taylor went to Japan, where she likely studied Japanese color woodcut methods with Helen Hyde. She broadened her study of color printmaking methods when she spent summers in Provincetown, Massachusetts, in 1915 and 1916, learning the white line technique of B. J. O. Nordfeldt. In 1916 and 1920, she joined expeditions of the New York Zoological Society to British Guiana, where she sketched tropical vegetation, which she later featured in woodcuts. During World War I she devoted herself to service with the Red Cross in France. While residing in New York from 1920 to 1929, Taylor exhibited her woodcuts nationally. In 1929 she moved to Charleston and created woodcuts and linoleum cuts of views of that city along with those reflecting her world travel.[1] New York galleries exhibited her prints in 1938 and 1941. Publicity for one of these exhibitions noted her "swinging, flamboyant style of drawing," and "richly decorative effect."[2]

Taylor is primarily known for her boldly colored botanicals and southern agricultural scenes in linoleum prints, which she made in the 1940s as illustrations for the book *This Our Land* (1949), a history of the South Carolina Agricultural Society. Most of her Charleston street scenes include human figures, many featuring the flower women carrying their baskets on their head or selling their produce at market. *St. Philips* is somewhat unusual in Taylor's relief oeuvre in that it is solely architectural. However, in its simple but bold, striking design with strong contrasts, *St. Philips* is typical of her best prints. She views the church of the oldest congregation in Charleston from the western cemetery to highlight the grill pattern of the gate. This pattern juxtaposes a central semicircle with curvilinear embellishment against strong verticals of the bars, posts, and columns of the church in the background that point upward toward otherworldly realms. The large dark posts act like sentinels protecting humble memorials to the dead in the darkness on the left.

Notes

1. "Chronology of Anna Heyward Taylor's Life," Anna Heyward Taylor file, Columbia Museum of Art, Columbia, SC; Severens, *Anna Heyward Taylor,* 4–5; Severens, *Charleston Renaissance,* 30–32.
2. "Southern Artist Exhibits Block Prints," *Art Digest,* November 15, 1938, 2; "Events Here and There," *New York Times,* November 16, 1941.

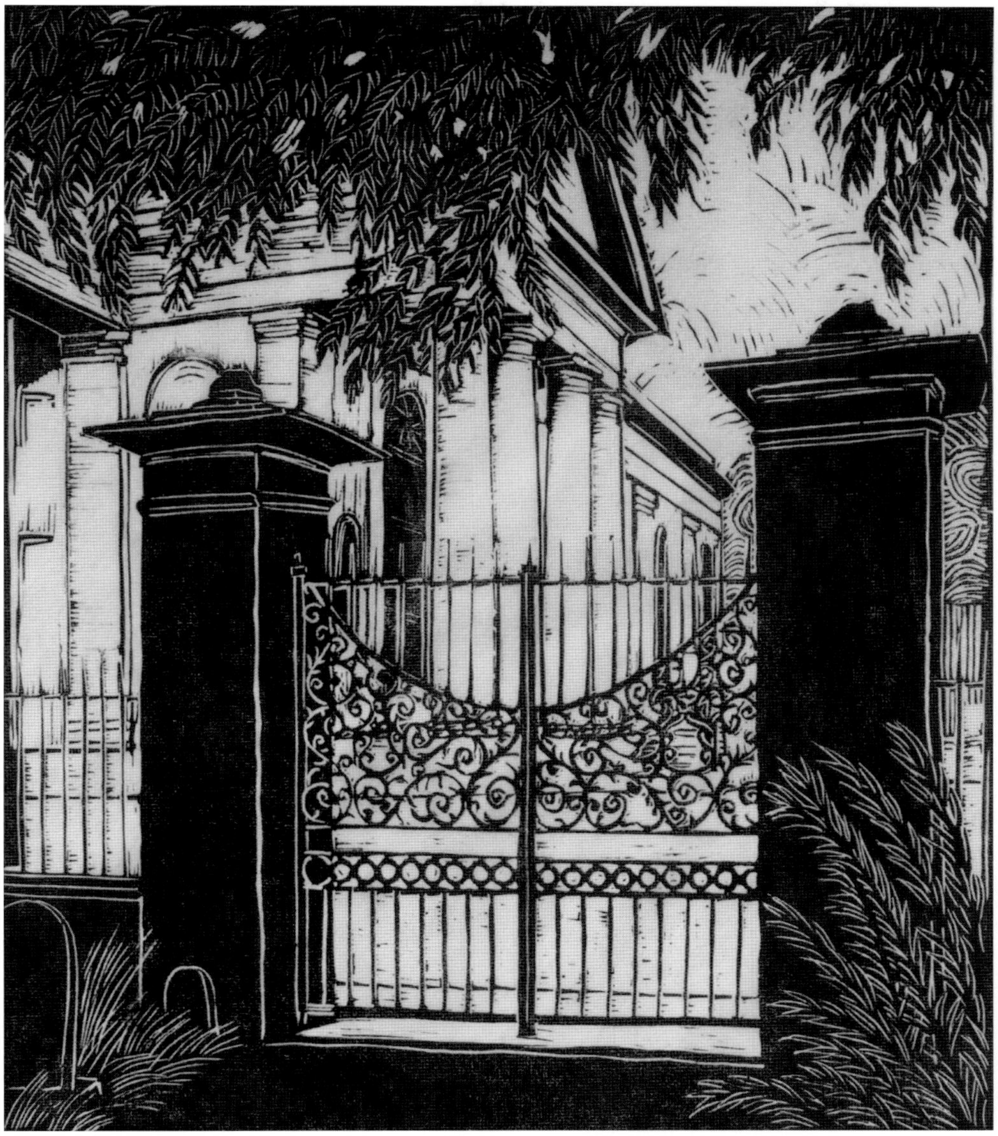

18. Anna Heyward Taylor, *St. Philips Church,* woodcut, 1934, 10 ⅛ x 9 ¼ in., collection of Lynn Barstis Williams.

Elizabeth O'Neill Verner (1883–1979)

A native of Charleston, Elizabeth O'Neill Verner studied at the Pennsylvania Academy of the Fine Arts from 1901 to 1903, a student of Thomas Anshutz during her second year. She taught school for a year in Aiken, South Carolina, then returned to her native Charleston, where she lived for the rest of her life. Her friend John Taylor Arms sparked her interest in etching, which she learned under the tutelage of her friend Alice Ravenel Huger Smith after a brief foray in woodcuts. She was a founding member of the Charleston Etchers' Club in 1923. When her husband died suddenly in 1925 followed shortly thereafter by the death of her mother, Verner found herself a widow with no financial support for herself and her children. Alice Smith gave her encouragement and confidence that she could support herself and her family as a professional artist so she purchased her own etching press, set up a workshop, and enlisted the help of her children in pulling prints.[1] She was able to earn her living selling to the many northern winter residents and tourists who visited Charleston.[2] Continuing to make etchings through the 1940s, she compiled several books from these images, which she spiced with her own commentary. With the help of her grandson, she completed some print editions in later years and produced over 260 etched images during her career as an artist.[3]

Charleston's architectural heritage, which Elizabeth Verner worked to preserve, became the focus of her etching oeuvre. Here that heritage manifests itself in the Daniel Ravenel house, an example of a Charleston dwelling type, whose projecting entrance supports a double-tiered portico, which Verner highlights. The small black figures in the foreground are also typical of her Charleston architectural etchings. Of particular importance for Verner was the black woman at work, who often walks, stands, or sweeps outside a walled compound with emphasis on an elegant facade of doorways, gates, and balconies. The black woman balancing the flower basket on her head, trailed by a child with a wagon on the sidewalk was a frequent figure complex in her Charleston views. Verner also made etched portraits and depicted the surrounding Lowcountry with its plantation houses, cabins, moss-hung oaks, and fieldworkers, giving an idealized vision of life in the South Carolina low country. According to her daughter, Elizabeth Hamilton, Verner often said, "The South has something to say"; her etchings became a voice from one corner of the old South, singing its attractions.[4]

Notes

1. Unpublished typescript "Elizabeth O'Neill Verner," Tradd Street Press, Charleston, SC; Lynn Robertson Myers, "Doing and Creating: A Biographical Sketch," in *Mirror of Time: Elizabeth O'Neill Verner's Charleston,* ed. Lynn Robertson Myers, 7–15 (Columbia: McKissick Museum, University of South Carolina, 1983); Yuhl, *A Golden Haze of Memory,* 75–76.
2. Dennison, "Art of the American South," 154–66; Yuhl, *A Golden Haze of Memory,* 78–80.
3. Elizabeth Hamilton interview with author, March 1994; Severens, "To Sell the City of Charleston," 41.
4. Elizabeth Hamilton interview with author, March 1994.

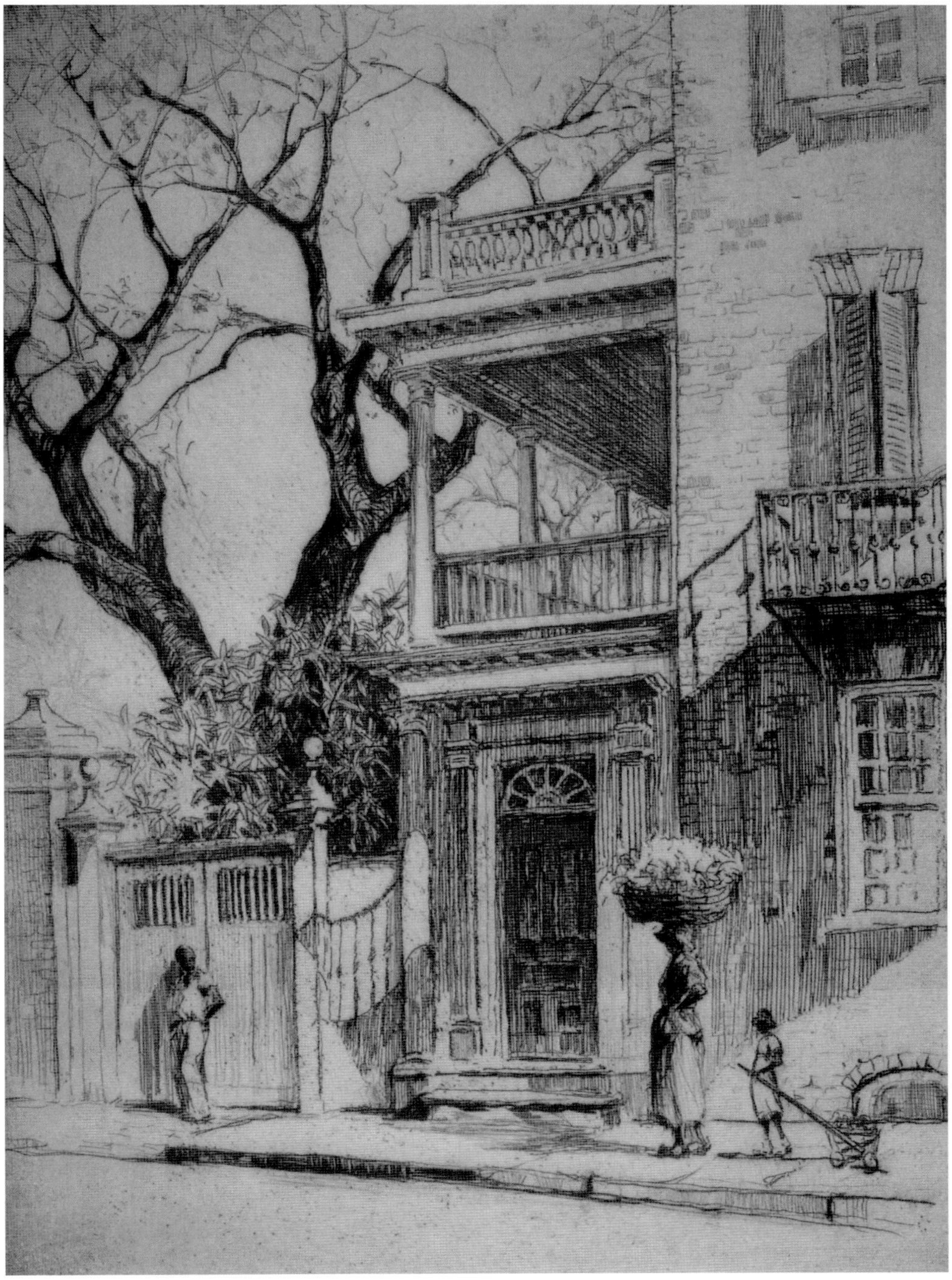

19. Elizabeth O'Neill Verner, *Ravenel Doorway, Charleston,* etching, c. 1930, 6 ⅞ x 5 in., art © Tradd Street Press/Licensed by VAGA, New York, NY, and from the collection of Lynn Barstis Williams.

Christopher Aristide Desbouillons Murphy (1902–1973)

Christopher A. D. Murphy was the son of two prominent Savannah artists, Christopher Patrick Hussey Murphy and Lucile Desbouillons Murphy, who gave him his initial art training. He learned etching from Joseph Pennell, to whom he was introduced when Pennell came to Savannah to visit a friend of his father. In 1921 the younger Murphy went to New York and studied with Pennell at the Art Students League and continued his studies at the Beaux-Arts Institute of Design in New York. After his studies Murphy worked with an architect, who taught him the fundamentals of architectural drawing. A Tiffany fellowship allowed him to travel and further his knowledge of etching. In 1931 he returned to Savannah, where he remained for the rest of his life, working as an artist and teaching classes at Armstrong College, a vocational school, and an art school, Telfair Academy.[1]

In 1925 Murphy began a project to record the life of Savannah in etchings. He created over 250 plates depicting various sections of the city seen from its streets as well as the outlying areas, a project that ended in the 1950s.[2] His training in architectural drawing is evident in these Savannah views, many of which featured historic buildings, as in *Chatham Academy.* Chatham Academy was Savannah's earliest school, chartered in 1788, and established in the edifice we see here in 1813.[3] Murphy places the Academy's Greek Revival portico in the background with casual sketches of human figures scattered in the middle ground. The figures provide scale, but also suggest that in the heart of Savannah, modern life blended well with its historic past. Compared to other coastal etchers, Murphy's stroke tended to be loose and straight as seen in the tree on the right. He etched a balanced view of Savannah, showing African American neighborhoods and modern construction along with imposing, high-style dwellings.[4]

Notes

1. Chambers, *Art and Artists of the South,* 136.
2. Ann Marshall, "Murphy Left Legacy of an Artist," *Savannah News Press,* October 28, 1973; King and DeLorme, *Looking Back*, 77.
3. Joseph Frederick Waring, *Cerveau's Savannah* (Savannah: Georgia Historical Society, 1973), 63.
4. See Murphy, *Savannah, Etchings and Drawings,* passim.

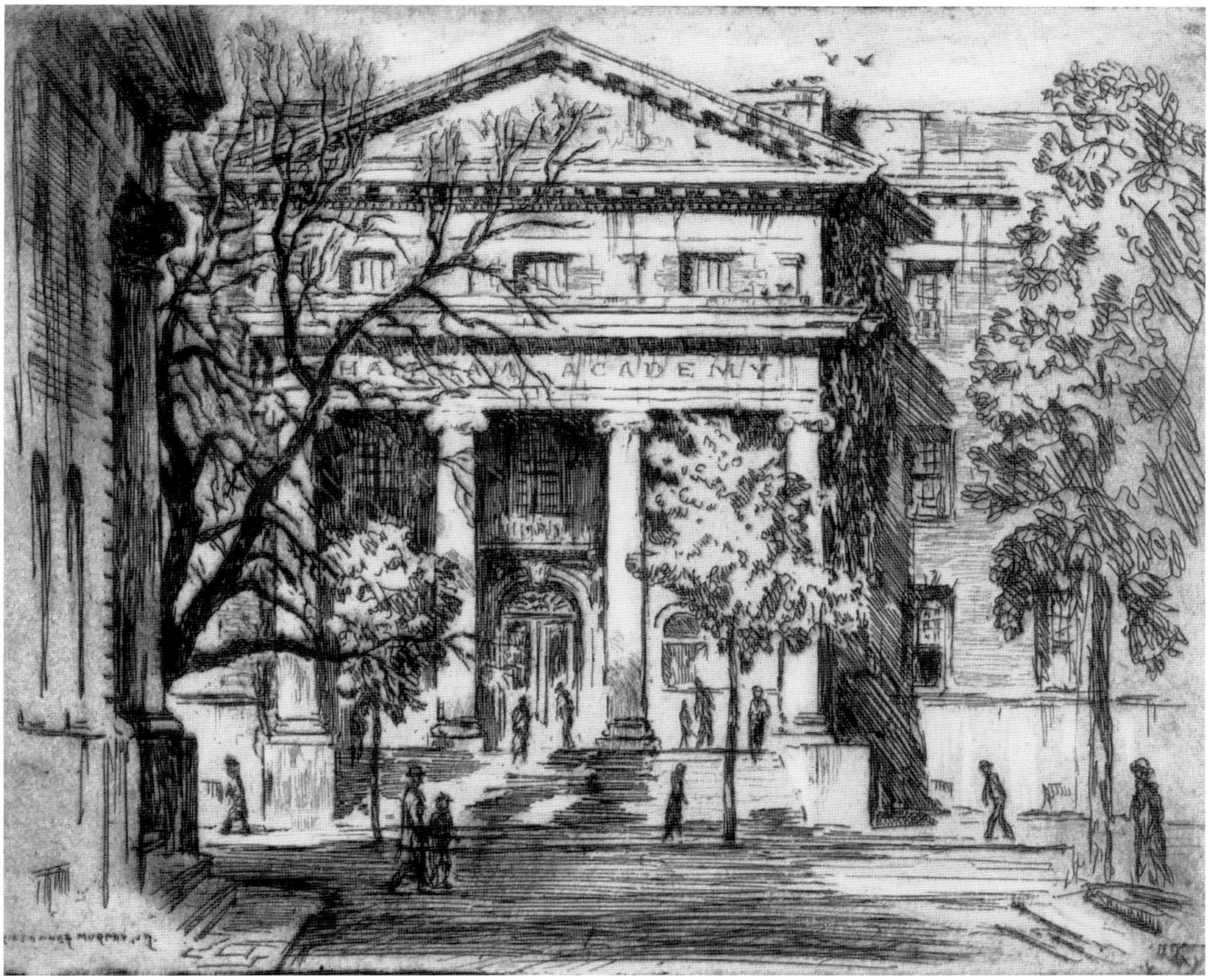

20. Christopher Murphy, *Chatham Academy,* etching, 6 x 8 in., courtesy of Christopher Cole Murphy and from the collection of the Morris Museum of Art, Augusta, Georgia.

Marian Francis Acker (Macpherson) (1906–1993)

Marian Acker was born in Mobile, where she lived all of her life, except for three years of study at the Vesper George School of Art in Boston. She graduated with honorable mention from that institution in 1931, after which she went to Provincetown, where she studied etching with W. H. W. Bicknell. Upon her return to Mobile, Acker set up a studio with an etching press next door to her family home, the historic mansion of Madame Le Vert, and behind the office of her father, a physician.[1]

Observing that so much of Mobile's historic architectural heritage was threatened by neglect and progress, Acker launched a project to record such buildings, usually stylized residences of the upper class, churches, and monumental public structures. In 1932 she published her first book, *Prints of the Past from Old Mobile,* which included a selection of reproductions of her etchings accompanied by her poetic description and historical background on the facing page. In 1938 her second book, *Etchings of Old Mobile,* appeared in a similar format. Visits to friends in Montgomery and Tuscaloosa resulted in several etchings of homes there. Acker sold individual impressions from her studio and often gave them as gifts for occasions such as weddings. Commercial contracts for her ink drawings and Mardi Gras art, along with marriage, four children, and a full social calendar, left little time to exhibit her prints. She also published *Glimpses of Old Mobile* (in at least six editions between 1946 and 1983), a small paperback guidebook that celebrated Mobile's architectural heritage in which some of her etchings were reproduced. By the 1950s she abandoned etching for ink drawings and watercolors.

A number of Acker's etchings focus on the Creole cottage, a form of vernacular architecture, which was associated with the French colonial tradition on the Gulf Coast.[2] *St. Michael Street* appeared in her book *Prints of the Past* under the title *Creole Cottage.* As Acker did not print her etchings in editions but as the need arose, titles vary. *St. Michael Street* is typical of her architectural views, which highlight the facade of an individual structure at a slight angle or from the front. Here the angular view highlights the side entrance to the front gallery in the center of the composition. In the text she wrote, Acker describes the dwelling as "wrapped in the romance of the past" with "rich and fragrant memories."[3]

Notes

1. Stephen J. Goldfarb, "Etched in Time: The Art of Marian Acker Macpherson," *Alabama Heritage* no. 73 (Summer 2004): 8–13.
2. See Gamble, *The Alabama Catalog,* 37–41.
3. Acker, *Prints of the Past,* n.p.

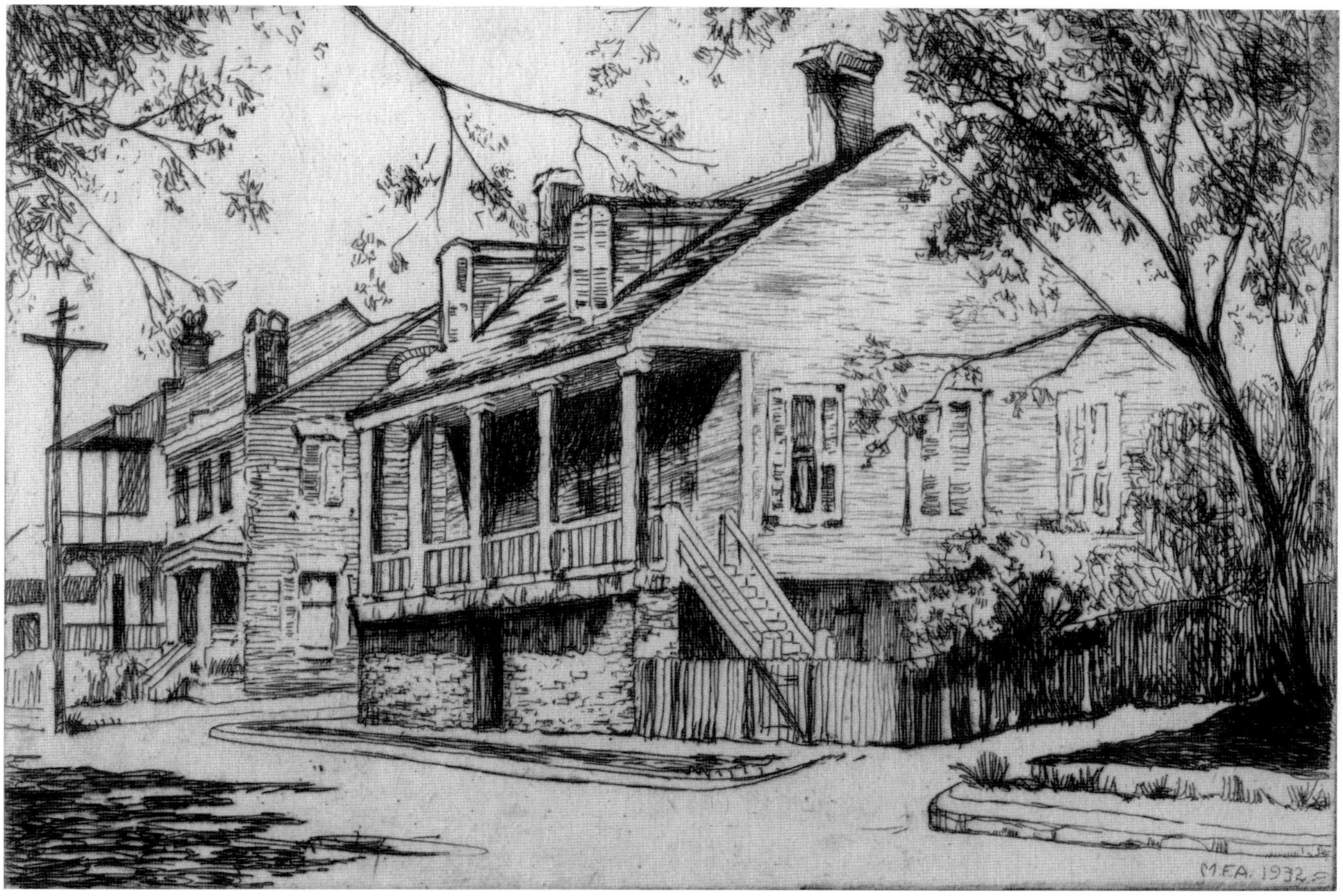

21. Marian Francis Acker, *St. Michael Street, Mobile,* etching, 1932, 4 ¼ x 6 ½ in., courtesy of the Estate of Marian A. Macpherson and MAM Arts, partnership and from the collection of Mr. and Mrs. Thomas B. Van Antwerp.

Samuel Chamberlain (1895–1975)

In his personal memoir *Etched in Sunlight* (1968), Samuel Chamberlain detailed his long career recording traditional architecture in drawings, lithographs, etchings, drypoints, and photographs, many of which he used to illustrate the numerous books he wrote on historic architecture. After studying at the University of Washington, from 1913 to 1915, where he registered as a civil engineering major, Chamberlain entered the School of Architecture at Massachusetts Institute of Technology in 1915. He left in 1917 to join the ambulance corps of the American Field Service in France, an experience that whetted his appetite for European architecture as well as French cuisine. Returning to MIT after his tour of duty, he soon left to begin a career as a free-lance architectural draftsman in watercolor and drawing. He returned to France a number of times, eventually purchasing a house, and traveled from there to other European locales to record historic architecture.[1]

Chamberlain learned lithography and intaglio methods of printmaking in Parisian studios around 1924 and began to publish numerous European architectural vistas, primarily in etching and drypoint, based on his extensive travels. He won a Guggenheim fellowship to study intaglio printmaking at the Royal College of Art in London in 1928, after which he returned to France to live. In the mid-1930s Chamberlain returned to MIT to serve as lecturer in the graphic arts in the School of Architecture and began to render more American architectural subjects in his prints.

Among Chamberlain's numerous architectural printmaking projects, that to celebrate the restoration of Williamsburg was particularly felicitous. William Perry, the lead architect in the restoration effort, commissioned him to produce etchings of major restored buildings to be sold on site. In traveling to Williamsburg to sketch in 1938, Chamberlain made his first trip to the South, which he described as "an interlude" that beamed "a ray of pure sunshine."[2] He produced eight drypoints of buildings, both restored and unrestored, between 1938 and 1940. The apothecary's shop is really the Prentis Co. Store, built from 1739 to 1740 and initially restored in 1928–31.[3] At the time Chamberlain sketched the building, it was interpreted as an apothecary shop. Choosing a distant, lateral view of the building, the middle in a row of three, Chamberlain is less interested in its architectural features than in creating an elegant ambiance for the site.

Notes

1. Chamberlain, *Etched in Sunlight*, passim.
2. Chamberlain, *Etched in Sunlight*, 102–4.
3. George Yetter, *Williamsburg Before and After* (Williamsburg, VA: Colonial Williamsburg Foundation, 1998), 100.

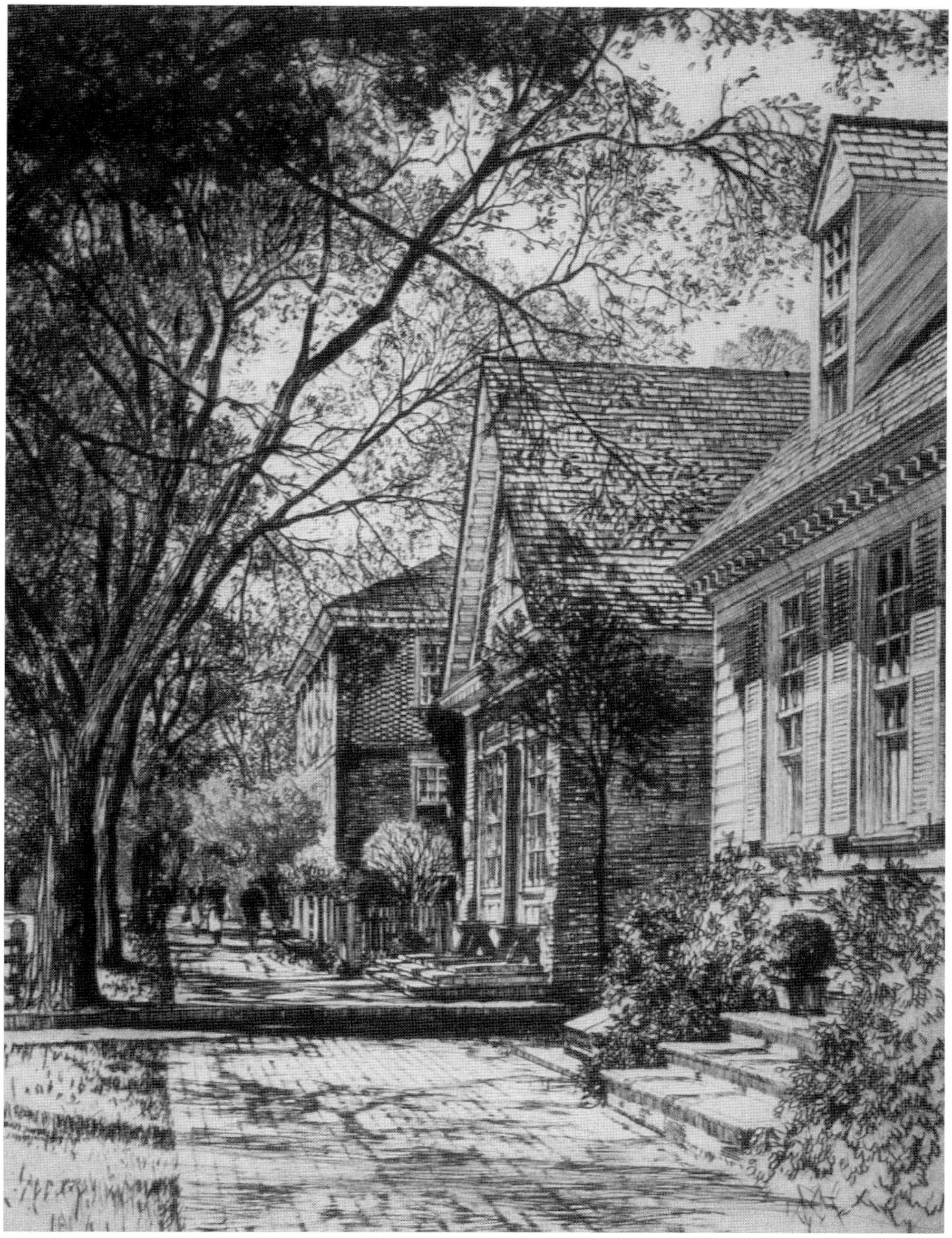

22. Samuel Chamberlain, *Apothecary's Shop, Williamsburg,* drypoint, 1938, 12 ¼ x 9 ½ in., collection of the Colonial Williamsburg Foundation.

(Sarah) Mabel Pugh (1891–1986)

One of North Carolina's most celebrated artists in her day, Mabel Pugh grew up in Morrisville, near Raleigh. After graduating from Peace College in Raleigh in 1913, she went to the Art Students League and continued her studies for five years at the Pennsylvania Academy of the Fine Arts. She competed and won a Cresson scholarship, which allowed her to travel and study for four months in Europe.[1]

In 1925 Pugh made her first block prints in Morrisville from sketches made on her European travels, and with the encouragement of the curator of prints at the New York Public Library, she exhibited them the following year in the International Print Makers Exhibition in Los Angeles. Her skill with block prints enabled her to launch a career as an illustrator that began when she sold three prints to *McCall's* magazine in 1925. Subsequent color block prints appeared on the jackets of popular novels. She wrote and illustrated *Little Carolina Blue Bonnet* (1933), a book for children based on her North Carolina childhood. When the head of the art department at Peace College died, Pugh accepted a request to replace her in 1936 and remained to teach and work there until she retired in 1960.[2]

Although Pugh considered lithography one of her major media, most of her print oeuvre appears to have been done on linoleum and wood blocks. She made simple floral compositions with bold use of tonal contrast, but most of her imagery comprised scenic views of place—whether Europe, New York, or North Carolina. During her years working in New York, she returned to the Raleigh area during summers to visit relatives and friends. With an umbrella for protection from the southern sun, she made sketching junkets to other towns, such as Greensboro, and more rural locations. Pugh claimed she delighted in portraits of homes as much as people, and some of her block prints feature North Carolina's historic monuments. During the summer of 1931 she traveled to Stokes County, North Carolina, to sketch an old rock house of a Revolutionary War colonel.[3] That sketch resulted in *Rock House Ruins,* a linoleum cut, which displays a somewhat more expressionistic style than most of her print oeuvre, but like her best relief prints has a simple, bold design.

Notes

1. Foushee, *Art in North Carolina,* 178; Biographical data sheet, Mabel Pugh file, North Carolina Museum of Art.
2. "Miss Mabel Pugh to Illustrate Books," *Raleigh News and Observer,* December 10, 1926; Betsy Marsh, "A Legend at Peace, Miss Pugh Retires to Allow More Time for Other 'Work,'" *Raleigh News and Observer,* May 26, 1960.
3. Betty Rose Thomas, "Mabel Pugh Is Now 'Back Home' after Busy Winter in New York," *Raleigh News and Observer,* May 19, 1935; Anne Cantrell White, "North Carolina Woman Wins Fame as an Artist," *Greensboro Daily News,* October 18, 1931; "Art Exhibit Open at Woman's Club," North Carolina Artists file, North Carolina State Library.

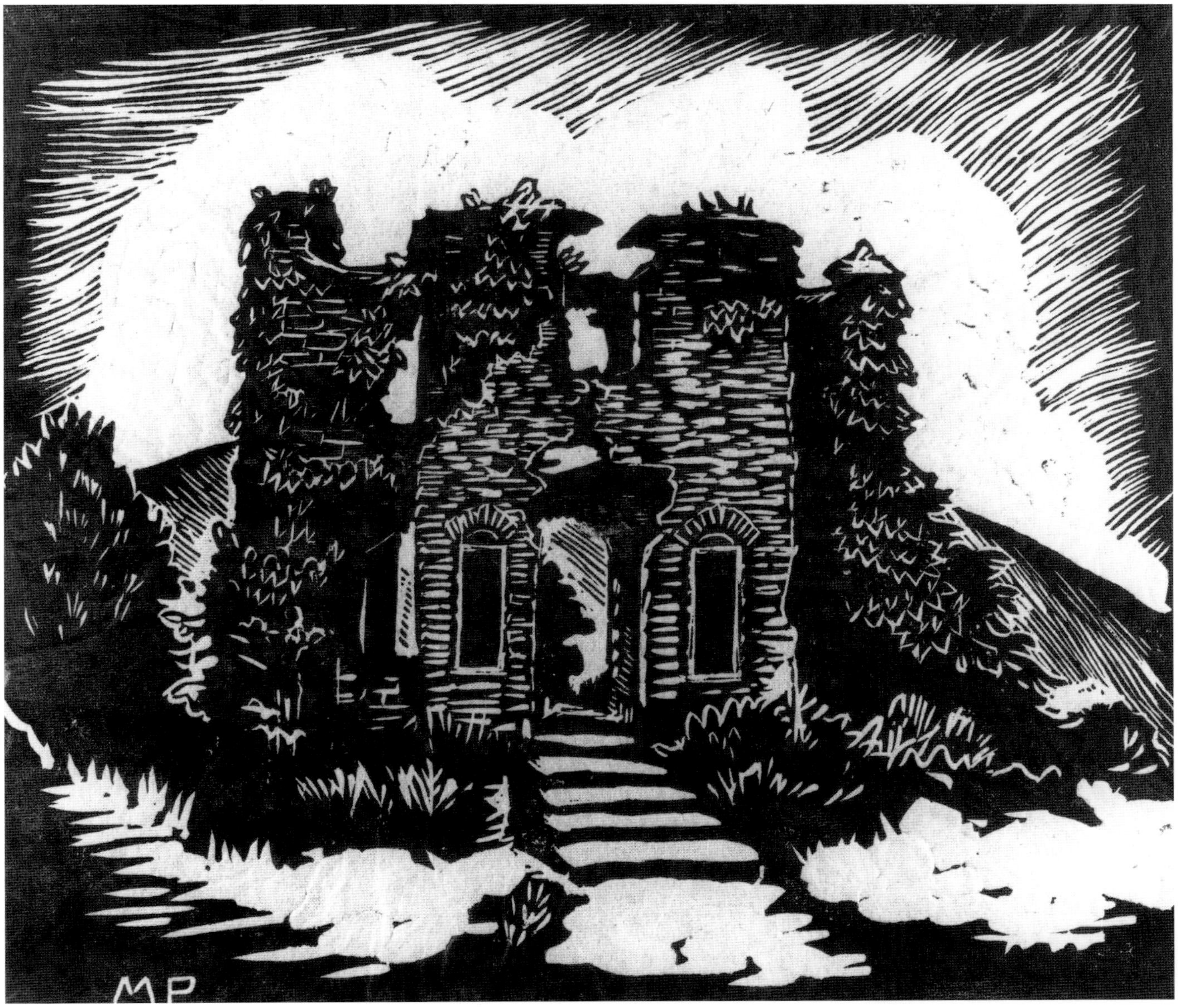

23. Mabel Pugh, *Rock House Ruins,* linoleum cut, c. 1931, 9 x 10 ½ in., photography produced by the North Carolina Museum of Art from the collection of the North Carolina Museum of Art, Raleigh, NC.

Ernest Alexander Pickup (1887–1970)

Although Ernest Pickup wanted to become an artist from an early age, his father had other ideas. He forced his son to quit school after the fifth grade, arranging for him to become a typesetter's apprentice so he would learn the father's trade of printing. Born in Shelbyville, Tennessee, Pickup moved with his family to Brooklyn, then to Baltimore, back to Brooklyn, and finally to Nashville. He ordered a correspondence course in art with his mother's approval and practiced to develop skill as a draftsman while hiding from his father in the attic. In 1912 he set out on his own to become a commercial artist, and two years later opened his free-lance studio. He built a successful commercial art business, but when the Great Depression struck, his commissions withered. To occupy his time he began making relief prints and joined the Nashville Studio Club. Sophonisba Hergesheimer encouraged him to exhibit his prints, which he did on both a regional and national level. When commercial work became available in the 1940s, he gave up his relief printmaking to return to his work as a commercial artist.[1]

Most of Pickup's relief prints were wood engravings with white lines on a black ground. He tried etching as well. The majority of his prints reflect places of interest in Nashville or the rural area of Brentwood, south of Nashville, where he lived with his wife and daughters. *Afternoon on the Statehouse* shows downtown Nashville in the early 1930s with its Greek Revival capitol designed by architect William Strickland in the background. Pickup's view juxtaposes the imposing capitol with a humble house situated below in the middle ground. The artist explained, "Long before 'urban renewal' came to Nashville, Tennessee's lovely State House towered majestically above the shanties, dirty streets, and neglected area that lay at the foot of Capitol Hill." The print was chosen for an exhibition at the Corcoran Gallery in Washington, DC in 1932.[2] Pickup also made landscapes highlighting trees and portraits with one genre scene of a street musician in Nashville during the years of the Great Depression.

Notes

1. Beverly St. John, comp., "The Life and Work of Ernest Alexander Pickup Artist," unpublished typescript; Beverly St. John telephone interview with author, July 7, 2000; Sophonisba Hergesheimer letter to Ernest Pickup, October 4, 1942 (in possession of Beverly St. John).
2. St. John, "The Life and Work of Ernest Alexander Pickup Artist," n.p.

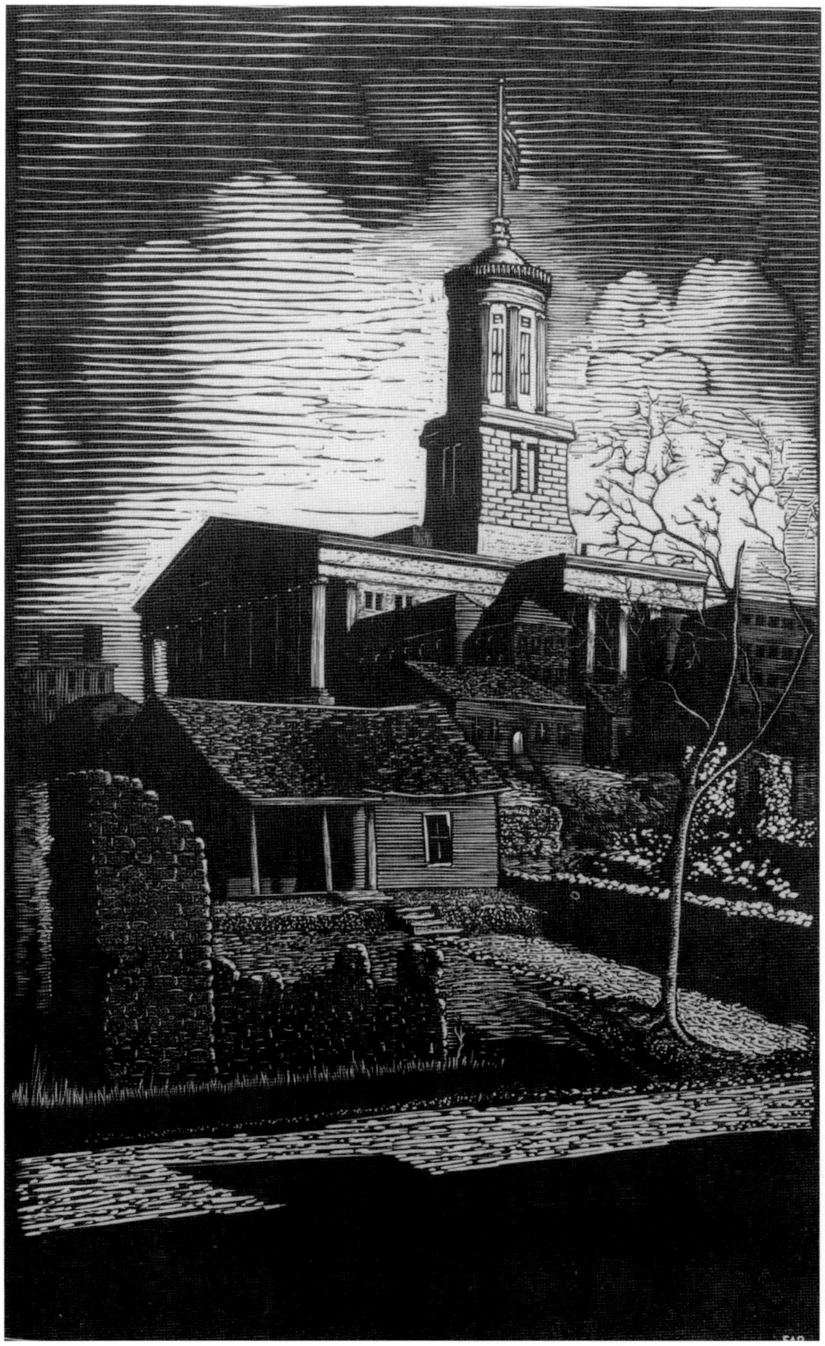

24. Ernest Pickup, *Afternoon on the Statehouse, Nashville,* wood engraving, c. 1932, 12 ¼ x 8 in., courtesy of Beverly St. John and from the collection of Lynn Barstis Williams.

Richard Blauvelt Coe (1904–1978)

Born and reared in Selma, Alabama, Richard Coe studied architecture at the University of Cincinnati but turned to drawing and painting. In 1922 he won a *Birmingham News* scholarship to study art at the Grand Central School of Art in New York. After a year, he went to Boston to attend the School of the Museum of Fine Arts, where he remained for six years studying with Philip Hale. At the end of his studies, he was awarded the Page traveling scholarship, which allowed him to spend two years in Europe, maintaining a studio in Florence.[1]

Coe developed an interest in etching, and when he returned to Birmingham in 1934, he established a studio with an etching press in the Five Points area and produced a considerable number. He joined the Dixie Art Colony where he taught etching and exhibited impressions with the Southern States Art League, through which he won awards, although he exhibited nationally as well.[2] He served as director of the Federal Arts Project of the WPA in Alabama but at the end of the 1930s left Alabama for New York City. In New York he became an editor for the McCall's Corporation and taught art on the side in his studio as well as at various institutions in the area.[3]

Coe's initial interest in architecture is evident in his etchings of Birmingham, which constitute rare print views of that industrial city. His views of the city were varied and included steel mills, the downtown business district, historic houses in the Five Points district, and African American residents at work and play in their neighborhoods. Frequently, he projected views of the city from the surrounding mountains as in the view here, which shows a variety of urban architectural structures with particular emphasis on huge, partially empty gasholders in the middle ground. Tall buildings lightly etched in the background are rare views of skyscrapers in prints of the Southeast. Coe experimented with the etched line and often wiped his plates to achieve variations in tone to evoke atmosphere and light. His etchings of Birmingham were printed in small editions, usually from four to eight impressions.

Notes

1. Dolly Dalrymple, "Winner of News Art Scholarship Returns on Visit," unidentified newspaper clipping, Birmingham artists' file, Tutweiler Collection, Birmingham Public Library.
2. Williams, "The Dixie Art Colony," 9.
3. Elizabeth Metcalf file, Alabama Department of Archives and History. See also Eiland, "Picturing the Unvictorious," 41, 43–44.

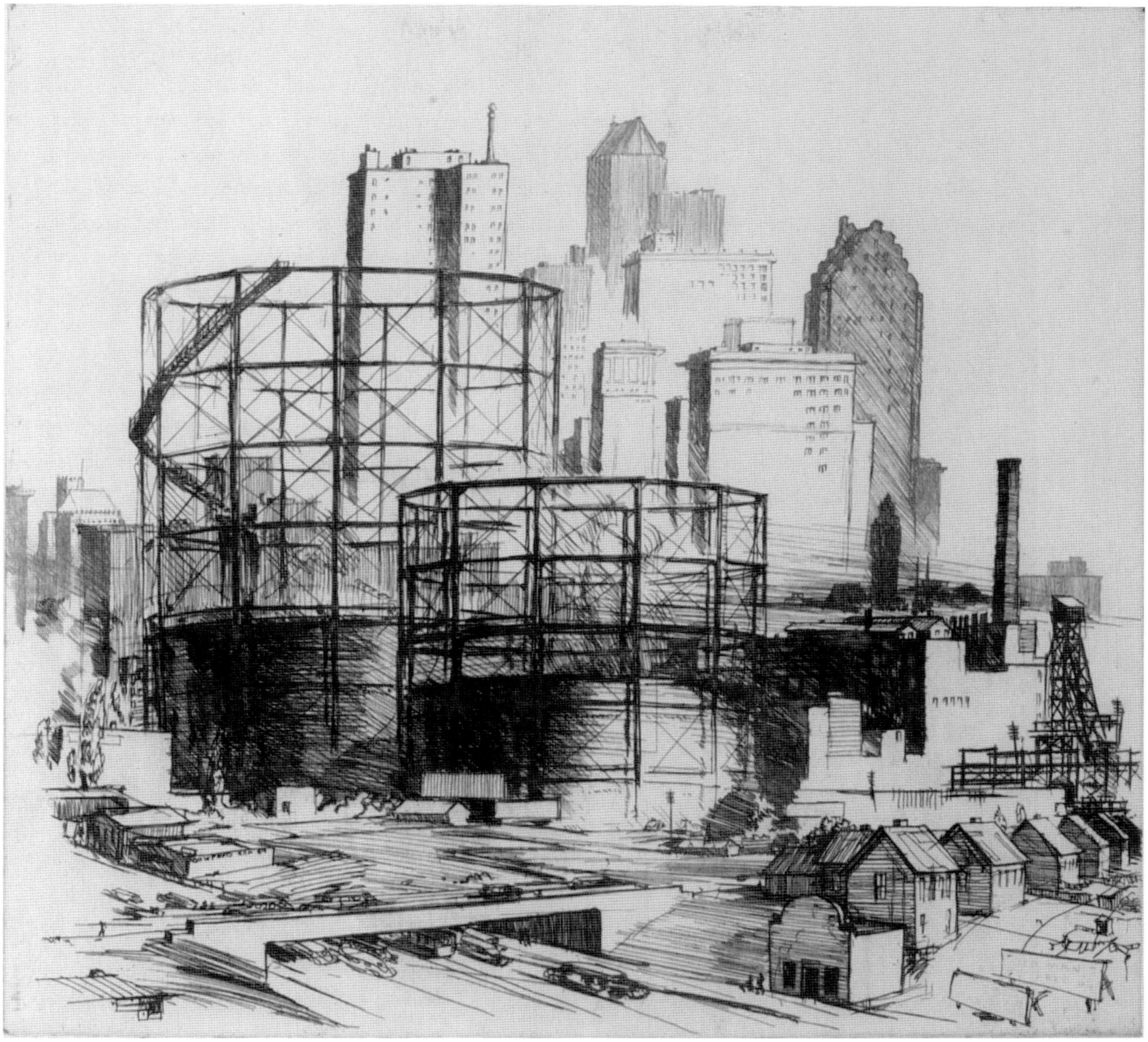

25. Richard Coe, *Birmingham,* etching, 7 ⅞ x 8 ½ in., courtesy of John K. Coe and from the collection of John K. Coe.

Julius John Lankes (1884–1960)

J. J. Lankes can be considered the prime exponent of the artistic revival of the traditional woodcut in the South. He received his first art instruction by correspondence, then continued at the Art Students League of Buffalo, New York, where he grew up, as well as the School of the Museum of Fine Arts in Boston. While working as a foreman in the drafting room of an arms factory in Buffalo during World War I, he taught himself to make woodcuts, discovering that a small gouge used to "checker gun stocks" could also be used to incise a design in a section of an apple tree limb. By 1917 Lankes settled on the woodcut as his favored artistic medium and used it to earn his living as a commercial artist, making bookplates, greeting cards, letterheads, and business cards.[1]

Moving to Hilton Village in the tidewater area of Virginia in 1925, Lankes began to depict local historic architecture and rural Virginia scenes. His subjects included many of the homes and churches of Williamsburg just before the massive restoration project began. *Virginia Farmhouse* was modeled on a house situated on the James River owned by a farmer named Massey.[2] Lankes depicted the same house from a frontal viewpoint in another woodcut titled *Massey's House* that he included in his book *Virginia Woodcuts* (1930). The distant, lateral viewpoint we see here allows inclusion of extensions in the form of shed rooms and a separate outbuilding in the back. It conveys a sense of isolation in the rural countryside as well as a modicum of prosperity. Lankes also delineates tree forms, which he silhouettes against a white area of sky behind the house. The triangular structure of the entire ensemble endows it with a sense of stability, bound to the land. Lankes continued his woodcuts of Virginia scenes until 1941.[3] He was also an important book illustrator. Early in his career he illustrated Rossa Belle Cooley's post–Civil War memoir, *Homes of the Freed* (1926), which included his four images of black tenant farmers.

Notes

1. Welford Dunaway Taylor, "Julius John Lankes: Virginia Woodcut Artist," *Virginia Cavalcade* 26 (Summer 1976): 4–19. According to J. B. Lankes, the artist's son, Lankes made only woodcuts, not wood engravings as some sources have asserted; J. B. Lankes e-mail to author, August 16, 2004.
2. J. B. Lankes e-mail to author, August 13, 2004.
3. Welford Dunaway Taylor, *Woodcut Art of J. J. Lankes* (Boston: David R. Godine, 1999), ix–xi, 20–22, 61.

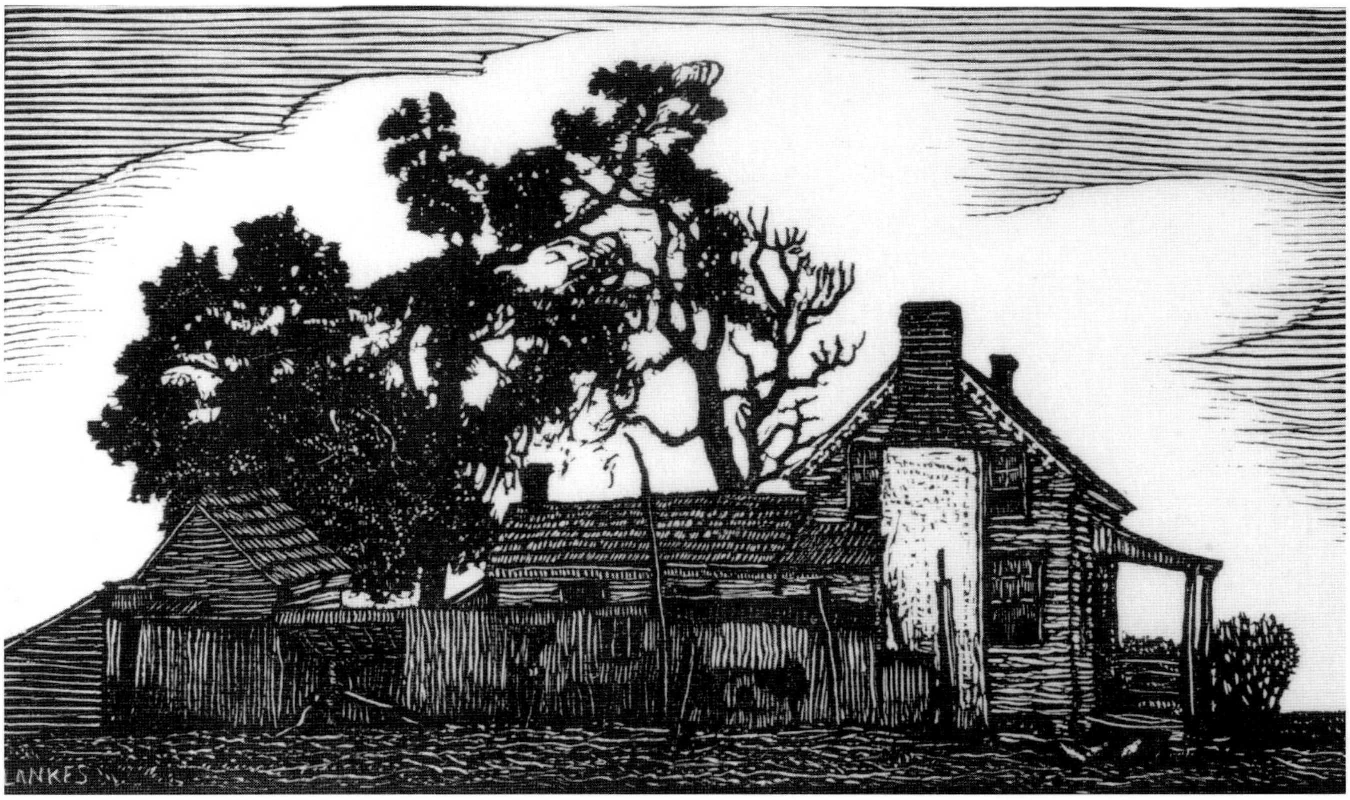

26. J. J. Lankes, *Virginia Farmhouse,* woodcut, 1926, 4 x 7 in., courtesy of the children of J. J. Lankes and from the collection of Lynn Barstis Williams.

Mary Wallace Kirk (1889–1978)

Born in Tuscumbia, Alabama, Mary Wallace Kirk lived at her family home, Locust Hill, the subject of her autobiography of the same title, from the age of four until her death. She obtained a college degree from Agnes Scott College in Decatur, Georgia, where she attended from 1907 to 1911, and served on its board of trustees for most of her adult life. Her art studies began with Alabama artist Lucille Douglass and continued with Harry Sternberg, with whom she studied etching at the Art Students League in New York. Although she mentioned her etching teacher (probably Sternberg) becoming "somewhat annoyed" with her sunny scenes of the South, they charmed a reviewer for the *New York Times,* who noted a gallery exhibition of her "unpretentious etchings," specifying *Fence with Tin Cans* as "among the best."[1] Kirk exhibited her etchings primarily in the South with the Alabama Art League and the Southern States Art League, and she sold them locally from a studio in her home into the 1960s. She also published several small volumes of poetry.

Humble vernacular houses along with allied structures, some displaying folk crafts practiced by the people who inhabited the dwellings, became the focus of Kirk's etchings. *Fence with Tin Cans* illustrates this emphasis, although it displays an example of the "I" house—two stories tall, one room deep—instead of the one-story cabin we usually see in Kirk's etchings.[2] Kirk brings the fence that surrounds the dwelling to the foreground to reveal the folk art it displays: a simple, yet ingenious arrangement of tin cans on posts that is probably derived from the southern "bottle trees," a remnant of African culture whereby bottles on stripped trees provided housing for spirits.[3] The human figure, here a child who is barely discernable sitting on the porch in the distance, was a rare element in Kirk's etchings. Kirk collected a number of her etchings to illustrate her prose. The text of *Cabins and Characters* (1969) discusses the unpretentious houses near her home and their inhabitants, who were probably tenants on her property in Tuscumbia.

Notes

1. Kirk, *Locust Hill*, 69; "In Graphic Vein," *New York Times,* March 18, 1945.
2. See O'Malley, "Functional Aspects of Folk Housing" See also, Gamble, *Alabama Catalog,* 29–32.
3. See Jim Martin, "Bottle Trees," *Encyclopedia of Southern Culture,* 495–96.

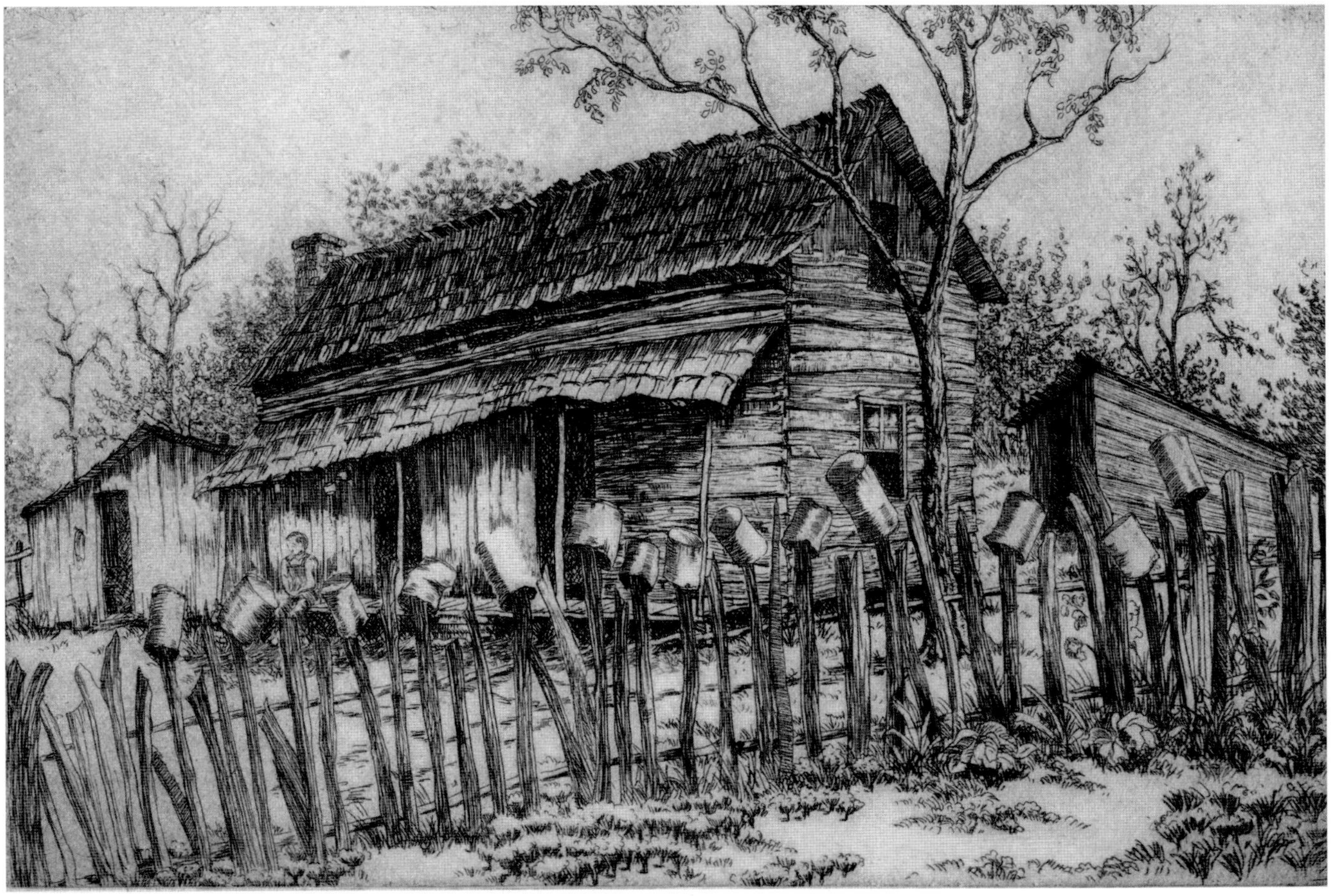

27. Mary Wallace Kirk, *Fence with Tin Cans,* etching, c. 1945, 5 ¾ x 8 ¾ in., courtesy of Gordon S. Rather Jr. and from the collection of Martha M. Kracke.

Knute Heldner (1875–1952)

The story of Knute Heldner's odyssey as a painter became legendary in New Orleans. A native of Sweden, Heldner enlisted in the Swedish Royal Navy at an early age but deserted when he landed in Boston. He found a job as a dishwasher and painted in his spare time. Moving on, he worked as a guide in the woods of Wyoming, then as a cook in lumber camps in Minnesota, all the while continuing to paint. He saved up enough money to attend the Minneapolis School of Fine Arts, which he later followed by study at the Art Institute of Chicago and the Art Students League in New York. After more odd jobs, Heldner decided to devote himself to art, setting up a studio in Duluth, Minnesota. He and his wife spent the winter of 1923–24 in New Orleans, and, like many artists visiting the Quarter, continued to winter in the city during the following years, returning to Duluth for the summer months. After traveling and studying in Europe from 1929 to 1932, the Heldners returned to New Orleans, where they settled permanently. Somewhere along the way, Heldner picked up printmaking, which he practiced in etching, woodcut, and lithography, undoubtedly to supplement his income, which was in short supply throughout his life.[1]

Most of Heldner's prints appear to be etchings along with drypoint. Working on the Louisiana WPA during the late 1930s, he completed twelve. He made the usual French Quarter scenes highlighting historic buildings as well as swamp vistas, his specialty as a southern landscape painter. His swamp views included the standard motifs seen in *Crayfishers Shack:* the humble cabin among tall, moss-hung cypress along with the bayou skiff and sometimes small human figures. Here the drypoint mellows the scene. However, Heldner's graphic iconography spanned a fairly broad range. His etchings, woodcuts, and lithography were often genre scenes highlighting the life of the lower classes—going fishing, coaxing a mule, or driving a mule-drawn cart. Others are unusual testimony in prints of the South that depict the down-and-out suffering from hunger and unemployment during the Depression in New Orleans: those on a breadline, scavengers, or a street person sleeping on a park bench in Jackson Square. His etching oeuvre extended to figures playing sports as well.

Notes

1. Sources conflict as to Knute Heldner's birth date and as to whether he came to this country in 1892 or 1902. The facts of his life here have been gleaned from the following sources: "Heldner Funeral Is Set for Today; Noted Artist Succumbs," *New Orleans Times-Picayune,* November 6, 1952; "Knute Heldner," *New Orleans Times-Picayune,* November 7, 1952; Elliot Hebert, "The Legacy of Knute Heldner: A Quiet Artist Leaves Us Beautiful Landscapes and a Stirring Story," *Dixie Roto Magazine, New Orleans Times Picayune,* December 7, 1952, 7–8, 10.

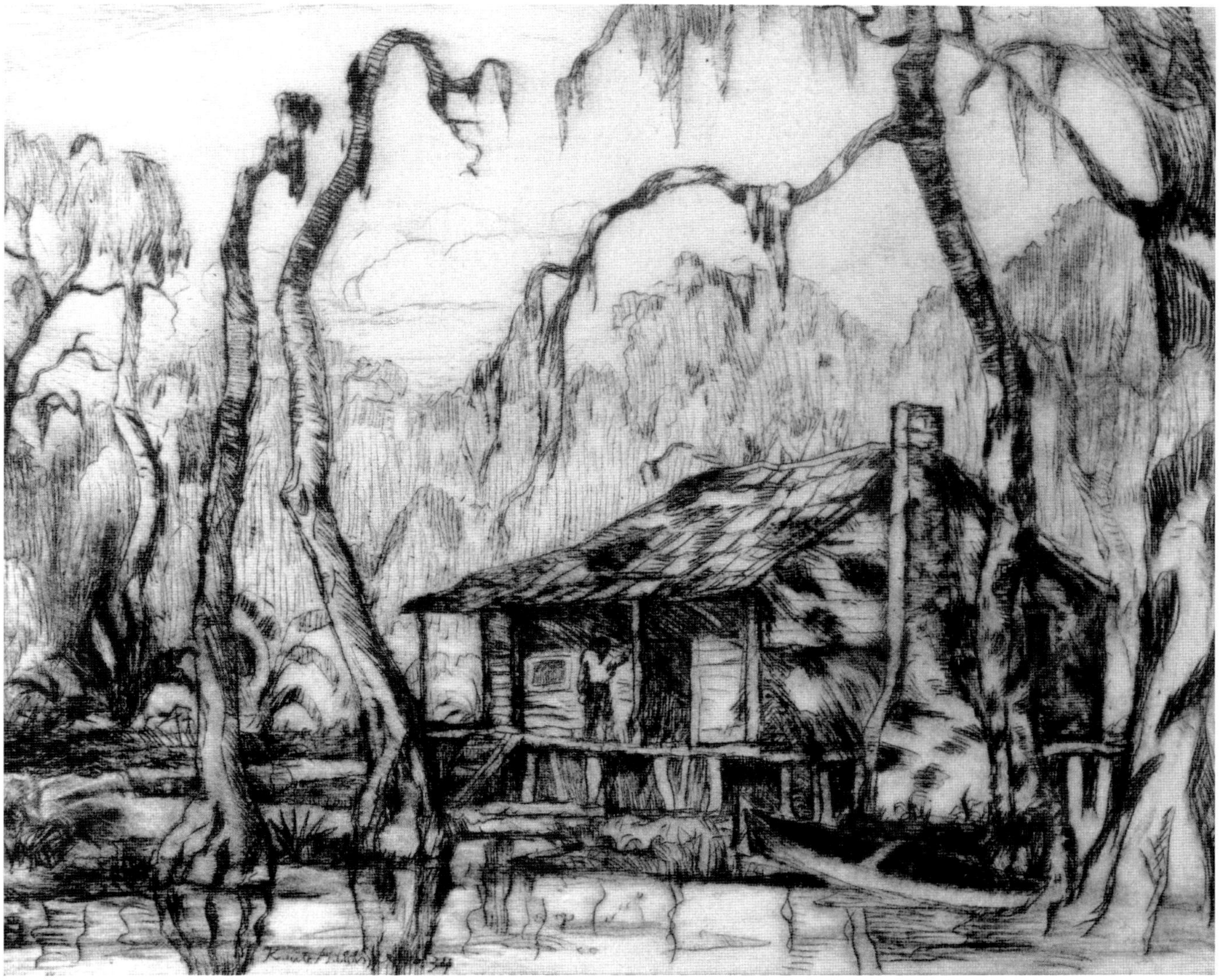

28. Knute Heldner, *Crayfishers Shack,* etching with drypoint, 1934, 7 x 9 in., Historic New Orleans collection, Museum/Research Center, accession no. 1999.15.2.

Clare Veronica Hope Leighton (1898–1989)

By the time she began to explore the South, Clare Leighton had established an international reputation as one of the best English illustrators in wood engraving. Born in London to a father who authored boys' adventure stories and a mother who wrote romantic fiction, she studied drawing and painting at the Brighton School of Art and the Slade School in London. However, only by enrolling in a course at the Central School did she learn wood engraving, the medium in which she achieved distinction. Her career as an illustrator began when she sold a wood engraving to H. N. Brailsford, the editor of a socialist periodical, *The New Leader,* in 1924. She continued to produce wood engravings, specializing in scenes of preindustrial labor. While illustrating numerous books of others, she also wrote a number of her own, including *The Farmer's Year* (1933), *Four Hedges* (1935), and *Country Matters* (1937). To publicize her work, Leighton made several lecture tours to the United States that included the American South.[1]

To distance herself from a failing relationship with Brailsford as well as war in Europe, Leighton decided to move to the United States in 1939. Soon after her arrival, she contracted with Macmillan for a book presenting her impressions of the South. Leighton wrote that she undertook the project to establish roots in her adopted country and unite with her new land. She chose the South because it had retained more of its agrarian folkways, a major theme of her prints. From 1939 to 1941 she lived in Baltimore, where she returned to write and make wood engravings after her travels through the South. In 1941 she stopped in Chapel Hill, North Carolina, on her way to the mountains to sketch and decided to move to that community. The following year Leighton's book, which she titled *Southern Harvest,* was published.[2] From 1943 to 1945 she served as a visiting lecturer in art and aesthetics at Duke University, where she illustrated the Frank C. Brown Collection of North Carolina Folklore.[3] In 1950 Leighton left North Carolina to reside in Connecticut and undertake new projects.

The text of *Southern Harvest* shows that Leighton traveled through Alabama, Mississippi, and Louisiana. She created the small wood engraving *Po' White Cabin* in fifty impressions and used it to illustrate her encounter with a family of poor whites somewhere in Alabama. The text makes it clear Leighton was particularly drawn to the wife of the family and her burden of raising a large family, whose activities she describes in the text.[4] Both the deep and mountain South were populated with large families often occupying small cabins, such as we see here. The illustration does not emphasize such large family size, however, as the view has narrowed to encompass the dwelling in the style of a dogtrot cabin on a rock foundation.[5] A woman stands on the porch to the right of the central hall, her hand on the head of the sole child, standing nearby.

Notes

1. Patricia Jaffé, *Wood Engravings of Clare Leighton* (Cambridge, England: Silent Books, 1992), 7–13; Carolyn Hickman, "Clare Leighton and the American South," *Duke University Libraries* 17, no. 3 (Spring–Summer 2004): 8–13. The exhibition catalog *Clare Leighton: An Exhibition: American Sheaves, English Seed Corn* contains the most complete list of her prints to date.
2. A second edition of *Southern Harvest* on "wartime paper" and in smaller format was published by Victor Gollancz in Britain in 1943. David Leighton letter to author, August 25, 2004.

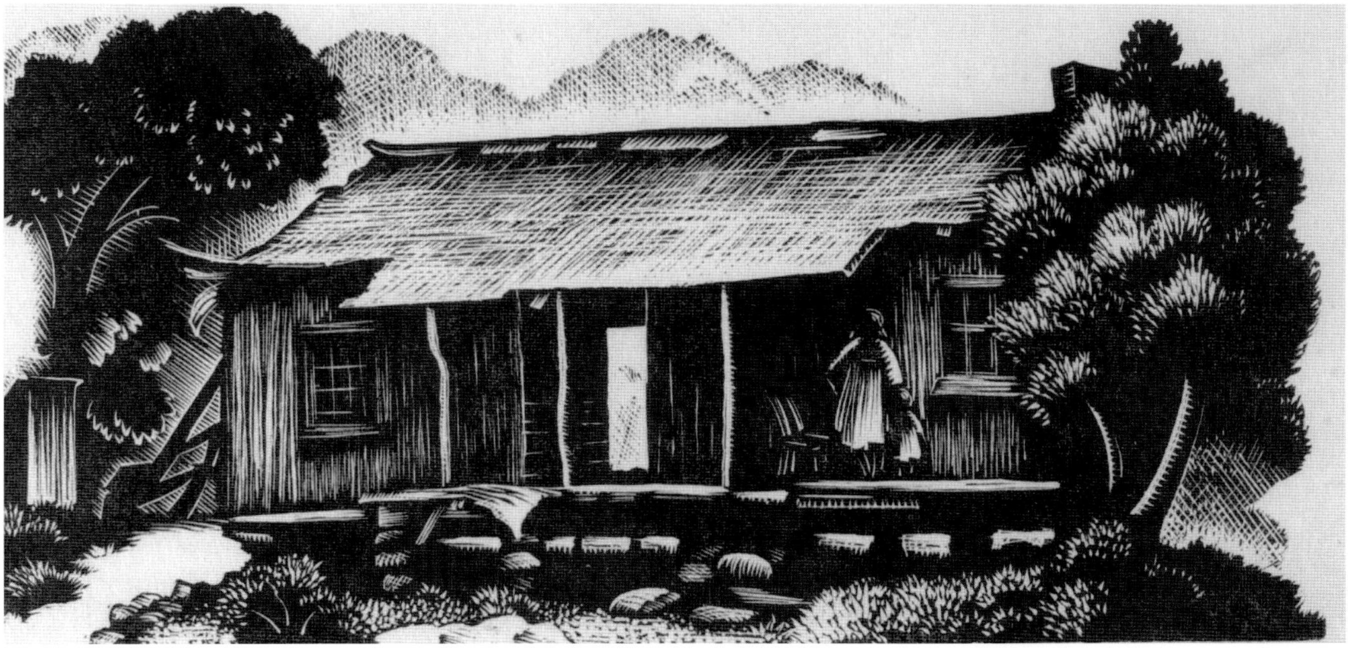

29. Clare Leighton, *Po' White Cabin,* wood engraving, c. 1941, 2 ½ x 5 ¼ in., courtesy of David Leighton and from the collection of Stephen Goldfarb.

3. Carolyn Hickman, "Graphic Images and Agrarian Traditions: Bayard Wootten, Clare Leighton, and Southern Appalachia," in *Graphic Arts and the South: Proceedings of the 1990 North American Print Conference,* ed. Judy L. Larson, 257–68; see *The Frank C. Brown Collection of North Carolina Folklore* (Durham, NC: Duke University Press, 1952–64).
4. Leighton, *Southern Harvest,* 101.
5. For a description of the dogtrot cabin, see Gamble, *Alabama Catalog,* 24–29.

Claude Clark (1915–2001)

Claude Clark was primarily a painter, but the New Deal arts program gave him opportunity to learn printmaking as well. Born near the southeastern Georgia community of Rockingham, Clark spent his early years as the child of a tenant farmer who frequently moved his family from place to place in south Georgia and north Florida to find suitable work. In 1923, when Clark was eight years old, his father moved his family of ten children to Philadelphia, where relatives lived. Clark attended public schools in Philadelphia and after graduating from high school, attended the Pennsylvania School of Industrial Arts from 1935 to 1939 and also studied at Philadelphia's Barnes Foundation.[1]

When the WPA established an art project in Philadelphia, Clark signed on. He was assigned to the Easel Painting Division, but used the graphic arts workshop to make prints as well.[2] Around 1941 he became good friends with Raymond Steth, and the two decided to set up their own studio. With the lithography press that he acquired for the studio, Steth printed lithographs for Clark.[3] Clark also used the carborundum etching and mezzotint processes pioneered by Dox Thrash; however, relief appears to be his major print medium, one he could continue in later years without a press. In 1948 Clark returned to the South to teach at Talladega College in Talladega, Alabama, where he established an art department. During his years at Talladega he made at least one linoleum cut of a painting each year. Leaving Alabama for California in 1955, he worked to earn college degrees, first a bachelor's from Sacramento State College and later a master's degree from the University of California at Berkeley. Clark continued make carborundum etchings until 1958 and linoleum cuts until the mid-1960s.[4]

Clark's southern background is reflected in images of sharecroppers done during the period that he worked on the Philadelphia WPA, perhaps due to the influence of Dox Thrash, who frequently depicted poor rural blacks in a cabin setting. However, Clark's sharecroppers in the cabin setting are usually white. Typically he seats them on the steps of a cabin. Although white sharecroppers did outnumber blacks, black artists rarely depicted white figures, although white artists freely depicted blacks. In this woodcut the man sits on the steps of what appears to be an open shed, while his wife stirs a pot on a stove in the shadows in the interior. The strong vertical and horizontal lines in the framing wood planks suggest a crude strength in the lives of the shack inhabitants.

Notes

1. Rev. Daima M. Clark, "Claude Clarke's Biography," available at www.claudeclark.com /Claude_Clark/bio.html, accessed October 2002.
2. See Medley-Buckner, "Fine Print Workshop of the Philadelphia Federal Art Project," 42, 45, 51.
3. Raymond Steth interview by Marge Kline, April 28, 1990, typescript, Raymond Steth papers, Smithsonian Archives of American Art, 37, 63.
4. Claude Lockhart Clark e-mail to author, October 1, 2002.

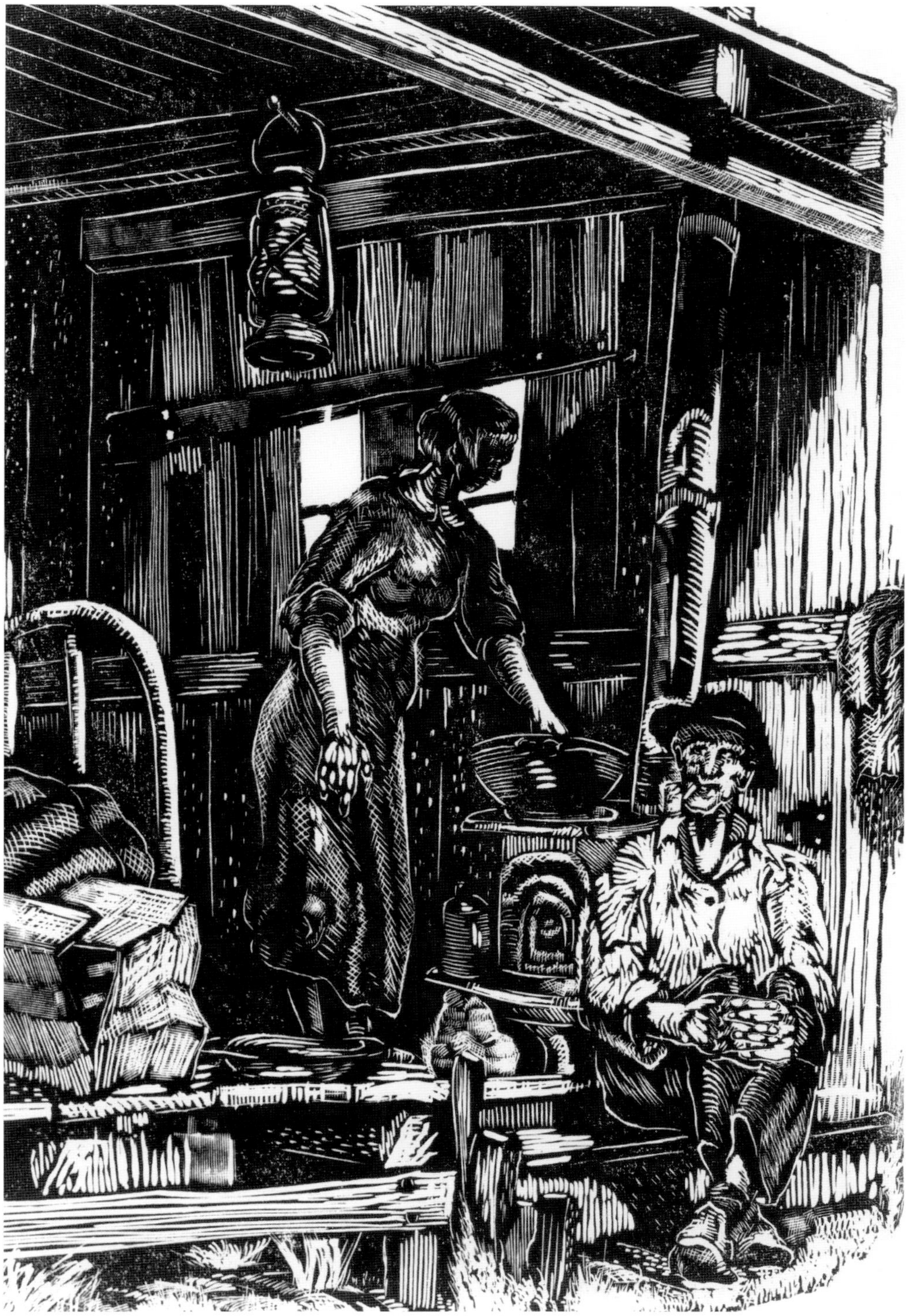

30. Claude Clark, *Sharecroppers,* woodcut, c. 1940, 9 ⅞ x 7 in., collection of the Saint Louis Art Museum; gift of Federal Works Agency, Works Projects Administration.

Richard Zoellner (1908–2003)

Born in Portsmouth, Ohio, and raised in Cincinnati, Richard Zoellner became one of Alabama's outstanding modernist lithographers during the later phase of his printmaking career. He won a scholarship to the Cincinnati Art Academy and later, a Louis Comfort Tiffany fellowship, which allowed him to study in New York.[1] From his father, who was a jeweler, Zoellner learned to engrave, a skill which facilitated his ability to teach himself intaglio methods of printmaking from a book. Likewise he got a part-time job with a firm in Cincinnati that made circus posters, which gave him a background for lithography, in which he was also largely self-taught. From 1933 to 1942, he had his own studio in Cincinnati where he made traditional, black-and-white lithographs between painting commissions.[2]

In 1942 Zoellner joined the military and was assigned to its Regional Studies division of the Tennessee Valley Authority near Knoxville. In spare moments he sketched his first southern subjects and used these in his prints. After the war in 1945, he accepted a position at the University of Alabama in Tuscaloosa, where he remained until his retirement in 1978. There he established a printmaking program. Teaching students forced him to learn more about various print media, and this expanded the range in which he worked as an artist. He began to work more in intaglio in the late 1940s. Zoellner remained in Tuscaloosa after his retirement, continuing his printmaking career.

Smokey [sic] *Mountains,* which represents a scene in east Tennessee, is typical of Zoellner's early scenic lithographs in its broad panoramic view and realistic style using a subtle range of tonal values. His few other southern subjects in a traditional representational mode were figure studies: one of an old woman he saw at a market in nearby Knoxville and another of the child of his black maid in Tuscaloosa.[3] Toward the end of the 1940s, Zoellner, like other young southern printmakers, began moving toward abstract styles in large color prints. The theme of the guitar player, which he attributed to his experiences hearing music in Alabama, remained as a recurring motif through many years of his graphic work. His standard edition size was twelve.

Notes

1. Karen I. Peterson Henricks, *Richard Zoellner,* Alabama Artists Series, Number One (Jacksonville, AL: Jacksonville State University, 1989), 7.
2. Richard Zoellner interview with author, Tuscaloosa, AL, March 2, 2000.
3. On the woman in Knoxville, see Reese, *American Prize Prints of the 20th Century,* 217.

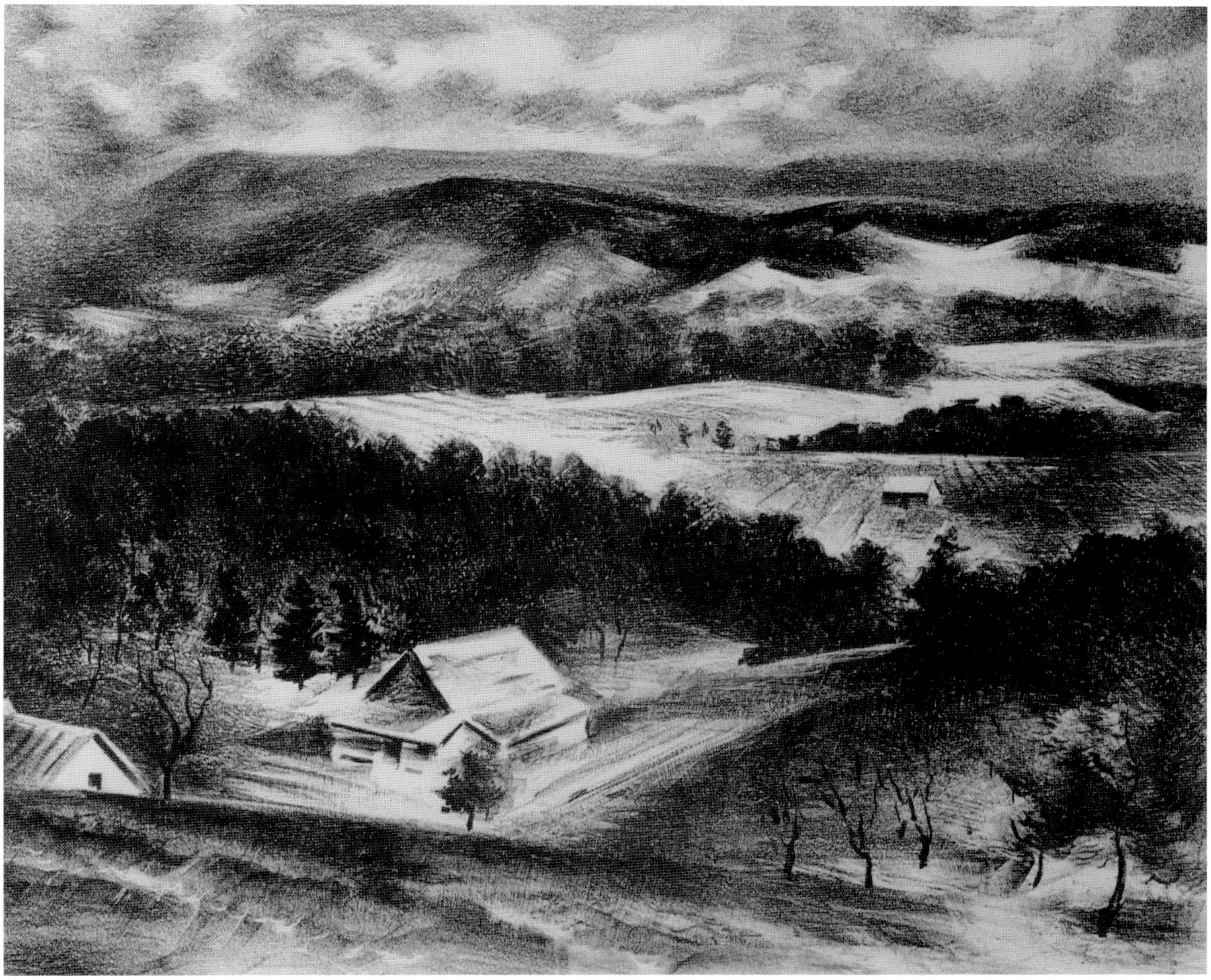

31. Richard Zoellner, *Smokey Mountains,* lithograph, c. 1942, 9 ⅞ x 12 ¾ in., courtesy of Willita S. Goodson Zoellner and from the collection of Lynn Barstis Williams.

Buell Whitehead (1919–1994)

Buell Whitehead was one of a number of southern artists who took up lithography shortly after World War II. Born in a small fishing community near Panama City, Florida, Whitehead grew up on a farm near Fort Myers, where his family raised cattle and hogs. Throughout his rough-and-tumble early years of hunting, fishing, raising cattle, and selling wood, dirt, and shells from a truck, he drew avidly, showing his potential as an artist. After graduating from high school, Whitehead worked for a year before he entered the University of Florida in 1938. Military service during World War II interrupted his studies, though he finally received a BFA with honors in 1945.

Only after college graduation did Whitehead make prints. Under the GI Bill, he attended Otis Art Institute in Los Angeles, where he taught himself lithography; the school had a press but no one to teach lithography. When he came across a prospective buyer for color prints, he taught himself the art of color lithography as well. In the late 1940s and early 1950s Whitehead traveled widely in the West and the South, selling his prints to hotels and stores as decorative accessories, framing around three thousand per year. In 1950 he returned to the University of Florida to obtain an MFA. As financial support and separation from his family was difficult, he turned to real estate development after 1953, constructing mobile home parks, but continued to work as an artist on the side.[1]

Alabama Road is one of Whitehead's earliest prints, and like so many lithographs of the 1930s and 1940s, it has a corresponding painting, which he titled *Erosion.* The kind of erosion illustrated here by the rift in the hillside in the center of the image area is termed "gully erosion," which is associated with bad farming practice. Lines in the gully lead the eye toward a pool of water in the lower foreground, which makes the road difficult to traverse. A name on the signpost directs the traveler to Dothan, Alabama. Many of Whitehead's early color lithographs lean in the opposing direction of romantic landscapes with floral blooms in the foreground, which may have been directed toward sales as decorative works.

Notes

1. Buell Whitehead letter to M. Lee Stone, M. Lee Stone Fine Prints, San Jose, CA, copy in possession of author; Stone and Press Gallery, New Orleans, Catalog #18, March 1993.

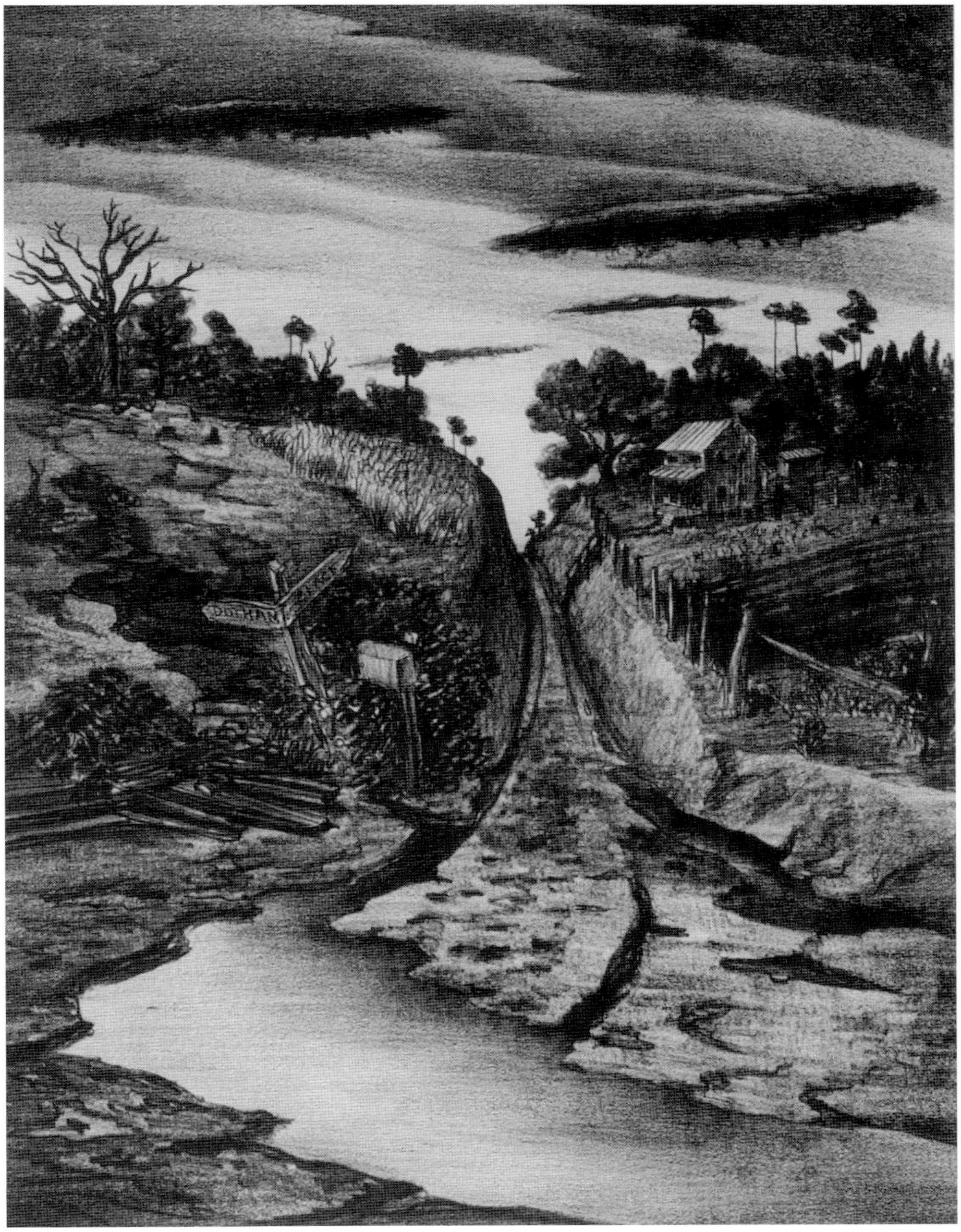

32. Buell Whitehead, *Alabama Road,* lithograph, 1946, 9 ¼ x 7 ⅜ in., collection of Lynn Barstis Williams.

James Edward Routh (b. 1918)

James Routh was born in New Orleans, but during his youth, his family moved to Atlanta, where he first studied art at Oglethorpe University. From 1936 to 1940 Routh studied printmaking under Harry Sternberg at the Art Students League and worked as Will Barnett's assistant in lithography. In 1940 he received a Julius Rosenwald fellowship, which allowed him to travel throughout the South. He bought a used car and set out on the path laid out by Jonathan Daniels in his book *A Southerner Discovers the South* (1938), traveling north from Atlanta through the Tennessee Valley in Alabama to the Mississippi Delta and down to New Orleans.[1] On a second, shorter trip he traveled with his friend Lamar Baker southward to the Okefenokee Swamp. Back home in Atlanta, he set up a print workshop in his parents' garage and made lithographs of the southern views he captured in sketches and photographs of his travels. These were printed in editions of twelve to fifteen impressions. World War II brought a halt to his printmaking career; after the war he abandoned printmaking to work full-time as a commercial artist for Delta Airlines.[2]

Routh made a number of lithographs featuring panoramic views with tiny female figures picking cotton in an expanse of ordered rows; a number were of the Mississippi Delta. The scene pictured here, however, is of the hilly terrain of Henry County, Georgia, just south of Atlanta. One day in 1940 he set out to visit a girlfriend in the area and stopped to do a pen-and-ink sketch of workers picking cotton. When he returned home, he made a lithograph from that sketch.[3] Routh's view shows cotton rows advancing right up to the house to maximize output of the ubiquitous southern staple, a situation often required by agreement between tenant or sharecropper and landlord.[4]

Other lithographs focusing on humble homes resulted from his observations in the Atlanta area. Routh also showed concern with devastated land in a few of his lithographs: *Erosion,* which shows destructive, deep gullies in South Georgia, and *Copper Hill,* which depicts the smelting plant just over the Georgia border in Tennessee whose fumes ravished the land.[5] Nor did he neglect southern industry as he also pictured an Atlanta steel mill, a cotton gin, and oil derricks in Mississippi.

Notes

1. Phagan, "Tours and Visits of the South," 193–94.
2. James Routh letter to author, August 17, 1993; Stone and Press Gallery, New Orleans, LA, Catalog #14, September 1991.
3. James Routh telephone interview with author, August 26, 1996.
4. John B. Boles, *The South through Time: A History of an American Region,* 2nd ed., 2 vols. (Upper Saddle River, NJ: Prentice Hall, 1999), 2:403.
5. "Works of James E. Routh, b. 1918," *Journal of the Print World* (Summer 1999): 36.

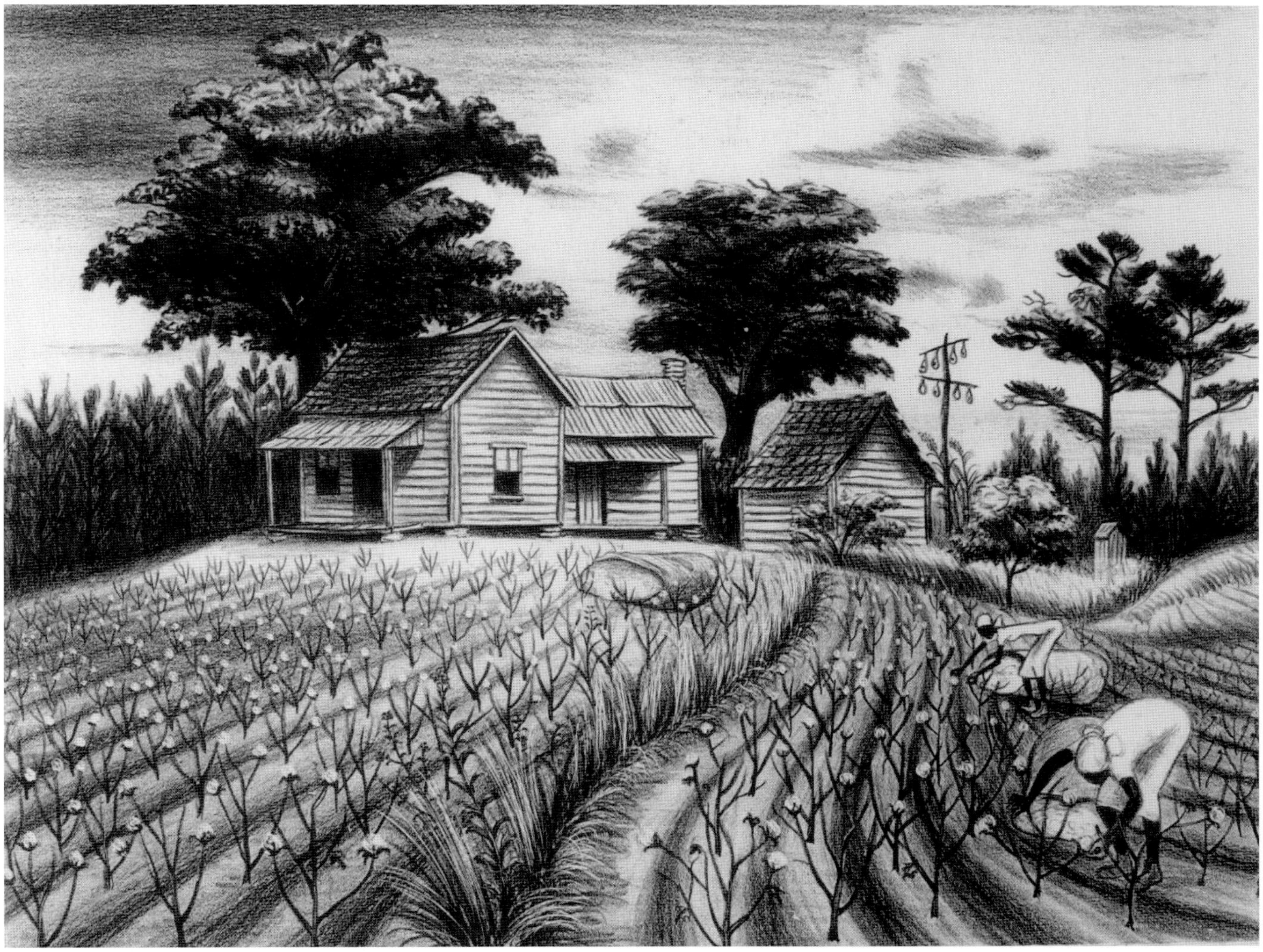

33. James Routh, *Cotton Farm,* lithograph, c. 1940, 8 ⅝ x 11½ in., courtesy of James Routh and from the collection of Lynn Barstis Williams.

Thomas Hart Benton (1889–1975)

One of the regionalist triumvirate that *Time* magazine hailed in a 1934 issue, Thomas Hart Benton was the major artist from outside the South to make the South an important subject of his prints.[1] The biographical data relating to Benton's early art training and orientation—his turn from European modernism toward rural American culture—are well known. Benton's interest in the South derives from two events in his life: the acquaintance he made with young, southern men while stationed at a naval base in Norfolk, Virginia, in 1918 toward the end of World War I and his father's death in 1924, which sparked interest in his family's southern roots in the upper South and Texas. In 1928–29 Benton made the first of numerous sketching trips through the South from which he produced lithographs.[2] He recounted his adventures and observations in his well-known autobiography *An Artist in America* (1937), which includes a long section on southern life and culture illustrated by his drawings.[3]

Benton began to make lithographs in 1929 after meeting George Miller in New York. Those depicting southern scenes date from the late 1930s through 1952. Most depict rural scenes of the upper South: North Carolina, Tennessee, as well as Arkansas. *Back from the Fields* is one of the minority from the Deep South. His catalogue raisonné indicates that this is a Louisiana scene, which shows "cotton pickers returning home after the last bags picked." Like most of Benton's lithographs, this lithograph relates to a painting of the same subject.[4] A degree of melodrama pervades Benton's scene of cotton farmers at work. Two thin, male figures, awkwardly bowed with large cotton sacks, stagger toward a cabin on thin limbs, walking on the fingertips of an ominous hand of black shadow. Heat pervades the scene from a warm tone in the paper background. A woman receiving the bounty stands partially hidden in a broad arc of deep shadow on the porch of the cabin.

Notes

1. See "U.S. Scene," *Time,* December 24, 1934, 24.
2. Gruber, *Thomas Hart Benton and the American South*, 18–19, 21.
3. *An Artist in America* went through four editions, the final one published in 1983 was posthumous.
4. Creekmore Fath, ed. and comp., *The Lithographs of Thomas Hart Benton* (Austin: University of Texas Press, 1969), 15.

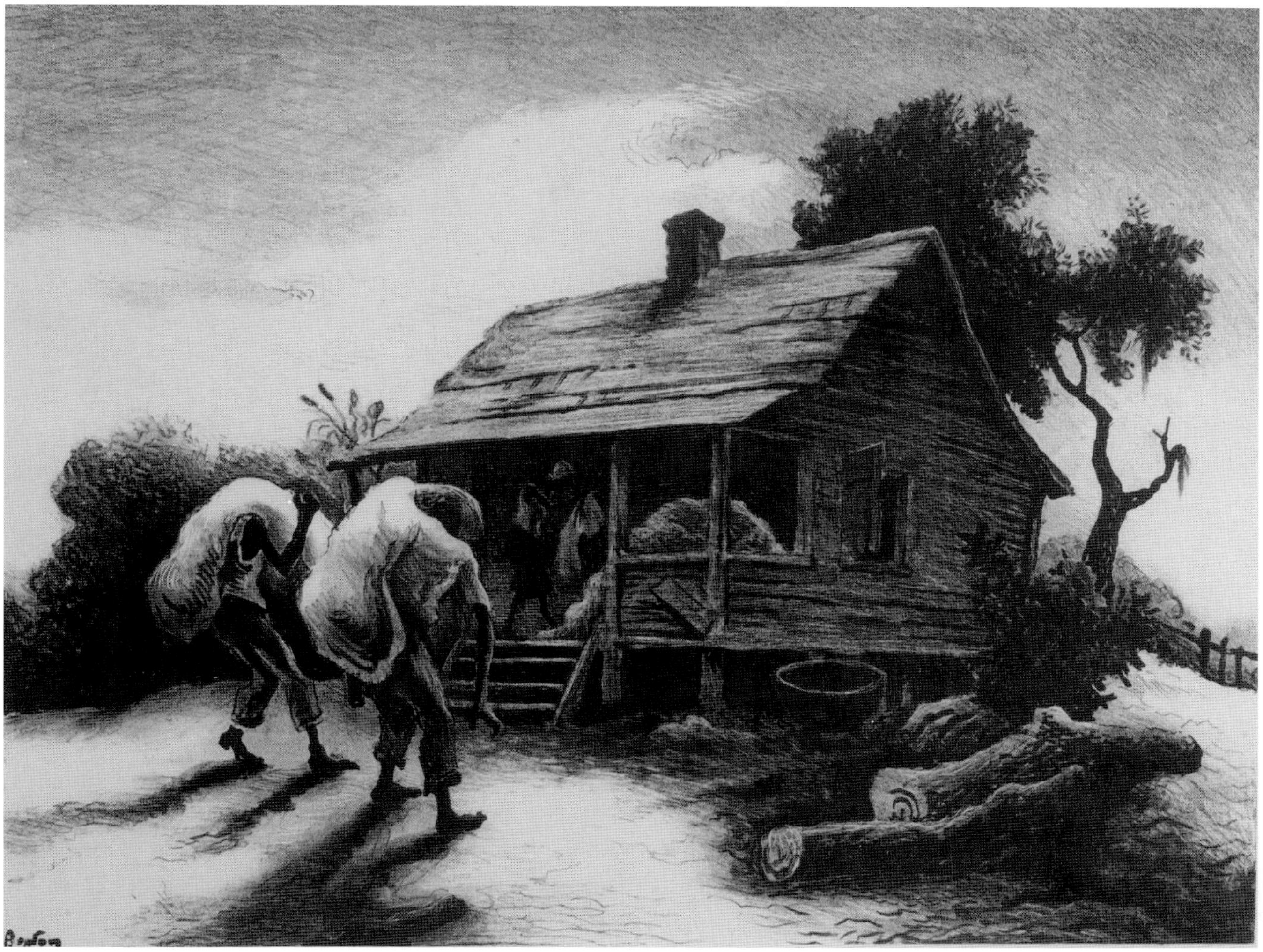

34. Thomas Hart Benton, *Back from the Fields,* lithograph, 1945, 9 ⅞ x 12 ⅞ in., © T. H. Benton and R. P. Benton Testamentary Trusts/UMB Bank Trustee/Licensed by VAGA, New York, NY, and from the collection of Lynn Barstis Williams.

Robert Gwathmey (1903–1988)

A highly recognized southern printmaker, Robert Gwathmey left his native Richmond, Virginia, in 1925 to study at the Maryland Institute College of Art in Baltimore for a year, followed by fours years at the Pennsylvania Academy of the Fine Arts. From 1931 to 1937 he taught at Beaver College in Pennsylvania, then at the Carnegie Institute of Technology in Pittsburgh. In 1942 he settled in New York and began teaching at the Cooper Union School of Art where he remained until 1968. He maintained contact with the South during visits to see family members. Moving away from the South and associating with artists on the political left allowed Gwathmey to achieve a critical perspective on his native region, particularly its racial mores. In 1944 he received a Julius Rosenwald grant, which he used to spend a summer on a tobacco farm near Rocky Mount, North Carolina. He worked in the field alongside black sharecroppers and made paintings and serigraphs from his sketches.[1] From that time on, southern culture became a major subject of his art.

Gwathmey's serigraphs have achieved renown as some of the most successful early applications of the commercial screen-print medium to the fine art print. The serigraph *Tobacco Farmers* illustrates why.[2] The formal composition hangs on heavy black lines formed by hoes plunging into the ground from the left and zigzagging across the picture space linking figures with a bipartite background. Parallel lines of the clothed black figures create a network defining angular shapes to suggest the intensity and harshness of the labor. Gwathmey orchestrates color as well, with saturated primary hues and value contrast to highlight figures against land and sky in the same warm hues but of less saturated intensity. Large tobacco plants with contrasting green in the lower foreground splay at the viewer with ferocious vigor. Four of Gwathmey's serigraphs made during the 1940s depict black field laborers cultivating tobacco. *Non Fiction,* made in 1945, assails racism by harsh imagery of entrapment, barbed wire entangling children, set against gaily clad minstrel imagery. Gwathmey continued his southern themes through the 1970s, but increasingly he turned to lithography.

Notes

1. Michael Kammen, *Robert Gwathmey: The Life and Art of a Passionate Observer* (Chapel Hill: University of North Carolina Press, 1999), 3.
2. See Reba White Williams, "Prints of Robert Gwathmey," in *Hot Off the Press: Prints and Politics,* ed. Linda Tyler and Barry Walker, 33–55 (Albuquerque: University of New Mexico Press, 1994), which includes a catalogue raisonné of Gwathmey's prints. That catalogue raisonné establishes the title *Tobacco Farmers* for this serigraph. See also Williams and Williams, *American Screenprints,* 21, 24, 42.

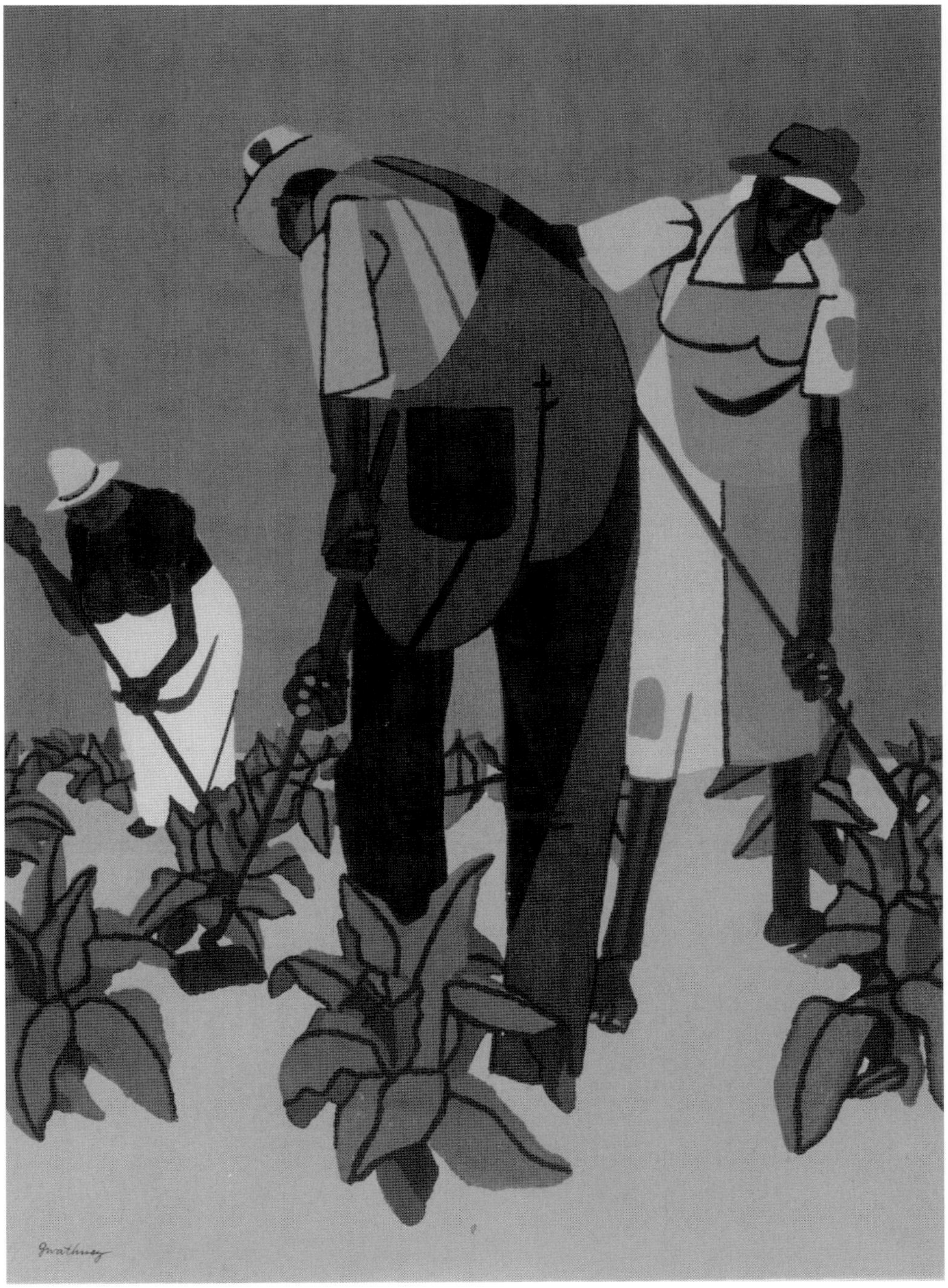

35. Robert Gwathmey, [Tobacco Farmers], serigraph, 1947, 13 ½ x 10 ½ in., art © Estate of Robert Gwathmey/Licensed by VAGA, New York, NY, and from the collection of Lynn Barstis Williams.

Lamar Baker (1908–1994)

In 1935, after obtaining a degree in commerce from the night school of the Georgia School of Technology in Atlanta (now Georgia State University), and studying at the High Museum School of Art, Lamar Baker moved to New York to study at the Art Students League. At the League, Baker studied intaglio printmaking and lithography with Harry Sternberg. During summers he returned home to Atlanta and often visited his grandfather's estate in rural Waverly Hall, Georgia, where four black tenant families lived. He made many sketches that were studies of the cotton plant and other scenes around him. One summer, which appears to have been in 1937, he talked a neighbor in Atlanta who was supervisor of a textile mill into letting him enter the factory to sketch its workers and operations. The result of these summer experiences was his Cotton Series in eleven lithographs and five aquatints with etching that he made from 1938 to 1943. Baker worked as a commercial artist in New York after finishing studies at the League, then returned to Atlanta in 1951. He moved to Columbus, Georgia, in 1952 to work as a commercial artist, settling on his grandfather's estate at Waverly Hall.[1]

Baker used the modern montage as a basis for organizing realistically defined images and segments of space related to cotton agriculture and the textile industry in the South. Often a close-up view of one central image or image complex serves as the focus around which other minor images and segments of space are displayed to explore one particular theme related to the South's cotton economy. A pattern of imagery of entrapment in ropes, threads, chains, and spider webs unifies much of the series to suggest the central problem of the South: its dependence on the cotton cultivation and the textile economy, which binds the common worker, men and women, white and black, as well as the owners and managers. Rope imagery appears in *Field Hands* in the chain of hands, which are pulled into cropped, spinning disks in a large image complex representing textile mill labor. The chain is juxtaposed against imagery of field labor in the corners on the left with a window suggesting the transition. Textile mills were introduced in the South to take advantage of the large, ready work force of poor whites who had difficulty competing with black tenant labor in farming. Often workers moved back and forth between the two types of work.[2] The diagonal of interlocking hands parallel to the pair picking cotton emphasizes the draw of industry in spite of the repetitious nature of the work.[3] Baker also made a few more traditional, realistic views of the South, such as one of the Okefenokee Swamp, which he explored with his printmaker friend James Routh.

Notes

1. Lamar Baker, *Recollections of an Art Student* (New York: Vantage Press, 1990), 53, 84–85; Karol Lawson, "From Cotton Fields to Cotton Mills: Lamar Baker's Lithographs on Labor, 1938–1941," *Georgia Historical Quarterly* 81 (1997): 498–501.
2. Tindall, *Emergence of the New South,* 339.
3. See Lynn Barstis Williams, "Imagery of Entrapment in the Cotton Series of Lamar Baker," *Print Quarterly,* 23 (2006): 391–408.

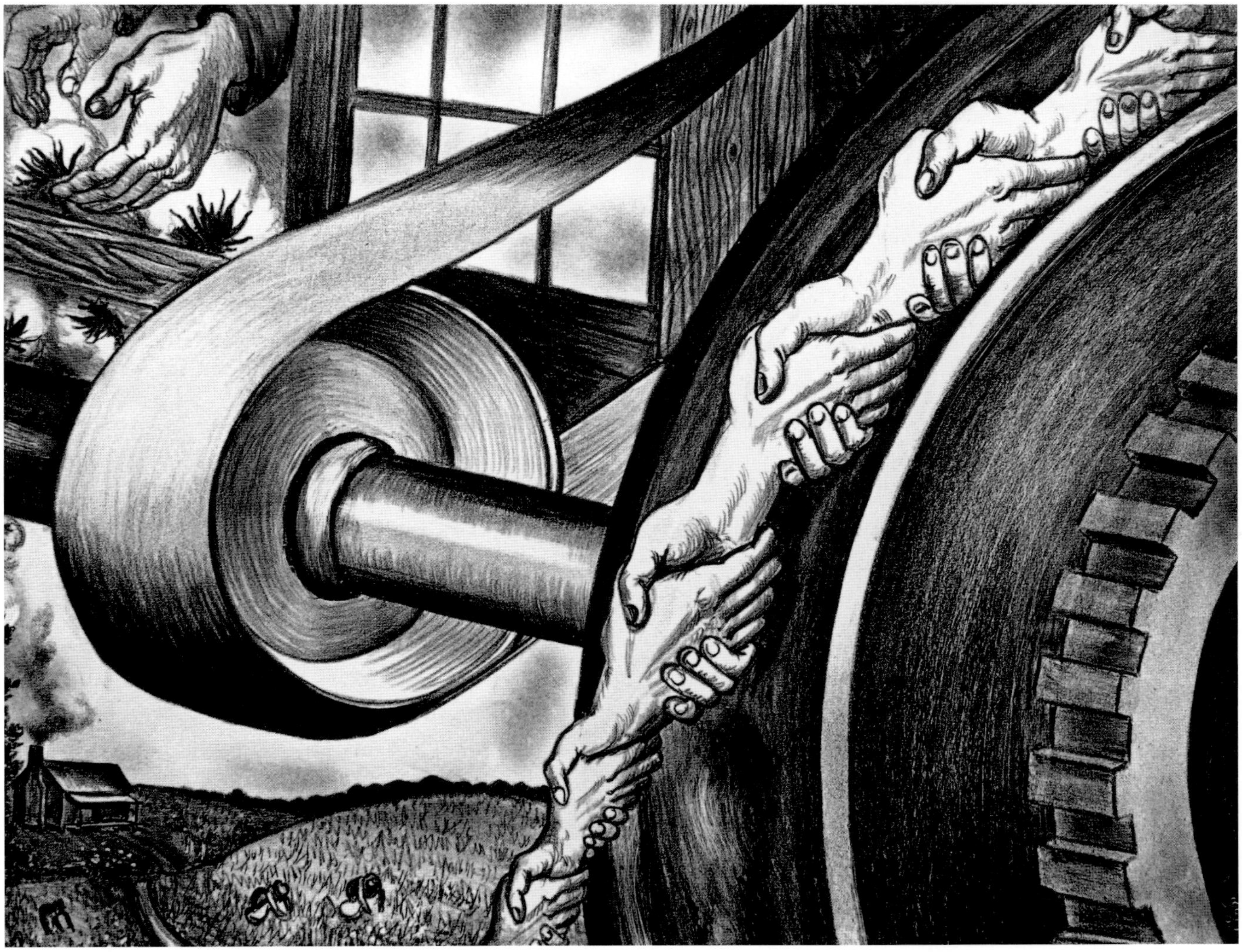

36. Lamar Baker, *Field Hands,* lithograph, 1940, 9 x 12 in., courtesy of the Columbus Museum and from the collection of the Columbus Museum, Columbus, Georgia; museum purchase.

John Roderick Dempster MacKenzie (1865–1941)

Roderick MacKenzie stands as one of Alabama's most distinguished artists whose artistic career shifted from anchor points in Mobile, Europe, and India. Of Scottish heritage, MacKenzie's family immigrated to Mobile from London in 1872 when he was seven years old. Through a scholarship provided by Mobile supporters, he studied at the School of the Museum of Fine Arts in Boston. After further study in Paris, he accepted a commission from an art dealer to paint sporting scenes in India in 1892. Once there, he received other commissions and remained for twelve years, traveling through much of the Indian subcontinent. He drew on his Indian experiences through etchings and monochrome monotypes that were probably made after he returned to London to live from 1908 to 1913.[1]

When he returned to the United States in 1914, a Mobile friend encouraged him to return to Mobile. He did so and opened an art school in 1917, where he taught etching. In 1921–22 MacKenzie visited his brother in Fairfield, Alabama, a Birmingham suburb, and obtained permission from the Tennessee Coal, Iron, and Railroad Co. to enter its mills to depict steel production. These visits resulted in a series of pastels in the early 1920s and a series of lithographs completed in the early 1930s.

MacKenzie's lithographs of work in the Birmingham steel mills may have been made as a way to earn some needed money during the Great Depression. A corporation in Birmingham purchased a set, which they hung on the walls of their branch offices. Most are in black and white, but MacKenzie hand colored a number of them as well. Most impressive are those with warm blue, yellow, or pink hues, built up through applications of transparent water-based color to suggest the heat, fumes, and murky atmosphere of the mills. *Soaking Pit* shows a worker watching as hoists lower steel ingots into hot, steaming, soaking pits prior to hot rolling into the final steel product.[2] MacKenzie often includes a male worker alongside a large piece of equipment for scale to emphasize the size of machinery. His color prints are notable for their large format, unusual in prints before 1945.

Notes

1. *John Roderick Dempster MacKenzie (1865–1941): A Retrospective* (Mobile: Mobile Museum of Art, 1997), 4–8, 18–22.
2. John Springer e-mail to author, July 6, 2004.

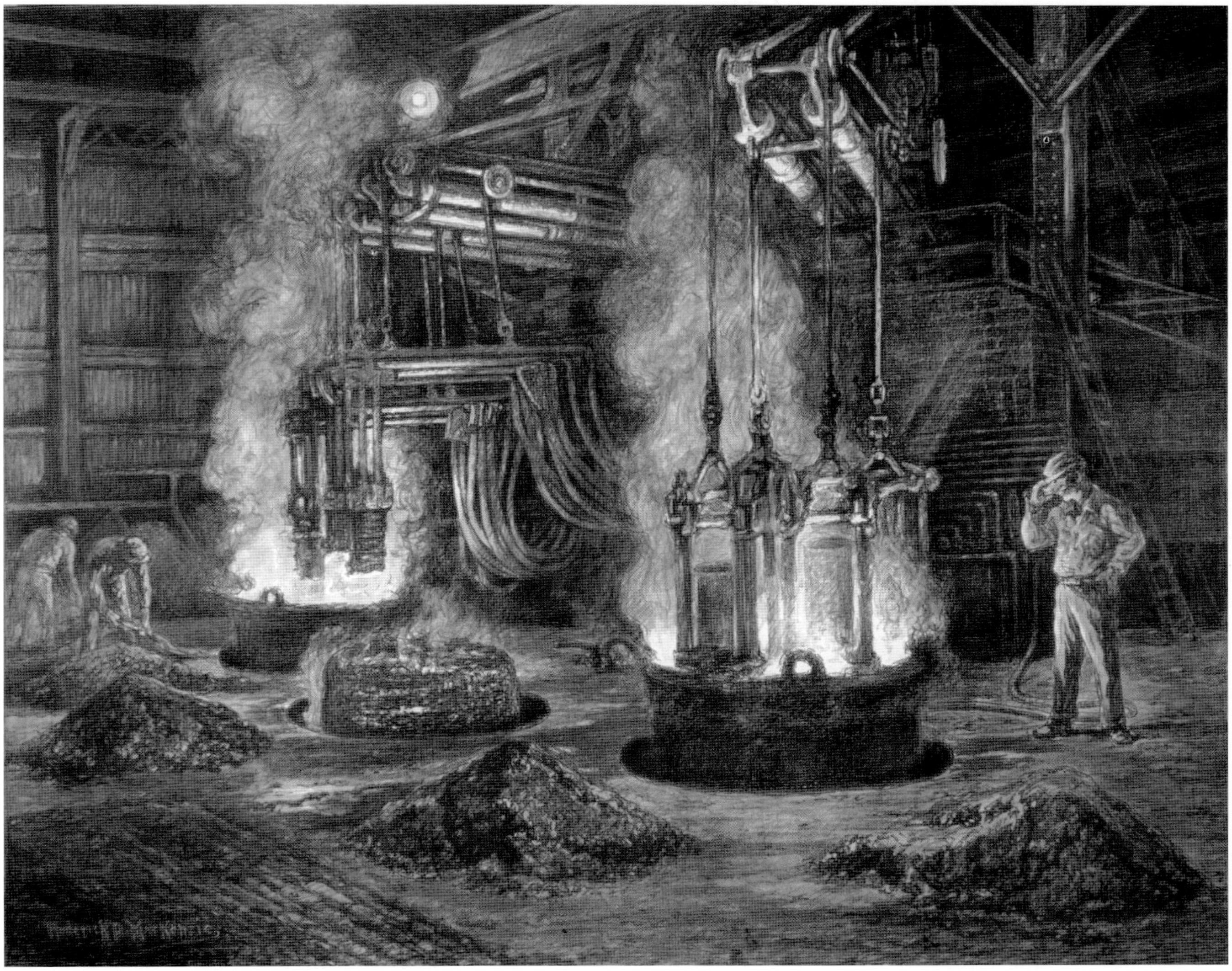

37. Roderick MacKenzie, *Soaking Pit,* hand-colored lithograph, c. 1932, 28 ¼ x 36 in., collection of the Birmingham Museum of Art, Alabama; gift of Mr. Herbert Ryding.

Celia Cregor Reid (1895–1956)

Celia Cregor Reid came to St. Augustine in 1926 when her husband of two years accepted a position with Flagler's Florida East Coast Railroad, and she remained there for the rest of her life, raising a family of three children. Born and reared in Springfield, Kentucky, she earned a BS from the University of Kentucky with a major in home economics. She went on to the Art Institute of Chicago, the Carnegie Institute of Technology in Pittsburgh, and the Maryland Institute College of Art in Baltimore for art training. Woodcuts were just one of many art media that Reid practiced. In addition to watercolors and oils, she made pottery, metal jewelry, and engraved pewter plates with scenes of St. Augustine.[1] She was an early member of the Arts Club of St. Augustine in 1931, exhibited frequently with the organization, and worked tirelessly for it. She also exhibited her prints with the Southern States Art League, and some were exhibited nationally as well.[2]

In her backyard Reid had a studio, which housed the press she used to print her wood carved plates. A turning point in her print production occurred at some time in the 1940s when she began having a printing company in town steel-face her hard wood plates so she could print editions of several hundred. The plates she had steel-faced were usually small ones that she made primarily for Christmas and greeting cards.

Like most St. Augustine printmakers Reid depicted views with historic St. Augustine architecture, but she also rendered boats, which were mainstays of the city's substantial shrimping industry at the time.[3] *Shrimp Boat, Evening, St. Augustine, Florida* suggests the industry offered employment to a considerable number of workers, as we see many small figures busy at work on a boat at dock. Like Reid's best woodcuts, the view shows complex, bold, black-and-white design, seen in the hull of the boat with its shadow as well as the strong diagonal of the sail against horizontals and verticals in other segments of the scene.

Notes

1. Celia Rose telephone interviews with author, November 14, 17, and 29, 2005.
2. Torchia, *Lost Colony,* 14–15, 17, 104–5.
3. Celia Rose telephone interviews with author, November 14 and 17, 2005; e-mail communication November 18, 2005.

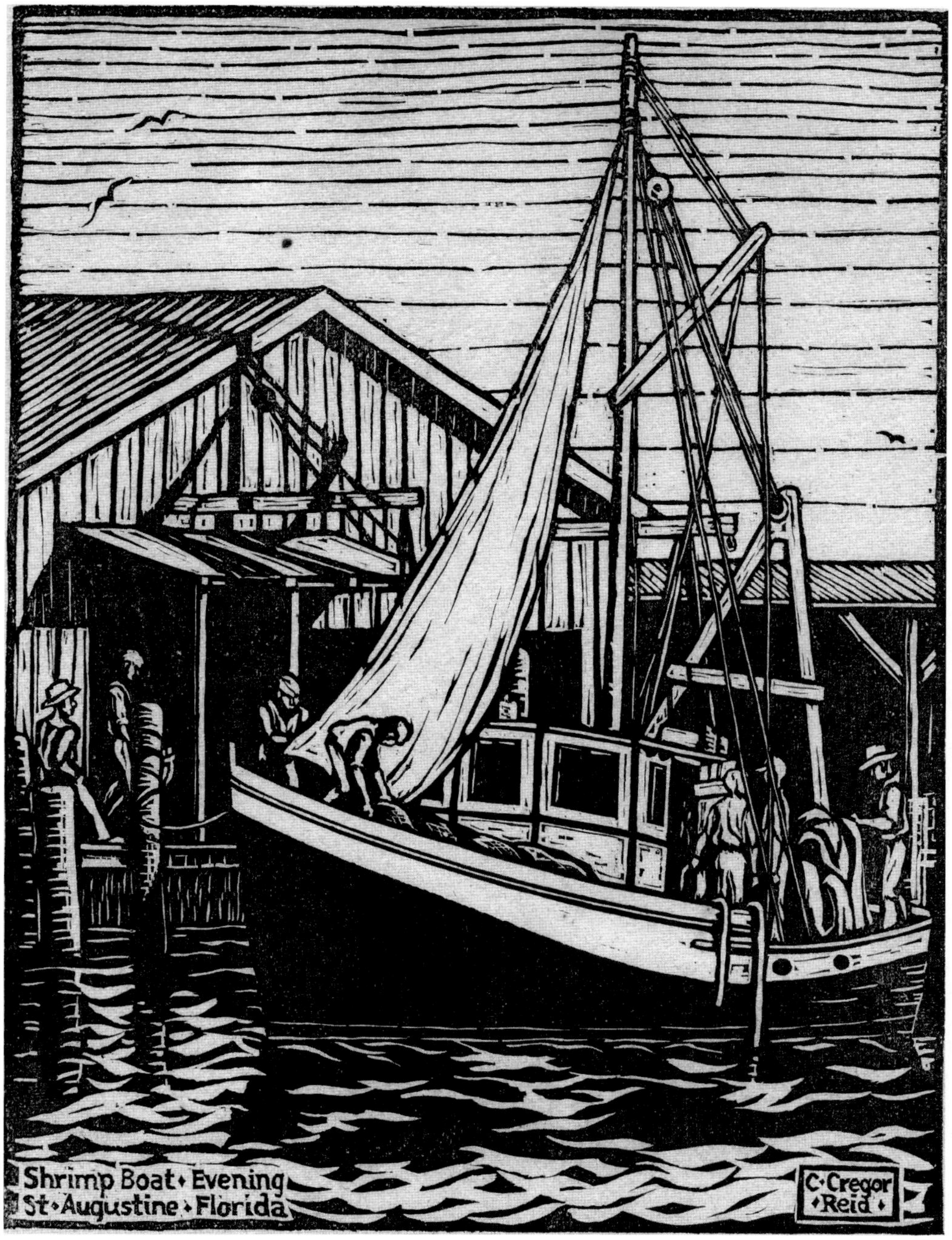

38. C. Cregor Reid, *Shrimp Boat, Evening, St. Augustine, Florida,* woodcut, 10 ⅝ x 8 ¼ in., courtesy of Celia Rose and from the collection of Celia Rose.

Doris Alexander (Thompson) (1906–1995)

Born and reared in Mobile, Alabama, Doris Alexander studied art under that city's most distinguished artist, Roderick MacKenzie. She lived in Montgomery from 1940 to 1944 and during two of those years participated in the Dixie Art Colony, founded through the Montgomery Museum. A woman artist in Birmingham, whose name she could not remember years later, introduced Alexander to lithography sometime during her years living in central Alabama. During summers and winters in 1944 and 1945 and following summer sessions, Alexander studied lithography under Raphael Sabatini at the Tyler School of Art of Temple University and began experimenting with multiplate, color lithography. She followed her husband, a minister, to Columbia, South Carolina, in 1945. There she bought a lithography press and began printing her own editions by herself, one of the few women artists to do so. When her husband retired in 1968, Alexander moved with him back to the Mobile area, settling in Magnolia Springs on the eastern shore of Mobile Bay, and continued making lithographs until 1989.[1] She was an active member of the National Association of Women Artists, the American Color Print Society, the Guild of South Carolina Artists, and the Alabama Art League, with which she exhibited.[2]

Alexander matured as a lithographer in the late 1940s, when printmakers in the South began to move beyond realistic scenes with local associations to emphasize design with universal implications. *Granite Quarry* reveals both older and newer impulses. Granite quarries did exist in the area near Columbia, South Carolina, and other lithographs of the artist, such as a more documentary view that featured gas towers in Columbia, show that she depicted such semi-industrial, local work.[3] Here workers are barely evident as tiny silhouettes in the background, a common visual strategy to provide scale. Alexander uses the small figures to emphasize the massive size of the quarry rock formation in the foreground, which she patterns in a bold, pinwheel design. Black wedges between rock clusters spiral out toward the viewer to add a disquieting, ominous mystery to the scene. She won an award for this lithograph from the Alabama Art League in 1950.[4] Alexander's basically realistic iconography during the 1940s varied: the natural landscape and floral blooms, ballerinas, black figures, and architectural structures from various places where she resided.

Notes

1. Doris Alexander Thompson interview with author, March 10, 1995; Doris Alexander Thompson letter to author, March 1995; "Mrs. Thompson's Art Makes Fine Display at Museum," *Montgomery Advertiser,* October 5, 1946.
2. Katherine A. McIver, *Doris Alexander Thompson and the Dixie Art Colony* (Birmingham: Visual Arts Gallery, University of Alabama at Birmingham, 2004), 10.
3. "Lithographs are on Display at Museum," Scrapbook, Alabama Art League, Special Collections and Archives, Auburn University.
4. "Anniversary Tea at Museum to Be Given by Art League," Scrapbook, Alabama Art League.

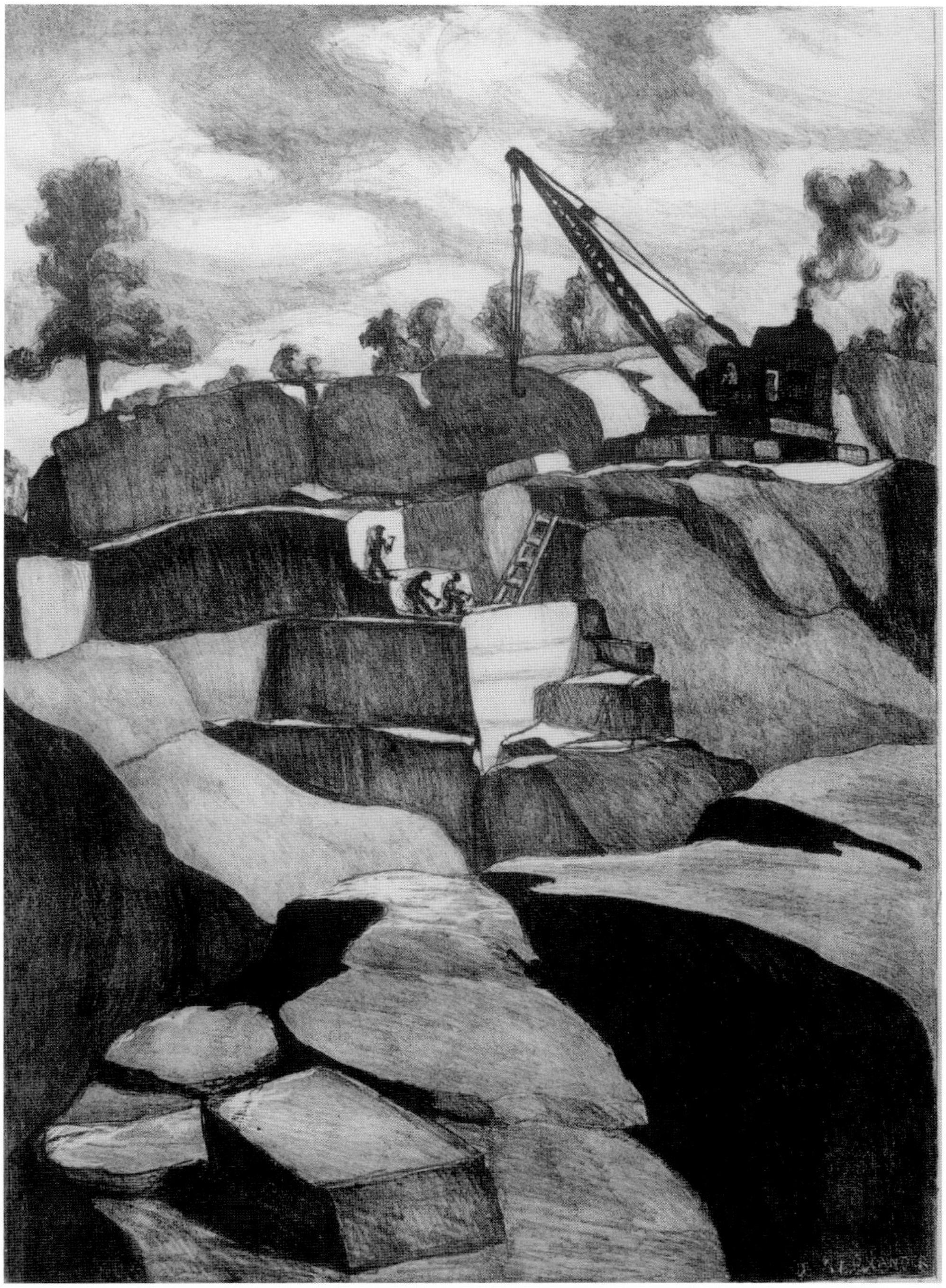

39. Doris Alexander, *Granite Quarry,* lithograph, 1949, 13 ⅜ x 9 ¾ in., collection of Stephen Goldfarb.

Georges Schreiber (1904–1977)

Georges Schreiber was a superb illustrator, specializing in the human figure, who transferred his skills to oil, watercolor, and lithography. Born in Brussels to German parents, he witnessed atrocities during World War I as his family fled to Germany in 1914 with the outbreak of war, only to return to Belgium when the Germans invaded that country. After studying at academies in Elberfeld, Berlin, and Düsseldorf, followed by travels throughout Europe, Schreiber became a free-lance illustrator in 1925 for a newspaper in Cologne. In 1928 he traveled to New York on an assignment and decided to remain. He continued to work as an illustrator for New York newspapers, specializing in sketches of well-known personalities.[1]

From 1936 to 1939 Schreiber made three major trips across the country through all forty-eight states, sketching people and landscapes. Back in New York he composed scenes combining both, creating a lithograph, watercolor, and oil of a single scene. Titles of the lithographs, which Associated American Artists printed, are derived from the corresponding paintings, as Schreiber did not title the print versions. A 1970 exhibition catalog lists twenty-six lithographs made from 1940 to 1948, eight of which have titles associated with the South. Several others have been associated with the South from titles of the paintings; such is the case with *Evening in North Carolina.*[2]

Most critical discussion of Schreiber's work before 1950 comments on his paintings; an exhibition of his southern paintings describes them as "documents of the poorer regions of the South."[3] Schreiber's lithographs lean toward rural scenes. He frequently situates a large figure in the foreground against a broad expansive landscape to suggest rural isolation. A number feature a white, farm woman in frontal or lateral view with suggestions of her hard lot. *Evening in North Carolina* is an elaboration of this theme. Schreiber adds dramatic tension by positioning the figure of a young, black male at the opposite end of the picture plane from that of the woman and on a lower level. The resulting composition uses these figures in the multilevel setting to establish polarities of class, race, gender, age, and psychology in the rural South.

Notes

1. "Georges Schreiber," *American Artist,* April 7, 1943, 10.
2. *Georges Schreiber: Symphonic Variations 1971–73,* Kennedy Galleries, 1973; *The Graphic Work of Georges Schreiber,* Kennedy Galleries, 1970; *Georges Schreiber Watercolors, 1969–79,* November 24–December 16, 1970, Kennedy Galleries. Georges Schreiber papers, Smithsonian Archives of American Art, Reel #2673. This lithograph is sometimes given the title *Evening in South Carolina* due to a title discrepancy in the above exhibition catalogs.
3. "Traveler Schreiber Paints Southern Journey," *Art Digest,* April 1, 1943, 11.

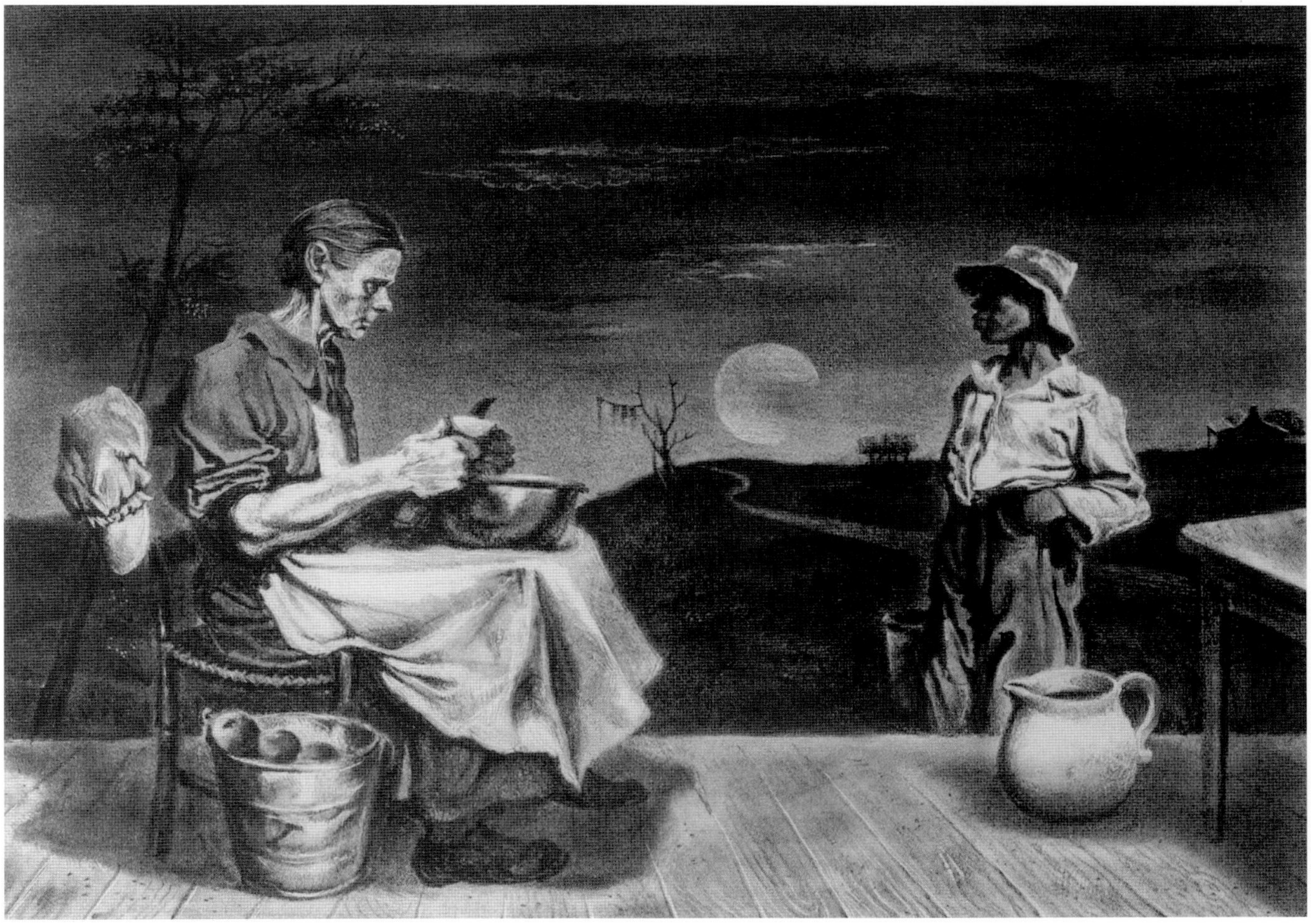

40. Georges Schreiber, [Evening in North Carolina], lithograph, 1947, 9 ½ x 13 ¼ in., courtesy of the Estate of the Artist and the Susan Teller Gallery, New York, and from the collection of Stephen Goldfarb.

Dox Thrash (1892–1965)

Born in Griffin, Georgia, Dox Thrash grew up in a former slave cabin on the outskirts of town. He studied art through correspondence since educational opportunities for blacks were severely limited in the rural South. In 1909 Thrash began traveling and doing odd jobs to earn his way until he settled in Chicago in 1911. In 1914 he began taking night classes at the Art Institute of Chicago and continued through 1923, though service with the American Expeditionary Forces in France interrupted his studies from 1917 to 1919. Thrash left Chicago in 1922 for more years of travel, often as a hobo, intending to "observe, draw, and paint the people of America."[1] In 1925 he settled in Philadelphia, where he lived for the rest of his life. He studied printmaking with Earl Horter in the early 1930s at the Graphic Sketch Club.[2] In 1937 he began working at the WPA graphic arts workshop in Philadelphia, where he, Hugh Mesibov, and Michael Gallagher experimented with the carborundum stone in intaglio processes and used it for many of the prints they produced on the program.[3]

Thrash reflected his rural southern heritage in his prints primarily through images of the tenant or sharecropper's cabin, which he knew firsthand from his boyhood. The catalogue raisonné of his prints shows that he began delineating the image in etching and linocuts, then progressed to the dark, muted tonalities of his carborundrum prints done on the WPA workshop. *Monday Morning Wash* is the culmination in this process in color. Like many of his cabin prints it shows the crude, dilapidated housing in which poor black and white people lived in the South. He frequently included human figures that associated cabin architecture with work, particularly that of women. *Monday Morning Wash* highlights laundry work, the most labor intensive of household chores before electric appliances, which was commonly relegated to black women in the South. The paths that cross in the foreground lead to the sturdy figure in the center, balancing a load of laundry on her head, an image similar to that seen in coastal urban views.

Notes

1. *Dox Thrash: An Exhibition from the Collection of the Print and Picture Department of the Free Library of Philadelphia,* May 17–29, 1987, n.p.
2. Ittmann, *Dox Thrash*, 1–13, 130–39.
3. See Jerry Wood, "A New Print Process," *Crisis,* December 1940, 379, 389, and Medley-Buckner, "Carborundum Mezzotint and Carborundum Etching," 34–45.

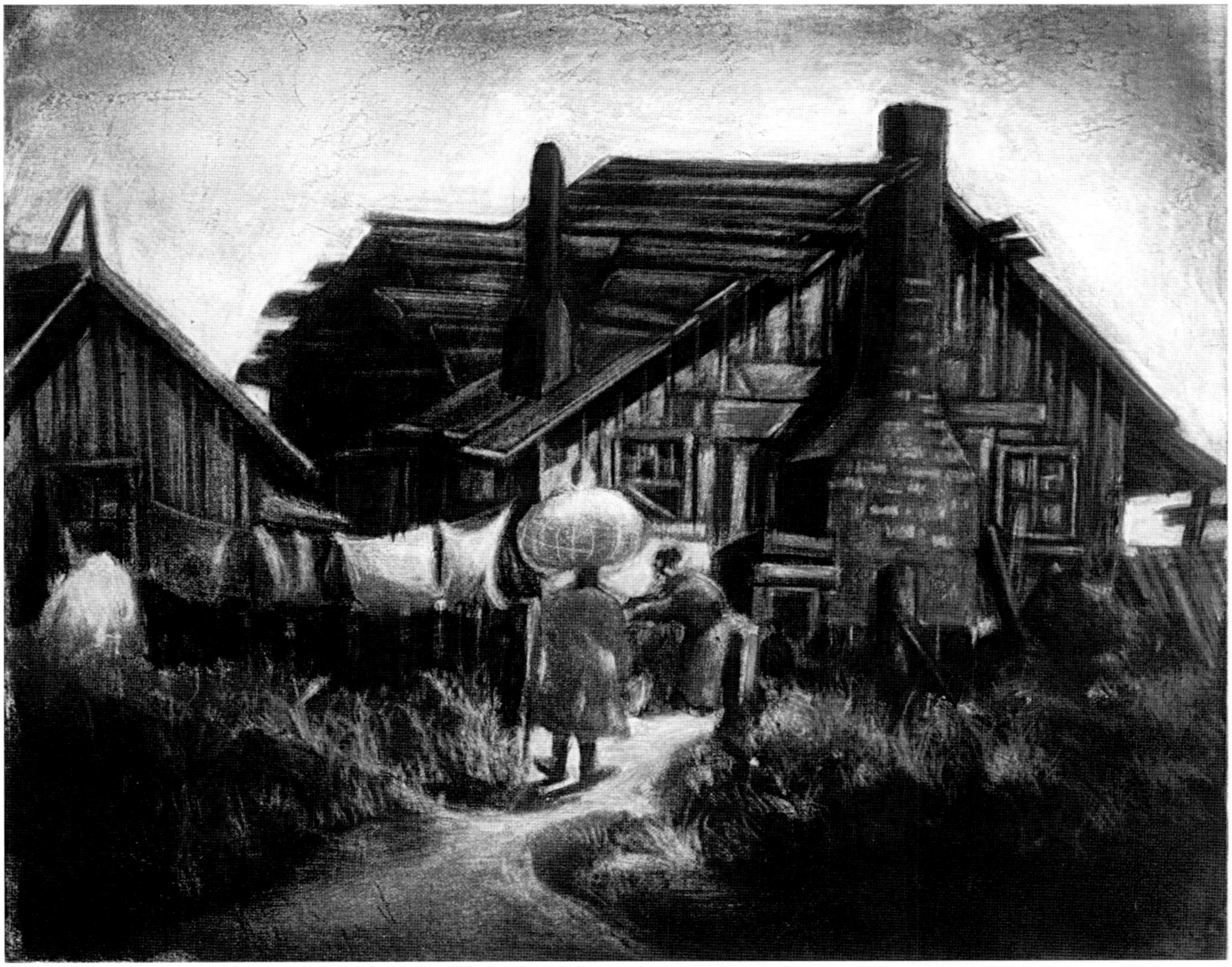

41. Dox Thrash, *Monday Morning Wash,* color carborundum mezzotint, c. 1939, 11 x 14 in., collection of the Philadelphia Museum of Art purchased with the Thomas Skelton Harrison Fund.

William Henry Johnson (1901–1970)

William Henry Johnson has been one of the most celebrated of all African American artists for his distinctive, colorful style in both painting and serigraphs. Johnson grew up in Florence, South Carolina. Because of his artistic bent and an uncle living in New York City, he went to New York at age seventeen. After working several years, he studied for three years at the National Academy of Design. Through the influence of Charles Hawthorne, one of his instructors at the Academy, Johnson began spending summers at the Cape Cod School of Art that Hawthorne had founded in Provincetown. In 1926 Hawthorne helped Johnson finance study in Paris. On a trip to the south of France, Johnson met his future wife, Holcha Kracke, a Danish weaver, whom he married in 1930. They settled in Denmark and traveled widely throughout Europe. Johnson's art during this European period was strongly influenced by the expressionist movement. During the 1930s he made numerous woodcuts in a crude, simple, and bold style with heavy lines reminiscent of the German expressionists.[1]

Sensing threatening political developments in Europe, Johnson returned to New York with his wife in 1938. In 1939 he joined the WPA's Federal Arts Project at the Harlem Community Art Center, creating and teaching painting. At this center Johnson was introduced to screen printing and produced a large number of serigraphs. His style began to change, reflecting the influence of southern folk art.[2] Straight lines predominate, contrasting with a few simple curvilinear forms with strong color contrasts. Moreover, the rural African American farm family became a prominent subject. His black figures bear excessively thin limbs with large hands and feet, suggesting both their poverty and capability. In *Deep South* we see the basic visual elements of his southern iconography: the farming couple, their traditional implements, and a simple shack set in a collage-like composition with bold design.[3]

Notes

1. Richard J. Powell, *Homecoming: The Art and Life of William H. Johnson* (New York: Rizzoli, 1991), passim. In *Homecoming* Powell discusses Johnson's life and painting extensively but only briefly mentions his block prints and never mentions his serigraphs.
2. Powell, *Homecoming,* 141.
3. The Smithsonian American Art Museum owns another impression of this serigraph, which bears the title *Farmers Day of Rest.*

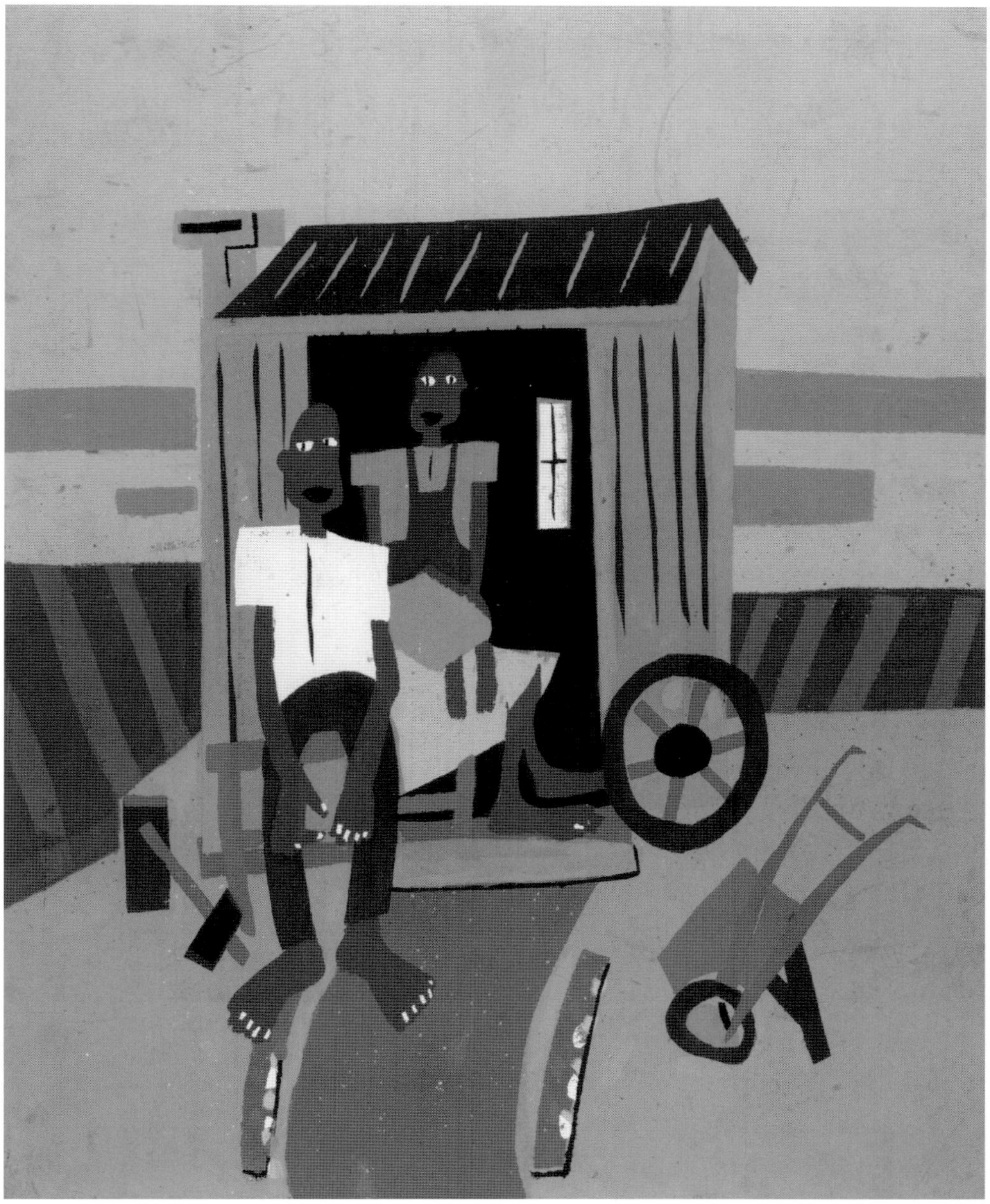

42. William Henry Johnson, *Deep South,* serigraph, c. 1940, 17 ⅛ x 14 ⅛ in., collection of the Smithsonian American Art Museum; gift of the Harmon Foundation.

Wilmer Angier Jennings (1910–1990)

Wilmer Jennings was the outstanding printmaking student of Hale Woodruff at Morehouse College and Atlanta University during the 1930s. Jennings was an Atlanta native, raised in a prosperous middle-class family. Hoping he would become an artist, his mother nurtured his talent by providing her son with art lessons, supplies, and books during his early years. Such parental encouragement bore fruit, as he made prints from linoleum as early as sixteen or seventeen years of age, before he met Woodruff.[1] After graduating from high school in Atlanta, Jennings enrolled in Morehouse College in 1931, where he earned a degree in mathematics and studied relief printmaking with Woodruff. After graduation in 1934, he taught math, then received a John Hope fellowship to study at the Rhode Island School of Design from 1935 to 1936. He returned to Atlanta to teach at Booker T. Washington High School, but headed back to Providence after only one year of teaching. Jennings lived in Providence the rest of his life, earning his living as a jewelry designer, and only returned to Atlanta for visits.[2]

Although Jennings did work in intaglio and lithography, his major print medium was relief: linoleum cuts, woodcuts, and wood engravings. Like other black southern printmakers, such as his mentor Hale Woodruff, he suggests his southern past through rural views of agricultural labor and rickety wooden architecture. In *Lazy Bones* we see an elongated male figure sprawled on the steps of what appears to be a ramshackle cabin in a twisted "S" curve. According to some authorities, lazy bones was a popular theme in African American art and literature among writers and artists.[3] Jennings treats this theme in a somewhat jocular, satiric manner. The thoroughly relaxed man appears to be in socks, suggesting he is not about to get up and around to do the domestic labor implied by other objects in the scene—laundry on the line, an iron pot on the fire, and a stack of wood under the steps—which is likely that of an unseen, female consort. Through his exaggeration of the figure Jennings may be satirizing a racial, geographic, or gender stereotype of the poor as lazy.

Notes

1. Corrine Jennings letter to author, October 15, 1993.
2. Elliott, *Pressing On,* 16–17.
3. Ibid., 22.

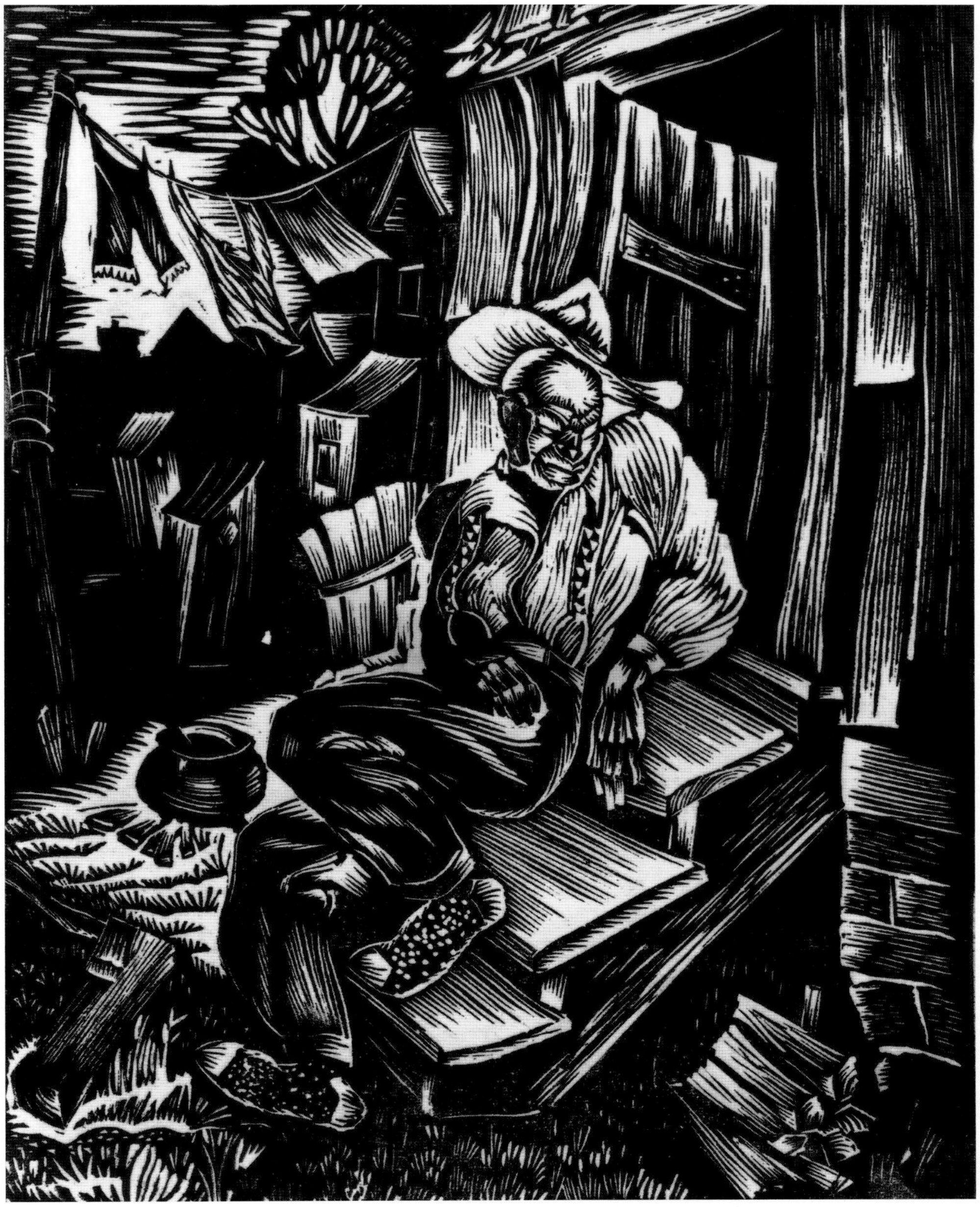

43. Wilmer Jennings, *Lazy Bones,* woodcut, c. 1939, 10 ½ x 8 ½ in., courtesy of Corrine Jennings and from the collection of the Metropolitan Museum of Art; gift of Reba and Dave Williams.

Caroline Wogan Durieux (1896–1989)

Born into a New Orleans French Creole family, Caroline Durieux demonstrated her independent spirit by convincing her parents to support her training at the Pennsylvania Academy of the Fine Arts after studies at Newcomb College instead of furnishing lavish festivities and attire for a debut.[1] Durieux married shortly after her studies and followed her husband first to Havana, where they lived from 1920 to 1926, then to Mexico City for a decade. In 1936 they returned to New Orleans where Durieux resumed a career in lithography that began in 1930 during a year's residence in New York. After viewing a sample of her drawings, Carl Zigrosser, a promoter of American printmaking, encouraged her to try lithography, as he did many other artists. Upon her return to Mexico City, Durieux found a printer at the Senefelder Lithographic House and began producing the distinctive satirical lithographs that became her hallmark.[2] She began teaching full-time at Newcomb in 1938 and became director of the Louisiana WPA/FAP in 1939. Moving on to a teaching position at Louisiana State University in 1942, she established a printmaking program there, and like other southern printmakers after 1950, drifted toward experimental work. One result was a patent for the electron print in 1957.[3]

Durieux is unique in the South for her distinctive satirical style, which featured close-ups of the human figure with exaggerated features rendered in either a spare linear style or one with full modeling through areas of tone, such as we see here. In the 1940s the superior stance of her satirical strain gave way to a more empathetic, elegiac infusion of her imagery as she used the human figure to visualize responses to war and oppression, often using human features for visual metaphors. *Desirée,* made in 1947, unites the satirical with the elegiac strains. The title, composed of a French past participle, suggests a New Orleans cultural context: the French heritage with freer sexual mores than those in other parts of the South. Her image of the older white woman with atypical congruities, such as delicate lace near muscular limbs, denotes a satirical strategy, but the sagging figure with the dour, drawn face deters a smile or laugh in the viewer's response.

Notes

1. Earl Retif, "Rare Works by Caroline Wogan Durieux," *Arts Quarterly* 11 (1989): 12, 18.
2. Richard Cox, *Caroline Durieux: Lithographs of the Thirties and Forties* (Baton Rouge: Louisiana State University Press, 1977), 6.
3. See Stacy V. Jones, "New Radioactive Ink for Artists Allows Many Easy Reproductions," *New York Times,* February 9, 1957; Ann Michelle Moore, "Life and Work of Caroline Spelman Wogan Durieux (1896–1989)," master's thesis, Tulane University, 1992, 36–46.

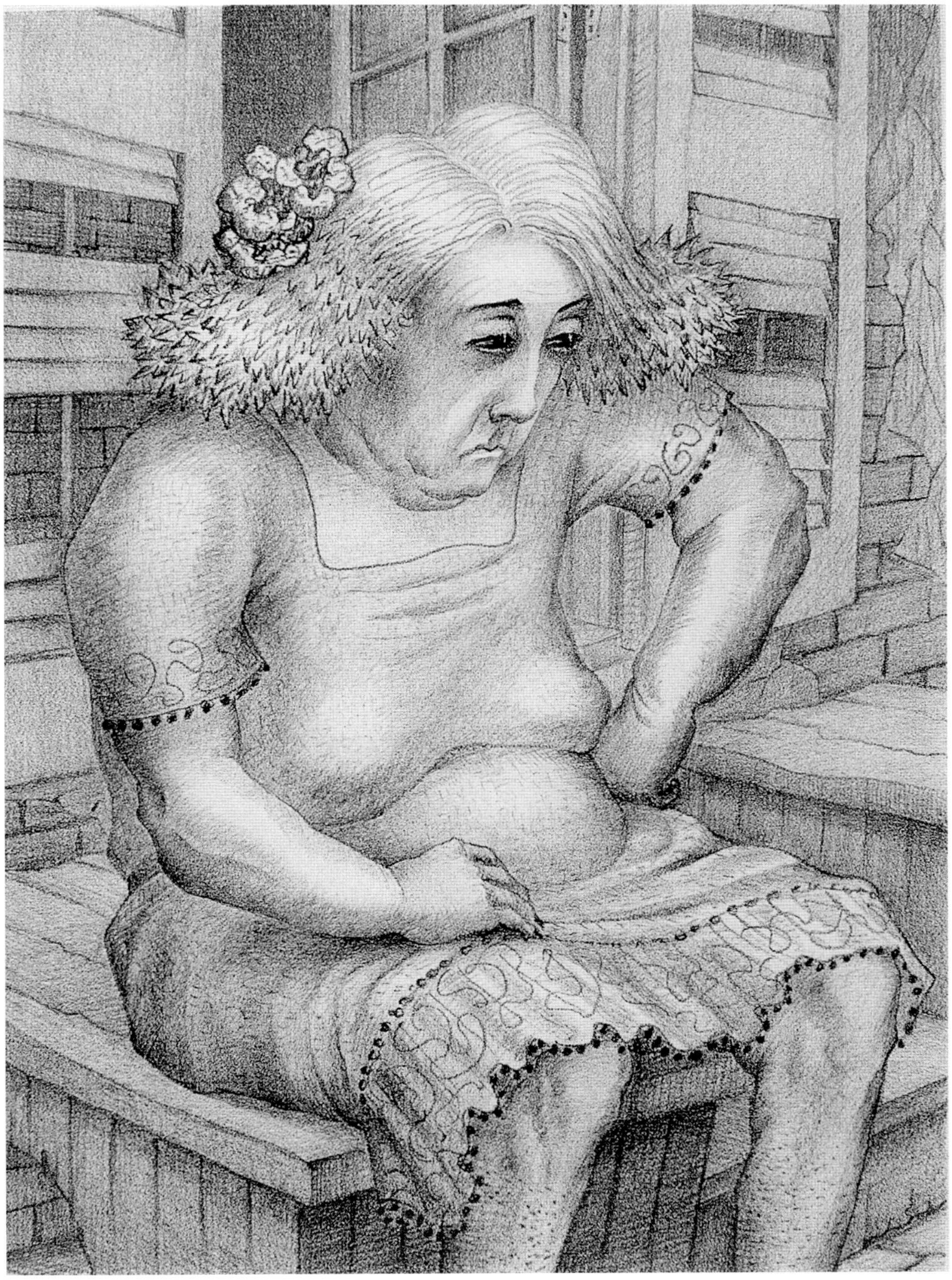

44. Caroline Durieux, *Desirée,* lithograph, 1947, 12 ¾ x 9 ½ in., collection of the Louisiana State University Museum of Art; gift of the artist.

Anne Wilson Goldthwaite (1869–1944)

Born not long after the Civil War to a distinguished Montgomery family, Anne Goldthwaite remembered her early Alabama years as a time when "all men were without hope of a better future." In search of that better future, her father moved his family to Dallas, Texas. However, when both her parents died in the early 1880s, Anne and her siblings returned to Montgomery to live with an aunt, who recognized and encouraged Anne's artistic talent. When an uncle who worked as a cotton factor in New York offered to finance her art training, she moved to New York around 1892.[1]

Anne Goldthwaite's printmaking career began when she applied for a job with Cheltenham Press and learned that the owner needed an etcher. She tried to learn by teaching herself from a book, then decided to take a course in the medium. She studied etching under the tutelage of Charles Mielatz at the National Academy of Design.[2] After studying and working in Paris from 1906 to 1913, Goldthwaite returned to New York, where she frequently exhibited her etchings. A bronze medal she won at the Panama Pacific International Exposition in 1915 signaled her achievement in this medium. In 1922 she joined the faculty at the Art Students League, where she became a favorite instructor of etching until shortly before her death. She studied lithography under Charles Locke at the League from 1925 to 1926 and increasingly shifted to that medium during the 1930s.[3]

During her early years, Anne Goldthwaite explored parts of Montgomery, such as Court Square and the African American district of Boguehomme, to sketch her observations. After she moved to New York, she returned to Montgomery during the summer to visit family and friends. In 1920 she began to make etchings from her southern sketches, and her scenes of southern life and landscape have been adjudged among her finest work.[4] Her sketch-like style consisted of loose, delicate lines in an impressionist manner reminiscent of Whistler. Extensive areas of white paper are left free of inked lines to suggest intense sunlight and accompanying heat subsuming figures and objects, which are sometimes barely visible, as in the background of the scene of Boguehomme.[5] In the 1920s Goldthwaite also made architectural views of New Orleans, and throughout her printmaking career she depicted family members and friends in portrait etchings. In the 1930s her figures become more emphatic in loosely executed lithographs consonant with national trends.

Notes

1. Goldthwaite memoirs quoted by Breeskin, *Anne Goldthwaite: A Catalogue Raisonné of the Graphic Work,* 15–20.
2. Goldthwaite memoirs quoted by Breeskin in ibid., 21–22.
3. Adelyn Breeskin, *Anne Goldthwaite, 1869–1944* (Montgomery AL: Montgomery Museum of Fine Arts, 1977), 11–17; Dennison, "Art of the American South," 302–6.
4. Margaret Lynne Ausfeld, "Introduction," in Breeskin, *Anne Goldthwaite,* 10.
5. There is a corresponding painting to this etching, titled *Street in Boguehomme,* which is owned by the Montgomery Museum of Art.

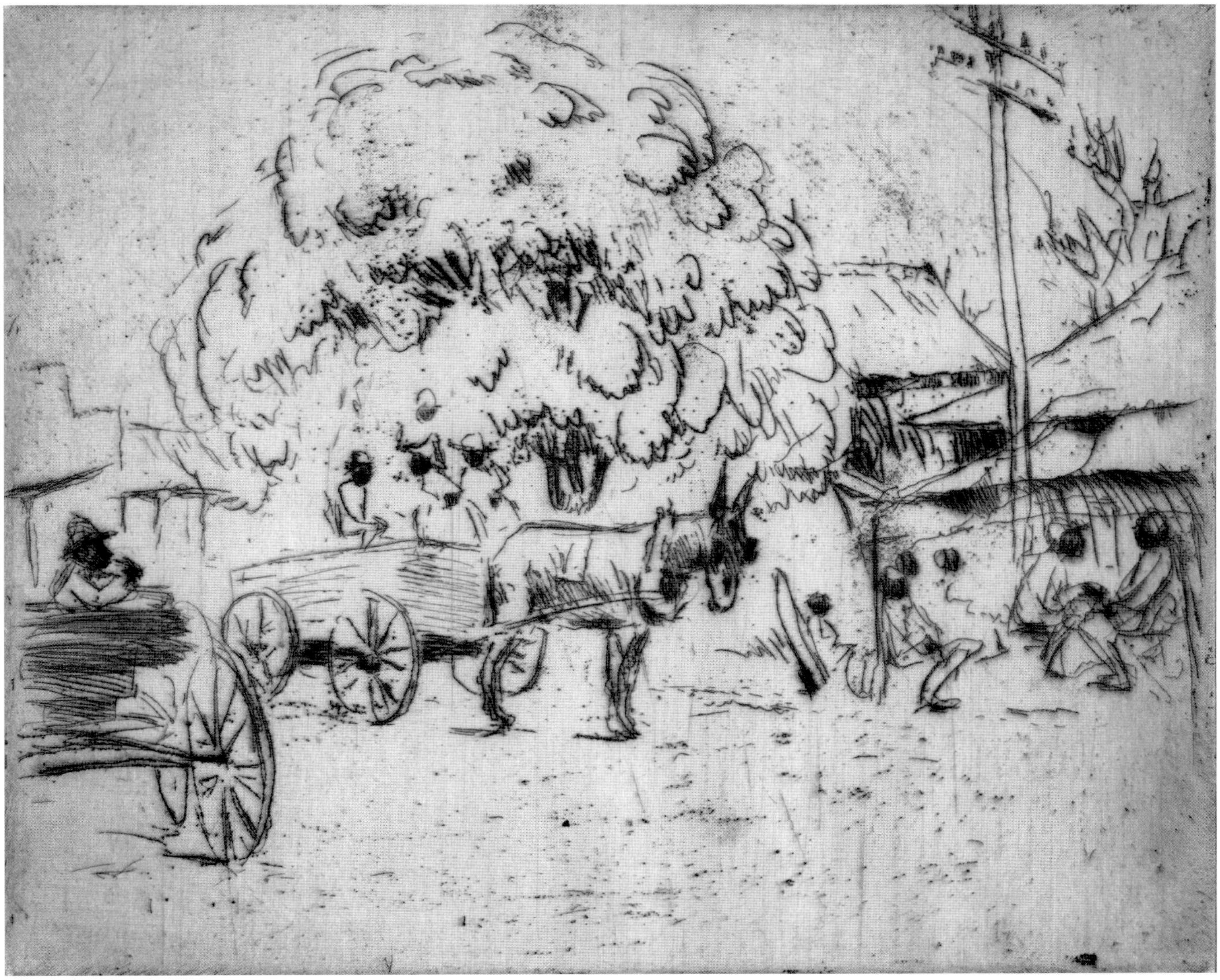

45. Anne Goldthwaite, *Street in Boguehomo* [Boguehomme], etching, c. 1920, 6 x 7 ⅜ in., collection of Stephen Goldfarb.

Mildred Nungester (Wolfe) (b. 1912)

When she was three years old, Mildred Nungester moved with her family from Ohio to Decatur, Alabama, where she lived until she married in 1944. She studied art, her true love, at the Alabama College for Women in Montevallo (now University of Montevallo) but prepared herself to become a history teacher because her father thought artists could not earn a living. While teaching history in Alabama public schools, she began attending Dixie Art Colony summer sessions in 1935, where her instructor, Kelly Fitzpatrick, nurtured her talent in drawing and painting.[1]

When she went to the Art Students League in 1938, Nungester studied etching, aquatint, and lithography to save some money as she thought materials for printmaking would be less expensive than those for painting.[2] In 1942 she went to Colorado Springs Fine Art Center to earn an MFA, studying lithography with Lawrence Barrett and Adolf Dehn. She learned to print her own work in hopes of someday acquiring a press. When Nungester married Karl Wolfe, whom she met earlier at the Dixie Art Colony, she moved with him to Jackson, Mississippi, in 1945. She abandoned lithography because she could not afford the printing equipment or find anyone to print for her. Instead she began making color prints from linoleum blocks beginning around 1950 and printing them by hand.[3]

Many of Nungester's lithographs are based on her sketches of scenes she saw in Alabama, particularly in or near her home in Decatur or rural central Alabama, where the Dixie Art Colony was located. She often traveled by train and sketched views from train windows as well as in stations, where she spent hours waiting to board, and sketched to pass the time. Her lithograph *Station* is a composite composition made from various sketches, most of them done at the train station in her home town of Decatur.[4] Epitomized by the nun in the center of the composition who is too engrossed in her newspaper to notice those in close proximity to her, the scene reflects the anonymity associated with modern urban life as all the figures appear absorbed by their own private preoccupations.

Notes

1. See Williams, "Dixie Art Colony, 12–13; see also Elizabeth Wolfe, ed., *Mildred Nungester Wolfe,* introduction by Ellen Douglas, (Jackson: University Press of Mississippi, 2005).
2. Mildred Nungester Wolfe letter to author, April 22, 1998.
3. Wolfe interview with author, August 4, 1993.
4. Wolfe letter to author, March 24, 1996.

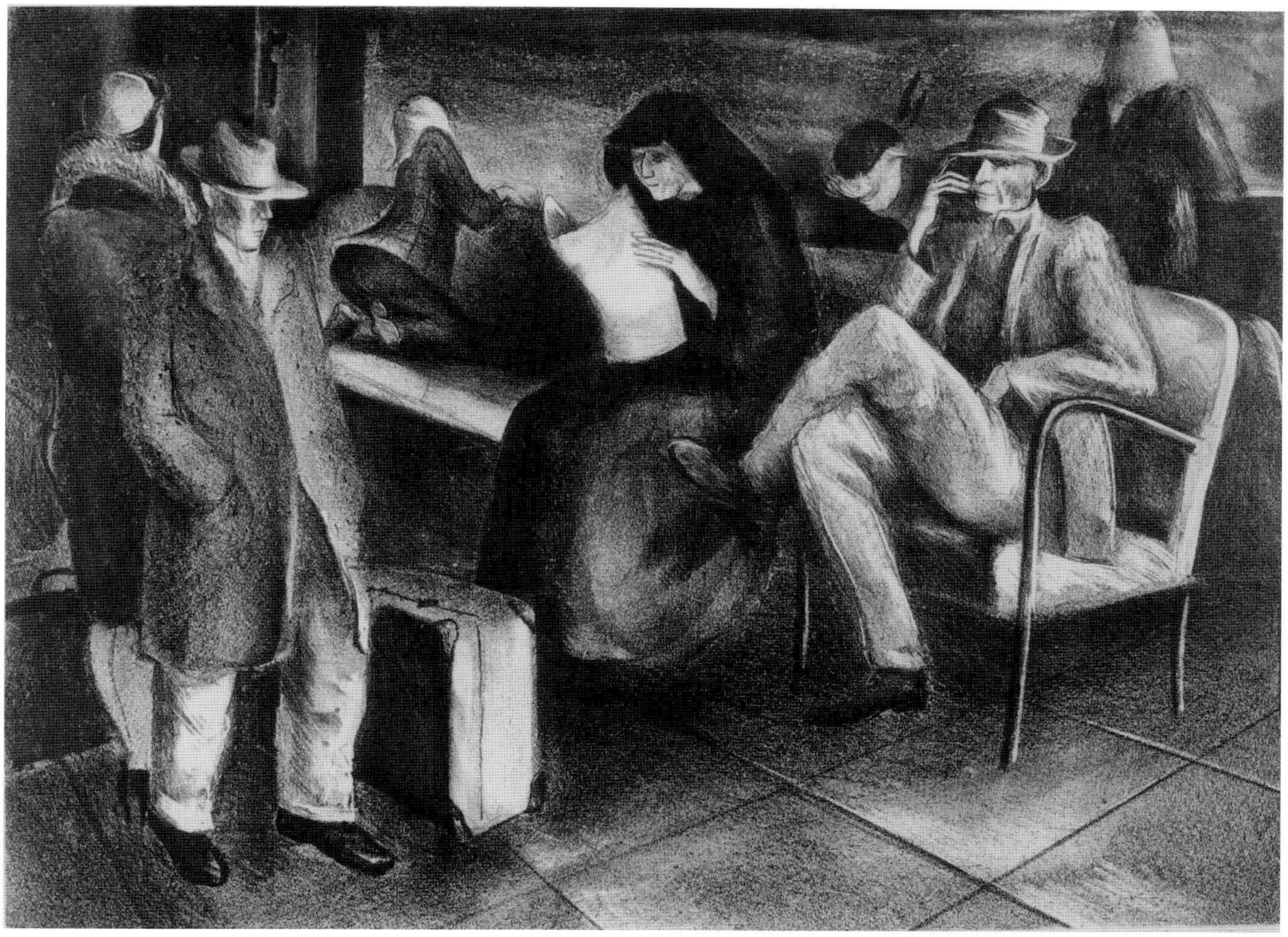

46. Mildred Nungester, *Station,* lithograph, 1943, 9 ¼ x 12 ⅞ in., courtesy of Mildred Nungester Wolfe and from the collection of Lynn Barstis Williams.

Elizabeth Catlett (b. 1915)

A native of Washington, DC, who has lived in Mexico since 1947, Elizabeth Catlett is rarely viewed as a southern artist. However, this acclaimed African American woman printmaker spent some early years of her career in the South. After graduating from Howard University in 1937, Catlett taught art for two years at a black high school in Durham, North Carolina, and supervised art programs for black elementary schools there as well. She then went on to the University of Iowa to earn an MFA in 1940, after which she headed the art department at Dillard University in New Orleans, remaining until 1942.[1] Catlett learned to make relief prints from James Lesesne Wells at Howard University. She was introduced to lithography, her other major print medium, at the Southside Community Art Center in Chicago in 1941 but perfected her skills when she studied under Harry Sternberg at the Art Students League in 1944. She received a Julius Rosenwald grant in 1945 and made a Black Woman Series in relief prints at the Taller de Gráfica Popular in Mexico City, where she went when her Rosenwald was renewed in 1946.[2] Catlett continued to make lithographs and relief prints in the following decades, achieving considerable recognition for her work.[3]

Catlett's sense of the injustice inflicted on African Americans was reinforced by her own experiences in New Orleans, to which one of the linoleum cuts in the Black Woman Series refers. In an interview Catlett recounted how she removed signs on city buses that restricted people of color, like that in the foreground of *I Have Special Reservations.* When Dillard students did the same and were arrested, Catlett contacted the NAACP to arrange for their legal defense.[4] The grim-faced woman in this linocut foreshadows Rosa Parks, whose refusal to give up her seat on a bus in Montgomery, Alabama, ignited a boycott of city buses in 1955. Other images in Catlett's early Black Woman Series suggest the inferior status and restricted opportunities that black women, like their male counterparts, suffered during the Jim Crow era of the South.

Notes

1. Phagan, "Tours and Visits of the South," 193.
2. Herzog, *Elizabeth Catlett,* 47.
3. See Jeanne Zeidler, ed., *Elizabeth Catlett: Works on Paper, 1944–1992* (Hampton, VA: Hampton University Museum, 1993), 6–14.
4. Herzog, *Elizabeth Catlett,* 24.

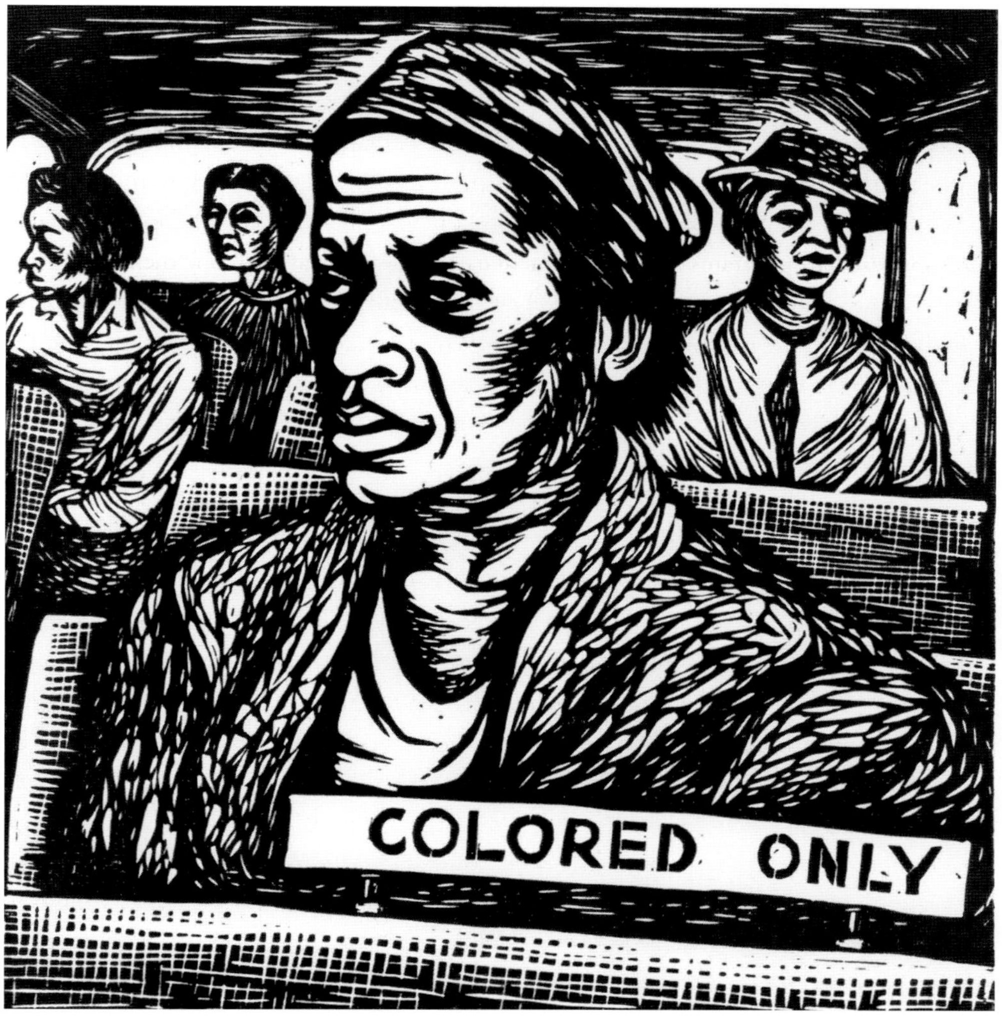

47. Elizabeth Catlett, *Black Women Series: I Have Special Reservations,* linoleum cut, 1946, 6 ¼ x 6 ¼ in., art © Elizabeth Catlett/Licensed by VAGA, New York, NY, and from the collection of the Hampton University Museum, Hampton, Virginia.

Homer Casteel (1919–1972)

Son of a prominent state official, his father having served as lieutenant governor of the state of Mississippi, Homer Casteel grew up in the Mississippi town of Canton. Like many artists, he began sketching at an early age and commenced formal art study through night classes at the Corcoran School of Art in Washington, DC, during the late 1930s. He graduated from the University of Mississippi in 1942, and then served in the Navy for the duration of World War II. After the war Casteel traveled in Europe and Mexico before going on to the Art Institute of Chicago from which he received a BFA in 1949, followed by an MFA in 1955. In 1956 he began teaching at Meridian Junior College (now Meridian Community College) in his home state and remained on the faculty until his early death at age fifty-three.[1]

Throughout his artistic career Homer Casteel had an abiding interest in the human figure. Early sketches of the black face in 1936 reveal an inclination to experiment. Casteel appears to have begun his printmaking career in etching shortly after World War II by modeling his own dour face. He progressed to other printmaking media, primarily relief and lithography, experimenting with the face, torso, and full figure. During these early years as a printmaker, Casteel took modernist liberties to simplify and distort proportions and positions of human anatomy as he moved further toward abstraction. The lithograph of a lynching scene shown here is one of his few early prints in which Casteel appears to have reflected his southern homeland and from a critical perspective that would have been daring for the time and place in which the work was created. Military service during the World War II as well as his travels abroad afterward likely fostered this viewpoint. Casteel creates a fresh rendition of a lynching scenario by softening edges and generalizing figures through abstraction. Through this stylistic strategy he points to shadowy circumstances, which usually surrounded such events to hide the identity of the perpetrators.

Notes

1. Black, *Art in Mississippi, 1720–1980,* 255–56; *Homer Casteel: Early Figurative Years* (Meridian, MS: Casteel Gallery, Meridian Community College, August 27–October 8, 1989), n.p.

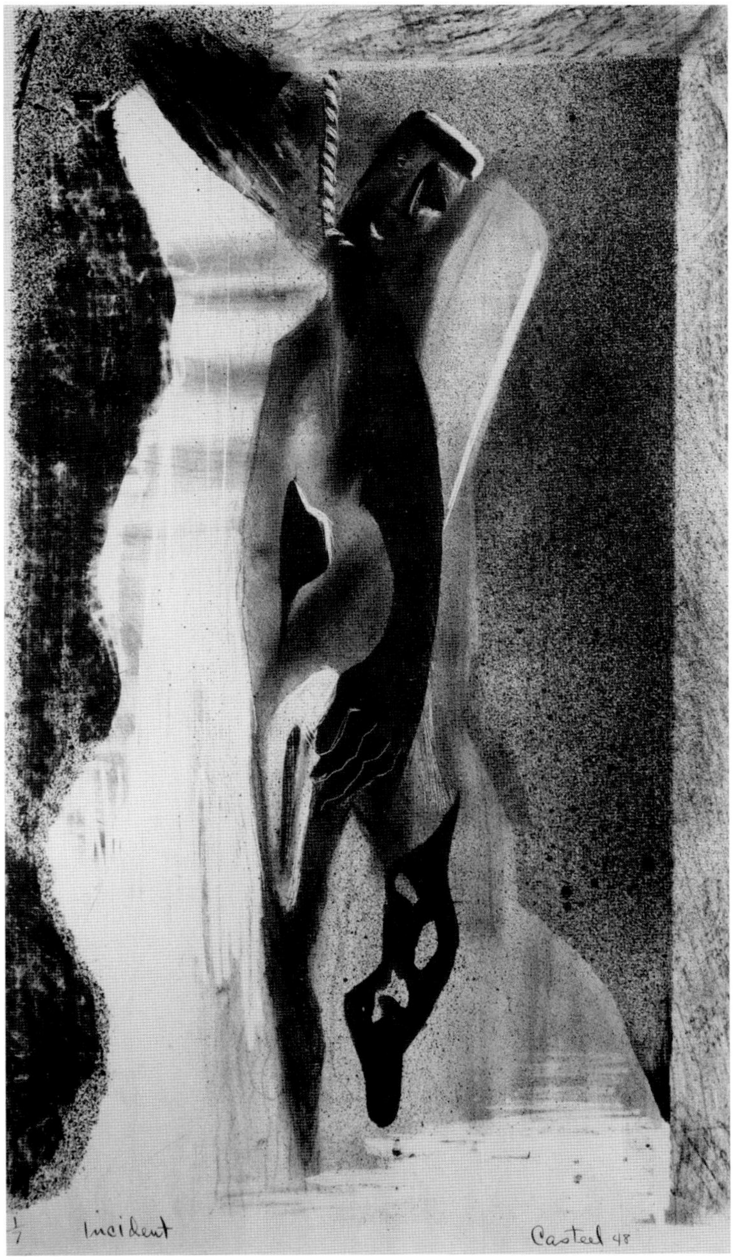

48. Homer Casteel, *Incident,* lithograph, 1948, 15 ¼ x 9 ⅛ in., courtesy of the Meridian Community College Foundation and from the Homer Casteel collection, Meridian Community College, Meridian, MS.

George Biddle (1885–1973)

George Biddle receives credit in American art history for urging his former schoolmate, President Franklin Delano Roosevelt, to create New Deal work programs for artists. Bearing genealogical connections to prominent Philadelphia and Virginia families, Biddle attended the prestigious private schools of Groton and Harvard. After earning a law degree from Harvard, he went to Paris to study art at the Académie Julien in 1911–12, continuing his studies at the Pennsylvania Academy of the Fine Arts from 1912 to 1914. Shortly after he made his first prints while studying with a professor Heinemann in Munich, Germany. After serving in France during World War I, Biddle settled in New York with a studio in Greenwich Village and residence at Croton-on-Hudson, but made numerous sketching trips elsewhere. He began to specialize in lithography, working with master printers, such as George Miller and Lawrence Barrett. In 1930 he traveled to Charleston and stayed long enough to sketch in the city and on Folly Beach. Three prints on southern themes resulted: A satirical etching titled *Folly Beach,* as well as two lithographs depicting both black and white lower classes: *Catfish Row* and *Poor Whites* respectively.[1]

The title of Biddle's most powerful southern print, *Alabama Code,* points to another southern location as the genesis of its imagery. According to his catalogue raisonné, Biddle considered the lithograph a political cartoon based upon the infamous Scottsboro Case. Although some critics point to historical figures in the case as models for the unflattering images of the large, white man holding a shrunken woman without a specific setting, it seems more likely the caricatured figures symbolically represent a specific brand of southern racism.[2] That racism entailed a pseudo-chivalric code that directed southern white males to overprotect southern white women, presumed sexually pure, against supposedly rapacious black males. The imagery is highly idiosyncratic in its treatment of a racial theme in prints.

Notes

1. George Biddle, *An American Artist's Story* (Boston: Little, Brown, 1939), passim; *George Biddle: An American Conscience: Prints and Unique Works on Paper from the 1920s to the 1960s,* Susan Teller Gallery, New York, December 3–30, 1999; Severens, *Charleston Renaissance,* 114–16, 189.
2. Martha Pennigar, *The Graphic Work of George Biddle with Catalogue Raisonné* (Washington, DC: The Corcoran Gallery, 1979), 7–8, 26–27; George Biddle papers, Smithsonian Archives of American Art, Reel #D127; Williams, "Images of Scottsboro," 55, 57.

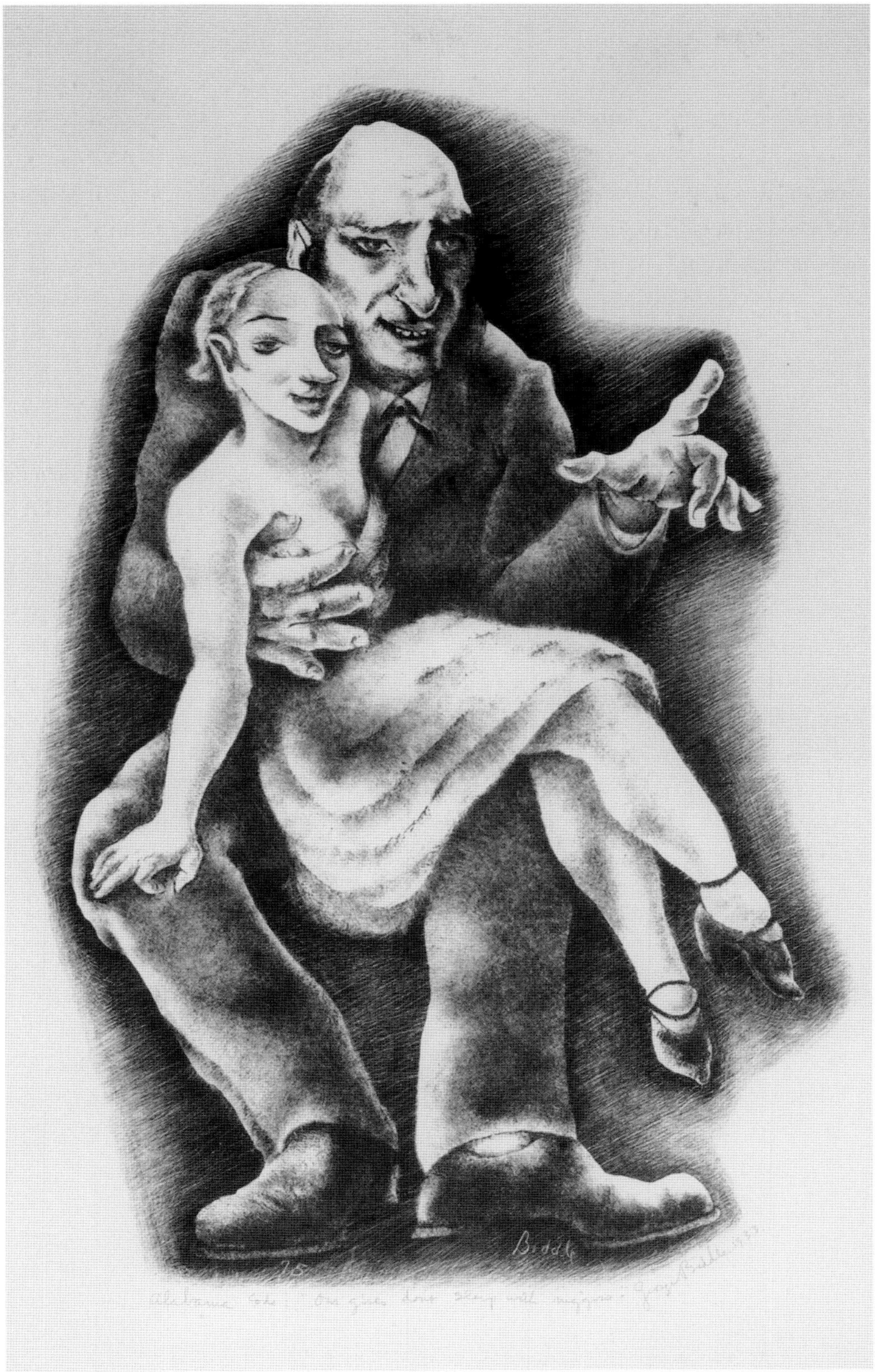

49. George Biddle, *Alabama Code—"Our Girls Don't Sleep with Niggers,"* lithograph, 1933, 13 3/8 x 9 1/2 in., courtesy of the Estate of the Artist and the Susan Teller Gallery, New York, and from the collection of Lynn Barstis Williams.

James Fowler Cooper (1907–1968)

After studying art with Elizabeth White at the University of South Carolina, from which he graduated in 1928, James Fowler Cooper went on to the Art Students League. In 1930 he returned home to Williamsburg County, South Carolina, where his family owned a farm, and began working at a bank in Kingstree, the county seat. He became interested in etching, due to its vogue in Charleston, teaching himself from books, though Alfred Hutty provided instruction as well. He used Elizabeth White's press until he was able to obtain his own. When his mother died in 1932, Cooper took over the family farm, where he set up an etching studio. He became proficient in all media of intaglio: aquatint, soft ground, and drypoint, in addition to etching. His subject matter ranged from people and architecture in rural Williamsburg County to the beach and coastal wildlife at nearby Pawley's Island, where he frequently visited and eventually built a second home. Cooper first exhibited his prints with the Southern Printmakers Society in 1936 and progressed to national shows in other parts of the country through 1942. He had a one-man show in New York in 1941, for which he received brief attention in the national media.[1]

Genre scenes featuring human figures of both races at work and play were fairly numerous in Cooper's etching oeuvre. He exhibited two genre etchings three times or more in national exhibitions: *Sausage Tomorrow* and *Saturday Night.* The latter was first exhibited in 1938 and honored in 1939 by acceptance in the World's Fair exhibition, which resulted in reproduction in the exhibition catalog.[2] Saturdays were market days in southern towns, when farmers came in their wagons, and later automobiles or trucks, to sell their produce, buy goods not produced on their farms, and to socialize. With chores done by sundown, they might devote the evening to socializing and other forms of amusement. In this distant, nocturnal view, Cooper manages to render a range of stance and gesture of a small crowd before a line of storefronts. A fine, delicate line suggests the close social interactions among black folk fostered by Saturday night in the small southern town.

Notes

1. Boyd Saunders and Stephanie Saunders, *The Etchings of James Fowler Cooper: An Illustrated Catalog* (Columbia: University of South Carolina Press, 1982), ix–xvii; Howard De Vree, "A Reviewer's Notebook," *New York Times,* April 27, 1941.
2. *American Art Today,* 259 (illustration 875).

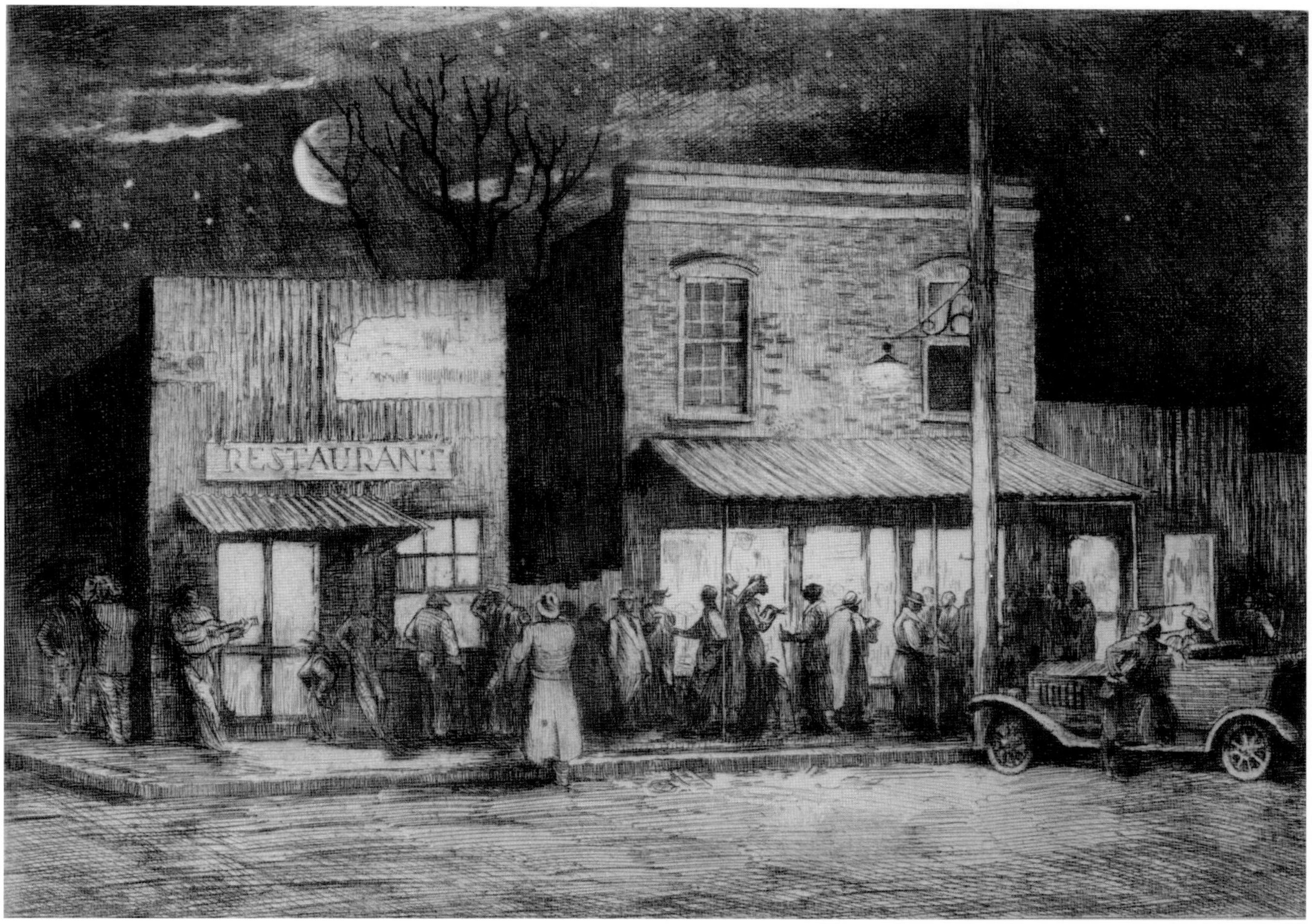

50. James Fowler Cooper, *Saturday Night,* etching, c. 1938, 5 ½ x 7 ⅞ in., courtesy of James F. Cooper Jr. and from the collection of Lynn Barstis Williams.

John McCrady (1911–1968)

John McCrady gained prominence as a painter of southern life, particularly of African American religious themes, based on several exhibitions in New York, one of which elicited criticism from the political left.[1] The son of an Episcopal minister, McCrady moved with his family from one parish to another in Mississippi and Louisiana, until they finally settled in Oxford, Mississippi. In 1932 he enrolled as a student at the Arts and Crafts Club in New Orleans after which he went to New York to study at the Art Students League on a scholarship. He returned to New Orleans in 1934, remaining there to work for the rest of his life.[2] His friend Caroline Durieux encouraged him to try lithography, and he made a small number of lithographs from 1941 to 1946, learning mostly on his own. He began by obtaining stones from Theodore Cuno in Philadelphia and shipping them back to Cuno to be printed. Associated American Artists asked to represent his work and printed five or six of his lithographs.[3] In 1947 McCrady also made a series of industrial scenes relating to oil refineries in Baton Rouge for Standard Oil Company of New Jersey.

A number of McCrady's lithographs reproduce his paintings done in the 1930s. He often depicted people, both white and black, having fun in demonstrative group interaction. Figures stride forth, swing limbs, and gesticulate with animation. *Carnival in New Orleans* highlights such group interaction and is distinctive for the fairly strong satire exemplified by the buxom, old woman with a mask, dancing in the line in the foreground. McCrady did an entire series of Mardi Gras drawings, many of which were reproduced for the book *Mardi Gras Day,* which he did with Caroline Durieux and Ralph Wickiser.[4] He is probably best known for his views of steamboats on the Mississippi, which have a quaint antiquarian touch, as well as that of a black spiritual, *Swing Low Sweet Chariot.*

Notes

1. "Loneliness Stirred His Brush to Activity," *Art Digest,* October 15, 1937, 12; Margaret Breuning, "John McCrady Interprets the South," *Art Digest,* June 1, 1946, 10; "A Reviewer's Notebook," *New York Times,* October 17, 1937. See Gambone, *Art and Popular Religion in Evangelical America,* 134–35, for a discussion of the leftist critique.
2. Keith Marshall, *John McCrady, 1911–1968* (New Orleans: New Orleans Museum of Art, 1975), 12–16.
3. Mary McCrady telephone interview with author, August 3, 1993.
4. Keith Marshall, *John McCrady* (New York: Henry Holt, 1948), 111.

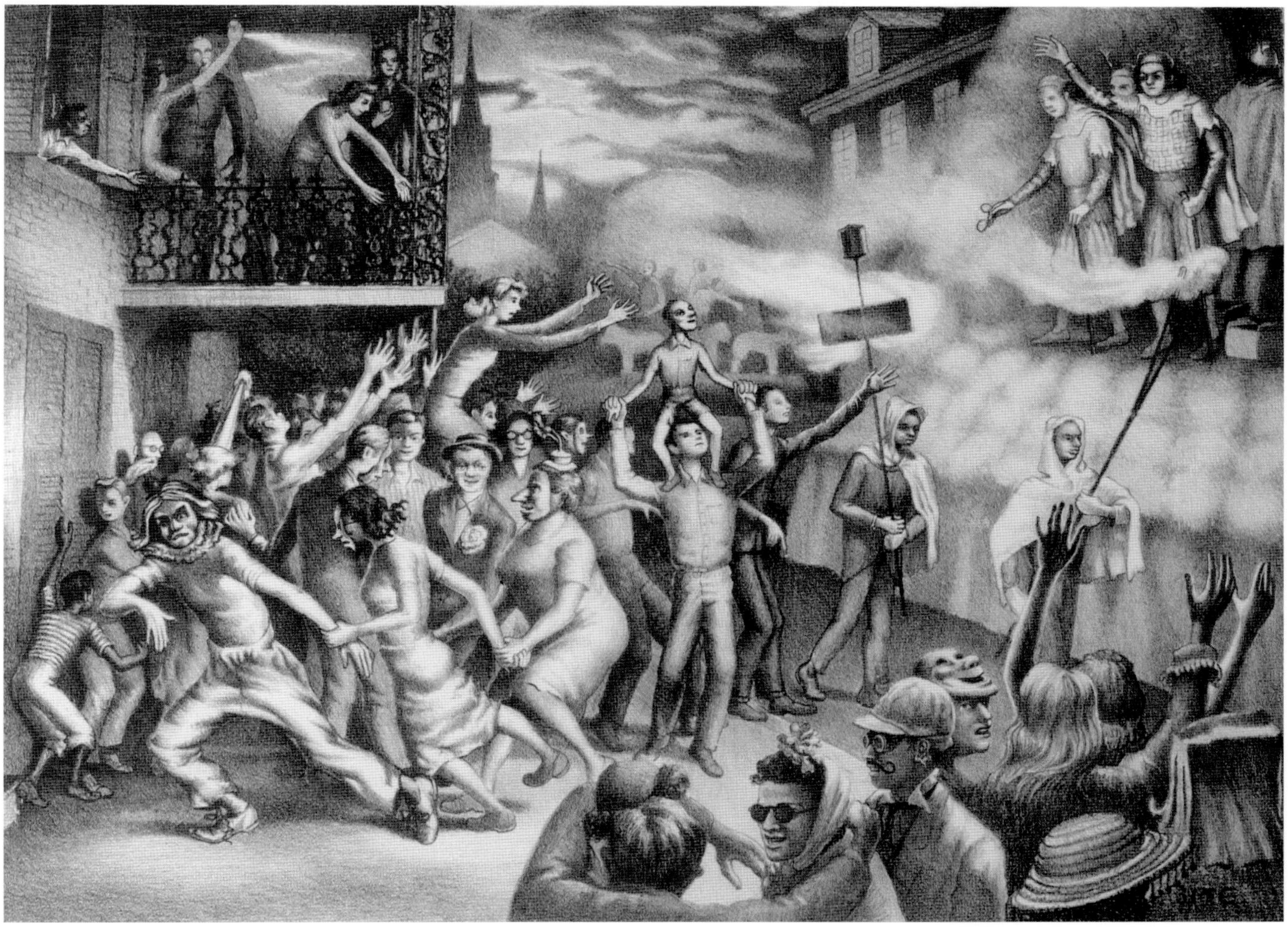

51. John McCrady, *Carnival in New Orleans,* lithograph, 1947, 8 ¾ x 12 ¼ in., collection of Lynn Barstis Williams.

Howard Norton Cook (1901–1980)

A Guggenheim fellowship allowed Howard Cook, a Massachusetts native, to realize a long-held desire to study the people of the South and portray them in their native setting. Beginning in 1924 Cook led an adventurous life traveling the far corners of the earth, while earning his living as an illustrator for various magazines. He studied etching from 1922 to 1923 with Joseph Pennell at the Art Students League and in 1929 learned lithography at the studio of Edmond Desjobert in Paris. A trip to New Orleans in 1926 resulted in his first print of the South, an etching of the French Quarter. When he traveled to New Mexico in 1926, he met his future wife, Barbara Latham, a fellow artist who was also a printmaker.[1] Cook received his first Guggenheim grant in 1932 to study in Taxco, Mexico. In 1934 Cook received a second Guggenheim, which granted the couple enough income to spend a year traveling from Virginia to Texas, remaining for appreciable amounts of time at various places along the way. Cook stated his objective as seeking the character of representative individuals influenced by social station and environment.[2] He made a large number of Conté crayon drawings of his observations on the journey, and a small number of lithographs, wood engravings, and aquatints resulted from them.[3]

In the winter of 1937, the Weyhe Gallery in New York exhibited the drawings and prints from his journey. Cook began publicizing his prints several months before the exhibition opened by publishing reproductions in various art periodicals. In his commentary supplied for the show, Cook said he found "a primitive, pre-industrial era" in the Cumberland mountains with "self reliant, fiercely independent mountaineers," along with "warm, sunny cotton fields of Alabama, its Negro rituals, agricultural exuberance and hillbillies."[4] *Fiddler's Contest* was among Cook's most reproduced prints of the South.[5] He attended a musical competition in Brookwood, Alabama, which he later described as "animated singing of folk-songs, ballads, dance jigs and the . . . feverish sawing of violins, guitar twanging" on a platform in the school assembly hall.[6] He made a colored, Conté crayon drawing as well as a lithograph from the event. His symmetrical, frontal composition structured on right angles for an ensemble of one fiddler with two guitar players suggests a more restrained, methodical approach to the music. Lines formed from strong tonal contrast sweep through drapery to create rhythmic patterns that emphasize legs thumping in time with the music.

Notes

1. Duffy and Duffy, *Graphic Work of Howard Cook,* 15–19.
2. "South by Southwest," *New York Times,* February 14, 1937.
3. Robert L. Gambone, "Howard Cook: From Drawings to Frescoes," *Bulletin: Georgia Museum of Art* 14 (Spring 1989): 3–4. A comparable study of Latham's prints has not been published, but evidence points to three wood engravings of the South. One is *North Carolina Mountain Woman,* another bears the title *Negro Group,* and yet another is a Texas scene.
4. "Critics Note Native Flavor in Cook's Prints," *Art Digest,* March 1, 1937, 24.
5. Reproductions appeared in *Parnassus,* February 1937, 19; *Art Digest,* March 1, 1937, 24; and *Magazine of Art,* March 1937, 180. Only *Southern Mountaineer* appeared as often during the 1930s in art periodicals.
6. Duffy and Duffy, *Graphic Work of Howard Cook,* 135.

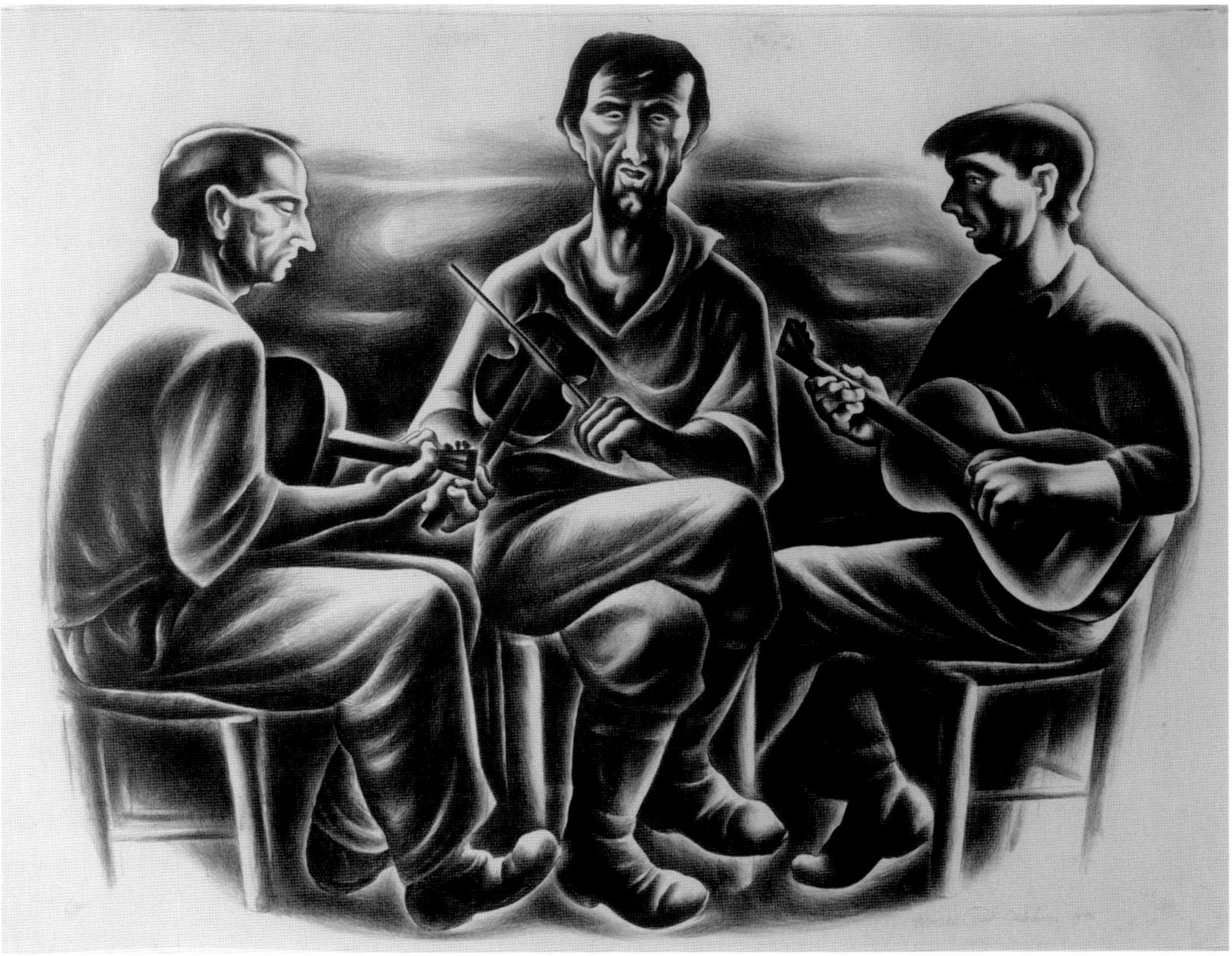

52. Howard Cook, *Fiddler's Contest,* lithograph, 1935, 14 ⅛ x 17 ¾ in., courtesy of Betty and Douglas Duffy and from the collection of Lynn Barstis Williams.

Palmer Schoppe (1912–2001)

Born in Wood Cross, Utah, Palmer Schoppe moved to Santa Monica, California, with his family in 1920 when he was eight years old. Inspired by a high school art teacher who encouraged a career in art, he enrolled at UCLA after graduating from high school in 1929. Disappointed because the university had no art department, he left after the first year. He signed up with the Merchant Marine and left San Francisco on a freighter bound for Australia and the South Seas. In 1931 Schoppe enrolled in the Yale University School of Fine Arts but, dissatisfied with its traditional art training, left after only a semester and headed to New York. There he enrolled at the Art Students League and studied with Thomas Hart Benton and Jean Charlot. When his studies were finished in 1934, he decided to return home to California via the South that included stops in Charleston and New Orleans.[1]

According to an interview he later gave, the cold gloomy weather in the Northeast motivated him to choose a southern route more than a desire to depict the South. He traveled to Charleston and "fell in love with the city." Attending a performance of black choral groups, Schoppe met the woman who coordinated the event; she invited him and a friend to visit her cabbage farm on Wadmalaw Island, where Schoppe encountered a Gullah community. He sketched its members as they went about their daily lives. After he returned to Los Angeles, he worked with Lynton Kistler, an important California printer for artists, on a portfolio of eleven lithographs based upon his sketches and memories.[2]

Most of the lithographs in Schoppe's *Carolina Low Country Portfolio* present black figures engaged in activities that reflect traditional folkways. He depicts them as bony and muscular, vigorous and animated. Limbs and facial expressions are sometimes exaggerated to emphasize the physical and spiritual energy he saw in the Gullah folk. *Grapevine Twist,* a nocturnal scene before a cabin, reflects Schoppe's interest in African American music, which he discovered at clubs in New York.[3] Here he shows the communal nature of Gullah life as young and old join in to dance or clap to the rhythm of the drums.

Notes

1. "An Interview with California Artist Palmer Schoppe," Stary-Sheets Gallery, Irvine, CA, summer 1993; "Palmer Schoppe: Watercolors, Lithographs and Drawings: 1930s–1960s," Tobey Moss Gallery, Los Angeles, CA, July 15, 1993; "Palmer Schoppe: Good Vibes, Paintings, Lithographs, Drawings, 1930s to 1990s," Tobey Moss Gallery, Los Angeles, CA, January/February 1997.
2. Severens, *Charleston Renaissance,* 116–20.
3. "Palmer Schoppe Rhythms and Jazz at Tobey Moss Los Angeles," *Journal of the Print World* 8 (Fall 1985): 1.

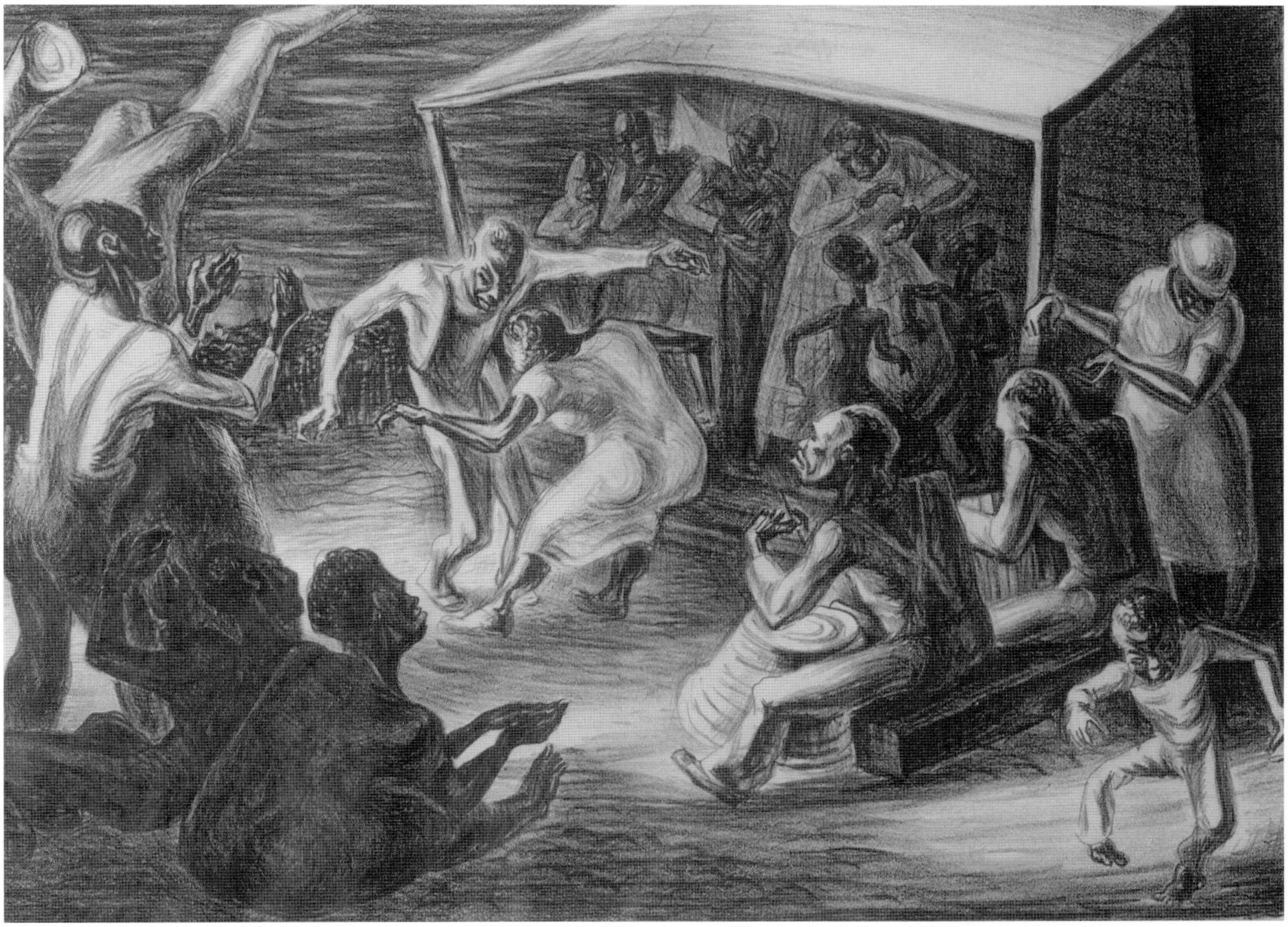

53. Palmer Schoppe, *Grapevine Twist,* lithograph, 1935, 9 x 12 ⅞ in., collection of Lynn Barstis Williams.

Polly Knipp Hill (1900–1990)

Polly Knipp received a BA in art from Syracuse University and soon after married George Snow Hill, a fellow art student. In 1922 the couple traveled to Paris. Encouraged by her husband, Polly studied etching at the Academy Colarossi, where she made numerous prints. The Hills returned to New York in 1927, and there they established a studio. Three years later they moved to St. Petersburg, Florida, although, for many years, they may have lived there only in the winters. In her Florida studio Polly Hill had her own etching press. In addition to etching and aquatint, she produced a number of small drypoints using a roulette.[1] In the late 1940s the Hills purchased a house in Highlands, North Carolina, where they also had studios, and spent six months of the year there, undoubtedly summers. In her later years Hill watercolored some of her prints and also authorized additional editions from some plates.[2]

To a great extent Polly Hill focused on a communal, traditional world showing a group of people involved in some joint activity. Frequently this was a world of women with children nearby, engaged in such activities as harvesting cherries, placing pies in a cold cellar, shaking a cat on a quilt, or birthing a child. Such is the case with *June Flood in Arcadia,* whose high viewpoint encompasses numerous small figure groups, mostly children, who are taking advantage of a minor disaster by turning a flooded yard in front of a cottage into a wading pool, while adults look on or visit. The setting is undoubtedly Arcadia, Florida, about seventy-five miles southeast of St. Petersburg. Other genre scenes by Hill depict crowds in public spaces, such as beaches or parks suggesting the land of leisure, which Florida was becoming, or life in the mountain South, which she probably knew from her second home in North Carolina. She also made simple landscape etchings featuring southern trees and other vegetation on riverbanks.

Notes

1. "Polly Knipp Hill," unpublished typescript; Polly Knipp Hill file, Museum of Fine Arts, St. Petersburg, FL; Ellen Fulton, "Polly Knipp Hill's Already at Work on New Etching of Typical St. Petersburg Scene," *St. Petersburg Times,* June 4, 1944.
2. Enee Abelman e-mail to author, July 26, 2000.

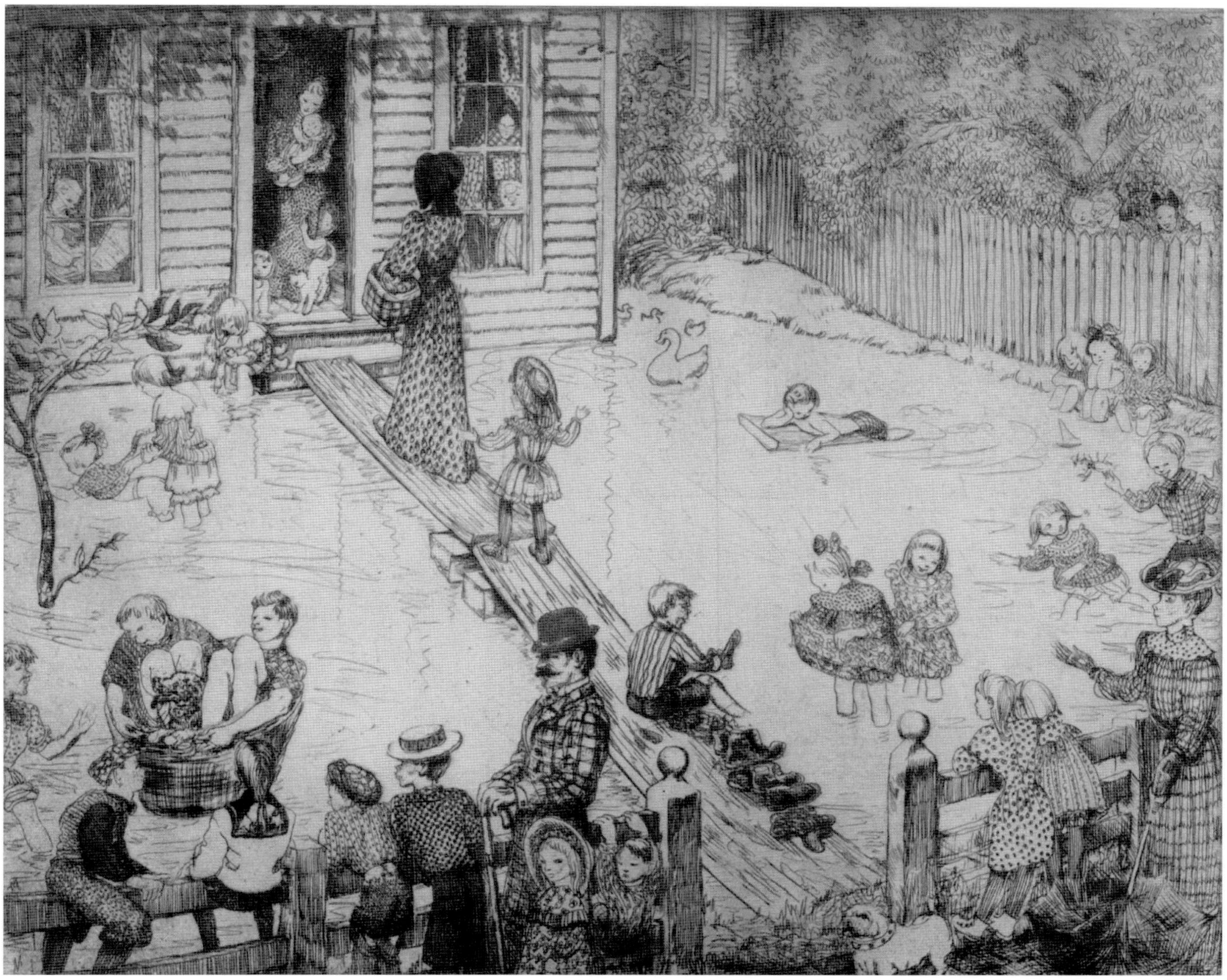

54. Polly Knipp Hill, *June Flood in Arcadia,* etching, 8 ⅝ x 10 ⅝ in., courtesy of Richard A. Beach and from the collection of Lynn Barstis Williams.

(William Kay) Kent Hagerman (1893–1978)

Kent Hagerman became a celebrated commercial etcher in his adopted Florida homeland of Lakeland. Born in Ohio to a father who was a minister-turned-lawyer, his family moved from place to place. Hagerman attended the Cleveland Institute of Art from 1913 to 1915. He then began a career as a designer for a lighting fixture firm until the military demanded his service in World War I. Shipped to France where he studied at the Sorbonne and visited museums during leave, he inhaled gas during combat and was sent to Denver, Colorado, to recuperate in a veterans' hospital. Because his lungs could not tolerate the fumes from paint, Hagerman took up etching and sculpture as substitutes for painting. After the war he and his brother established a commercial engraving company in Denver, specializing in newspaper and magazine illustration.

Looking for a location for winter vacations, Hagerman considered Lakeland, Florida, where his family had visited during his youth. The Lakeland Chamber of Commerce convinced him of the city's merits, so Hagerman and his wife arrived for a visit in 1933 and continued to visit in subsequent years. In 1936 the couple decided to make Lakeland their permanent home. Setting up a studio above his garage, Hagerman continued his commercial art business, making advertisements for magazines and etchings for various companies. He also produced etchings for his personal pleasure, which he gave as gifts to friends and customers. Identifying himself primarily as a commercial artist, he never accepted an invitation for a solo exhibition during his lifetime.[1] Signatures on his etchings evolved from William Kay Hagerman to Kay Hagerman to Kent Hagerman in the 1940s.

Some of Hagerman's etchings of Florida present urban architectural views, but the most interesting depict local industries as well as Florida pastimes. He made a series on the production of cypress lumber for a company in Jacksonville and another on shipbuilding for a firm in Tampa. *Florida Tusker* is part of a series emphasizing Florida sports, which he completed for the Florida Electric Supply Company to give as Christmas gifts to their customers and promote Florida as the land of leisure in the mid-1940s. Hagerman deeply etches the animals in a dramatic confrontation in the foreground while a diagonal of foliage sweeps to the hunters lightly etched in the background, ready to fire. The card, which accompanied *Florida Tusker,* noted that wild hogs are legal game in three areas of the state and any hunter who could snag these "mean, cantankerous devils" could be "justifiably proud." Others etchings in this series depict bear hunting, football, horse racing, and water skiing.

Notes

1. Ruth Daughtrey, "Kent Hagerman, Etcher Extraordinary, among Coterie of Nationally Famous Lakelanders," *Lakeland Ledger,* February 8, 1948; Ruth Daughtrey, "Artist Backs Chamber Drive," n.d.; "Etchings of Florida by Kent Hagerman, 1893–1978"; "The Work of Wm. Kay Hagerman," December 26, 1941; Jeff Kline, "Kent Hagerman's Life Has Revolved around Art," *Lakeland Ledger,* March 12, 1975. Kent Hagerman file, Polk Museum of Art.

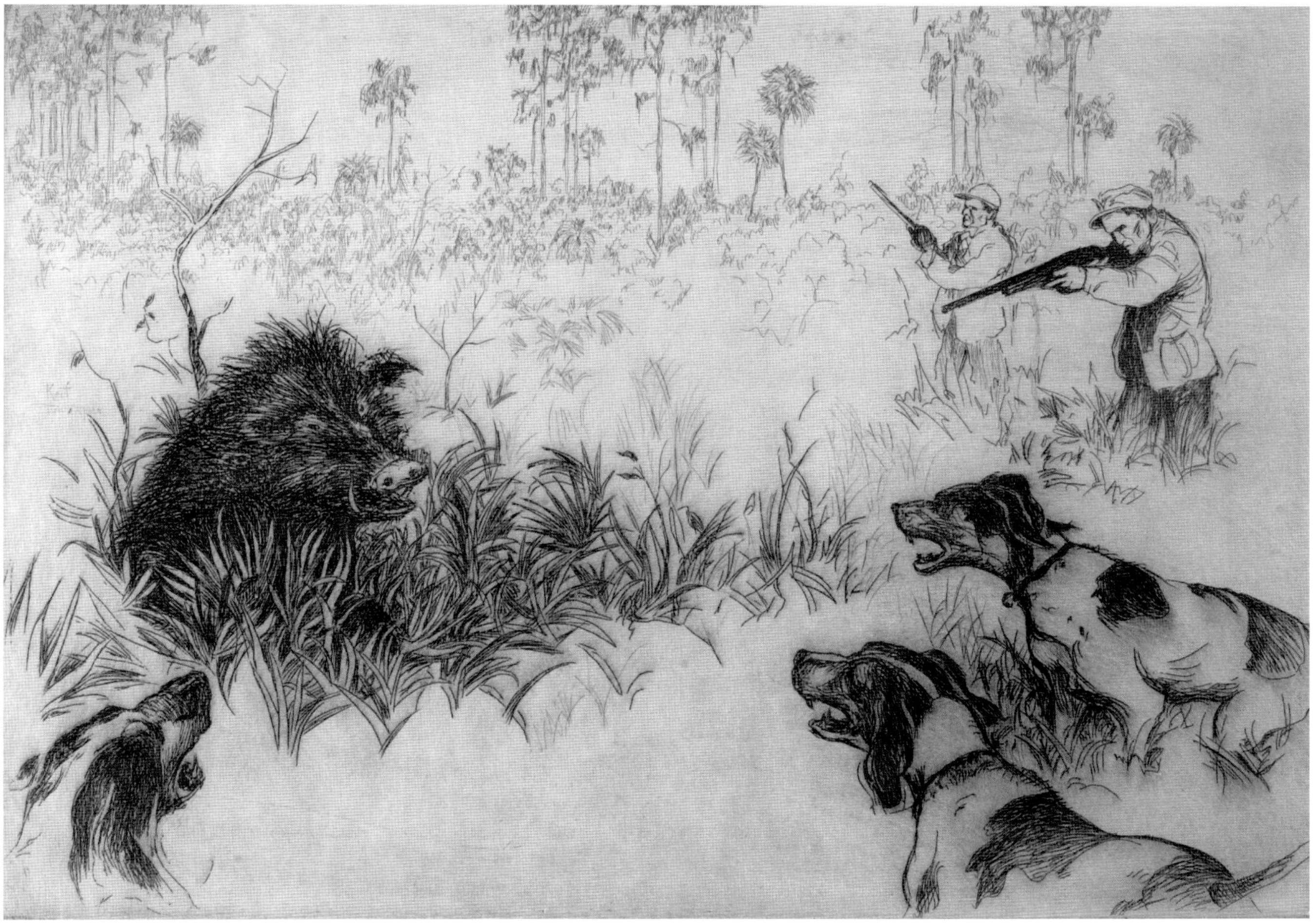

55. Kent Hagerman, *Florida Tusker,* etching, c. 1945, 6 ⅝ x 9 ½ in., collection of Lynn Barstis Williams.

Raymond Steth (1916–1997)

Although he was born near Norfolk, Virginia, Raymond Steth spent much of his early childhood working on a large farm, which his uncle operated as a sharecropper near Rocky Mount, North Carolina, his mother's family home. In 1925, he moved to Philadelphia and joined relatives in an ethnically diverse neighborhood. Attending public school in Philadelphia, he often drew during his classes, sometimes to the annoyance of his teachers. He had his first art training at the Graphic Sketch Club, and, when he reached high school, he was among those recognized as artistically talented and was encouraged to attend extension classes during evenings. When his mother returned to live with her family in North Carolina for four or five years during the 1930s, Steth renewed his contact with the South as he traveled there to visit her often.

After working as a vaudeville sign painter, Steth joined the Philadelphia WPA in 1939 and was placed in the Graphic Arts Division due to the quality of his drawings. Working as an apprentice under the supervision of Michael Gallagher, he learned lithography as well as intaglio processes of etching and aquatint. He also worked with Dox Thrash and utilized the carborundum print process Thrash and Gallagher pioneered. Steth bought his own lithography press for an independent studio he shared with Claude Clark. Most of his prints were lithographs and included a wide variety of images, many reflecting industrial life in Philadelphia. Serving in the Navy during World War II, he headed a graphic arts unit that made silkscreen posters; he resumed lithography after the war.[1]

Steth liked to draw groups of people engaged in various activities. He made only a small number of prints, mostly lithographs, which reflected his southern background, but his images of southern life are distinctive for prints of the era. *Despair, Apostolic* and *Heaven on a Mule* reflected southern, black religious experience. *Southern Barbeque,* a nocturnal view of a hog split open and cooking over an open pit, is a rare view of a traditional southern country feast in which blacks usually served as cooks. Steth made this lithograph from a drawing; the view reflected his close-knit, extended family on a farm in the South.[2] It is one of the few prints by a black artist before 1950 whose title specifies a specifically southern geographic setting.

Notes

1. Raymond Steth interview by Marge Kline, April 28, 1990, 1–78. Raymond Steth papers, Smithsonian Archives of American Art, Reel #4780.
2. Steth interview by Kline, 10–11; Gary D. Ford, "Barbeque," *Encyclopedia of Southern Culture,* 676.

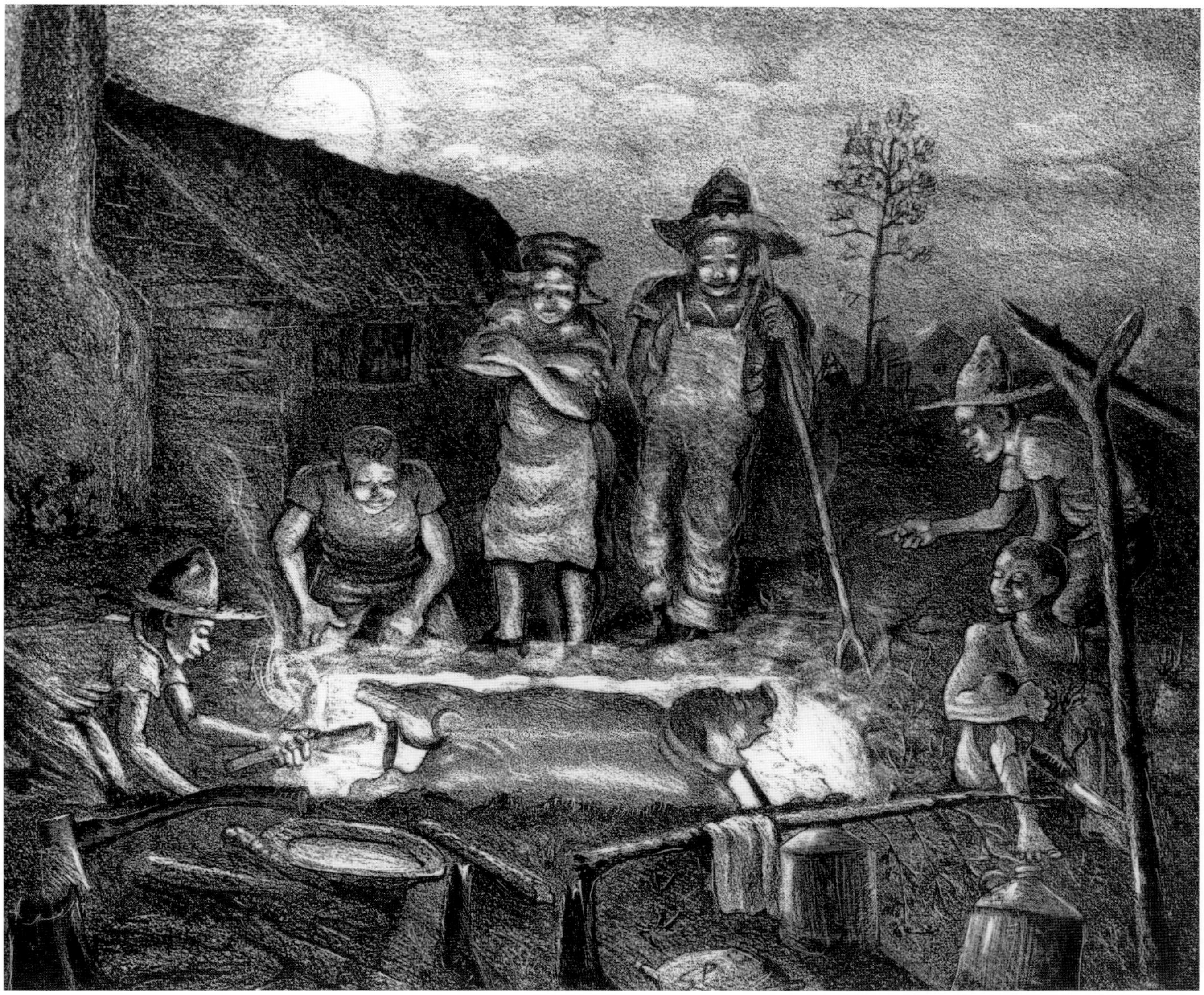

56. Raymond Steth, *Southern Barbeque,* lithograph, c. 1940, 8 x 9 ⅞ in., collection of the Saint Louis Art Museum; gift of Federal Works Agency, Works Projects Administration.

Frank Hartley Anderson (1890–1947) and Martha Fort Anderson (1885–1968)

A Boston native, Frank Hartley Anderson practiced his varied artistic talents in Birmingham, Alabama. After studies at the Art Institute of Chicago and Harvard with Henry Vincent Hubbard and Warren Manning, Anderson came to Birmingham in 1909 to assist in laying out the district of Fairfield and to develop the city's master plan. Remaining to work as an architect and landscape designer, he married Martha Fort, the first art instructor at the University of Alabama, in 1923. By 1930 he was making woodcuts and had a gallery on the first floor of their home, which he designed and where he sold his own work and that of other artists.[1]

When the Depression eliminated opportunities for architectural work in Birmingham, Anderson signed up with the Public Works of Art Program on which he made twenty-three woodcuts. A number illustrated themes in American history, probably destined for the public schools. Among the others were genre scenes, a number of which were designed with the aid of his wife Martha. The best among all these have bold design with strong contrast in black and white.[2] He entered several depicting African American experience in national shows. *Negro Preachin'* won first prize at a national exhibition of American block prints in 1935—the same year Anderson organized the Southern Printmakers Society for which he served as secretary.

Anderson offered *Church Supper,* his best-known woodcut, as the first presentation print for the first Southern Printmakers rotary exhibition. Martha designed the composition using their cook as a model for three female figures. Frank had already sketched in a figure for the preacher when Martha arrived home with a better version from her sketch of a black preacher made while riding a streetcar.[3] The print won first prize in the Southern States Art League annual in 1937. The American Society of Etchers chose it for an international exhibition sent to Scandinavian countries, while the New York Public Library selected it for purchase among the best prints of the year. The composition represents the Andersons' highest achievement for its sensitive portrayal of African American figures in the foreground who spar in serious conversation, even debate, through their eating utensils.

Notes

1. "Frank Hartley Anderson," *Journal of the Birmingham Historical Association* 7, no. 3–4 (November 1982): 37; Williams, "An Artistic Blend, Frank and Martha Anderson," 14–23.
2. Lucia Giddens, "Woodcut by Birmingham Artist Wins First Prize," *Birmingham Post,* January 21, 1935; Martha Prince telephone interview with author, March 1997; Jordan Prince letter to author, November 25, 2000.
3. Lucia Giddens, "Cosmopolitan Group Used as Models for Art Exhibit," *Birmingham Post,* March 13, 1935.

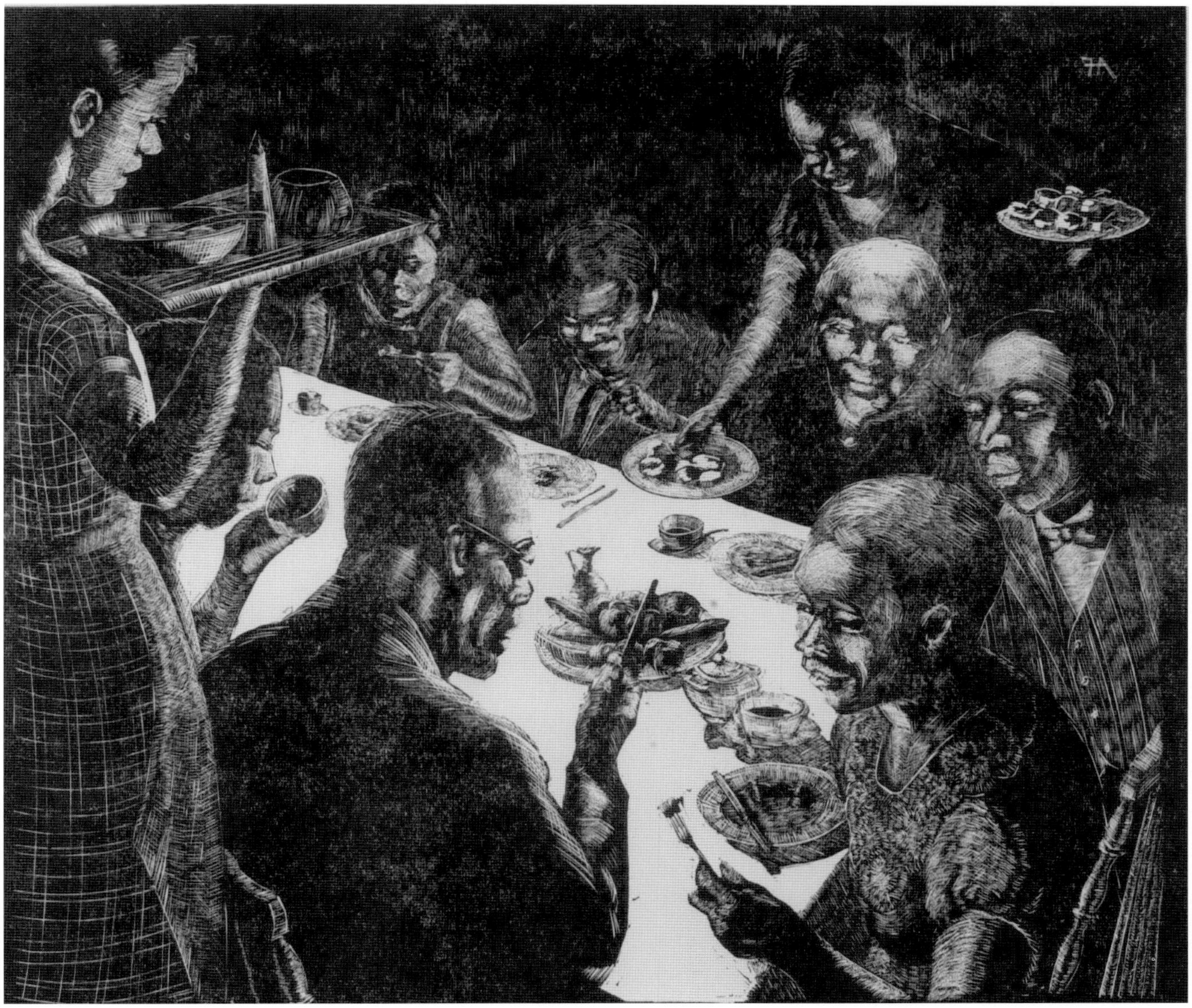

57. Frank Hartley Anderson, *Church Supper,* wood engraving, c. 1934, 10 ½ x 12 ⅜ in., courtesy of the Martha Prince Estate and from the collection of Lynn Barstis Williams.

Frank Besedick (1913–1987)

Eatonville, Florida, the oldest all-black community in the United States, is generally associated with Zora Neale Hurston, who grew up there and made the town the imaginative setting for her fiction. Eatonville was also the setting for a series of prints by Cincinnati artist Frank Besedick, who visited the community when he was a resident artist at the Maitland Art Center in nearby Orlando from 1940 to 1941.

Besedick grew up in Hamilton, Ohio. Through a scholarship he won from *Scholastic Magazine,* he studied at the Vesper George School of Art in Boston from 1933 to 1936, after which he was awarded a Tiffany Foundation scholarship for the academic year of 1936–37. From 1938 to 1939 he made etchings and worked in lithography on the WPA/FAP in New York City, followed by studies at the National Academy of Design in 1940.[1] Ernest Roth, an etcher and friend of André Smith, who directed the Maitland Art Center, recommended Besedick for an appointment at Maitland, where he experimented with watercolor and worked in all three major print media: etching, woodcut, and lithography.[2] After serving in the military during World War II, Besedick returned to Cincinnati.

In many of his prints of Eatonville and elsewhere, Besedick explored how groups of people interact spontaneously and simultaneously. In the etching *Eatonville on Sunday,* we see a number of different social interactions in the yard before a church. The most prominent group standing in the foreground appear engaged in conversation and display the sense of community and sociability a church ideally fosters. Other small groups of people display more distinctive forms of sociability: greeting each other through hand gestures, guiding a child, and examining an object while seated together under a tree. Besedick emphasizes that his Eatonville figures are African American through facial physiognomy, but he also suggests middle-class status through their Sunday attire in this scene. Although Besedick experimented with printmaking at Maitland, his style remained firmly traditional and conservative, as in his Eatonville etchings.

Notes

1. *The Federal Art Project,* 28; Beall, *American Prints in the Library of Congress,* 66–67.
2. Katherine Besedick letter to author, June 13, 1994.

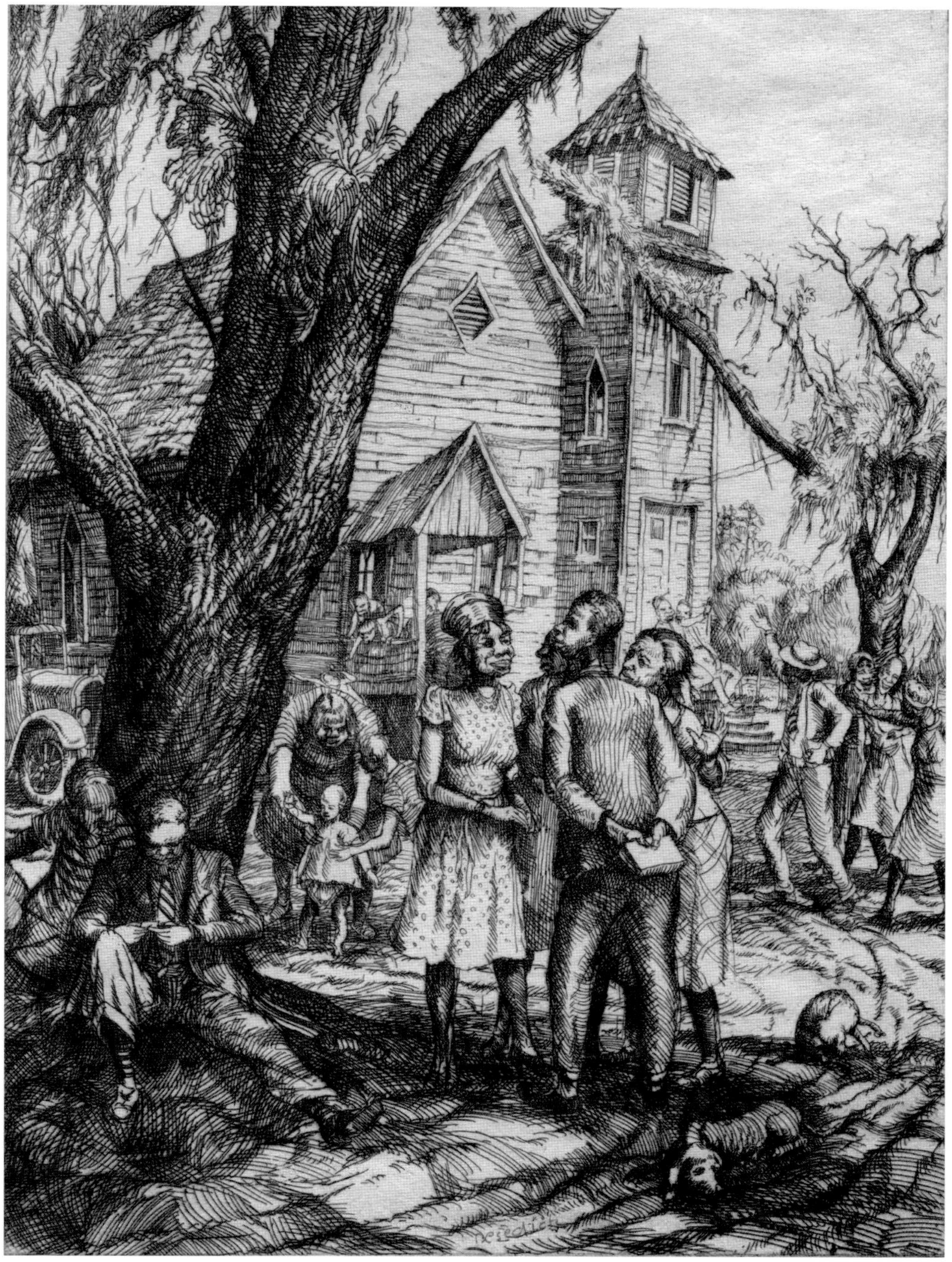

58. Frank Besedick, *Eatonville on Sunday,* etching, c. 1941, 7 ⅞ x 6 ⅜ in., courtesy of Katherine Besedick and from the collection of Lynn Barstis Williams.

Prentiss Hottel Taylor (1907–1991)

Born and raised in Washington, DC, Prentiss Taylor studied etching at the Art Students League under Anne Goldthwaite and progressed to lithography around 1930. Shortly after, he became friends with black writer Langston Hughes through a mutual friend, Carl Van Vechten. Soon after their friendship began, the Scottsboro case erupted in the national media, catapulting southern racism to artistic attention. Taylor and Hughes joined the throng of artists and writers who launched a defense of the nine accused black youths through their art. They collaborated to produce a booklet titled *Scottsboro Limited,* for which Taylor contributed four lithographs to illustrate a skit and three short poems by Hughes. They published the book in 1932 and donated profits from the sale to the Scottsboro defense effort.[1]

The second phase of Taylor's southern subjects began soon thereafter when he attended the MacDowell Art Colony in New Hampshire in 1932 and met Josephine Pinckney, a Charleston author who invited him to Charleston. Taylor arrived in May 1933 and stayed through the summer.[2] In 1934 he made lithographs from his sketches on the Public Works of Art Project (PWAP) in New York. Taylor focused on the black community of Charleston, and three of his lithographs depict their religious services. In 1940 he added to this series exploring black religious expression with *"—In Whom I Am Well Pleased,"* which was also based on his experiences in Charleston.[3] The title is a quotation from the Bible (Mark 1:11) where the heavens open and the spirit like a dove descends, as we see in the lithograph. The scene typifies Taylor's portrayal of ecstatic religious expression through outstretched arms in a wide "U" shape. Such figuration is also evident in his views of interior church services as well as several of the lithographs in the Scottsboro series. In this baptism scene, concentric circles formed by outstretched arms, branching trees, and arcs in the sky suggest the close-knit African American community supporting the initiate and the holy spirit with which that community unites.

Notes

1. See Bruce Kellner, "Working Friendship: A Harlem Renaissance Footnote," in Ingrid Rose and Roderick S. Quiroz, *Lithographs of Prentiss Taylor: A Catalogue Raisonné,* ed. Patrice La Liberté, 11–18 (Bronx, NY: Fordham University Press, 1996), for a detailed examination of their collaboration; for a broad examination of Scottsboro art see Williams, "Images of Scottsboro," 50–67.
2. Severens, *Charleston Renaissance,* 76.
3. Rose and Quiroz, *Lithographs of Prentiss Taylor,* 94.

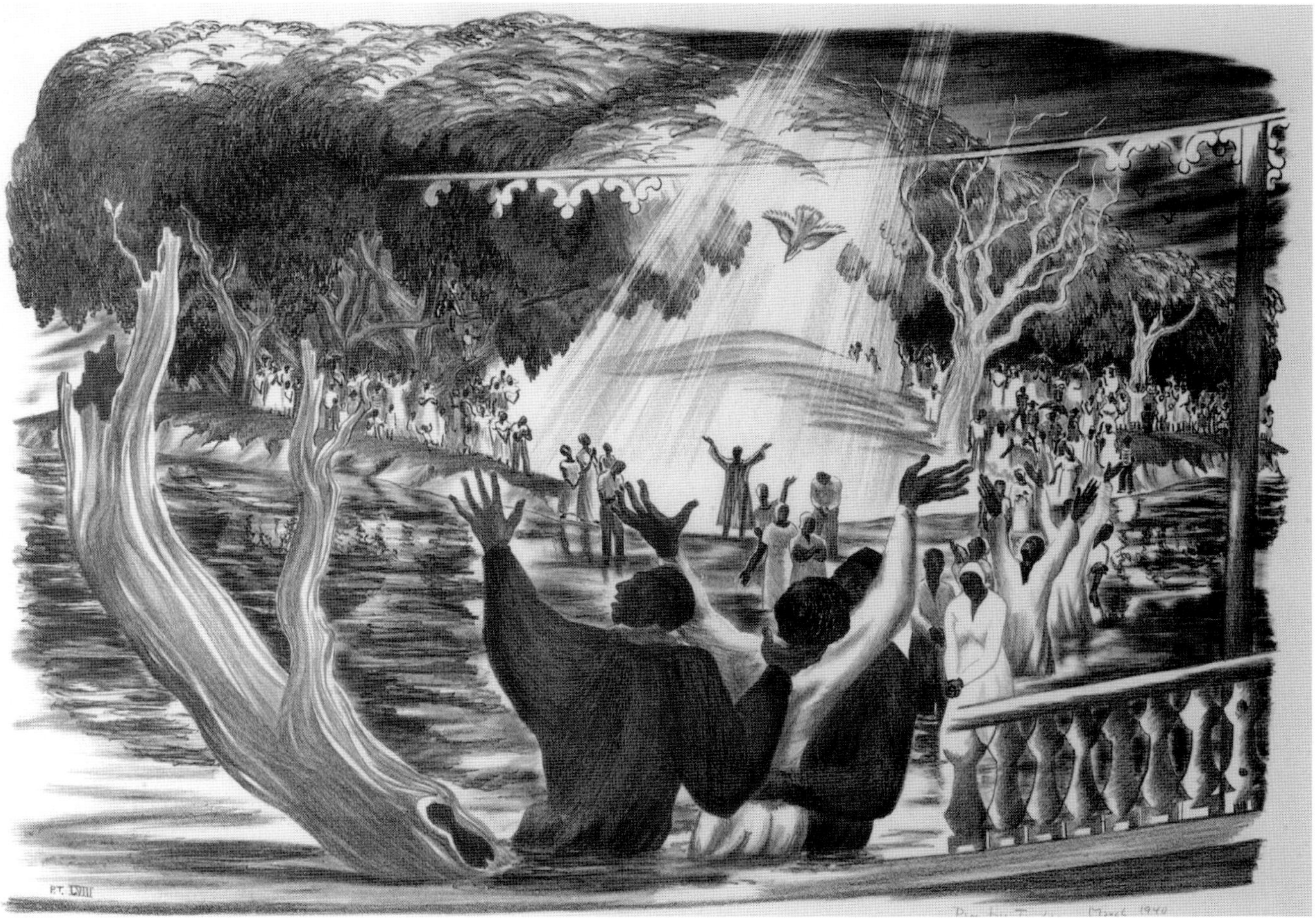

59. Prentiss Taylor, *"—In Whom I Am Well Pleased,"* lithograph, 1940, 10 ½ x 15 in., courtesy of Roderick S. Quiroz and from the collection of Lynn Barstis Williams.

Carroll Cloar (1913–1993)

Carroll Cloar grew up on a farm in the community of Gibson Bayou in rural Arkansas, just south of the Ozarks near Earle. By the age of fifteen he had lost both parents, though a small stipend through inheritance made a broad artistic education possible. After graduating from Southwestern College (now Rhodes College) in Memphis in 1934, he toured Europe, visiting many of its museums. With the intention of becoming a comic strip artist, he entered the Art Students League in 1936. He studied lithography under Harry Sternberg, who was, according to Cloar, "the first teacher who saw anything in me, who really felt I could be an artist." Cloar sent home for photographs of relatives and began an autobiographical series of lithographs in editions of twenty-five. They featured dour-faced figures of family members as well as images of himself against his native Arkansas background. On the basis of this series, the Art Students League awarded him a MacDowell fellowship in 1940. He used the money to travel to Mexico, where he worked at the graphic arts workshop Taller de Gráfica Popular. Cloar gave up printmaking at the end of the 1940s to devote himself to painting.[1]

The Preacher shows the montage compositional structure that Cloar often used to integrate various figures and scenes into the image area.[2] He structures some of these compositions around a central figure, as we see here. The dark pyramid shape formed by the frontal stance of the upper torso dominates the composition and suggests the stability of the preacher's position. The preacher was very likely modeled on Brother Ed, his family's visiting preacher, who, according to Cloar, "declared a foot washing once a year, preached at camp meetings and brought sinners flocking to the altar with his pleading."[3] His forthright stare from dark shadows suggests an undaunted, somewhat demonic spirit, and his hands, closure and control.

Notes

1. Patricia Cloar telephone interview with author, March 26, 1994; Guy Northrup, *Hostile Butterflies and Other Paintings* (Memphis: Memphis State University Press, 1977), 24–28.
2. *Hostile Butterflies* lists the title of this print as *Preacher of Holiness.*
3. "Backwoods Boyhood," *Life,* January 22, 1948, 80–81.

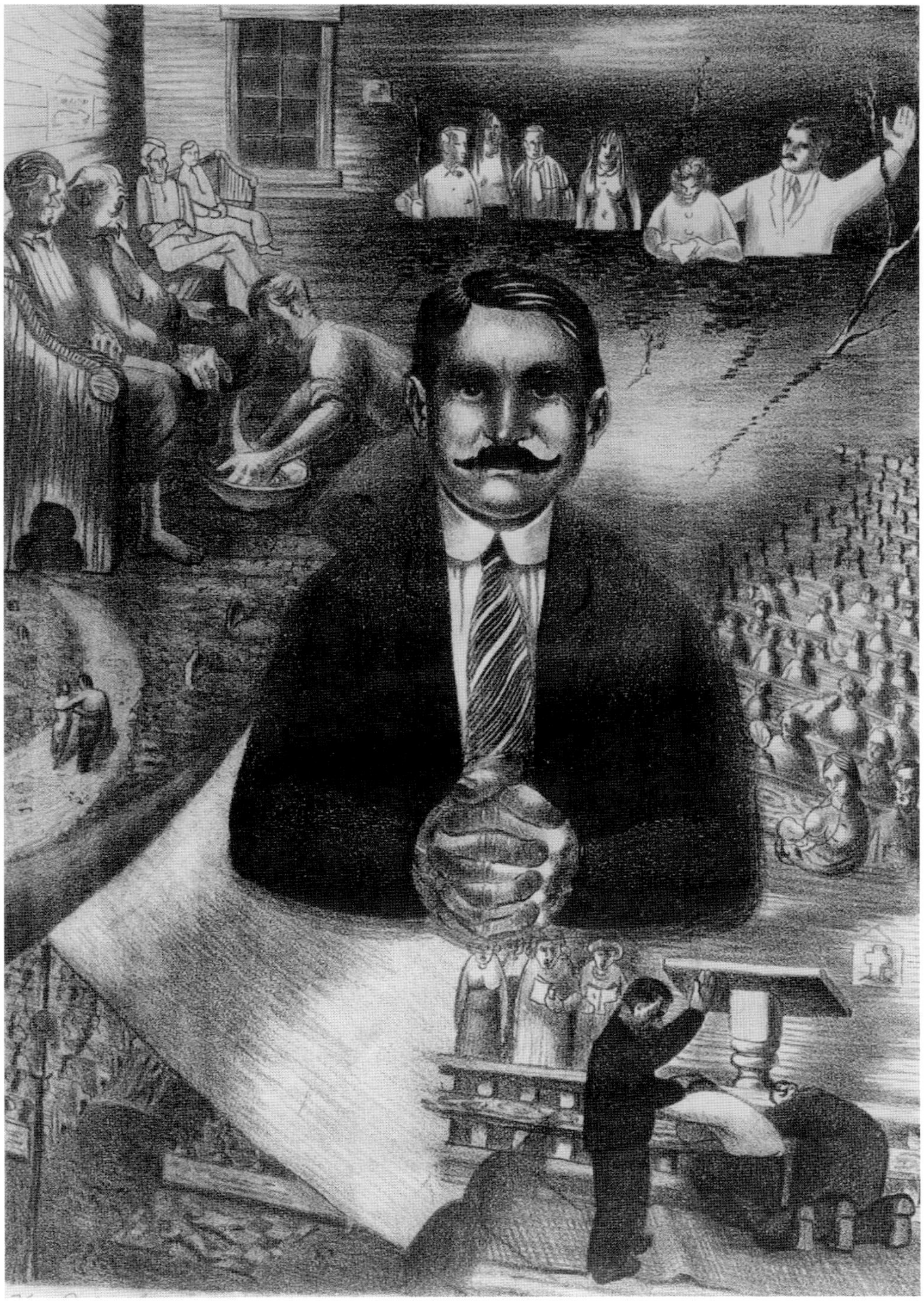

60. Carroll Cloar, *The Preacher,* lithograph, 1939, 11 ⅝ x 8 ½ in., © Estate of Carroll Cloar and from the collection of Lynn Barstis Williams.

Appendix: Southern Connections
An Index and Dictionary to Printmakers

Following the list of institutions below are artists who have biographical connections with the South or southern images. Public collections are listed if at least three prints have been located there, although they have not been systematically surveyed for every printmaker listed. Sources include clipping files listed in the bibliography as well as articles and monographs listed there. If information came primarily from one monograph or book, that source has been identified.

Amistad Research Collection, Tulane University; New Orleans, LA
Atlanta University; Atlanta, GA
Averett University Library; Danville, VA
Birmingham Public Library; Birmingham, AL
Brooks Memorial Art Gallery; Memphis, TN
Butler Center for Arkansas Studies, Main Library of the Central Arkansas Library System; Little Rock, AR
Charleston Museum; Charleston, SC
Cheekwood Museum of Art; Nashville, TN
Colonial Williamsburg Foundation; Williamsburg, VA
Columbia Museum of Art; Columbia, SC
Columbus Museum; Columbus, GA
Converse College; Spartanburg, SC
Duke University Libraries; Durham, NC
Free Library of Philadelphia; Philadelphia, PA
Georgetown University Library Special Collections, Georgetown University; Washington, DC
Georgia Museum of Art, University of Georgia; Athens, GA
Gibbes Museum of Art; Charleston, SC
Guilford College; Greensboro, NC
Hampton University Art Museum; Hampton, VA
High Museum of Art; Atlanta, GA
Historic New Orleans Collection; New Orleans, LA
Jule Collins Smith Museum of Fine Art, Auburn University; Auburn, AL
Lakeland Public Library; Lakeland, FL
Library of Congress; Washington, DC

Library of Virginia; Richmond, VA
Louisiana State Museum; New Orleans, LA
Louisiana State University Museum of Art; Baton, Rouge, LA
Marsh Museum, University of Richmond; Richmond, VA
McKissick Museum of Art, University of South Carolina; Columbia, SC
Meridian Community College; Meridian, MS
Metropolitan Museum of Art; New York, NY
Mobile Museum of Art; Mobile, AL
Montgomery Museum of Art; Montgomery, AL
Morris Museum of Art; Augusta, GA
New Orleans Museum of Art; New Orleans, LA
New York Public Library Prints and Photographs; New York, NY
Newark Museum; Newark, NJ
North Carolina Museum of Art; Raleigh, NC
Ogden Museum of Art; New Orleans, LA
Orlando Museum of Art; Orlando, FL
Philadelphia Museum of Art; Philadelphia, PA
Polk Museum of Art; Lakeland, FL
Saint Louis Art Museum; St. Louis, MO
Schomberg Center for Research in Black Culture; New York, NY
Smithsonian American Art Museum; Washington, DC
South Carolina State Museum; Columbia, SC
Spartanburg County Museum of Art; Spartanburg, SC
St. Augustine Historical Society, St. Augustine, FL
State Library of Louisiana; Baton Rouge, LA
Sumter County Museum; Sumter, SC
University of Alabama at Birmingham, Art Gallery; Birmingham, AL
University of Delaware Library; Newark, DE
University of Memphis; Memphis, TN
University of North Carolina; Chapel Hill, NC
University of Wisconsin-Whitewater, University Library; Whitewater, WI
Virginia Historical Society; Richmond, VA
Virginia Museum of Fine Arts; Richmond, VA
Virginia State Library; Richmond, VA
Walter Anderson Museum of Art; Ocean Springs, MS

Abrams, William Ross (b. 1920). Born in Richmond, VA. Graduated from Richmond Professional Institute (now part of Virginia Commonwealth University) in 1942 and studied at the Art Students League 1946–50 after having served in the military. In later years he received a Guggenheim grant and taught art at the Richmond Professional Institute as well as Rutgers University. Made color woodcuts in a semi-abstract style in the late 1940s. Collections: Virginia Museum.

Acker (Macpherson), Marian Francis (1906–1993). Born in Mobile, AL. See p. 80.

Adams, Wayman (1883–1959) Born in Muncie, IN. A well-known portrait painter, Adams began making annual trips to New Orleans to sketch black subjects in 1916. From 1929 to 1931 he made lithographs of black church services there: *The Offering* (1929) and *The Hymn* (1930). Source: Gambone. See also: Falk; Smith, *American Printmakers;* Williams, *American Printmakers.*

Albee, Grace (1890–1985). Born in Scituate, RI. A northeastern wood engraver, Albee made at least two wood engravings of South Carolina: *No Parking South Carolina* and *Suburban Charleston.* See: Falk; Smith, *American Printmakers;* Williams, *American Printmakers.* Collections: Georgetown.

Albers, Josef (1888–1976). Born in Bottrop, Germany. During his residence in Black Mountain, NC, where he taught at the college, 1933–49, he made totally abstract relief prints, lithographs, and drypoints. Source: Danilowitz. See also: Falk; Smith, *American Printmakers;* Williams, *American Printmakers.*

Alexander (Thompson), Doris (1906–1995). Born in Mobile, AL. See p. 116. Collections: Georgia, Mobile, Ogden.

Alston, Charles (1907–1977). Born in Charlotte, NC. Specialized in lithographs. *Deserted House* has been repeatedly associated with the South. See: Culpepper; Falk; King-Hammond; Smith, *American Printmakers; Alone in a Crowd;* Williams, *American Printmakers.*

Anderson, Frank Hartley (1890–1947). Born in Boston, MA. See p. 152. See: Falk; Smith, *American Printmakers;* Williams, *American Printmakers.* Collections: Birmingham, Library of Congress, Montgomery.

Anderson, Walter Inglis (1903–1965). Born in New Orleans, LA. See p. 42. See: Falk; Smith, *American Printmakers.* Collections: Brooks, Walter Anderson.

Angell, Lydia B. Member of the Louisiana Society of Etchers with which she exhibited. Titles indicate she focused on Vieux Carré architecture.

Arnold, Frank McIntosh (1867–1932). Born or lived in Orlando, FL. Etcher. See: Falk.

Austen, Carl Frederick (1917–1999). Born in Waukegan, IL. Visited St. Augustine during the early 1940s and established residence shortly thereafter. Made lithographs of St. Augustine street scenes with historic architecture in the background. Source: Torchia.

Avent, Mayna Treanor (1868–1959). Born in Nashville, TN. See p. 46. See: Falk.

Avery, Milton (1893–1965). Resident artist at Maitland Art Center during winters 1949–50 and 1950–51 where he made monotypes. See: Falk; Moser; Smith, *American Printmakers;* Williams, *American Printmakers.*

Babcock, Loren—See Barton

Bailey, Henrietta Davidson (1874–1950). Born in New Orleans, LA. See p. 52. See: Falk.

Baker, Lamar (1908–1994). Born in Atlanta, GA. See p. 110. See: Culpepper; Falk; Katz; Phagan, "American Scene in Georgia"; Smith, *American Printmakers;* Williams, *American Printmakers.* Collections: Columbus, High, Philadelphia, Mobile.

Ball, Mary Wilson (1892–1984). Born in Charleston, SC. Worked in etching, drypoint, and lithography. Source: Davis. See also: Falk; Severens, *Charleston Renaissance.* Collections: Morris.

Barton (Babcock), Loren (1893–1975). Born in Oxford, MA. Made four etchings of New Orleans Vieux Carré scenes from 1922 to 1924. See: Falk; Smith, *American Printmakers;* Williams, *American Printmakers.*

Benton, Thomas Hart (1889–1975). Born in Neosho, MO. See p. 106. See: Culpepper; Falk; Phagan, "Tours and Visits"; Pohl; Smith, *American Printmakers;* Williams, *American Printmakers.*" Collections: Georgetown, Library of Congress.

Besedick, Frank (1913–1987). Born in Hamilton, OH. See p. 154. See: Falk; Smith, *American Printmakers;* Williams, *American Printmakers.*

Biddle, George (1885–1973). Born in Philadelphia, PA. See p. 136. See: Culpepper; Falk; Pohl; Smith, *American Printmakers;* Williams, *American Printmakers.* Collections: Library of Congress.

Bird, Esther Brock (b. 1899). Studied at the Pratt Institute, the Art Students League, and etching with Arthur Dow at Columbia. Lived in Richmond for a period of time where she became a member of the Richmond Art Club. Made lithographs *Urbana River, Virginia* and *Tourists Home* of African Americans, which suggests a southern scene. See: Smith, *American Printmakers.*

Bohrod, Aaron (1907–1992). Born in Chicago, IL. Received a Guggenheim fellowship for 1936–37, which allowed him to travel to the South. Several lithographs resulted. One is known as *New Orleans Street Scene* and another *New Orleans Vista.* See: Culpepper; Falk; Phagan, "Tours and Visits"; Smith, *American Printmakers;* Williams, *American Printmakers.*

Bowman, David. Founding member of the Louisiana Society of Etchers with which he exhibited etchings, drypoints, and aquatints.

Brisac, Edith Mae (1894–1974). Born in Walton, NY. From 1929 to 1933 taught art at Alabama College for Women in Montevallo (now University of Montevallo), and it was likely during those years that she made a linoleum cut *Birmingham from Red Mountain.* She moved on to Denton, TX, to teach at Texas Woman's College (now Texas Woman's University) and exhibited prints there, joining the all female Texas Printmakers. See: Falk; Powers; Smith, *American Printmakers; Texas Painters; Texas Printmakers.*

Brook, Alexander (1898–1980). Born in Brooklyn, NY. From 1938 to 1943, he had a studio in Savannah, GA. At least one lithograph *Willie Mae* is likely from that period, as, according to King, he often depicted the local children who visited his studio. See: Culpepper; Falk; King; Phagan, "American Scene in Georgia"; Smith, *American Printmakers;* Williams, *American Printmakers.*

Brown, Don (1899–1958). Born in Taylor, TX. Taught at Centenary College in Shreveport,

LA, from 1934 until his death. Made etchings and drypoints, many of Caddo Lake area. Source: Stewart. See also: Falk; Powers; Smith, *American Printmakers;* Williams, *American Printmakers.*

Brown, Samuel Joseph (1907–1994). Born in Wilmington, NC. Worked on the Philadelphia WPA graphic arts workshop. Taught in Philadelphia. See: Falk; Smith, *American Printmakers;* Williams, *American Printmakers; Alone in a Crowd.*

Buell, Alice Standish (1892–1964). Born in Oak Park, IL. Spent 1927–28 in New Orleans with her husband who came on business. During that year taught an etching class at Arts and Crafts Club and later became a member of the Louisiana Society of Etchers with which she exhibited. Created numerous etchings of the Vieux Carré, many small in size. In subsequent years, she spent winters in New Orleans and still later she had a studio on Sanibel Island, FL, among other places. See: Falk; Smith, *American Printmakers;* Williams, *American Printmakers.* Collections: Historic New Orleans.

Buhmann, Max. Made a few etchings and linocuts in the 1920s in association with the Charleston Etchers' Club. Source: Davis. See also: Severens, *Charleston Renaissance.* Collections: Charleston Museum.

Cady, Harrison (1877–1970). Born in Gardner, MA. Worked as a newspaper artist and illustrator. Lived in Brooklyn and later settled in Rockport, MA. In the 1920s and 1930s, he traveled in the Smoky Mountains of North Carolina, which he pictured in etchings and drypoints that emphasize the mountain folk. Source: Reese. See also: Falk; Smith, *American Printmakers.*

Casteel, Homer (1919–1972). See p. 134. See: Falk. Collections: Meridian.

Castleden, George (1861–1945). Born in Canterbury, England. First visited New Orleans in 1901; in 1921 he established a studio in the French Quarter where he remained until 1936. In that year he moved to Charleston, SC, remaining there until his death. Castleden depicted historic architecture of the French Quarter in his etchings. See: Falk; *Knute Heldner and the Art Colony.* Collections: Historic New Orleans.

Catlett, Elizabeth (b. 1915). Born in Washington, DC. See p. 132. See: Falk; Phagan, "Tours and Visits"; Smith, *American Printmakers; Alone in a Crowd;* Williams, *American Printmakers.* Collections: Hampton.

Chamberlain, Samuel (1895–1975). Born in Cresco, IA. See p. 82. See: Falk; Smith, *American Printmakers;* Williams, *American Printmakers.* Collections: Colonial Williamsburg.

Clancy, Joe Wheeler (1896–1976). Born in Birmingham, AL. Studied at Alabama Polytechnic Institute (now Auburn University). Around 1940 he was making lithographs and serigraphs. As a member of the Dixie Art Colony in Alabama, he taught serigraphy and was visiting instructor at Huntingdon College in Montgomery in 1941. See: Falk.

Clark, Claude (1915–2001). Born in Rockingham, GA. See p. 98. See: *Alone in a Crowd;* Smith,

American Printmakers; Williams, *American Printmakers.* Collections: Newark, Free Library, Philadelphia, Saint Louis.

Clements, Gabrielle De Veaux (1858–1948). Born in Philadelphia, PA. Wintered in Charleston, possibly as early as 1901 and became one of the founders of Charleston Etchers' Club. Made etchings but none are known to be southern scenes. See: Davis; Falk; Severens, *Charleston Renaissance;* Smith, *American Printmakers;* Williams, *American Printmakers.*

Cloar, Carroll (1913–1993). Born near Earle, AR. See p. 158. See: Falk; Smith, *American Printmakers;* Williams, *American Printmakers.* Collections: University of Memphis.

Cobb, Kate McKinley (1888–1971). Born in Athens, GA, where she lived at least through the 1930s. Made block prints that were exhibited with the Southern States Art League during the 1930s. Reviewers commented that her prints were in the Japanese style. See: Falk.

Coe, Richard Blauvelt (1904–1978). Born in Selma, AL. See p. 88. See: Culpepper; Falk.

Cook, August (1897–1990). Born in Philadelphia, PA. Went to Converse College, Spartanburg, SC, in 1924 to head the art department and remained there for forty-two years. Made etchings, linocuts, and wood engravings, most of Vermont. Source: Davis. See also: Falk; Smith, *American Printmakers;* Williams, *American Printmakers.* Collections: Converse.

Cook, Howard (1901–1980). Born in Springfield, MA. See p. 142. See: Culpepper; Falk; Phagan, "Tours and Visits"; Smith, *American Printmakers;* Williams, *American Printmakers.* Collections: Smithsonian.

Cooper, James Fowler (1907–1968). Born in Kingstree area of South Carolina. See p. 138. See: Culpepper; Falk; Severens, "South Carolina and the American Scene"; Smith, *American Printmakers;* Williams, *American Printmakers.*

Crawford, Ralston (1906–1978). Born in St. Catherines, ON, Canada. Resident at Maitland Art Center in 1938, during which time he made prints. In 1940 he made his earliest color lithograph *Overseas Highway,* based on his painting of the causeway to Key West. See: Falk; Freeman; Smith, *American Printmakers,* Williams, *American Printmakers.*

Curry, John Steuart (1897–1946). Born near Dunavant, KS. Curry's lithograph *Mississippi Noah* is a southern scene and a lynching scene, *Fugitive,* has been associated with the South. See: Cole; Culpepper; Falk; Phagan, "Critical Views"; Smith, *American Printmakers;* Williams, *American Printmakers.*

Davenport, Carson Sutherlin (1908–1972). Born in Danville, VA. Made etchings, drypoints, and lithographs from the late 1930s and 1940s. His entry for 1939 World's Fair was a Virginia scene but later work does not appear strongly local. Resident at the Maitland Art Center in Orlando in 1938. Taught at Averett University from 1943 to 1969. See: Falk; Smith, *American Printmakers;* Williams, *American Printmakers.* Collections: Averett.

Davidson, Theresa Sherrer (1893–1986). Born in Marion, OH. Received BA (1914) and MA (1915) from Oberlin. Married author Donald Davidson in 1918. Received her LLB (1922) and PhD (1943) from Vanderbilt. Made linoleum cuts and exhibited two of these with the Southern States Art League in 1938. Illustrated Davidson's books *The Tennessee* and *The Long Street: Poems.*

Dawson, Charles Clarence (1889–1981). Born in Warrenton or Bruns, GA. Studied at Tuskegee, Art Students League, and Art Institute of Chicago. In 1933 he privately published *ABC of Great Negroes,* which included twenty-six original linoleum cuts of black leaders. See: Falk; Smith, *American Printmakers.*

Dehn, Adolf (1895–1968). Born in Waterville, MN. Made a number of trips to the South. Most of his southern images in lithographs were extracted from a trip to Key West: *Street Scene, Key West* (1942); *Pelicans at Key West* (1947); and *Queen of Key West* (1949) according to Lumsdaine's catalogue raisonné. He also made lithographs of Black Mountain, NC. See: Falk; Lumsdaine; Phagan, "Tours and Visits"; Pohl; Smith, *American Printmakers;* Williams, *American Printmakers.*

Dotterer, Selma Tharin (1904–2001). Born in Charleston, SC. Studied etching with Alfred Hutty and became a member of the Charleston Etchers' Club in 1924. Made etchings of dancers, which reflected her professional career as a dancer in New York, though she stopped doing etchings when she left for New York to become a dancer in 1927. See: Davis; Severens, *Charleston Renaissance.*

Douglass (or Douglas), Lucille Sinclair (1878–1935). Born in Tuskegee, AL. Lived in Birmingham, 1891–1909, studied in Europe 1909 to 1913. After 1920 she lived in China and New York. Her etchings were scenes of China and Angkor done in the 1920s. Source: Ingham. See also: Falk; Smith, *American Printmakers;* Williams, *American Printmakers.* Collections: Library of Congress, Metropolitan.

Durieux, Caroline Wogan (1896–1989). Born in New Orleans, LA. See p. 126. See: Cox, "Genre Art"; Culpepper; Falk; Smith, *American Printmakers;* Williams, *American Printmakers.* Collections: Louisiana State University, New York Public Library, Ogden, State Library of Louisiana.

Durkee, Florence (1879–1971). From Talisheek, LA. Lived in New Orleans where she made etchings and drypoints of the French Quarter. Member of the Louisiana Society of Etchers with which she exhibited drypoints.

Dwight, Mabel (1875–1955). Born in Cincinnati, OH. See p. 60. See: Culpepper; Cox, "Genre Art"; Falk; Pohl; Smith, *American Printmakers;* Williams, *American Printmakers.*

Freund, Harry Louis (1905–1999). Born in Clinton, MO. Lived in Little Rock, AR, in the 1930s. Made at least one relief print of Arkansas: *Vendor Arkansas.* See: Falk; Smith, *American Printmakers;* Williams, *American Printmakers.*

Gelb, Jan (Jeanette) (1906–1978). Born in New York City. Wife of Boris Margo and resident artist at Maitland Art Center in 1947. Some archival evidence indicates that she made prints while there. See: Falk; Smith, *American Printmakers.*

Giddens, Philip Harris (1898–1972). Born in Cuthbert, GA. An architect who worked in Atlanta and often traveled to Europe, he made architectural etchings, many of which are distinguished because they picture eastern Europe. See: Falk; Smith, *American Printmakers.* Collections: Columbus.

Goldthwaite, Anne Wilson (1869–1944). Born in Montgomery, AL. See p. 128. See: Falk; Smith, *American Printmakers;* Williams, *American Printmakers.* Collections: Montgomery, Smithsonian.

Gorelick, Boris (1912–1984). Born in Russia. *Strange Fruit* appears to be Gorelick's only print of the South. See: Pohl; Smith, *American Printmakers;* Williams, *American Printmakers.*

Gwathmey, Robert (1903–1988). Born in Manchester, VA (near Richmond). See p. 108. See: Falk; Katz; Phagan, "North Carolina and Virginia"; Smith, *American Printmakers;* Williams, *American Printmakers.* Collections: Metropolitan.

Hagerman, (William Kay) Kent (1893–1978). See p. 148. Born in Ohio. Collections: Polk, Lakeland.

Hale, Ellen Day (1855–1940). Born in Worchester, MA. During her winter visits to Charleston, she made a number of soft ground color etchings of African Americans in street scenes. See: Davis; Falk; Severens, *Charleston Renaissance;* Smith, *American Printmakers;* Williams, *American Printmakers.* Collections: Morris.

Hancock, (James) Carl (1868–1966). Born in Springfield, TN. A self-taught etcher, he moved to Arkansas at an early age and settled in Rose City in the environs of Little Rock. His wife taught school, he made his living as an artist, and the couple spent summers in New Orleans. Many of his etchings depict Little Rock scenes while others feature the French Quarter as well as St. Francisville, LA. Restrikes have been made of a few Arkansas etchings. Those exhibited with the Southern States Art League in the mid-1930s suggest a wider span of iconography. Collections: Butler Center, Historic New Orleans.

Hart, George Overbury (Pop) (1868–1933). Born in Cairo, IL. A vagabond artist, he shared an apartment with Jules Pascin in the French Quarter in 1917. Made etchings, aquatints, and lithographs in the 1920s, a few of which were figure studies and genre scenes of New Orleans such as *Springtime in New Orleans, The Gallery, French Opera House, New Orleans.* One known as *Mammy* might be associated with the South. Source: Gilbert. See also Falk; Smith, *American Printmakers;* Williams, *American Printmakers.*

Hassam, (Frederick) Childe (1859–1935). Born in Boston, MA. Made a few architectural etchings of Charleston and Virginia. See: Falk; Severens, *Charleston Renaissance;* Smith, *American Printmakers;* Williams, *American Printmakers.*

Healy, William John. Member of the Louisiana Society of Etchers with which he exhibited.

Heldner, Knute (1875–1952). Born in Vederslow, Sweden. See p. 94. Restrikes from etching plates were made in the mid-1970s; some are stamped "Whisnant Gallery." See: Falk; *Knute Heldner and the Art Colony;* Williams, *American Printmakers.* Collections: Historic New Orleans, Louisiana State Museum.

Henderson, Ernest M. (1905–1998). Born in Greenville, SC. Lived in Birmingham, AL, where he was an editor of the *Birmingham News* and teacher at Birmingham Southern College during the 1930s. Made etchings that were exhibited with the Southern States Art League in 1929 and 1930, but it is difficult to determine from titles to what extent he made scenes of the South. See: Falk.

Hergesheimer, Ella Sophonisba (1873–1943). See p. 48. See: Falk; Smith, *American Printmakers;* Williams, *American Printmakers.* Collections: Cheekwood, University of Delaware.

Hicken, Philip (1910–1985). Born in Lynn, MA. Visited Alabama and Georgia and made a few genre scenes in serigraphs. See: Falk; Smith, *American Printmakers;* Williams, *American Printmakers.*

Hill, Polly Knipp (1900–1990). Born in Ithaca, NY. See p. 146. See: Falk; Smith, *American Printmakers;* Williams, *American Printmakers.* Collections: Library of Congress.

Hobbs, Morris Henry (1892–1967). Born in Rockford, IL. See p. 62. See: Falk; *Knute Heldner;* Smith, *American Printmakers;* Williams, *American Printmakers.* Collections: Historic New Orleans, Library of Congress, Morris, Ogden.

Hoehn, Werner Conrad (1882–1940). Born in New Orleans, LA, where he lived during his adult years. Worked in lithography and drypoint. Made a number of portraits of black subjects as well as southern scenes, which were exhibited with the Southern States Art League in the late 1930s. See: Falk.

Holloway, Jenelsie. Studied art at Spelman College under Hale Woodruff. Taught art at Spelman for thirty-nine years. Made lithographs for which she won a prize in Atlanta University art annual in 1944.

Horter, Earl (1881–1940). Born in Philadelphia, PA. Began to produce etchings of New Orleans shortly after he began working in this medium in 1910 and progressed to aquatint. He also made etchings of historic tidewater Virginia homes probably in the 1930s. See: Falk; Ittmann; Smith, *American Printmakers;* Williams, *American Printmakers.*

Hoshall, Mercedes Erixon (b. 1904). Born in Minnesota. Lived in Heidelberg, Germany, and Charleston. Made relief prints. Beginning in the 1920s taught art education at the University of Oklahoma.

Howard, Willie. Made lithographs on the Louisiana WPA in New Orleans.

Howell, Catherine (b. 1892) Born in East Feliciana Parish, LA. Made lithographs on the Louisiana WPA. See: Falk.

Howorth, (Emma) Louise. Born in Kosciusko, MS. Lived in Montgomery, AL, and Meridian, MS. Made linoleum cuts. See: Falk.

Huntley, Victoria Ebbels Hutson (1900–1971). Born in Hasbrouck Heights, NJ. See p. 40. See: Falk; Smith, *American Printmakers;* Williams, *American Printmakers.*

Hutty, Alfred Heber (1877–1954). Born in Grand Haven, MI. See p. 72. See: Culpepper; Falk; Severens, "South Carolina and the American Scene"; Smith, *American Printmakers;* Williams, *American Printmakers.* Collections: Gibbes, Library of Congress, Morris, Ogden.

Hyde, Helen (1868–1919). Born in Lima, NY. Spent the winter of 1916 in Charleston. Made black-and-white lithographs as well as color etchings of the area from 1917 to 1919. Many are of black family life with emphasis on children. See: Mason. See: Falk; Smith, *American Printmakers;* Williams, *American Printmakers.*

Irvine, Sadie (Sarah Agnes Estelle) (1887–1970). See p. 54. Born in New Orleans, LA. See: Falk. Collections: Louisiana State Museum, Louisiana State University.

Jackley, F. Dano (b. 1900). Born in Franklin, IN. An architect who lived in St. Augustine and depicted the city in architectural etchings. See: Falk.

Jaques, Bertha Evelyn (1863–1941). Born in Covington, OH. An etcher who depicted views around the world, Jaques made one known etching of New Orleans and one of St. Augustine. See: Czestochowski; Falk; Smith, *American Printmakers.*

Jennings, Wilmer (1910–1990). Born in Atlanta, GA. See p. 124. See: Culpepper; Falk; King-Hammond; Smith, *American Printmakers; Alone in a Crowd.* Collections: Metropolitan.

Johnson, William Henry (1901–1970). Born in Florence, SC. See p. 122. See: Falk; Severens, "South Carolina and the American Scene." Collections: Metropolitan, Smithsonian.

Jones, Lawrence Arthur (1910–1996). Born in Lynchburg, VA. Instructor and chair of the art department at Dillard University, 1936–40. Made etchings on the Louisiana WPA, some of which were southern scenes. In 1940 received a Julius Rosenwald fellowship that he used to work at the Taller de Gráfica Popular in Mexico City, after which he made lithographs. Taught art at Fort Valley State College, GA, until 1949, when he took a position heading the art department at Jackson State Teachers College (now Jackson State University) in Jackson, MS, where he remained until 1979. See: Black, *Art in Mississippi;* Falk; Fax; *Alone in a Crowd.* Collections: Metropolitan.

Kappel, Philip (1901–1981). Born in Hartford, CT. Made numerous etchings of New Orleans that were collected in his book *Louisiana Gallery: The River Country and New Orleans* (1950). See: Falk; Smith, *American Printmakers;* Williams, *American Printmakers.*

Kirk, Mary Wallace (1889–1978). Born in Tuscumbia, AL. See p. 92. See: Falk.

Kiser, Jesse Dorrance (1922–1997). Born in Nuyaka, OK. Moved to Gardendale, AL. Received a BA in art from Alabama Polytechnic Institute (now Auburn University) and taught art as an instructor. Made lithographs of southern scenes with black figures.

Kofler, John George. Member of the Louisiana Society of Etchers with which he exhibited.

Lankes, Julius John (1884–1960). Born in Buffalo, NY. See p. 90. A son, J. B. Lankes, made restrikes stamped "Imp JBL," which some museum collections include. Some posthumous impressions have also been made. See: Falk; Phagan, "North Carolina and Virginia"; Smith, *American Printmakers;* Williams, *American Printmakers.* Collections: Library of Congress, Marsh, Virginia Historical Society, Virginia State Library.

Latham, Barbara (1896–1989). Born in Walpole, MA. Studied at the Norwich, CT, art school. Traveled throughout South with husband Howard Cook in 1934 on his Guggenheim grant. Made at least two wood engravings associated with the trips: *North Carolina Mountain Woman,* and one titled *Negro Group* is possibly a southern scene. See: Falk; Smith, *American Printmakers;* Williams, *American Printmakers.*

Law, Margaret Moffett (1871–1956). Born in Spartanburg, SC. Graduated from Converse College in 1895. After teaching art in Maryland, she returned to Spartanburg in 1930 to serve as art supervisor of the city schools. Maintained studios in Spartanburg and Lake Summit, NC. Experimented with etching, drypoint, aquatint, lithography, and linoleum cuts, both in black-and-white and color. Began exhibiting her prints, which were primarily genre scenes, in 1923. See: Culpepper; Falk; *Work Song.* Collections: Spartanburg.

Lazzell, Nettie Blanche (1878–1956). Born near Maidsville, WV. Taught in West Virginia but traveled to Provincetown summers, where she learned the white-line woodblock method from Oliver Chaffee. She exhibited in St. Augustine, became a member of the Arts Club and created two prints of the city in 1940, which suggests she visited in that year. See: Clarkson; Falk; Shapiro; Smith, *American Printmakers;* Torchia.

Lee-Smith, Hughie (1915–1999). Born in Eustis, FL, but moved to Cleveland at an early age. Made lithographs and linoleum cuts. See: Falk.

Leighton, Clare Veronica Hope (1898–1989). Born in London, England. See p. 96. See: Falk; Smith, *American Printmakers.* Collections: Duke, University of North Carolina.

Lewis, Arthur Allen (1873–1957). Born in Mobile, AL. An illustrator who was considered one of the foremost woodcut artists of the period, he spent the first four years of his life in Mobile. He also made etchings. See: Falk; Smith, *American Printmakers;* Williams, *American Printmakers.*

Lewis, Lalla Walker (b. 1912). Born in Greenwood, MS, and lived there. Studied at the Mississippi State College for Women (now Mississippi University for Women). Made linoleum cuts of southern scenes. *Liberty Act, Southern Snow, Up the Levee,* and *Loading Cotton* were exhibited with the Southern States Art League in the mid-1930s. See: Falk.

Lillie, Ella Fillmore (1884–1972). Born in Minneapolis MN. Lived in Vermont where she had a studio for many years. Some biographical information indicates that she spent her later years in St. Petersburg, FL. Made a series of lithographs depicting the Georgia Sea Islands and Augusta, GA, around 1949. See: Falk; Smith, *American Printmakers;* Williams, *American Printmakers.* Collections: Georgia, Library of Congress.

Locke, Walter Ronald (1883–1949). Born in Winchester, MA. See p. 58. See: Falk; King and DeLorme. Collections: High, Ogden, Orlando.

Logan, Velma Kidd (1912–1991). Born in Birmingham, AL, where she continued to live. Studied with Ellsworth Woodward at Newcomb. Made some linoleum cuts. See: Falk.

Loving, Eugene E. (1908–1971). Born in Round Rock, TX. See p. 64. Collections: Guilford, Historic New Orleans, Ogden.

MacKenzie, John Roderick Dempster (1865–1941). Born in London, England. See p. 112. See: Falk. Collections: Birmingham, Mobile, University of Alabama at Birmingham.

Macpherson, Marian Francis Acker—See Acker

Manuel, Margaret. Born in Scotland. Made etchings of the Cumberland Mountains in Tennessee in the 1930s. See: Smith, *American Printmakers.*

Margo, Boris (1902–1995). Born in the Volochisk, Ukraine. Immigrated to Montreal then settled in New York in 1930. He and his wife were resident artists at Maitland during the winter of 1947 and made monotypes and possibly the surrealist cellocuts for which he is known. He continued to winter in Florida and established the Creative Art Seminar in Orlando. See: Falk; Moser; Smith, *American Printmakers.*

Marshall, (James) Duard (b. 1914). Born in Northwest, AR. Attended the Kansas City Art Institute where he studied lithography under John de Martelly and Thomas Hart Benton. See: Smith, *American Printmakers.*

Mayer, Henry (Hy) (1868–1953). Born in Worms on Rhine, Germany. An illustrator and etcher he returned to St. Augustine in 1947 after an absence of five years. Source: Torchia. See also: Falk.

Mayfield, Robert Bledsoe (1869–1934). Born in Carlinville, IL. After serving as an apprentice artist for the *St. Louis Dispatch,* Mayfield went to New Orleans in 1891 to become the assistant editor of the *Times Democrat.* Made a considerable number of small etchings of the French Quarter and New Orleans docks. See: Falk.

McCrady, John (1911–1968). Born in Canton, MS. See p. 140. See: Cox, "Genre Art"; Falk; Smith, *American Printmakers;* Williams, *American Printmakers.*

Meissner, Leo John (1895–1977). Born in Hamtrack, MI. Made several wood engravings of North Carolina and Florida, which were done in the early 1950s. See: Falk. Collections: Library of Congress.

Merrick, Richard L. (1903–1986). Born in Coconut Grove, FL. Taught art at the University of Miami in the 1930s and in 1940 became head of the art department. Made etchings at Key West on the Florida WPA. Also made woodcuts. See: Falk; Smith, *American Printmakers.*

Merrill, Katherine (1876–1962). Born in Milwaukee, WI. Went to Charleston in 1928 from New York to teach at Carolina Art Association School. Made at least six etchings of Charleston scenes. Returned to Charleston to winter for several years. In the late 1930s she worked on the Florida WPA in Jacksonville and later became a resident of Tampa. Source: Davis. See also: Falk; Ray; Smith, *American Printmakers.*

Mikell, Minnie (Mrs. Alexander B.) (1891–1987). Born in Charleston, SC. Studied etching under Alfred Hutty at Carolina Art Association, and then under Joseph Pennell at the Art Students League. One of the founding members of Charleston Etchers' Club. Exhibited etching, drypoint, and aquatint in architectural studies, landscapes of coastal scenes, and nudes. See: Davis; Severens, *Charleston Renaissance.*

Milhollen, Hirst Dillon (1906–1970). Born in Philomont, VA. Lived in Alexandria, VA. Curator of photographs at Library of Congress and expert on Civil War photography, he made some etchings of small-town Virginia life in the 1930s and 1940s. See: Falk.

Millet, Clarence (1897–1959). Born in Hahnsville, LA. See p. 68. See: Falk. Collections: Historic New Orleans.

Morgan, F(ranklin) Townsend (1883–1965). Born in Brooklyn, NY. Made etchings on the WPA in Florida. Depicted various sites in Florida in etching and drypoint. See: Falk; Smith, *American Printmakers.* Collections: Library of Congress.

Morley, Hubert (1888–1951). Born in La Crosse, WI. Made architectural etchings of the French Quarter. See: Falk; Smith, *American Printmakers.*

Mueller, Lola Pace (1889–1949). Born in Atlanta, GA, but moved to San Antonio, TX, where she lived in the 1940s. Made lithographs, which she exhibited with the Southern States Art League in 1944. See: Falk.

Muller-Uri, Hildegard (1894–1990). A leader of the artists' colony in St. Augustine and a founder of the Arts Club, she made etchings and woodcuts of the town. See: Falk; Torchia.

Murphy, Christopher A. D. (1902–1973). Born in Savannah, GA. See p. 78. See: Falk; Smith, *American Printmakers.* Collections: Morris.

Nelms, Marjory Collison (1902–1983). Born in Washington, DC. Spent part of her childhood and adult life in Charleston. While living in Charleston in 1927, she exhibited three lithographs with the Charleston Etchers' Club. See: Davis; Falk under Collison.

Newhall, Harriet (1874–1934). Born in Topeka, KS. An etcher who worked in Provincetown, she joined the St. Augustine Arts Club in 1940. Source: Torchia. See: Falk.

Nungester (Wolfe), Mildred (b. 1912). Born in Celina, OH. See p. 130. Restrikes are being printed at Wolfe Studio, Jackson, MS. See: Culpepper; Falk under Wolfe; Eiland; Smith, *American Printmakers;* Williams, *American Printmakers.* Collections: Montgomery.

O'Keeffe, Ida Ten Eyck (1889–1961). Born in Sun Prairie, WI. Studied at the University of Virginia and Columbia where she received her BS and MA degrees in fine arts. Taught art at a school for girls in Valle Crucis, NC, and served as head of the fine arts department at Athens College, Athens, AL, in 1936–37. She made monotypes, as a hobby, that were exhibited in Charlotte, NC, in 1936. North Carolina and other parts of the country where she lived appear as subjects of her monotypes. See: Falk; Smith, *American Printmakers.*

Oliver, Edith Walker (1889–1979). Born in Chicago, IL. She visited St. Augustine in 1933 and became a permanent resident when she married in 1935 and active in the Arts Club. Depicted historic St. Augustine architecture in small etchings, hand colored. See: Torchia.

Orr, Louis (1879–1961). Born in Hartford, CT. Created finely textured architectural etchings of European cathedrals and historic southern architecture. He made some of Duke University buildings. See: Falk; Smith, *American Printmakers.*

Page, Grover (1892–1958). Worked for the *Louisville Courier-Journal* in the 1930s. Exhibited wood engravings with the Southern States Art League in 1938, 1939, and 1941. See: Falk.

Peacock, Jean Eleanor. Born in Norfolk, VA. Lived in Richmond, VA. Exhibited two linoleum block prints with the Southern States Art League in 1939. See: Falk.

Pearce, George E. (1889–1976). Born in New Orleans, LA, where he was active during the 1930s. Made small linoleum cuts of historic New Orleans architecture, some in color. A number of them appeared in Arthur's *Old New Orleans.* See: Falk. Collections: Historic New Orleans.

Peirce, Gerry (1900–1969). Born in Jamestown, NY. Lived in New Orleans where he became a founding member of the New Orleans Art League in 1927 and taught etching at the New Orleans School of Art. At some point during the 1930s, he moved to Philadelphia and entered commercial art. Moved to Tucson in 1939 where he remained for the rest of his life. Made etchings and drypoints of the French Quarter. See: Falk; Smith, *American Printmakers.*

Pescheret, Leon René (1892–1961). Born in Chiswick, England. Settled in Whitewater, WI. Made etchings, many large and in color, of many parts of the United States and Europe including the South: New Orleans, Williamsburg, Charleston, the Low Country, and the mountains of North Carolina and Tennessee. See: Falk; Smith, *American Printmakers;* library.uww.edu. Collections: University of Wisconsin–Whitewater.

Pickup, Ernest Alexander (1887–1970). Born in Shelbyville, TN. See p. 86. See: Falk.

Pittman, Hobson (1899–1972). Born near Epworth, NC. Took private art lessons in Tarboro, NC, 1912–16. After the death of his parents in 1918, he moved to Coatesville, PA, to live with his sister. He later went to Philadelphia where he began teaching and studying etching with Earl Horter in 1931. He appears to have worked primarily in relief, making still lifes in wood or linoleum. See: Falk; Smith, *American Printmakers.*

Pugh, (Sarah) Mabel (1891–1986). Born in Morrisville, NC. See p. 84. See: Falk; Hickman; Smith, *American Printmakers.* Collections: North Carolina.

Ravenscroft, Ellen (1876–1949). Born in Jackson, MS. Lived in St. Louis in early 1920s. Spent summers in Provincetown. Moved to New York in 1926 where she appears to have spent the rest of her life, continuing to spend summers in Provincetown. Made color woodcuts. See: Falk; Smith, *American Printmakers.*

Reed, Willie Lucille (Rowe) (1914–1986). Lived in New Orleans in early 1940s where she became a member of Louisiana Society of Etchers. She worked in various media of intaglio and made some color relief prints. Made architectural etchings of the French Quarter; in 1944 and 1945 she exhibited Mexican scenes in aquatint with the Southern States Art League. See: Smith, *American Printmakers*, under Rowe.

Reid, Celia Cregor (1895–1956). Born in Springfield, KY. See p. 114. See: Falk; Williams, *American Printmakers.*

Reinike, Charles Henry (1906–1983). Born in New Orleans, LA, where he continued to live. An etcher, Reinike was a founding member of the Louisiana Society of Etchers with which he exhibited. He and his wife started a school, the Reinike Academy of Art, in New Orleans until 1944 and an art colony in St. Francisville, LA. See: Falk. Collections: Louisiana State Museum.

Reisman, Philip (1904–1992). Born in Warsaw, Poland. Reisman made a trip through the South on the WPA and his etching *South* resulted. Considered a New York urban realist, this etching appears to be the only print he did of the South. See: Hemingway; Smith, *American Printmakers;* Williams, *American Printmakers.*

Rhett, Antoinette Francesca (1884–1964). Born in Baltimore, MD. See p. 44. See: Falk; Severens, *Charleston Renaissance.* Collections: Gibbes.

Richards, Charles (1906–1992). Born in the Mississippi Delta north of Vicksburg. Grew up in Memphis and came to New Orleans in 1927 as a newspaper reporter and illustrator. Moved on to work on newspapers in New York, Kansas City, and elsewhere. Studied at the Kansas City Art Institute and at the Art Students League with Will Barnett. Returned to New Orleans in 1945. Made etchings, some of the French Quarter, and monotypes. See: Falk. Collections: Historic New Orleans.

Ripley, Aiden Lassell (1896–1969). Born in Wakefield, MA. Grew up in Boston. In 1936 his dealer, Sportsman's Gallery of Art and Books of New York, sponsored the first of many winter trips south to paint plantations and hunting preserves of preserves in Georgia, the Carolinas, and Florida. Made etchings of hunting scenes. Source: Chambers. See also: Falk; Smith, *American Printmakers;* Williams, *American Printmakers.* Collections: Morris.

Rohland, Caroline Speare (1885–1965). Born in Boston, MA. With her husband Paul lived in New Orleans, Beaufort, SC, and Florida. Made a number of lithographs of southern scenes including *Darkie's Mardi Gras, Plaza—St. Augustine, FL,* and *Southern Morning* in the late 1920s and early 1930s. Southern blacks and their lives were her frequent subject. See: Falk; Smith, *American Printmakers.*

Rohland, Paul (1884–1953). Born in Richmond, VA. Lived in Richmond where he worked for a photo engraving company until 1900 when his family moved to Philadelphia. In addition to work executed in France, California, New Mexico, and the West Indies, he spent 1926 in New Orleans, several years painting in and around Beaufort, SC, and also resided in Florida. Made lithographs, woodcuts, and monotypes. See: Falk; Smith, *American Printmakers.*

Routh, James Edward (b. 1918). Born in New Orleans, LA. See p. 104. See: Phagan, "Tours and Visits"; Smith, *American Printmakers.* Collections: Georgia.

Rowe—See Reed, Willie Lucille

Ruellan, Andrée (b. 1905–2006). Born in New York City. Visited Charleston and made one lithograph, *City Market, Charleston,* in 1939. See: Keyes.

Rumph, Alice Edith (1877–1957). Born in Rome, GA. Lived in Birmingham, AL, from 1887 until 1916 when she moved to Virginia and other locations to take various teaching positions, the longest in Orange, NJ, from 1922 to 1942. Made etchings, usually architectural, of various southern locations as well as other areas where she lived and traveled. Most noteworthy were those depicting landmarks of Colonial Williamsburg. Source: Ingham. See also: Falk.

Ryder, Chauncey Foster (1869–1949). Born in Danbury, CT. Studied at the Art Institute of Chicago and the Académie Julien. In 1907 he moved to New York and spent summers in a home in New Hampshire. He began to travel widely and created drypoints, most of them landscapes, depicting what he saw. He made one landscape of Virginia mountains and around eight Tennessee and North Carolina mountain views, some with dwellings embedded in the scenes. According to an early catalog, at least some were executed as early as 1920. See: Falk; Smith, *American Printmakers;* www.raisonné.org.

Schoppe, Palmer (1912–2001). Born in Wood Cross, UT. See p. 144. See: Falk; Smith, *American Printmakers.* Collections: Gibbes.

Schreiber, Georges (1904–1977). Born in Brussels, Belgium. See p. 118. See: Culpepper; Falk; Katz; Phagan, "Tours and Visits"; Reese; Smith, *American Printmakers;* Williams, *American Printmakers.*

Schutz, Marian C. Member of the Louisiana Society of Etchers with which she exhibited, focusing on scenes of the Vieux Carré in etchings.

Shackelford, Shelby (1899–1987). Born in Halifax, VA. Began making prints in the early 1930s. Most have been described as wax prints, but one linocut is a very distinctive image of mechanization of cotton production, *Rust Cotton Picker Comes to the South.* See: Falk; Smith, *American Printmakers;* Williams, *American Printmakers.*

Sharpe, H(erbert) Alvin (1910–1982). Born in southern Kentucky.

Simons, Albert (1890–1980). Born in Charleston, SC, where he practiced architecture. Member of Charleston Etchers' Club with which he exhibited etchings of European scenes in the 1920s. See: Davis; Severens, *Charleston Renaissance.*

Smith, Albert Alexander (1896–1940). Born in New York City but after 1920 lived in Europe. No biographical connection with the South has been established, but of his etchings and lithographs, a number have been associated with the South through titles or in subjects such as cotton picking or outdoor baptism. His etching *Plantation Melodies* (1923) and the lithograph *Sunday—Southern States* (1930) are the most definitively connected. See: Falk; Leininger-Miller; Reynolds and Wright; Smith, *American Printmakers.*

Smith, Alice Ravenel Huger (1876–1958). Born in Charleston, SC. Made color woodcuts from 1917 to 1919 and etchings 1923 to 1924. Created color woodcuts in the Sosaku Hanga manner of Japanese printmakers with some southern lowland scenes. Her etchings are fairly conventional architectural and natural scenes of the Charleston area. See: Falk; Severens, *Alice Smith* and *Charleston Renaissance;* Smith, *American Printmakers.* Collections: Gibbes.

Smith, Charles William (1893–1987). Born in Lofton, VA. See p. 50. See: Culpepper; Severens, "South Carolina and the American Scene"; Falk; Smith, *American Printmakers.* Collections: Greenville, Library of Virginia, New York Public, South Carolina State Museum, Virginia Museum of Fine Arts.

Smith, Jules André (1880–1959). Born in Hong Kong. Grew up in Germany, Boston, and New York. Studied architecture at Cornell. He taught himself etching, which he stopped doing in 1935 due to failing eyesight. Became a winter resident in Maitland, FL, and in 1937 established the Maitland Art Research Studio. Made at least one etching with drypoint of the South. See: Falk; Smith, *American Printmakers;* Williams, *American Printmakers.*

Sternberg, Harry (1904–2001). Born in New York City. *Southern Holiday* was his only southern image of the 1920–40s period. In later life he made an autobiographical series in woodcut. One lynching scene in the series was titled *Strange Fruit.* See: Falk; Smith, *American Printmakers;* Williams, *American Printmakers.*

Steth, Raymond (1916–1997). Born in Norfolk, VA. See p. 152. See: Culpepper; Falk; King-Hammond; Smith, *American Printmakers; Alone in a Crowd;* Williams, *American Printmakers.* Collections: Free Library, Newark, Philadelphia, Saint Louis.

Story, Hal. Made lithographs on the Louisiana WPA.

Surendorf, Charles Frederick (1906–1979). Born in Richmond, IN. See p. 70. See: Falk; Smith, *American Printmakers;* Williams, *American Printmakers.*

Suydam, E. H. (Edward Howard) (1885–1940). Born in Vineland, NJ. A Philadelphia-based printmaker he made etchings of the French Quarter, many of which appeared in Saxon's *Fabulous New Orleans.* See: Falk; Smith, *American Printmakers.*

Swett, Ruth Doris (1901–1966). Born in Southern Pines, NC. Lived there as well as Winter Park, FL, and Maine. Made etchings. See: Falk; Smith, *American Printmakers.* Collections: Library of Congress.

Sykes, (William) Maltby (1911–1992). Born in Aberdeen, MS. Moved to Birmingham in 1916. Studied lithography with Wayman Adams and George Miller in New York in the 1930s and intaglio in Paris with Stanley William Hayter after World War II. In the 1940s he made realistic lithographs of Mexican scenes, military life, and musical performances, as well as imaginative interpretations of biblical figures. Began to teach art at Alabama Polytechnic Institute in 1941 and established the printmaking program there. See: Falk; *Spirit of the Modern.* Collections: Georgia, Jule Collins Smith.

Tannahill, Mary Harvey (1863–1951). Born in Warren County, NC, on family plantation. Moved with her family to New York in 1865. Made color woodblocks in Provincetown with white-line technique. See: *Eight Southern Women;* Falk; Smith, *American Printmakers.*

Tatum, Howard. Made architectural etchings of Charleston in the 1930s and 40s. Collections: Gibbes.

Taylor, Anna Heyward (1879–1956). Born in Columbia, SC. See p. 74. See: Falk; Severens, "South Carolina and the American Scene"; Smith, *American Printmakers;* Williams, *American Printmakers.* Collections: Columbia, Gibbes.

Taylor, Prentiss Hottel (1907–1991). Born in Washington, DC. See p. 156. See: Culpepper; Falk; Severens, "South Carolina and the American Scene"; Smith, *American Printmakers;* Williams, *American Printmakers.* Collections: Georgetown, Library of Congress, Smithsonian.

Thompson, Doris Alexander—See Alexander

Thompson, Walter Whitcomb (1882–1948). Born in Palatka, FL; lived in Mayesville, SC. See: Falk.

Tharin, Selma—See Dotterer

Thrash, Dox (1892–1965). Born in Griffin, GA. See p. 120. See: Culpepper; King-Hammond; Smith, *American Printmakers; Alone in a Crowd;* Williams, *American Printmakers.* Collections: Free Library, Metropolitan, Philadelphia, Saint Louis.

Turnbull, James Baare (1909–1976). Born in St. Louis, MO. Turnbull produced at least a few lithographs that are critical views of the South: *Southern Democracy* and a view of a chain gang with moss-hung trees in the background. Another view of sharecroppers sleeping in a shack may also be of the South. See: Falk; North and Goddard; Smith, *American Printmakers;* Williams, *American Printmakers.*

Turtle, Arnold (1892–1954). Born in Birmingham, England. In 1922 came to Chicago. Made etchings of the French Quarter. Collections: Historic New Orleans.

Verner, Elizabeth O'Neill (1883–1979). Born in Charleston, SC. See p. 76. See: Culpepper; Falk; King and DeLorme; Severens, *Charleston Renaissance* and "South Carolina and the American Scene"; Smith, *American Printmakers;* Williams, *American Printmakers.* Collections: Gibbes, Library of Congress, Morris.

Vorst, Joseph Paul (1897–1947). Born in Essen, Germany. Created lithographs of cotton and tobacco workers as well as of a chain gang. See: Falk; Smith, *American Printmakers.*

Waring, Leila (1876 –1964). Born in Charleston, SC. Made etchings with the Charleston Etchers' Club. See: Davis; Falk; Severens, *Charleston Renaissance.*

Warren, Elizabeth Boardman (1886–1980). Born in Bridgeport CT. Studied etching in England and with W. H. W. Bicknell in Provincetown. Began wintering in St. Augustine in 1934 with her husband Tod Lindenmuth and became residents when they purchased a house there in 1940. Depicted historic St. Augustine in numerous etchings and drypoints. Member Southern Printmakers Society. Source: Torchia. See also: Falk. Collections: St. Augustine.

Webb, Alonzo C. (1888–1975). Born in Nashville, TN. Spent most of his life in Europe and created architectural etchings of Europe and American skyscrapers in the 1920s. See: Falk; Smith, *American Printmakers.*

Weber, Frederick T(heodore) (1883–1956). Born in Columbia, SC, but spent most of youth in New York and Finland due to father's employment. In 1930s made etchings of European and New York views (streets, architecture, and landscape). See: Falk; Smith, *American Printmakers;* Williams, *American Printmakers.* Collections: Library of Congress.

Webster, Hutton, Jr. (1910–1956). Born in Lincoln, NE. In 1941 he became resident artist at Maitland Research Studio where he made a series of color monotypes featuring black figures. See: Falk; Smith, *American Printmakers.*

Wells, James Lesesne (1902–1993). Born in Atlanta, GA. Grew up in Florida. Made black-and-white linocuts in the 1920s and moved to wood engravings. Created lithographs in the 1930s and 1940s. Many biblical subjects, which suggest his background as the child of a preacher. See: Falk; Powell, "Talking with James Lesesne Wells"; Smith, *American Printmakers; Alone in a Crowd; American Printmakers.* Collections: Amistad.

Wells, Jane McClintock (1903–1993). Born in Charleston, SC. Graduated from Wellesley College. Joined the Charleston Etchers' Club in 1927 and exhibited relief prints. See: Davis; Falk; Severens, *Charleston Renaissance.*

Whaley, Edna Reed (1884–1979). Born in New Orleans, LA. Studied at Newcomb from 1901 to 1906. Later lived in Columbia, SC, during the 1930s. Last residence Lexington, SC. Made black-and-white as well as color woodcuts, many close-up images of floral blooms and some of sailboats. See: Falk. Collections: Morris.

White, Elizabeth (1893–1976). Born in Sumter, SC, where she lived most of her life. Studied intaglio with Frank Nankiwell in New York and with Alfred Hutty in Charleston and Woodstock. Taught in Sumter public schools and beginning in 1926 at the University of South Carolina. Made etchings, drypoints, and aquatints, which she exhibited with the Southern States Art League in the 1930s. Trees in a southern setting appear as her most frequent subject. See: Culpepper; Falk; Katz; Severens, "South Carolina and the American Scene"; Smith, *American Printmakers;* Williams, *American Printmakers; Work Song.* Collections: McKissick, Sumter.

Whitehead, Buell (1919–1994). Born Panama City, FL. See p. 102.

Whitelaw, Robert N. S. (1905–1975). Born in Charleston, SC, and educated at College of Charleston and the National Academy of Design. Studied under Alfred Hutty. Worked with William Beebe in the 1920s. Joined the Charleston Etchers' Club in second year and exhibited etchings. See: Davis; Severens, *Charleston Renaissance.*

Wickiser, Ralph Lewanda (1910–1998). Born in Greenup, IL. Taught graphic arts at Louisiana State University, 1938–57, and made lithographs. Became a member of the New Southern Group in New Orleans in 1940. See: Falk.

Wilcox, Edith. Part of a small group of women printmakers in Syracuse, NY, she spent time in Florida and pictured its architecture in a small body of woodcuts.

Wilimovsky, Charles A. (1885–1974). Born in Chicago, IL. Made small relief prints of French Quarter scenes and some with KKK images. See: Falk.

Willson, James Mallory (1890–1962). Born in Kissimmee, FL. Taught at the Norton School of Art, Palm Beach, 1946–50s. Made etchings of European subjects. See: Falk; Smith, *American Printmakers.*

Wolfe, Mildred Nungester—See Nungester

Woodruff, Hale Aspacio (1900–1980). Born in Cairo, IL. See p. 56. The Robert Blackburn workshop reprinted eight of the linoleum blocks from the original plates in the late 1990s and the plates were struck afterwards. Earl Washington made wood or linoleum prints after Hale Woodruff's original scenes but signing his own name to them. See: Culpepper; Falk; King-Hammond; Smith, *American Printmakers;* Williams, *American Printmakers.* Collections: Atlanta University, Metropolitan, Schomberg.

Woodward, Ellsworth (1861–1939). Born in Bristol County, MA. Made etchings as early as the 1880s. Woodward was particularly active as an etcher during his retirement in the 1930s when he made restrikes from earlier plates and new ones as well. His subjects included Vieux Carré architectural views, particularly the French Market, as well as figure studies. See: Falk; Smith, *American Printmakers;* Williams, *American Printmakers.* Collections: Historic New Orleans, Ogden.

Woodward, William (1859–1939). Born in Sekonk, MA. Came to New Orleans in 1884 to teach at Tulane. In the 1930s he made drypoints from Fiberloid, plastic-like sheets, which his brother Ellsworth printed. Many reproduced his Vieux Carré crayon drawing done 1890–1910s. A collected edition was for the benefit of the Vieux Carré Commission in 1936 and was used for his book *French Quarter Etchings,* published in 1938. Other drypoints depict scenes from the Mississippi coast and the mountain South. He exhibited his prints in the late 1930s. See: Falk; Smith, *American Printmakers;* Williams, *American Printmakers.* Collections: New Orleans.

Woolley, Guy Livingston (1892–1970). Born in Brooklyn, NY. Lived in New York until 1918, when he became vice president of a bank in New Orleans. Took up etching in 1940 under the tutelage of Morris Henry Hobbs and migrated to other intaglio media such as aquatint and mezzotint. He was known for his mezzotints, which he began to make in 1947. Collections: Historic New Orleans.

Wright, George Hand (1872–1951). Born in Philadelphia, PA. Lived in Westport, CT. Some information indicates he lived and worked in Louisiana as well. Made etchings of New Orleans and the surrounding swamp area. See: Falk; Smith, *American Printmakers.*

Yeomans, Walter Curtis (1882–1972). Born in Avon, IL. Lived in St. Augustine and made architectural etchings of the city. See: Falk.

Zoellner, Richard Charles (1908–2003). Born in Portsmouth, OH. See p. 100. See: Falk; Smith, *American Printmakers.*

Glossary of Print Media

THE FOLLOWING ARE DEFINITIONS of printmaking media used during the period under consideration in this book:[1]

INTAGLIO: A generic term that refers to all forms of printmaking whereby a metal plate is incised with a design by various types of tools and ink is placed in the grooves below the surface. The plate is printed by a rolling or etching press where it is pressed with considerable force against a piece of soft dampened paper. The basic methods of intaglio used by artists associated with the South:

Aquatint: An etching process that creates areas of tone when rosin is dusted or floated in a solvent on the metal plate, then heated so it will adhere. When the plate is immersed in the acid bath, acid bites through the exposed uniformly small spots between the resin particles so an even area of tone will be produced. Aquatint is often combined with etching.

Drypoint: The artist incises the plate directly with a special tool, raising a burr or metal residue. The burr holds ink and prints as a fuzzy, velvety line. Drypoint is often combined with etching.

Etching: The artist draws the design through an acid-resistant, waxy ground covering a metal plate so that metal is exposed in the design. The plate is then dipped in an acid bath, which eats through the exposed lines to incise them. The artist can stop out lines that he wants to print lightly and re-etch others to create deeper lines that will hold more ink to print darker and wider. The protective ground is removed with a solvent.

Mezzotint: An intaglio process that creates areas of tone when the artist roughens the surface of a copper plate with a tool called a rocker so it prints black, then selectively smoothes other areas to create an image. Few artists associated with the South used this process.[2]

PLANOGRAPHIC**:** or flat surface printing processes are of three basic types during the period under consideration here:

Lithograph: Relies on the chemical diversity of oil and water in the printing process. A drawing with a greasy crayon or liquid called "tusche" is made on a limestone slab or metal plate. A solution of gum arabic and nitric acid applied to the surface affixes the image to the plate and keeps it from spreading when it is rolled with ink. The plate is then dampened with a wet sponge, which the greasy image repels. When a greasy ink is rolled on the surface, it adheres to the image area but is repelled by the water everywhere else.

Monotype: A single print made by pressing a sheet of paper against a metal or glass plate on which an image or design has been drawn with printer's ink or oil plate. A press may or may not be used to print.[3]

Serigraph: A term applied to screen prints, which are intended as works of art. It refers to a stencil process in which colored ink is spread through a gauze or mesh screen, often made of silk, onto areas that are not blocked out by the application of a glue or varnish. Colored ink is pressed through the screen onto the paper under it. When the screen has been made of silk, the term "silkscreen" is sometimes used for the resulting print.[4]

RELIEF: A generic printmaking category that refers to the process by which a raised surface is inked and printed. The artist cuts away the area around the design so it prints white. During the first half of the twentieth century, artists used wood or linoleum for relief printmaking. Relief prints may be printed by hand with a spoon, or spoon-shaped wooden burnisher, or with any press except a rolling or etching press. They are sometimes called block prints, a term that some authorities reserve only for those from wood or linoleum while others accept it in relation to both. Because of such ambiguity this author avoids using the term. Those referred to in this book are in the following media:

Linoleum cut: The plate is made of linoleum, which is softer and more easily cut than wood; however, like wood it cannot accept a great deal of detail. Linoleum plates are often backed by wood. As in a woodcut the artist cuts away the area to be printed white.[5] The abbreviated term "linocut" is also used for a linoleum cut.

Woodcut: Using a tool called a gouger, the artist cuts away the area that is to print white on the plank or lengthwise side of a piece of wood, leaving the raised area to be printed as a black line.[6] The term "woodblock" is also commonly used for the medium but is not used in this book.

Wood engraving: The plate for a relief print is made from the end grain or cross section of wood, usually boxwood or maple, which is harder and can accept more detail than the lengthwise grain. Small pieces of wood are frequently glued together. The artist cuts narrow furrows in the wood, traditionally with a burin, the same tool used by a metal engraver. The furrows print as white lines, while the area that is not cut is inked and prints black. As a result, wood engravings print as white lines on a predominantly black background.

Selected Bibliography

Books and articles cited more than once in the text and referred to in Southern Connections are listed.

Unpublished sources

Manuscript Collections

Alabama Department of Archives and History, Montgomery, AL
  Elizabeth Metcalf file
Alderman Library, University of Virginia, Charlottesville, VA
  Special Collections Department, Charles William Smith papers
Amistad Research Center, Tulane University, New Orleans, LA
  Hale Woodruff papers
Auburn University Libraries, Special Collections and Archives, Auburn, AL
  Alabama Art League, scrapbook
Birmingham Public Library, Birmingham, AL
  Archives Department
  Frank Hartley Anderson file
  Tutweiler Collection
  Richard Coe file
Columbia Museum of Art, Columbia, SC
  Anna Heyward Taylor file
Hill Memorial Library, Louisiana State University, Baton Rouge, LA
  Special Collections, Caroline Durieux interview, 1975
Howard Tilton Library, Tulane University, New Orleans, LA
  Louisiana Collection, vertical files
Maitland Art Center, Maitland, FL
  Archives
Morris Museum of Art, Augusta, GA
  Clarence Millet file
Museum of Fine Arts, St. Petersburg, FL
  Polly Knipp Hill file
North Carolina Museum of Art, Raleigh, NC
  Mabel Pugh file
North Carolina State Library, Raleigh, NC

North Carolina artists file
Polk Museum of Art, Lakeland, FL
Kent Hagerman file
Smithsonian Archives of American Art
Anne Goldthwaite papers
George Biddle papers
Georges Schreiber papers
Holger Cahill papers
Raymond Steth papers
State Correspondence Files: Alabama, Florida, Georgia, Louisiana, North Carolina, South Carolina, Tennessee, Virginia
WPA/FAP
Sumter Gallery of Art, Sumter, SC
Elizabeth White file
Surendorf Gallery, Murphys, CA
Surendorf, Charles. "Artist Autobiography," unpublished typescript.
Tennessee State Library and Archives, Nashville, TN
Ella Sophonisba Hergesheimer file
Tucson Museum of Art, Tucson, AZ
Gerry Peirce file
Virginia Museum of Fine Arts, Richmond, VA
Charles William Smith file
Williams Research Center, Historic New Orleans Collection, New Orleans, LA
Arts and Crafts Club file
Louis Oscar Griffith file
Morris Henry Hobbs file
Charles Richards file
Alvin Sharpe file
G. Livingston Woolley file

Theses and Dissertations

Barkemeyer, Estelle. "Ellsworth Woodward: His Life and Work." Master's thesis, Tulane University, 1942.

Davis, Gwen Shepherd. "The Charleston Etchers' Club and Early South Carolina Printmakers." Master's thesis, University of South Carolina, 1982.

Dennison, Mariea Caudill. "Art of the American South, 1915–1945: Picturing the Past, Portending Regionalism." PhD diss., University of Illinois at Urbana–Champaign, 2000.

Kheel, Claudia. "Morris Henry Hobbs: Printmaker, 1892–1967." Master's thesis, Tulane University, 1994.

Knowles, Susan Williams. "A. C. Webb: Artist/Architect." Master's thesis, Vanderbilt University, 1986.

Stoelting, Winifred Louise. "Hale Woodruff, Artist and Teacher: Through the Atlanta Years." PhD diss., Emory University, 1979.

Published Sources

Books and Booklets

Acker, Marian Francis. *Etchings of Old Mobile.* Mobile, AL: Gill Printing and Stationary, 1938.

———. *Prints of the Past from Old Mobile.* Mobile, AL: n.p., 1932.

Adams, Clinton. *American Lithographers, 1900–1960: The Artists and Their Printers.* Albuquerque: University of New Mexico Press, 1983.

Alone in a Crowd: Prints of the 1930s–40s by African-American Artists: From the Collection of Reba and Dave Williams. 2nd rev. ed. N.p.: Washburn Press, 1993.

American Art Today: Gallery of American Art Today, New York World's Fair. Poughkeepsie, NY: Apollo, 1987. Reprint of 1939 catalog.

Apel, Dora. *Imagery of Lynching: Black Men, White Women, and the Mob.* New Brunswick, NJ: Rutgers University Press, 2004.

Arthur, Stanley Clisby. *Old New Orleans.* Edited by Susan Cole Doré. Gretna, LA: Pelican, 1990. Based on 1944 edition.

Beall, Karen F., et al., comps. *American Prints in the Library of Congress: A Catalog of the Collection.* Baltimore, MD: Johns Hopkins Press for the Library of Congress, 1970.

Benton, Thomas Hart. *An Artist in America.* Foreword and Afterword by Matthew Baigell. 4th rev. ed. Columbia: University of Missouri Press, 1983.

Bianco, George D. *The Prints of Philip Reisman: A Catalogue Raisonné.* Bedford, NY: Bedford Press, 1992.

Black, Patti Carr. *Art in Mississippi, 1720–1980.* Jackson: University Press of Mississippi in association with the Mississippi Historical Society and the Mississippi Department of Archives and History, 1998.

Bragg, Jean, and Susan Saward. *The Newcomb Style: Newcomb College Arts and Crafts and Art Pottery: Collector's Guide.* New Orleans: Jean Bragg Gallery, 2002.

Cash, W. J. *The Mind of the South.* New York: A. A. Knopf, 1941.

Chamberlain, Samuel. *Behold Williamsburg: A Pictorial Tour of Virginia's Colonial Capital.* New York: Hastings House in cooperation with Colonial Williamsburg, 1947.

———. *Etched in Sunlight: Fifty Years in the Graphic Arts.* Boston: Boston Public Library, 1968.

Chambers, Bruce W. *Art and Artists of the South: The Robert P. Coggins Collection.* Columbia: University of South Carolina Press, 1984.

Clark, Thomas D. *The Emerging South.* 2nd ed. New York: Oxford University Press, 1968.

Clarkson, John. *Blanche Lazzell.* Provincetown, MA: Provincetown Cape Cod Pilgrim Memorial Association, 1989.

Cole, Sylvan, ed. *The Lithographs of John Steuart Curry: A Catalogue Raisonné.* New York: Association of American Artists, 1976.

Cox, Richard. *Southern Works on Paper, 1900–1950.* [Baton Rouge]: n.p., 1981.

Craven, Thomas, ed. *A Treasury of American Prints: A Selection of One Hundred Etchings and Lithographs by the Foremost Living American Artists.* New York: Simon and Schuster, 1939.

Danilowitz, Brenda. *The Prints of Josef Albers: A Catalogue Raisonné, 1915–1976.* Foreword by Nicholas Fox Weber. New York: Hudson Hills Press in association with the Josef and Anni Albers Foundation, 2001.

Delehanty, Randolph. *Art in the American South: Works from the Ogden Collection.* Baton Rouge: Louisiana State University Press, 1996.

Dixon, Brandt V. B. *A Brief History of H. Sophie Newcomb Memorial College, 1887–1919: A Personal Reminiscence.* [New Orleans]: Hauser Printing Co., 1928.

Driskell, David C. *The Other Side of Color: African American Art in the Collection of Camille O. and William H. Cosby Jr.* San Francisco: Pomegranate, 2001.

Duffy, Betty, and Douglas Duffy. *Graphic Work of Howard Cook: A Catalogue Raisonné.* Bethesda, MD: Bethesda Art Gallery, 1984.

Eight Southern Women: Blanche Lazzell, Josephine Marien Crawford, Nell Choate Jones, Clara Weaver Parrish, Alice Ravenel Huger Smith, Helen M. Turner, Mary Harvey Tannahill, Anne Goldthwaite. Greenville, SC: Greenville County Museum of Art and Charleston, SC: Gibbes Art Gallery, 1986.

Elliott, Claude L. *Pressing On: The Graphic Art of Wilmer Jennings, September 29, 2000–January 7, 2001.* Providence: Museum of Art, Rhode Island School of Design, 2000.

Encyclopedia of African-American Culture and History. Edited by Jack Salzman, David Lionel Smith, and Cornel West. 5 vols. New York: Macmillan Library Reference, 1996.

Encyclopedia of Southern Culture. Edited by Charles Reagan Wilson and William Ferris. Chapel Hill: University of North Carolina Press for the Center for the Study of Southern Culture at the University of Mississippi, 1989.

Falk, Peter Hastings, and Audrey Lewis, eds. *Who Was Who in American Art, 1564–1975: 400 Years of Artists in America.* 3 vols. Madison, CT: Sound View Press, 1999.

Fax, Elton C. *Seventeen Black Artists.* New York: Dodd, Mead, 1971.

The Federal Art Project: American Prints from the 1930s in the Collection of the University of Michigan Museum of Art. Ann Arbor: University of Michigan Museum of Art, 1985.

Fite, Gilbert C. *Cotton Fields No More: Southern Agriculture, 1865–1980.* Lexington: University Press of Kentucky, 1984.

Flynt, J. Wayne. *Dixie's Forgotten People: The South's Poor Whites.* Bloomington: Indiana University Press, 1979.

Foushee, Ola Maie. *Art in North Carolina: Episodes and Developments, 1585–1970.* Chapel Hill, NC: n.p., 1972.

Freeman, Richard B. *The Lithographs of Ralston Crawford.* Lexington: University of Kentucky Press, 1962.

Gamble, Robert. *The Alabama Catalog: Historic American Buildings Survey: A Guide to the Early Architecture of the State.* Tuscaloosa: University of Alabama Press, 1987.

Gambone, Robert. *Art and Popular Religion in Evangelical America, 1915–1940.* Knoxville: University of Tennessee Press, 1989.

Gilbert, Gregory. *George Overbury "Pop" Hart: His Life and Art.* New Brunswick, NJ: Rutgers University Press and the Jane Voorhees Zimmerli Art Museum, 1986.

Goldfield, David R. *Cotton Fields and Skyscrapers: Southern City and Region, 1607–1980.* Baton Rouge: Louisiana State University Press, 1982.

Graphic Works of the American Thirties: A Book of 100 Prints. New York: Da Capo Press, 1977. Reprint of *America Today: A Book of 100 Prints Chosen and Exhibited by the American Artists' Congress* published by Equinox Cooperative Press in 1936.

Gruber, J. Richard. *Thomas Hart Benton and the American South.* Augusta, GA: Morris Museum of Art, 1998.

Hale Woodruff: 50 Years of His Art. New York: The Studio Museum in Harlem, April 20–June 24, 1979.

Hancock, Carl. *Etchings, Dry-Points, Sketches.* New Orleans: Peerless Press, 1938.

Harris, Michael D. *Colored Pictures: Race and Visual Representation.* Chapel Hill: University of North Carolina Press, 2003.

Harris, Paul Rogers. *The Texas Printmakers.* Dallas: Meadows Museum, Southern Methodist University, 1990.

Hemingway, Andrew. *Artists on the Left: American Artists and the Communist Movement, 1926–1956.* New Haven, CT: Yale University Press, 2002.

Herzog, Melanie Anne. *Elizabeth Catlett: An American Artist in Mexico.* Seattle: University of Washington Press, 2000.

Hosmer, Charles B. *Preservation Comes of Age;* Vol. II: *From Williamsburg to the National Trust, 1926–1949.* Charlottesville: University of Virginia Press for the Preservation Press, National Trust for Historic Preservation in the United States, 1981.

Ingham, Vicki Leigh. *Art of the New South: Women Artists of Birmingham, 1890–1950.* Birmingham, AL: Birmingham Historical Society, 2004.

Ittmann, John. *Dox Thrash: An African American Master Printmaker Rediscovered.* With essays by David R. Brigham, Cindy Medley-Buckner, and Kimberly Pinder. Philadelphia: Philadelphia Museum of Art, 2001. This work includes a catalogue raisonné.

Jones, Jacqueline. *Labor of Love, Labor of Sorrow: Black Women, Work, and the Family from Slavery to the Present.* New York: Basic Books, 1985.

Kane, Harnett T. *Queen New Orleans: City by the River.* New York: William Morrow, 1949.

Kappel, Philip. *Louisiana Gallery: The River Country and New Orleans.* New York: Putnam, 1950.

Katz, Harry L., ed. *Life of the People: Realist Prints and Drawings from the Ben and Beatrice Goldstein Collection, 1912–1948.* Essays by Bernard F. Reilly Jr. and Garnett McCoy. Washington, DC: Library of Congress, 1999.

Keyes, Donald D., with a critical essay by Marlene Park. *Andrée Ruellan.* Athens: Georgia Museum of Art, University of Georgia, 1993.

King, Pamela D., and Harry H. DeLorme. *Looking Back: Art in Savannah, 1900–1960.* Savannah, GA: Telfair Museum of Art, 1996.

Kirby, Jack Temple. *Rural Worlds Lost: The American South, 1920–1960.* Baton Rouge: Louisiana State University Press, 1987.

Kirk, Mary Wallace. *Cabins and Characters.* Birmingham, AL: Southern University Press, 1969.

———. *Locust Hill.* [Tuscaloosa]: University of Alabama Press, 1975.

Knute Heldner and the Art Colony in Old New Orleans. New Orleans: Jean Bragg Gallery, 2000. Catalog for sales exhibition, October 2000.

Kraft, June, and Norman Kraft. *Great American Prints, 1900–1950.* New York: Dover, 1984.

Lang, Gladys Engel, and Kurt Lang. *Etched in Memory: The Building and Survival of Artistic Reputation.* Introduction to paperback edition. Urbana: University of Illinois Press, 2001.

Lankes, Julius J. *Virginia Woodcuts.* Newport News, VA: Virginia Press, 1930.

———. *A Woodcut Manual.* New York: H. Holt, 1932.

Larson Judy L., ed., with the assistance of Cynthia Payne. *Graphic Arts and the South: Proceedings of the 1990 North American Print Conference.* Fayetteville: University of Arkansas Press, 1993.

Laughlin, Clarence John. *Ghosts along the Mississippi: An Essay in the Poetic Interpretation of Louisiana's Plantation Architecture.* New York: Scribner's, 1948.

———. *New Orleans and Its Living Past.* Boston: Houghton, Mifflin, 1941.

LeFalle-Collins, Lizzetta, and Leonard Simon. *The Portrayal of the Black Musician in American Art: March 7–August 14, 1987.* Los Angeles: California Afro-American Museum, 1987.

Leighton, Clare. *Southern Harvest.* New York: Macmillan, 1942.

Leininger-Miller, Theresa. *New Negro Artists in Paris: African American Painters and Sculptors in the City of Light, 1922–1934.* New Brunswick, NJ: Rutgers University Press, 2001.

Locke, Alain, ed. *The Negro in Art: A Pictorial Record of the Negro Artist and of the Negro Theme in Art.* Reprint. New York: Hacker Art Books, 1968.

The Long Weekend: The Arts and the Vieux Carré between the World Wars, 1914–1918: A Two Part Exhibition. Part I: *The 1920s: From Armistice to the Crash;* Part II: *The 1930s: From the Crash to Pearl Harbor.* New Orleans: Historic New Orleans Collection, 1993.

Lumsdaine, Joycelyn Pang, and Thomas O'Sullivan, eds. *The Prints of Adolf Dehn: A Catalogue Raisonné.* St. Paul: Minnesota Historical Society, 1987.

Lynn, Stuart M. *New Orleans.* New York: Bonanza, 1949.

Mason, Tim, and Lynn Mason. *Helen Hyde.* Washington, DC: Smithsonian Institution Press, 1991.

Masteller, Richard N. *"We the People?": Satiric Prints of the 1930s.* Walla Walla, WA: Donald H. Sheehan Gallery with Whitman College, 1989.

McElroy, Guy, with an essay by Henry Louis Gates Jr. *Facing History: The Black Image in American Art, 1710–1940.* San Francisco: Bedford Arts and Washington, DC: Corcoran Gallery of Art, 1990.

McNeely, Stanley Blake. *Bits of Charm in Old Mobile.* Mobile, AL: Gill Printing and Stationary, 1946.

Meech, Julia, and Gabriel P. Weisberg. *Japonisme Comes to America: The Japanese Impact on the Graphic Arts, 1876–1925.* New York: Harry N. Abrams in association with the Jane Voorhees Zimmerli Art Museum, Rutgers, State University of New Jersey, 1990.

Moser, Joann. *Singular Impressions: The Monotype in America.* Washington, DC: Smithsonian Institution Press, 1997.

Murphy, Christopher. *Savannah, Etchings and Drawings.* Columbia, SC: Bostick and Thornley, 1947.

Newcomb College Arts and Crafts Sales Exhibition: October 30–November 30, 1998. New Orleans: Jean Bragg Gallery, 1998.

North, Bill, and Stephen H. Goddard. *Rural America: Prints from the Collection of Steven Schmidt.* [Lawrence]: Spencer Museum of Art, University of Kansas, 1993.

Odum, Howard W. *Southern Regions of the United States.* Chapel Hill: University of North Carolina Press, 1936.

———. *The Way of the South: Toward the Regional Balance of America.* New York: Macmillan, 1947.

Ormond, Suzanne, and Mary E. Irvine. *Louisiana's Art Nouveau: The Crafts of the Newcomb Style.* Gretna, LA: Pelican, 1976.

Pennington, Estill Curtis. *Downriver: Currents of Style in Louisiana Painting, 1800–1950.* Gretna, LA: Pelican, 1991.

Phagan, Patricia, ed. *The American Scene and the South: Paintings and Works on Paper, 1930–1946.* [Athens]: Georgia Museum of Art, University of Georgia, 1996.

Poesch, Jessie, with Walter Bob and Sally Main Spanola. *Newcomb Pottery: An Enterprise for Southern Women, 1895–1940.* Exton, PA: Schiffer Publishing, 1984.

Pohl, Frances K. *In the Eye of the Storm: An Art of Conscience, 1930–1970.* San Francisco: Pomegranate, 1995.

Powdermaker, Hortense. *After Freedom: A Cultural Study of the Deep South.* New York: Viking, 1939.

Powell, Richard J. *Black Art and Culture in the 20th Century.* New York: Thames and Hudson, 1997.

Powell, Richard J., and Jock Reynolds. *To Conserve a Legacy: American Art from Historically Black Colleges and Universities.* Andover, MA: Addison Gallery of American Art, Phillips Academy, and the Studio Museum in Harlem, New York, 1999.

Powers, John E., and Deborah Powers. *Texas Painters, Sculptors and Graphic Artists: A Biographical Dictionary of Artists in Texas before 1942.* Austin, TX: Woodmont Books, 2000.

Preston, Howard Lawrence. *Dirt Roads to Dixie: Accessibility and Modernization in the South, 1885–1935.* Knoxville: University of Tennessee Press, 1991.

Prieto, Laura R. *At Home in the Studio: The Professionalization of Women Artists in America.* Cambridge, MA: Harvard University Press, 2001.

Ray, Lisa. *Southern Women Artists: From the Collections of the Columbia Museum of Art.* Columbia, SC: Columbia Museum of Art, 1990.

Reese, Albert. *American Prize Prints of the 20th Century.* New York: American Artists Group, 1949.

Reynolds, Gary A., and Beryl J. Wright. *Against the Odds: African-American Artists and the Harmon Foundation.* Newark, NJ: Newark Museum, 1989.

Robertson, Bruce. *Representing America: The Ken Trevey Collection of American Realist Prints.* Santa Barbara: University Art Museum, University of California at Santa Barbara, 1995.

Saunders, Boyd, and Ann McAden. *Alfred Hutty and the Charleston Renaissance.* Orangeburg, SC: Sandlapper Publishing, 1990.

Saxon, Lyle. *Fabulous New Orleans.* Introduction and notes by Robert Tallant and illustrated by E. H. Suydam. New Orleans: Robert L. Crager, 1952.

Severens, Martha R. *Alice Ravenel Huger Smith: An Artist, A Place, and a Time.* Charleston, SC: Carolina Art Museum, Gibbes Museum of Art, 1993.

———. *Anna Heyward Taylor: Printmaker.* [Greenville, SC]: Greenville County Museum of Art and Gibbes Art Gallery, 1987.

———. *The Charleston Renaissance.* Spartanburg, SC: Saraland Press, 1998.

———. *Greenville County Museum of Art: The Southern Collection.* Introduction by William H. Gerdts. New York: Hudson Hills Press in association with the Greenville County Museum of Art, 1995.

Shapiro, Barbara Stern. *From Paris to Provincetown: Blanche Lazzell and the Woodcut.* Boston: MFA Publications, a division of the Museum of Fine Arts, 2002.

Simkins, Francis Butler. *The Everlasting South.* [Baton Rouge]: Louisiana State University Press, 1963.

Smith, Charles William. *Abstractions.* New York: Johnson Company Publishing, 1939.

———. *Linoleum Block Printing.* Waynesboro, VA: Charles W. Smith Press, 1925.

———. *Old Charleston: Twenty-Four Woodcuts.* Richmond, VA: Dale Press, 1933.

———. *Old Virginia in Block Prints.* Introduction by John W. Rixey Smith. Richmond, VA: Dale Press, 1929.

———. *The University of Virginia: Thirty-Two Woodcuts.* Richmond, VA: Johnson Company Publishing, 1937.

Smith, Donald E. *American Printmakers of the Twentieth Century: A Bibliography.* Haworth, NJ: St. Johann Press, 2004.

The Spirit of the Modern: Drawings and Graphics by Maltby Sykes. Athens: Georgia Museum of Art, University of Georgia, 2004.

Stewart, Rick. *Lone Star Regionalism: The Dallas Nine and Their Circle, 1928–1945.* Austin: Texas Monthly Press and Dallas: Dallas Museum of Art, 1985.

Tallant, Robert. *The Romantic New Orleanians.* New York: E. P. Dutton, 1950.

Tannenbaum, Frank. *Darker Phases of the South.* New York: Putnam, 1924.

Tindall, George B. *The Emergence of the New South, 1913–1945.* [Baton Rouge]: Louisiana State University Press and the Littlefield Fund for Southern History of the University of Texas, 1967.

Torchia, Robert. *Lost Colony: The Artists of St. Augustine, 1930–1950.* St. Augustine, FL: Lightner Museum, 2001.

Vance, Rupert C. *All These People: The Nation's Human Resources in the South.* Chapel Hill: University of North Carolina Press, 1945.

Verner, Elizabeth O'Neill. *Prints and Impressions of Charleston: Forty-Eight Etchings.* Columbia, SC: Bostick and Thornley, 1939.

Vlach, John Michael. *Back of the Big House: The Architecture of Plantation Slavery.* Chapel Hill: University of North Carolina Press, 1993.

Watrous, James. *American Printmaking: A Century of American Printmaking, 1880–1980.* Madison: University of Wisconsin Press, 1984.

Wax, Carol. *The Mezzotint: History and Technique.* New York: Harry N. Abrams, 1990.

Williams, Lynn Barstis, comp. *American Printmakers, 1880–1945: An Index to Reproductions and Biocritical Information.* Metuchen, NJ: Scarecrow Press, 1993.

Williams, Reba, and Dave Williams. *American Screenprints.* New York: National Academy of Design, 1987.

Wilson, Raymond L. *Index of American Print Exhibitions, 1882–1940.* Metuchen, NJ: Scarecrow Press, 1988.

Woodward, William. *French Quarter Etchings of Old New Orleans.* New Orleans: Magnolia Press, 1938.

Wootten, Bayard, and Samuel Gaillard Stoney. *Charleston: Azaleas and Old Bricks.* Boston: Houghton, Mifflin, 1939.

Work Song. [Greenville, SC]: Greenville County Museum of Art, 1990.

Yuhl, Stephanie E. *A Golden Haze of Memory: The Making of Historic Charleston.* Chapel Hill: University of North Carolina Press, 2005.

Zigrosser, Carl, and Christa M. Gaehde. *A Guide to the Collecting and Care of Original Prints.* New York: Crown, 1968.

Articles and Chapters of Books

Brigham, David R. "Bridging Identities: Dox Thrash as African American and Artist." *Smithsonian Studies in American Art* 4 (1990): 27–39.

Brownell, Blaine A. "The Urban South Comes of Age, 1900–1940." In *The City in Southern History: The Growth of Urban Civilization in the South,* edited by Blaine A. Brownell and David R. Goldfield, 123–58. Port Washington, NY: Kennikat Press, 1977.

Cox, Richard. "Genre Art in Louisiana and Mississippi, 1930–1946." In Phagan, *American Scene and the South,* 103–33.

Culpepper, Angela, and Alan Vannoy. "Biographies and Major Sources." In Phagan, *American Scene and the South,* 243–63.

Eiland, William U. "Picturing the Unvictorious: The Southern Scene in Alabama, 1930–1946." In Phagan, *American Scene and the South,* 33–74.

Evaul, William H. "The Provincetown Printers: Genesis of a Unique Color-Woodcut Process." *Print Review* 18 (1984): 57–66.

Farmer, David, "The Printmakers Guild and Women Printmakers in Texas, 1939–1965." In *Prints and Printmakers of Texas: Proceedings of the North American Print Conference,* edited by Ron Taylor, 117–35. Austin: Texas State Historical Association, 1997.

Gregory, Ula Milner. "The Fine Arts." In *Culture in the South,* edited by W. T. Couch, 270–98. Chapel Hill: University of North Carolina Press, 1935.

Gruber, J. Richard. "Looking Forward, Looking Back: Painting in the South, 1900–1950." In *A Place Not Forgotten: Landscapes of the South from the Morris Museum of Art,* 27–40. Lexington: University of Kentucky Art Museum, 1999.

Hickman, Caroline Mesrobian. "Women and the Transformation of Art in Early 20th Century North Carolina." In *Nine from North Carolina,* 13–21. An exhibition organized by the North Carolina State Committee for presentation at the National Museum of Women in the Arts, Washington, DC, 1999.

Kainen, Jacob. "The Graphic Arts Division of the WPA Federal Art Project." In *The New Deal Art Projects: An Anthology of Memoirs,* edited by Francis V. O'Connor, 155–76. Washington, DC: Smithsonian Institution Press, 1972.

King-Hammond, Leslie. "WPA Black Printmakers: Southern Life, Social Realities, and the Modernist Impulse." In Phagan, *American Scene and the South,* 201–25.

Medley-Buckner, Cindy. "Carborundum Mezzotint and Carborundum Etching." *Print Quarterly* 16 (1999): 34–49.

———. "The Fine Print Workshop of the Philadelphia Federal Art Project." In *Dox Thrash: An African American Master Printmaker Rediscovered,* edited by John Ittmann, 43–51. Philadelphia: Philadelphia Museum of Art in association with the University of Washington Press, 2001.

O'Malley, James R. "Functional Aspects of Folk Housing: A Case for the 'I' House, Union County, Tennessee." *Tennessee Folklore Society Bulletin* 38 (March 1972): 1–4.

"Our New Day Begun: Atlanta's Black Artistic Heritage," *Atlanta History* 37 (Spring 1993): 33–43.

Phagan, Patricia. "The American Scene in Georgia." In Phagan, *American Scene and the South,* 75–102.

———. "Critical Views of the South by Northern Artists: Antilynching in the 1930s." In Phagan, *American Scene and the South,* 227–41.

———. "Introduction." In Phagan, *American Scene and the South,* 9–32.

———. "Tours and Visits of the South." In Phagan, *American Scene and the South,* 179–99.

Powell, Richard J. "Talking with James Lesesne Wells." *Print Review* 9 (1979): 65–75.

Rub, Timothy F. "American Architectural Prints." *Print Review* 18 (1984): 7–19.

Scardaville, Michael C. "Elizabeth O'Neill Verner: The Artist as Preservationist." In *Mirror of Time: Elizabeth O'Neill Verner's Charleston,* 17–25. [Columbia]: McKissick Museum, University of South Carolina, 1983.

Severens, Martha. "South Carolina and the American Scene." In Phagan, *American Scene and the South,* 135–68.

———. "Southern Scene." *American Art Review* 8 (February 2001): 112–19.

Williams, Lynn Barstis. "An Artistic Blend: Frank and Martha Anderson." *Alabama Heritage* no. 78 (Fall 2005): 14–23.

———. "The Dixie Art Colony." *Alabama Heritage* no. 41 (Summer 1996): 6–15.

———. "Images of Scottsboro." *Southern Cultures* 6 (Spring 2000): 50–67.

Endnotes

Notes to Chapter One

1. See Maybelle Mann, *Art in Florida: 1564–1945* (Sarasota, FL: Pineapple Press, 1999), 7–17; Harold. S. Sniffen, "Southern Views in Prints," *The Magazine Antiques* 60 (October 1951): 300–302.
2. For national historical trends, See Watrous, *American Printmaking,* 3–20.
3. See, for example, M. G. Van Rensselaer, "American Etchers," *The Century Magazine* 25 (February 1883): 483–99.
4. Jessie Poesch, "Growth and Development of the Old South: 1830–1900," in *Painting in the South, 1564–1980,* comp. David S. Bundy, (Richmond: Virginia Museum of Fine Arts, 1983), 74.
5. See entries in catalogs such as Rona Schneider's *American Painter Etchings, 1853–1908* (New York: Grolier Club, 1989), catalog for an exhibition, February 21–April 1, 1989, 29–34.
6. See Frederic A. Sharf, "St. Augustine: City of Artists: 1883–1895." *Antiques* 90 (August 1966): 221; Sandra Barghini, *Society of Painters: Flagler's St. Augustine Art Colony* (Palm Beach, FL: Henry Morrison Flagler Museum, 1998), n.p.; Susan Braden, *Architecture of Leisure: The Florida Resort Hotels of Henry Flagler and Henry Plant* (Gainesville: University Press of Florida, 2002), 78, 84.
7. Pennington, *Downriver,* 132–37.
8. George W. Cable, "Who Are the Creoles?" *The Century Magazine* 25 (1882–83): 385.
9. Joseph Pennell, *The Adventures of an Illustrator, Mostly in Following His Authors in America and Europe* (Boston: Little, Brown, 1925), 89–99.
10. Poesch, *Newcomb Pottery,* 9–14; Bragg and Saward, *The Newcomb Style,* 59.
11. Barkemeyer, "Ellsworth Woodward," 49–50.
12. "New York Woman's Etchings Charm Art World," *New York Evening Sun,* May 18, 1913. Anne Goldthwaite papers, Smithsonian Archives of American Art, Reel #D359.
13. Adams, *American Lithographers, 1900–1960,* 49.
14. Watrous, *American Printmaking,* 20–26.
15. Prieto, *At Home in the Studio,* 38; Meech and Weisberg, *Japonisme Comes to America,* passim.
16. Severens, *Charleston Renaissance,* 31–32.
17. Bragg and Saward, *Newcomb Style,* 5.
18. See Poesch, *Newcomb Pottery,* 40; Bragg and Saward, *Newcomb Style,* 13, 17.
19. Lang and Lang, *Etched in Memory,* 64–66; Wilson, *Index of American Print Exhibitions, 1882–1940,* 43, 181, 194, 331.
20. *Exhibition of Paintings and Etchings of New Orleans by Robert W. Grafton and Louis Oscar Griffith,*

Delgado Museum, 1916. This exhibition brochure can be found in the Louis Oscar Griffith file, Historic New Orleans Collection. See also Pennington, *Downriver,* 169, who mentions Griffith's visit in reference to painting.

21. Gideon Stanton letter to Ralph Pearson, August 17, 1921. Arts and Crafts Club file, folder 17, Historic New Orleans Collection.
22. Ibid.
23. See Antony Stanonis, "Always in Costume and Mask: Lyle Saxon and New Orleans Tourism," *Louisiana History* 42 (2001): 32–55; Laura Clark Brown, "New Orleans Modernism: The Arts and Crafts Club in the Vieux Carré, 1919–1939," *Louisiana History* 41 (2000): 327–29; James W. Thomas, *Lyle Saxon: A Critical Biography* (Birmingham, AL: Summa, 1991), 30–31; *Knute Heldner and the Art Colony in Old New Orleans,* 6–11; Tallant, *The Romantic New Orleanians,* 307–28.
24. *The Long Weekend,* Part I: *The 1920s,* n.p.
25. Nancy Sortore, "Gerry Peirce's Arizona," *Arizona Daily Star,* January 20, 1975. Gerry Peirce file, Tucson Museum of Art.
26. Hal Crowther, *Cathedrals of Kudzu: A Personal Landscape of the South* (Baton Rouge: Louisiana State University Press, 2000), 52.
27. Myrtie Engelkes telephone interview with author, January 6, 2006.
28. See *The Long Weekend,* Part II: *The 1930s,* n.p.
29. Lang and Lang, *Etched in Memory,* 72.
30. "Old New Orleans as Seen by Etcher Hobbs," *Art Digest,* October 15, 1939, 24.
31. Kheel, "Morris Henry Hobbs," 84, 88; Marmion, "The Banker Became an Artist," *New Orleans Times-Picayune,* May 13, 1951.
32. Charles Surendorf, "Artist Autobiography," 9–10; unpublished typescript, courtesy of Surendorf Gallery.
33. Gregory, "The Fine Arts," 285.
34. Before the First World War, the only fine prints associated with the city were the etchings of Charles Henry White, who visited the port in 1905 to depict its architecture for a book on American cities. He also did a number of etchings of New Orleans. Severens, *Charleston Renaissance,* 7–9.
35. For information on Alice Smith's contributions to the "Charleston Renaissance" see Severens, *Alice Ravenel Huger Smith: An Artist, a Place and a Time* and Yuhl, *A Golden Haze of Memory,* 60–74.
36. See Severens, *Charleston Renaissance,* 36–44; Severens, "To Sell the City of Charleston: The Visual Arts and the Charleston Renaissance," in *Renaissance in Charleston: Art and Life in the Carolina Low Country, 1900–1940,* ed. James M. Hutchisson and Harlan Greene, 35–50 (Athens: University of Georgia Press, 2003); Saunders and McAden, *Alfred Hutty and the Charleston Renaissance,* 43–56; Yuhl, *A Golden Haze of Memory,* 75–76.
37. Titles of books by Saunders and Severens bear this title. See Yuhl, *A Golden Haze of Memory,* 15–16 for a critical explanation of the term.
38. In a telephone interview with the author (March 1994), Selma Tharin Dotterer stated that she and Antoinette Rhett learned etching from Hutty.
39. The four others were Minnie Mikell, Antoinette Rhett, Leila Waring, and author John Bennett; see Severens, *Charleston Renaissance,* 36.
40. Severens states that the last exhibition was held in 1928; *Charleston Renaissance,* 44. However, Davis notes that the final exhibition took place in 1933; "The Charleston Etchers' Club and Early South Carolina Printmakers," 25.
41. "Chronology of Anna Heyward Taylor's Life," Anna Heyward Taylor file, Columbia Museum of Art, Columbia, SC; Saunders and McAden, *Alfred Hutty and the Charleston Renaissance,* 21–22; Severens, *Charleston Renaissance,* 4.

42. Yuhl, *A Golden Haze of Memory,* 75–76, 78–79; Lynn Robertson Myers, "Doing and Creating: A Biographical Sketch," in *Mirror of Time: Elizabeth O'Neill Verner's Charleston,* ed. Lynn Robertson Myers ([Columbia, SC]: McKissick Museum, University of South Carolina, 1987), 12; Dennison, "Art of the American South," 151–56.
43. Severens, *Charleston Renaissance,* 53–55, 76–79, 114–20.
44. See Torchia, *Lost Colony,* 11–38.
45. Robert Harper, Director, Lightner Museum, telephone interview with author, November 14, 2005.
46. Etchings of Elizabeth Verner illustrated DuBose Heyward's *Porgy* (1925), while four woodcuts of Lankes were used in Rossa Belle Cooley's *Homes of the Freed* (1926).
47. See Rainey, "Images of the South in *Picturesque America* and *The Great South,*" in *Graphic Arts and the South,* ed. Judy L. Larson with the assistance of Cynthia Payne, 185–215.
48. In *The Ardent Image: Book Illustration for Adults in America, 1920–1942* ([Toledo, OH]: Ward M. Canaday Center, University of Toledo, 1995), Judith M. Friebert notes that Rockwell Kent first produced a deluxe edition before the trade version of some of his books, while Lynd Ward had his own press, through which he produced hand-bound books: 13, 20–21. See also Roderick Cave's *The Private Press,* 2nd ed. (New York: R. R. Bowker, 1983) for a general history of the private press movement here and abroad. Charles William Smith, noteworthy as a book designer, included six original woodcuts in his book *Abstractions* (1939). The monograph is an oddity as poor black-and-white reproductions hardly complement the fine abstract, color woodcuts on thin, delicate, paper.
49. In addition to Hancock's *Etchings, Drypoints, and Sketches,* the OCLC Worldcat database lists three other publications by Hancock that appear to be pamphlets with unspecified publication data: *Old New Orleans Patios, Alleys and Stairways; Seeing New Orleans;* and *Old New Orleans.*
50. Complete citations to these books are in the bibliography.
51. See such photographic tours as those of Clarence Laughlin; Lynn, *New Orleans* (1949); or May Randlette Beck, *Ghosts of Old Mobile* (Mobile: Haunted Book Shop, 1946.)
52. Brownell, "The Urban South Comes of Age, 1900–1940" 128.
53. Jessie Poesch, "The Thirst for Self Expression: Women in the Visual Arts in the South, 1860–1960," in *A New Perspective: Southern Women's Cultural History from the Civil War to Civil Rights,* ed. Priscilla Cortelyou Little and Robert C. Vaughan (Charlottesville: Virginia Foundation for the Humanities, 1989), 44.
54. Sophonisba Hergesheimer letter to Ernest Pickup, October 4, 1942 (in possession of Beverly St. John); Beverly St. John interview with author, July 7, 2000.
55. In 1907, a group of Birmingham women organized the Birmingham Art Club, which remained active through the founding of the Birmingham Museum of Art in 1951. An earlier organization, the Birmingham Art League, was extant from 1891 to 1898. See Ingham, *Art of the New South,* 7–19, 124.
56. "Southern Printmakers Hold First Annual, Which Goes on Circuit," *Art Digest,* April 1, 1936, 22; "Advice to the South," *Art Digest,* December 1, 1935, 9.
57. Martha Prince letter to author, April 19, 1997.
58. Lang and Lang, *Etched in Memory,* 71–72.
59. *Art Digest,* April 1, 1936, 22; "Print Exhibit to Open Here," *Birmingham Post,* February 22, 1936.
60. *Art Digest,* June 1, 1938, 23.
61. See Williams, "An Artistic Blend," 23, for the final deathblow to the organization; *Art Digest,* October 1, 1942, 11; *Art Digest,* May 1, 1947, 12.
62. Powell, *Black Art and Culture in the 20th Century,* 49–50.
63. *Hale Woodruff,* 20.
64. Surendorf, "Artist Autobiography," 5–6.

65. Stoelting, "Hale Woodruff, Artist and Teacher," 75.
66. "Our New Day Begun," 33.
67. Robertson, *Representing America,* 12.
68. Watrous, *American Printmaking,* 108–15.
69. See "McCrady's Nostalgic Interpretations of the Deep South," *Art News,* October 23, 1937, 15–16.
70. Mildred Nungester (Wolfe) interview with author, August 4, 1993.
71. James Routh interview with author, December 17, 2005.
72. Preston, *Dirt Roads to Dixie,* 108, 139.
73. Gruber, *Thomas Hart Benton and the American South,* 8, 46; Phagan, "Tours and Visits of the South," 179–94.
74. See Cox, *Southern Works on Paper, 1900–1950,* 8; Preston, *Dirt Roads to Dixie,* 110–11.
75. Katz, *Life of the People,* 77; Hemingway, *Artists on the Left,* 90; Phagan, "Tours and Visits of the South," 179–99.
76. Eugene Balk, "The 'American Scene' Print and the Cartoon," *Print Quarterly* 40 (1994): 387.
77. Jonathan Harris, *Federal Art and National Culture: The Political Identity in New Deal America* (Cambridge: Cambridge University Press, 1995), 44–49.
78. I have scanned correspondence files on microfilm for most of the southeastern states; however, some of this correspondence is not very legible.
79. William S. Wood letter to Holger Cahill, February 19, 1936; Holger Cahill letter to Eve Alsman Fuller, May 6, 1936; Holger Cahill memorandum to Jacob Baker, May 6, 1936; [Frank J.] Cogan memorandum to [Thomas C.] Parker, July 16, 1936; Thomas C. Parker letter to Eve Alsman Fuller, July 18, 1936; Eve Alsman Fuller letter to Thomas C. Parker, August 22, 1939. WPA/FAP Central Correspondence Files: Florida; Smithsonian Archives of American Art, Roll #DC 23.
80. Richard Merrick interviewed by Richard K. Doud in Miami, FL, June 14, 1965. Typescript, Smithsonian Archives of American Art.
81. Adele Clark letter to Thomas C. Parker, November 2, 1938. WPA/FAP Central Correspondence Files: Virginia; Smithsonian Archives of American Art, Roll #DC 108.
82. *Long Weekend,* Part II: *The 1930s,* n.p.
83. Caroline Durieux, oral history interview, 1975. Transcript, Mss. 4700.0013. Special Collections, Hill Memorial Library, Louisiana State University, 2–4.
84. See Medley-Buckner, "Carborundum Mezzotint and Carborundum Etching," 34–49; Medley-Bruckner, "The Fine Print Workshop of the Philadelphia Federal Art Project," 44; King-Hammond, "WPA Black Printmakers," 207; Ittmann, *Dox Thrash,* 90–129.
85. See Kainen's account of the New York Art Project, which produced the largest number of prints, in "The Graphic Arts Division of the Federal Art Project," 155–76.
86. Adams, *American Lithographers,* 24–42.
87. James Routh letter to author, September 11, 1993.
88. Maltby Sykes, "Recollections of a Lithographile," *The Tamarind Papers* 6, no. 1 (Summer 1983): 40–47.
89. Mildred Nungester (Wolfe) letter to author, August 4, 1993.
90. James Routh letter to author, August 17, 1993.
91. "Mrs. Thompson's Art Makes Fine Display at Museum," *Montgomery Advertiser,* October 5, 1947.
92. Doris Alexander Thompson letter to author, May 26, 1995; Michael Crouse conversation with author, November 26, 2005.
93. Warree LeBron Archives in possession of LeBron family.
94. Danilowitz, *The Prints of Josef Albers,* 17.
95. Moser, *Singular Impressions,* 133. In *A History of Visual Art in Sarasota,* Pat Ringling Buck, Marcia Corbino, and Kevin Dean (Gainesville: University Press of Florida, 2003), 60, state that Margo

was an instructor at the center but there were no instructors or classes, only winter residents or Bok Fellows, as they were called, who did their own creative work. Richard D. Colvin e-mail to author, November 28, 2005. In *Printmaking,* Peterdi describes Margo's cellocut process as depositing a varnish made of plastic and dissolved in acetone on a metal or wood plate and working it with intaglio or relief methods, 239.

96. Mrs. Duke Bianca telephone interview with author, February 2, 1994; "Andre Smith," unpublished typescript, and handwritten list of Maitland artists; Maitland Art Center. Unfortunately the archives of the Maitland Center are scant, so documentary information is minimal.
97. See Fred C. Hobson Jr. *Serpent in Eden: H. L. Mencken and the South* (Chapel Hill: University of North Carolina Press, 1974), especially chapter 1.
98. See Hemingway, *Artists on the Left,* 1, 18, 55–56, 65, 90.
99. Harry Sternberg letter to author, [1994].
100. See Raymond J. Steiner, *Art Students League of New York: A History* (Saugerties, NY: CSS Publications, 1999), xx.
101. James Routh letter to author, August 3, 1993; Harry Sternberg letter to author, July 1994.
102. Harry Sternberg letter to author, March 1994.
103. Mildred Nungester (Wolfe) letter to author, March 22, 2000.
104. Amy Helene Kirschke, "The Southern States Art League: A Regionalist Artists' Organization, 1922–1950," *Southern Quarterly* 25 (Winter 1987): 1–23; Kirschke, "Elizabeth O'Neill Verner and the Southern States Art League," in *Mirror of Time: Elizabeth O'Neill Verner's Charleston,* ed. Lynn Robertson Myers ([Columbia, SC]: McKissick Museum, University of South Carolina, 1983), 30.
105. See Mary H. Phifer, "Southern Personalities: Elizabeth O'Neill Verner, Etcher," *Holland's: The Magazine of the South* 48 (October 1929): 14; "Artist Elizabeth White: A Compilation of Articles and Reviews by Margaret Britt," Sumter Gallery of Art, 1985.
106. See Yuhl, *A Golden Haze of Memory,* 6–15, 76–85; Dennison, "Art of the American South," 36, 64, 239.
107. Gregory, "Fine Arts," 285.
108. Charles W. Ramsdell, "The Southern Heritage," in *Culture in the South,* ed. W. T. Couch (Chapel Hill: University of North Carolina Press, 1935), 21–22.
109. Gregory, "Fine Arts," 286.

Notes to Chapters Two

1. George B. Tindall, "Mythology: A New Frontier in Southern History," in *The Idea of the South: Pursuit of a Central Theme,* ed. Frank E. Vandiver (Chicago: University of Chicago Press for William Marsh Rice University, 1964), 1.
2. Robert Dorman, *Revolt of the Provinces: The Regionalist Movement in America, 1920–1945* (Chapel Hill: University of North Carolina Press, 1993), 82–103; Phagan, "Introduction," *American Scene and the South,* 9–32.
3. See Poesch, *Newcomb Pottery,* 67; Delehanty, *Art in the American South,* 72.
4. See Frances Borzello, *A World of Our Own: Women as Artists since the Renaissance* (New York: Watson-Guptill, 2000), 62; Prieto, *At Home in the Studio,* 3, 8, 13.
5. Prieto, *At Home in the Studio,* 39.
6. See the following works by Severens: *Alice Ravenel Huger Smith,* 35–41; *Anna Heyward Taylor,* 5–11; *Charleston Renaissance,* 30–32, 34. See also Meech and Weisberg, *Japonisme Comes to America,* passim.

7. See Severens, *Alice Ravenel Huger Smith,* 39, for a reproduction of Smith's color woodcut *Moonlight on Cooper River.* Another Smith woodcut, *Mossy Tree,* shown in Severens, *Charleston Renaissance,* 24, exhibits similarities, although without the image of the moon.
8. See Saunders and McAden, *Alfred Hutty and the Charleston Renaissance,* 115–22, for images of Hutty's trees. In her dissertation Mariea Dennison claims that "the live oak became associated with the planter's domain, status and aristocracy"; "Art of the American South, 1915–45," 40.
9. Cited in Douglas Helms, "Soil and Soil Conservation," in *Encyclopedia of Southern Culture,* 362.
10. See Preston, *Dirt Roads to Dixie,* 133.
11. Courtney McGowan, Childs Gallery, e-mail to author, August 16, 2005.
12. See Hosmer, *Preservation Comes of Age,* 6.
13. Severens, *Charleston Renaissance,* 6–7, 65.
14. See Hosmer, *Preservation Comes of Age,* 232–74, 290–306; Yuhl, *A Golden Haze of Memory,* 20–52.
15. Scardaville, "Elizabeth O'Neill Verner" 18–19.
16. Pennington, *Downriver,* 157.
17. See Scardaville, "Elizabeth O'Neill Verner" 17–25, for a thorough discussion of this aspect of Verner's work.
18. See Hosmer, *Preservation Comes of Age,* 11–73.
19. Ingham, *Art of the New South,* 133.
20. Chamberlain, *Etched in Sunlight,* 103; Hosmer, *Preservation Comes of Age,* 4, 6, 11–55.
21. Anne Cantrell White, "North Carolina Woman Wins Fame as an Artist," *Greensboro Daily News,* October 18, 1931.
22. Watrous, *American Printmaking,* 31–32.
23. See Rub, "American Architectural Prints," 8–9.
24. "The Graphic Arts Division of the Federal Art Project," 155; Watrous, *American Printmaking,* 44.
25. Tallant, *Romantic New Orleanians,* 308, 327.
26. For contrasting views of this street by Verner and Hutty, see Severens, *Charleston Renaissance,* 58–59.
27. Robert Harper telephone interview with author, November 14, 2005.
28. Severens, *Charleston Renaissance,* 86; Yuhl, *A Golden Haze of Memory,* 83; Dennison, "Art of the American South," 161–66.
29. Jones, *Labor of Love, Labor of Sorrow,* 39.
30. Rub, "American Architectural Prints," 7.
31. Bohrod's New Orleans street scene can be seen in Phagan, "Tours and Visits of the South," 189, or Craven, *A Treasury of American Prints,* 15. The print itself does not bear a title.
32. For a view of this print see King-Hammond, "WPA Black Printmakers," 218, or Powell and Reynolds, *To Conserve a Legacy,* 238. According to King-Hammond, the original edition of this print bore the title *View of Atlanta; Alone in a Crowd,* 19.
33. Goldfield, *Cotton Fields and Skyscrapers,* 143.
34. James R. O'Malley and John B. Rehder, "The Two-Story Log House in the Upland South," *Journal of Popular Culture* 11 (1977–78): 904–15.
35. See O'Malley, "Functional Aspects of Folk Housing: A Case for the 'I' House, Union County, Tennessee," 1, 4.
36. Benton, *An Artist in America,* 198.
37. See Tindall, *The Emergence of the New South, 1912–1945,* 598–99.
38. See Jessie Poesch, "David Hunter Strother: Mountain People, Mountain Images," in *Graphic Arts and the South,* ed. Judy L. Larson with the assistance of Cynthia Payne, 69–70.
39. See Vlach, *Back of the Big House,* 160–64.

40. Kirby, *Rural Worlds Lost,* 175; see also Vlach, *Back of the Big House,* 160–64.
41. Brownell, "The Urban South Comes of Age, 1900–1940," 138.
42. See Jerah Johnson, "The Vernacular Architecture of the South: Log Buildings, Dog-Trot Houses, and English Barns," in *Plain Folk of the South Revisited,* ed. Samuel C. Hyde Jr. (Baton Rouge: Louisiana State University Press, 1997), 53; Rita Wall Turner uses the term "cat slide" in "The Vanishing Tenant Houses of Rural Georgia," *Georgia Historical Quarterly* 65 (1981): 252–54; Robert Gamble adopts "spraddle roof" in *The Alabama Catalog,* 41–43, and Terry G. Jordan "witche's hat," in *Texas Log Buildings: As Folk Architecture* (Austin: University of Texas Press, 1979), 86–89.
43. Dennison, "Art of the American South," 126.
44. Latham's wood engraving can be viewed in Mary Francey, *American Women at Work: Prints by Women Artists of the Nineteen Thirties* (Salt Lake City: Utah Museum of Fine Arts, University of Utah, 1991), 27, which assigns it the incorrect title *South Carolina Mountain Woman,* or in *Graphic Works of the American Thirties,* 25, where it appears under the correct title: *North Carolina Mountain Woman.*
45. See McElroy and Gates, *Facing History*, xi–xix; Harris, *Colored Pictures,* 41–47; LeFalle-Collins, *The Portrayal of the Black Musician in American Art.*
46. Bruce Chalmers, *Art and Artists of the South: The Robert P. Coggins Collection* (Columbia: University of South Carolina Press, 1984), 43. See also Paul Grootkerk, "Earth and Soil: Southern Art and the Cultivation of the Land," *Southeastern College Art Conference Review* 12 (1995): 353–62.
47. Cox, *Southern Works on Paper,* 2.
48. Harris, *Colored Pictures,* 41.
49. See also Phagan, "Introduction," *American Scene and the South,* 27; Dennison, "Art of the American South," 5, 112–16, 239–40.
50. Odum, *Southern Regions of the United States,* 59; Vance, *All These People,* 143.
51. Fite, *Cotton Fields No More,* 113.
52. See Rupert B. Vance, *Human Geography of the South: A Study in Regional Resources and Human Adequacy* (Chapel Hill: University of North Carolina Press, 1935), 182–83, 203.
53. Dennison, "Art of the American South," 107.
54. Ibid., 108–20.
55. See Severens, *Charleston Renaissance,* 101, for a view of Taylor's *Harvesting Rice;* see Verner, *Prints and Impressions of Charleston with Forty-Eight Etchings,* plate XVIII, for a view of *Low Country.*
56. Barbara Batson e-mail to author, May 20, 2003; Block, Ink, Paper: J. J. Lankes and Charles W. Smith, June 4, 2001–December 1, 2001.
57. "The Work of Wm. Kay Hagerman," December 26, 1941; "Kent Hagerman's Life Has Revolved around Art," [*Lakeland Ledger*], March 12, 1975. Kent Hagerman File, Polk Museum of Art.
58. A. Cash Koeniger, "Climate and Southern Distinctiveness," *Journal of Southern History* 54 (1988): 29–30.
59. James O. Breeden, "Disease as a Factor in Southern Distinctiveness," in *Disease and Distinctiveness in the American South,* ed. Todd L. Savitt and James Harvey Young, 1–28 (Knoxville: University of Tennessee Press, 1988).
60. See Vic Zink, *John Stockton De Martelly, 1903–1979* (Gaylord, MI: Mid-North Printing, 1990), 19, 31, 33, 38; *American Art Today,* 302; Dennison, "Art of the American South," 165–173.
61. Fite, *Cotton Fields No More,* 22.
62. Kirby, *Rural Worlds Lost,* 196.
63. Vance, *All These People,* 142
64. See Apel, *Imagery of Lynching,* 23–24, for the evolution of lynching as a common practice, a "semiofficial institution of terror," against blacks in the South.
65. See Hemingway, *Artists on the Left,* 20, for the founding of the John Reed Club and 64–67, for

the antilynching exhibition it organized; Parks, "Lynching and Antilynching: Art and Politics in the 1930s," *Prospects* 18 (1993): 311–65; Margaret Rose Vendryes, "Hanging on Their Walls: An Art Commentary on Lynching: The Forgotten 1935 Art Exhibition," in *Race Consciousness: African-American Studies for the New Century,* ed. Judith Jackson Fossett and Jeffrey A. Tucker, 153–76 (New York: New York University Press, 1997); Helen Langa, "Two Antilynching Art Exhibitions: Politicized Viewpoints, Racial Perspectives, and Gendered Constraints," *American Art* 13 (Spring 1999): 11–39; and Apel, *Imagery of Lynching,* 83–131, for in-depth histories of the two exhibitions.

66. Gorelick's *Strange Fruit* can be viewed in Pohl's *In the Eye of the Storm,* 52. For a history of the song, see David Margolick, "Strange Fruit," *Vanity Fair* 457 (September 1998): 310–20, or the book by the same author: *Strange Fruit: Billie Holliday, Café Society, and an Early Cry for Civil Rights* (Philadelphia: Running Press, 2000). See Williams, "Images of Scottsboro," 50–67, for reflections of the Scottsboro Case in art and literature.
67. See Apel, *Imagery of Lynching,* 113–17.
68. Christopher Murphy depicted a lynched figure hanging between buildings in an etching that appears to be based on a watercolor with the title *Alabama Episode,* both undated in the collection of the Morris Museum. Lamar Baker treated the theme of African American terror from an illuminated cross in his lithograph *Fright.* For an image of this print see Phagan, "The American Scene in Georgia," *American Scene and the South,* 94. Later, Caroline Durieux made a lithograph with an abstract pattern of pointed hoods and crosses, dated.
69. Ralph Wickiser, Caroline Durieux, and John McCrady, *Mardi Gras Day* (New York: Henry Holt, 1948).
70. See Torchia, *Lost Colony,* 105, for an image and explanation of what he erroneously labels a linoleum cut according to the artist's daughter.
71. *Picnic at the Beach* is reproduced in Beall et al., *American Prints in the Library of Congress,* 214.
72. Kirby, *Rural Worlds Lost,* 229.
73. Harris, *Colored Pictures,* 41.
74. Richard Zoellner interview with author, March 2, 2000.
75. Odum, *The Way of the South,* 165, 163.
76. Kirby, *Rural Worlds Lost,* 184.
77. Samuel S. Hill, "Religion," in *Encyclopedia of Southern Culture,* 1271; Gambone, *Art and Popular Religion in Evangelical America, 1915–1940,* 183–85.
78. See Robertson, *Representing America,* 54–55; Theophus H. Smith, "Spirituality," in *Encyclopedia of African-American Culture and History,* 5:2550.
79. See Walter L. Fleming, *The Religious and Hospitable Rite of Feet Washing* (Sewanee, TN: University Press at the University of the South, 1908. Reprinted from the *Sewanee Review,* January 1908), 12–15.
80. Benton, *An Artist in America,* 169.
81. Robertson, *Representing America,* 54.
82. Gambone, *Art and Popular Religion in Evangelical America,* 101, 135; see also Dennison's discussion of African Americans on the New York stage during the era in "Art of the American South," 70–79.
83. See Smythe et al., *The Carolina Low Country* (New York: Macmillan, 1931); Yuhl, *A Golden Haze of Memory,* 127–56.
84. See Benton's chapter on the South in *An Artist in America;* Cash, *The Mind of the South,* 439–40.
85. See Jones, *Labor of Love, Labor of Sorrow,* 5, 102.
86. Powell, *Black Art and Culture in the Twentieth Century,* 94.

87. See Richard Masteller, *"We the People?" Satirical Prints of the 1930's.*

88. See Flynt, *Dixie's Forgotten People,* passim.

Notes to Glossary

1. See Zigrosser and Gaehde, *A Guide to the Collecting and Care of Original Prints,* for more defined terms.
2. See Wax, *The Mezzotint.*
3. See Moser, *Singular Impressions.*
4. See Williams and Williams, *American Screenprints.*
5. See Smith, *Linoleum Block Printing.*
6. See Lankes, *A Woodcut Manual.*

Index

Page numbers in italics refer to illustrations

AAA. *See* Associated American Artists
Abrams, William Ross, 162
Académie Julien (Paris), 46, 136
Académie Moderne (Paris), 56
Académie Scandinave (Paris), 56
Academy Colarossi (Paris), 144
Academy of the Sacred Heart (New Orleans), 54
Acker, Marian Francis, 8, 17, 23, 27, 80, *81,* 162
Adams, Clinton, 14
Adams, Wayman, 162
African American printmakers, 11, 13, 56–57, 98–99, 120–25, 132–33, 150–51, 177
African Americans (subject), 26–27, 31, 36, 38, 76–77, 105–9, 121–25, 128, 138–39, 140, 144–45, 152–57, 168,
Agnes Scott College (Decatur, GA), 92
agriculture, 31–32, 104–109
Alabama, 3, 11, 18, 90–81, 92–93, 96–97, 100, 130–31, 136–37, 142–43, 164, 165
Alabama Art League, 116
Alabama College for Women (University of Montevallo), 130
Alabama Polytechnic Institute (now Auburn University), 171, 178
Albee, Grace, 10, 163
Albers, Josef, 15, 16, 163
Alexander, Doris, 14, 23, 116, *117,* 163
Allen, Lewis, 18
Alston, Charles, 163
American Color Print Society, 116
American Scene, 1, 12
American Society of Etchers, 6, 152
Anclote (FL), 58–59
Anderson, Frank Hartley, 9–10, 11, 36, 37, 152, *153,* 163
Anderson, Martha Fort, 152, *153*
Anderson, Walter Inglis, 8, 15, 16, 20, 21, 42, *43,* 163
Angell, Lydia B., 163
Anshutz, Thomas, 76
aquatint, 183
Arcadia, (FL), 28, 30, 146
architecture, 23–30, 62–99, 168, 170, 178, 179
Arms, John Taylor, 10, 76
Armstrong College, 78
Art Association of New Orleans, 52, 54
Art Institute of Chicago, 62, 68, 94, 114, 120, 134, 152
Art Students League, 3, 14, 40, 54, 68, 70, 78, 84, 92, 94, 110, 128, 130, 132, 138, 140, 142, 144, 158
Art Students League (Buffalo), 90
Arts and Crafts Club (New Orleans), 5, 52, 68, 140, 165
Arts and Crafts movement, 3
Associated American Artists, 11, 12, 118, 140
Atelier Duchâtel (Paris), 60
Athens College (Athens, AL), 11
Atlanta, 9, 10, 11, 27
Atlanta University, 11, 56, 124
Austen, Carl Frederick, 163
Avent, Mayna Treanor, 9, 15, 21, 46, *47,* 163
Avery, Milton, 16, 163

Bacher, Otto, 2
Bacon, Peggy, 35
Bailey, Henrietta, 4, 6, 21, 52, *53,* 163
Baker, Lamar, 12, 16, 31, 32, 104, 110, *111,* 163
Ball, Mary Wilson, 164

baptism, 37, 156–57
Barnes Foundation (Philadelphia), 98
Barnet, Will, 14
barns, 30, 101
Barrett, Lawrence, 130, 136
Barton, Loren, 5, 164
Bartram, William, 20
Baton Rouge, 32, 140
Beaux-Arts Institute of Design (New York), 78
Beaver College (PA), 108
Bennington College, 16, 50
Benton, Thomas Hart, 12, 29, 30, 31, 32, 37, 38, 106, *107,* 144, 164
Besedick, Frank, 16, 28, 30, 37, 154, *155,* 164
Best-Maugard, Adolfo, 42
Bicknell, W. H. W., 80
Biddle, George, 7, 16, 35, 136, *137,* 164
Biloxi (MS), 42
Bird, Esther Brock, 164
birds, 20, 40–43
Birmingham, 9, 14, 27, 32, 88–89, 112, 152, 164, 169
Birmingham Public Library, 10
Black Mountain College, 15
black printmakers. *See* African American printmakers
blacks (subject). *See* African Americans (subject)
Blanch, Arnold, 17
boats, 114–15, 140
Bohrod, Aaron, 27, 164
Bok Foundation, 15
books, 8–9, 23
Bowman, David, 6, 164
Brailsford, H. N., 96
Brisac, Edith Mae, 164
Brighton School of Art (Brighton, UK), 96
Brook, Alexander, 164
Brooklyn Society of Etchers, 4
Brown, Don, 164
Brown, Samuel Joseph, 13, 165
Buell, Alice Standish, 5, 165
Buhmann, Max, 165

cabins, 23, 27, 29–30, 94–97, 120
Cable, George Washington, 2, 5
Cady, Harrison, 23
Cahill, Holger, 12
California Society of Etchers, 4
Cape Cod School of Art, 122
Carnegie Institute of Technology, 108, 114
Carolina Art Association, 7, 72
Casteel, Homer, 35, 134, *135,* 165
Castledon, George, 5, 165
Catesby, Mark, 20
Catlett, Elizabeth, 16, 33, 132, *133,* 165
cemeteries, 25, 60, 70–71
Chamberlain, Samuel, 8, 9, 24, 82, *83,* 165
Charleston, 6–7, 15, 17, 20–23, 25–27, 44, 50, 72–77, 136, 144, 156
Charleston Etchers' Club, 7, 44, 72, 76, 165–67, 173
Charlot, Jean, 144
Chase, William Merritt, 74
Cheltenham Press, 128
Chicago, 62, 120
Chicago Society of Etchers, 4–7, 44
churches, 25, 30, 36, 72–75, 134–35, 154, 158–59
Cincinnati Art Academy, 100
Cincinnati School of Design, 46
Clancey, Joe, 15, 165
Clark, Claude, 11, 13, 30, 98, *99,* 150, 165
Clements, Gabriele de Veaux, 7, 166
Cleveland Institute of Art, 148
Cleveland Print Club, 4
Cloar, Carroll, 16, 37, 158, *159,* 166
Cobb, Kate McKinley, 166
Coe, Richard Blauvelt, 9, 27, 88, *89,* 166
College of Industrial Arts (Denton, TX) (Texas Woman's University), 40
Colophon, 26
Colorado Springs Fine Arts Center, 14, 17, 130
Columbia (SC), 14, 21
Columbia University, 40
Communist Party, 16
Converse College, 44, 166
Cook, Howard, 12, 36, 37, 142, *143,* 166
Cooper, James Fowler, 11, 22, 28, 31, 32, 35, 36, 138, *139,* 166
Cooper Union School of Art, 108
Corcoran Gallery, 86
Corcoran School (Corcoran College of Art and Design), 50, 134
cotton, 22, 31, 104–7
courtyards, 25, 66–69
Crawford, Ralston, 16, 166
Cresson grant, 42, 84
Cuno, Theodore, 140
Curry, John Steuart, 10, 37, 166
Cuthbert Rookery, 40

dancing, 145
Davenport, Carson Sutherlin, 15–16, 166
Davidson, Theresa Sherrer, 167
Dawson, Charles Clarence, 167

de Martelly, John, 33
Dean, J. Ernest, 62
Decatur (AL), 14, 130
Dehn, Adolf, 20, 36, 130, 167
Delgado Museum, 5
Desjobert, Edmond, 142
Dillard University (New Orleans), 132
Dixie Art Colony, 15, 88, 116, 130, 165
Dotterer, Selma Tharin, 44, 167
Douglass, Lucille, 18, 92, 167
Dow, Arthur Welsey, 52
Duke University, 96
drypoint 137
Durieux, Caroline, 6, 13, 14, 27, 35, 36, 126, *127,* 140, 167
Durkee, Florence, 167
Dwight, Mabel, 5, 21, 22, 32, 35, 37, 60, *61,* 67

Eatonville (FL), 28, 30, 37, 154
erosion, 22, 104
etching, 1–2, 3, 5–8, 12, 15, 24, 137, 183
Etching Revival, 1–2, 7, 24
Evans, Walker, 18
Everglades, 20, 40

farms. *See* agriculture
Federal Art Project. *See* Works Progress Administration
Fitzpatrick, J. Kelly, 130
Flagler, Henry, 2, 114
Florence, (SC), 122
Florida, 2, 7–8, 15, 20, 28, 32, 114, 146–49, 163, 173
flowers, 20–21, 44–49
Frank Brown Collection of North Carolina Folklore, 96
French Quarter, 3–6, 10, 13, 15, 23, 25, 62–70, 94, 142, 163, 165, 167, 168, 174, 177–79
Freund, Harry Louis, 167
Friedlander, Isaac, 37

Gallagher, Michael, 13, 120, 150
Galleon Club, 7
gates, 25–26, 67, 75, 77
Gautier (MS), 42
Gelb, Jan (Jeanette), 167
Georgia, 166, 172
Gibbes Memorial Art Gallery (Gibbes Museum), 7, 44
Giddens, Philip Harris, 168
Goldthwaite, Anne, 3, 5, 33, 128, *129,* 156, 168
Gorelick, Boris, 34,
Grafton, Robert 68
Grand Central School of Art (New York), 88
Graphic Sketch Club (Philadelphia), 150
graveyards. *See* cemetaries
Great Depression, 29, 33
Greenwood (MS), 171
Griffith, Louis Oscar, 5, 68
Guggenheim fellowship, 12, 82, 142
Gullah, 144
Gwathmey, Robert, 12, 14, 16, 32, 108, *109,* 168

Hagerman, Kent, 8, 11, 20, 27, 32, 35, 148, *149,* 168
Hale, Ellen Day, 7, 168
Hale, Philip, 88
Hamilton, Elizabeth, 76
Hancock, J. Carl, 5, 8, *28,* 168
Harlem Community Arts Center, 14, 122
Harlem Renaissance, 16
Harmon Foundation, 10, 56
Hart, George Overbury (Pop), 168
Harvard University, 136, 152
Hassam, Childe, 7, 168
Hawthorne, Charles, 122
Heade, Martin Johnson, 20
Healy, William John, 169
Heldner, Knute, 5, 13, 29, 30, 94, *95,* 169
Henderson, Ernest M., 169
Hergesheimer, Ella Sophonisba, 9, 15, 21, 46, 48, *49,* 86, 169
Hicken, Philip, 169
High Museum of Art, 10, 110
Hill, Polly Knipp, 8, 15, 28, 30, 35, 36, 146, *147,* 169
historic preservation, 19, 23, 62, 76, 78, 80
Hobbs, Morris Henry, 5, 6, 20, 24, 26, 35, 62, *63,* 64, 169
Hoehn, Werner Conrad, 169
Holloway, Jenelsie, 11, 169
Hopkins Institute of Art, 60
Horn Island, 20
Horter, Earl, 8, 24, 120, 169
Hoshall, Mercedes Erixon, 169
houses, 27, 28, 76–77, 85, 90–91. *See also* cabins
Howard University, 132
Howard, Willie, 169
Howell, Catherine, 13, 170
Howorth, (Emma) Louise, 170
Hubbard, Henry Vincent, 152
Hughes, Langston, 156
hunting, 148–49, 176
Huntley, Victoria Hutson, 7, 20, 27, 40, *41,* 170

Hurd, Peter, 37
Hurston, Zora Neale, 154
Hutty, Alfred, 7, 10, 22, 25, 26, 32, 44, 58, 72, *73,* 138, 170
Hyde, Helen, 4, 7, 74, 170

industry, 32, 88, 104, 112, 140
International Print Makers Exhibition, 84
Ipswich (MA), 52
Irvine, Sadie, 4, 6, 21, 22, 52, 54, *55,* 170

Jackley, Dano, 8, 170
Jackson (MS), 130
Jacksonville (FL), 12
Jacques, Bertha Evelyn, 7, 170
Jennings, Wilmer, 10, 11, 29, 30, 34, 37, 124, *125,* 170
Jim Crow laws, 10–11, 33
John Herron Art Institute (Indianapolis), 56
John Hope fellowship, 124
John Reed Club, 33
Johnson, William Henry, 14, 29, 31, 32, 36, 122, *123,* 170
Jones, Lawrence Arthur, 13, 170

Kainen, Jacob, 24
Kappel, Philip, 5, 9, 170
Kent, Rockwell, 10
Key West, 36, 167
Kirk, Mary Wallace, 11, 16, 28, 92, *93,* 171
Kiser, Jesse Dorrance, 171
Kistler, Lynton, 144
Kofler, John George, 171
Kracke, Holcha, 122
Kronberg, Louis, 58

Lakeland (FL), 8, 11, 27, 148
landscapes, 20, 22
Lankes, J. J., 8, 10, 24, 25, 27, 28, 90, *91,* 171
Latham, Barbara, 30, 36, 142, 171
Laughlin, Clarence, 18
Law, Margaret Moffett, 37, 171
Lazzell, Nettie Blanche, 8, 171
Lee-Smith, Hughie, 171
Leighton, Clare, 29, 30, 37, 96, *97,* 171
leisure activity, 35
Lewis, Arthur Allen, 171
Lewis, Lalla Walker, 171
Lillie, Ella Fillmore, 10, 172
Lindenmuth, Tod, 8
linoleum cuts, 1, 4, 11, 184
lithography, 1, 6, 12, 13–14, 184
Little Rock, (AR), 165
Locke, Charles, 128
Locke, Walter Ronald, 8, 11, 22, 58, *59,* 172
Logan, Velma Kidd, 172
Louisiana Society of Etchers, 6, 64, 68, 164, 175, 177
Louisiana State University, 126
Loving, Eugene, 5, 26, 64, *65,* 172
lynching, 33–34, 134–35

MacDowell Art Colony, 156, 158
MacDowell fellowship, 158
MacKenzie, Roderick, 15, 32, 112, *113,* 116, 172
magnolia, 21, 48–49
Magnolia Springs (AL), 116
Maitland Art Center, 15–16, 154, 166, 172, 177
Manuel, Margaret, 172
Manning, Warren, 152
Mardi Gras, 35, 66, 70, 80, 140–41
Margo, Boris, 16, 172
Marshall, (James) Durad, 172
Maryland Institute College of Art (Baltimore), 108, 114
Massachusetts Institute of Technology, 82
Mayer, Henry (Hy), 172
Mayfield, Robert Bledsoe, 3, 172
McCalls magazine, 84
McCrady, John, 11, 14, 32, 35, 38, 140, *141,* 172
McTyeire, Bishop Holland, 48
meals (communal), 36, 150
Meeker, Joseph, 20
Meissner, Leo John, 10, 173
Mencken, H. L., 16, 38
Meridian Junior College (Community College), 134
Merrick, Richard, 13, 173
Merrill, Katherine, 7, 173
Mesibov, Hugh, 13, 120
mezzotint, 183
Mielatz, Charles, 128
Mikell, Minnie, 173
Milhollen, Hirst Dillon, 173
Miller, George, 14, 106, 136
Millet, Clarence, 6, 15, 25, 26, 35, 68, *69,* 173
Minneapolis School of Fine Arts, 94
Mississippi, 134
Mobile, 8, 17, 23, 25, 27, 79–80, 112, 116
monotypes, 184
Montgomery, (AL), 128–29
Moran, Mary Nimmo, 2
Moran, Thomas, *2*
Morehouse College (Atlanta), 124

Morgan, F(ranklin) Townsend, 173
Morley, Hubert, 5, 173
Morris, William, 3. 8
mountains, 22–23, 46, 101, 172, 176
Mueller, Lola Pace, 173
mule, 33, 94
Muller-Uri, Hildegard, 173
Murphy, Christopher A. D., 8, 9, 23, 25, 26, 78, *79,* 173
Murphy, Patrick Hussey, 78
Murphy, Lucille Desbouillons, 78
music, 36, 142–43

NAACP, 33, 35
Nashville 9, 21, 27, 46, 56, 86–87
National Academy of Design, 3, 122, 128, 154
National Association of Women Artists, 116
National Institute of Arts and Letters, 40
Nelms, Majory Collison, 173
Newcomb College. *See* Sophie Newcomb College
New Deal Art Projects. *See* Works Progress Administration and Public Works of Art Project
Newhall, Harriet, 174
New Leader, 96
New Orleans, 2–3, 4, 9, 12–14, 20–23, 25, 27, 52, 54, 60, 62, 64, 66, 68, 70, 94, 126, 140, 142, 144. *See also* French Quarter
New Orleans Art Association, 5, 6
New Orleans Art League, 6, 64
New Orleans Museum of Art. *See* Delgado Museum
New Orleans School of Art, 5
New York, 12, 16, 24, 33, 34, 60, 74, 78, 88, 118, 122, 128, 146
New York Public Library, 84, 152
New York School of Fine Arts, 40
New York University, 56
New York Zoological Society, 74
Nordfeldt, B. J. O., 15, 46, 74
Norfolk, VA, 106
North Carolina, 84–85, 119, 163, 165, 174, 178
Nungester, Mildred, 11, 14, 17, 32, 33, 36, 38, 130, *131,* 174

Ocean Spring (MS), 8, 20, 42
O'Keeffe, Ida Ten Eyck, 11, 174
Okefenokee Swamp, 104, 110
Oglethorpe University (Atlanta), 104
Ohio State University, 90
Oldfields' plantation (Gautier, MS), 42
Oliver, Edith Walker, 8, 15, 174
Orlando, 15, 40, 154
Orr, Louis, 174
Otis Art Institute (Los Angeles), 102

Packard award, 42
Page, Grover, 174
Page Traveling Scholarship, 88
Panama Pacific International Exposition, 128
Parrish, Stephen, 2
Peace College (Raleigh), 84
Peacock, Jean Eleanor, 174
Peale, Charles Wilson, 48
Peale family, 21, 48
Pearson, Ralph, 5
Pearce, George E., 174
Peirce, Gerry, 5, 174
Pennell, Joseph, 2, *3,* 29, 78, 142
Pennsylvania Academy of Fine Arts, 42, 46, 76, 84, 108, 126, 136
Pennsylvania School of Industrial Art, 98
Perry, William, 24, 82
Pescheret, Leon René, 5, 7, 10, 23, 24, 30, 174
Philadelphia, 12–14, 98, 120, 150
Pickup, Ernest, 9, 11, 27, 86, *87,* 175
Pilot Town (LA), 29
Pinckney, Josephine, 156
Pittman, Hobson, 21, 175
Print Club of Philadelphia, 4
Printmakers Society of California, 4
Provincetown, 8, 15, 46, 74, 80, 122, 175
Public Works of Art Project (PWAP), 12, 152, 156
Pugh, Mabel, 4, 15, 21, 24, 25, 84, *85,* 175

quarries, 117

Raleigh (NC), 21
Ravenscroft, Ellen, 175
Reed, Willie Lucille (Rowe), 175
Reid, Celia Cregor, 8, 12, 32, 35, 114, *115,* 175
Reinike, Charles, 6, 175
Reisman, Philip, 12, 35, 175
religion, 36–38
Rhett, Antoinette, 7, 21, 44, *45,* 175
Rhode Island School of Design, 124
Richards, Charles, 175
Richmond (VA), 13, 32, 50, 162, 163
Ripley, Aiden Lassell, 176
roads, 12, 103
Rockefeller Foundation, 24
Rocky Mount (NC), 150
Rohland, Caroline, 30, 176
Rohland, Paul, 176
Rollins, College, 40

Roosevelt, Franklin Delano, 29, 136
Rose, Ruth Starr, 38
Rosenwald fellowship, 12, 56, 104
Roth, Ernest, 154
Routh, James, 12, 14, 16, 22, 31, 104, *105,* 110, 176
Royal College of Art (London), 82
Ruellan, Andrée, 176
Rumpf, Alice, 7, 24, 176
Ryder, Chauncey, 22, 176

Sabatini, Raphael, 116
Sacramento State College, 98
Savannah (GA), 8, 23, 25, 78–79, 164
Saxon, Lyle, 5
School of the Museum of Fine Arts (Boston), 88, 90, 112
Schoppe, Palmer, 7, 36, 144, *145,* 176
Schreiber, Georges, 7, 12, 27, 30, 32, 33, 118, *119,* 176
Schutz, Marian C., 177
Scopes Trial, 16, 38
Scottsboro case, 16, 35, 136, 156
screen-printing, 12, 13–14, 184
Senefelder Lithographic House, 126
serigraphs. *See* screen-printing
Seymour, Ralph Fletcher, 62
Shackelford, Shelby, 177
Sharpe, H. Alvin, 5, 13, 15, 25, 66, *67,* 177
Shearwater Pottery, 42
ships. *See* boats
Simons, Albert, 177
Slade School of Art (London, UK), 96
Smilie, George, 2
Smith, Albert Alexander, 177
Smith, Alice Ravenel Huger, 7, 15, 21, 44, 76, 177
Smith, Charles William, 4, 7, 8, 16, 21, 23–27, 32, *50–51,* 177
Smith, Jules André, 15, 154, 177
Smoky Mountains, 46
Society for the Preservation of Negro Spirituals, 38
Society for the Preservation of Old Dwellings, 23
Sophie Newcomb College, 3, 4, 6, 15, 52, 54, 126
Sorbonne, 148
South Carolina, 116, 138, 163, 171. *See also* Charleston
South Carolina Agricultural Society, 74
South Carolina College for Women, 74
Southern Printmakers Society, 9, 10, 138, 152
Southern States Art League, 5, 6, 9, 17, 44, 52, 54, 88, 92, 114, 152
Southside Community Art Center (Chicago), 132
Southwestern College (Rhodes College), 158
Standard Oil Co., 32, 140
Stanton, Gideon, 5
St. Augustine, 2, 7, 15, 23, 26, 32, 35, 114, 163, 170, 172, 174
steel industry 32, 112–13
steamboats. *See* boats
Sternberg, Harry, 16, *34,* 92, 104, 110, 132, 158, 177
Steth, Raymond, 13, 29, 36, 98, 150, *151,* 177
still life, 21, 48–51
Story, Hal, 13, 178
St. Petersburg, 8, 146
Strickland, William, 86
Studio Club of Nashville, 9, 86
Surendorf, Charles, 5, 6, 10–11, 25, 35, 36, 70, *71,* 178
Suydam, E. H., 178
swamps, 19–20, 62, 66, 94, 104, 110
Swett, Ruth Doris, 178
Sykes, Maltby, 14, 178

Talladega College (Talladega, AL), 11, 98
Taller de Gráfica Popular (Mexico City), 132, 158
Tannahill, Mary Harvey, 15, 21, 178
Tarpon Springs (FL), 8, 58
Tatum, Howard, 178
Taxco, Mexico, 142
Taylor, Anna Heyward, 4, 7, 15, 21, 25, 30–32, 74, *75,* 178
Taylor, Prentiss, 7, 34, 35, 156, *157,* 178
Telfair Academy, 78
Tennessee Coal, Iron and Railroad Co., 112
Tennessee Valley Authority, 11, 100
textile industry, 32, 110–11
Thompson, Doris. *See* Alexander, Doris
Thrash, Dox, 13, 27, 29, 30, 36, 120, *121,* 150, 178
Tiffany fellowship, 78, 100, 154
tobacco, 22, 108–9, 110–11
tourism, 5–8, 18, 25, 26
transportation, 33, 13–34
trees, 21–22, 52–61, 90
Tulane University, 3
Turnbull, James Baare, 179
Turtle, Arnold, 179
Tyler School of Art, Temple University, 116

University of Alabama, 100, 152
University of California, Berkeley, 98
University of California, Los Angeles, 144
University of Cincinnati, 88

University of Florida, 102
University of Iowa, 132
University of Kentucky, 114
University of Mississippi, 134
University of Virginia, 50
University of Washington, 82

Vanderbilt Agrarians, 19
Vanderbilt University, 48, 167
Verner, Elizabeth O'Neill, 7–10, 17, 22, 23, 25, 26, 30, 31, 37, 72, 76, *77*, 179
Vesper George School of Art (Boston), 80, 154
Vieux Carré. *See* French Quarter
Vieux Carré Commission, 23
Virginia, 8–9, 24, 27, 82–83, 90–91, 169, 173
Vorst, Joseph Paul, 179

Wadmalaw Island (SC), 144
Walker, William Aiken, 31
Walmsley, Elizabeth, 35
Waring, Leila, 179
Warren, Elizabeth Boardman, 8, 179
Waynesboro (VA), 50
Webb, Alonzo C., 179
Weber, Frederick T(heodore), 179
Webster, Hutton, Jr., 179
Wells, James Lesesne, 16, 132, 179
Wells, Jane McClintock, 179
Weyhe Gallery, 60, 142
Whaley, Edna Reed, 21, 180
Whistler, James McNeill, 128
White, Elizabeth, 22, 138, 180
Whitehead, Buell, 22, 102, *103*, 180
Whitelaw, Robert N. S., 180
Wickiser, Ralph Lewanda, 180
Wilcox, Edith, 180
Wilimovsky, Charles, 5, 180
Williamsburg, 9, 24, 82–83, 90
Williamsburg County (SC), 138
Willson, James Mallory, 180
windows, 21, 26
WPA/FAP. *See* Works Progress Administration
Wolfe, Mildred. *See* Nungester, Mildred
women printmakers, 3, 4, 17, 20–21, 40–41, 45–49, 52–55, 60–61, 74–77, 80–81, 84–85, 92–93, 96–97, 114–15, 116–17, 126–33
woodcuts, 1, 3–4, 11, 184
wood engravings, 1, 3–4, 184
Woodruff, Hale Aspacio, 10, 11, 15, 21, 22, 27, 34, 36, 56, *57*, 124, 169, 180
Woodstock (NY) art colony, 17
Woodward, Ellsworth, 3, 5, 9, 23, 181
Woodward, William, 3, 5, 8, 23, 181
Woolley, Guy Livingston, 181
Works Progress Administration/Federal Art Project, 12–13, 14, 56, 66, 88, 94, 98, 120, 122, 126, 150, 154, 165, 169, 170
World's Fair (1939 New York), 138
Wright, George Hand, 181

Yale University School of Fine Arts, 50, 144
Yeomans, Walter, 8, 181

Zigrosser, Carl, 12, 40, 60, 126
Zoellner, Richard, 14, 23, 30, 36, 100, *101*, 181